T O U R I N G

New South Wales

TOURING

New South Wales

BRUCE ELDER

NH
NEW
HOLLAND

First published in Australia in 2000 by
New Holland Publishers (Australia) Pty Ltd
Sydney • Auckland • London • Cape Town

14 Aquatic Drive Frenchs Forest NSW 2086 Australia
218 Lake Road Northcote Auckland New Zealand
24 Nutford Place London W1H 6DQ United Kingdom
80 McKenzie Street Cape Town 8001 South Africa

National Library of Australia Cataloguing-in-Publication Data:

Elder, Bruce.
Touring New South Wales

Includes index.
ISBN 1 86436 486 6

1. New South Wales—Tours. 2. New South Wales—Description and travel.
3. New South Wales—Guidebooks. I. Title.

919.4404

Publishing Manager: **Anouska Good**
Senior Editor: **Monica Ban**
Copy Editor: **Glenda Downing**
Design Concept: **Mandy Moss**
Cover Design: **Nanette Backhouse**
Layout: **Jenny Mansfield**
DTP Cartographer: **John Loubser**
Picture Researcher: **Kirsti Wright**
Reproduction: **Colour Symphony**
Printer: **Kyodo Printing**

PHOTOGRAPHIC CREDITS:

All photographs © Bruce Elder with the exception of:

Ted Mead: front cover—l & tl, back cover—t, p1, p108-9
John Meier: front cover—centre & br, back cover—b, p5
Shaen Adey/NHIL: p6, 12br, 13, 15t, 17, 19, 20, 21t, 32, 33t, 34-35, 44,
45bl, 80-81, 137bl, 138, 141, 147tl, 150br, 152-3, 154, 155br
Nick Rains/NHIL: p14, 15b, 18, 104, 105 **Anthony Johnson/NHIL:** p10-11
Vicki Hastrich/NHIL: p21b **NHIL:** p120, 155bl, 155t, 165br
Trevor Worden/photolibrary.com: p2-3, 128-9 **Geoff Higgins/photolibrary.com:** p70-71
Peter J. Robinson/photolibrary.com: p 88-89 **Jeffrey C. Drewitz/photolibrary.com:** p98-99
Robin Smith/photolibrary.com: p142-3

NHIL: New Holland Image Library
(b=bottom, t=top, l=left, r=right)

AUTHOR'S ACKNOWLEDGEMENTS

Large and complex projects like this book are inevitably a team effort.
This book would not be possible without the assistance of my tireless, meticulous and
hard-working researcher, Ivan Coates, and my wife, Kim. They both spent hundreds of
hours engaged in the tedious and exacting work of measuring distances and checking facts.
Without their patience and precision, this book would not exist.

CONTENTS

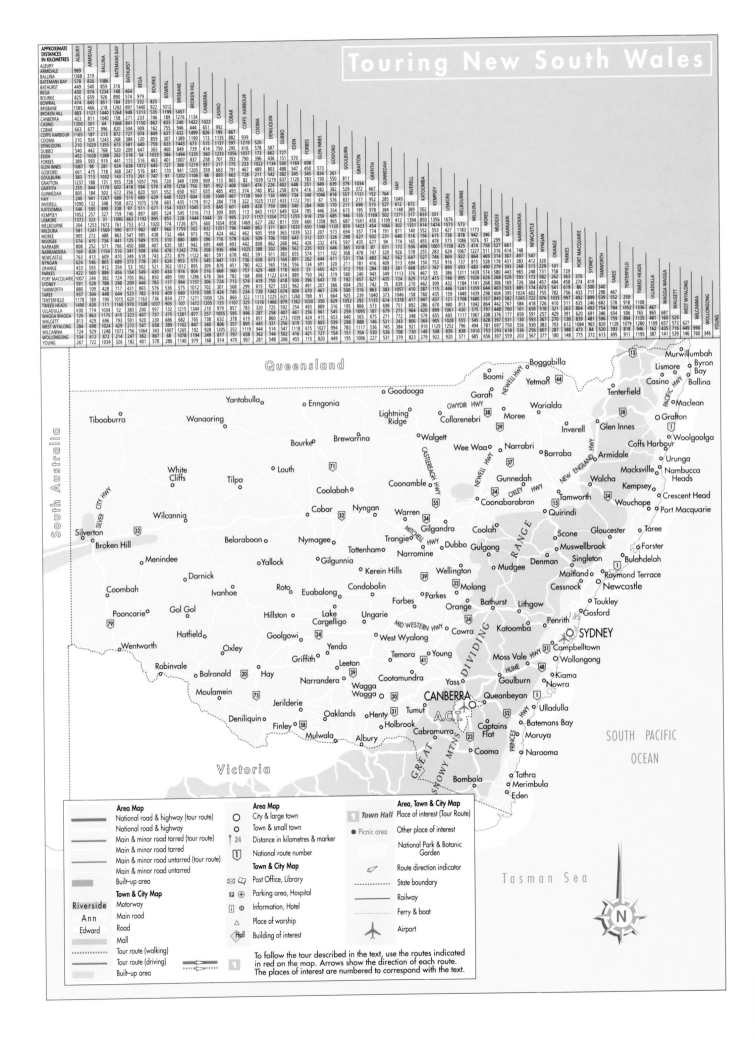

INTRODUCTION

*I*t is one of the strange inconsistencies of Australia that while more people live in New South Wales than in any other state, the people of New South Wales tend to take their holidays elsewhere. They are more likely to go to Bali than to go to Ballina; more likely to go to the Gold Coast than Gulgong; and more eager to go to Uluru than to Urunga.

It is therefore necessary to remind 'the locals' that their state is full of wonders which are keenly sought out by both the overseas and the interstate visitor. The traveller coming to New South Wales is eager to see the spectacular box canyons and the misty grey-blue of the Blue Mountains; they are happy to wander along the beaches; they explore the state's many national parks and make their way to the edge of great Australian deserts; and they know that the New South Wales coast offers some of the best diving and surfing in the world.

It is not surprising that New South Wales and Sydney are Australia's premier destinations for people travelling from overseas. Where else are you only 90 minutes away from something as spectacular as the Blue Mountains? Where else can you access beautiful golden beaches so easily and effortlessly?

This book provides the traveller to New South Wales with 71 self-contained tours. While most of these tours can be completed in a day, the distances involved will often invite the traveller to stop. It is also true, particularly in the case of the larger towns, that a single day would never do justice to the richness of their history.

New South Wales is a state of great diversity which changes as it moves westward. The coast is characterised, with very few exceptions, by beautiful beaches, rocky headlands and a narrow coastal plain. Beyond the coast lies the Great Dividing Range which, although low by world standards, is often rugged and sparsely populated. The Great Dividing Range tumbles into slopes to the west. This is the grazing country where farmers plant crops and graze sheep and cattle. Slowly these slopes give way to the vast western plains which comprise more than half of the state. This is the area described by the poet and short story writer, Henry Lawson, as 'the great grey plain' where low lying scrub on infertile red soils stretch to the horizon and where the rainfall is low except when the skies open with sudden and violent storms.

The aim of this book is to provide travellers in New South Wales with a rich cross-section of tours. The original intention was to attempt to create circular routes which allowed the traveller to return to their original destination before nightfall. It quickly became apparent that these self-imposed constraints would mean that some of the state's most beautiful countryside (particularly the outback) would have to be excluded.

While the vast majority of these journeys can be done on good sealed roads in a conventional vehicle, there are some where commonsense says that a four-wheel-drive vehicle is a good option. It is probably quite possible to do the Broken Hill–Menindee–Wilcannia tour in a conventional vehicle but it is easier and more comfortable to have the extra power that a four-wheel-drive provides.

All travellers should be aware that outback New South Wales is subject to extreme temperatures through the summer months and that journeys into the Snowy Mountains in winter require chains. There are times when many of the National Park roads are closed by snow and it is common to be refused entry if you do not have chains.

New South Wales is a truly wonderful state. Its diversity is breathtaking and its beauty, particularly the Blue Mountains, the coastal beaches, the quietness of the coastal hinterland rainforests and the seemingly infinite plains of the outback, lives in the memory of travellers long after their journey is over.

CHAPTER 1
SYDNEY AND ENVIRONS

1 HISTORIC SYDNEY

■ WALKING TOUR ■ 6KM ■ 4 HOURS ■ A WALK INTO SYDNEY'S HISTORIC PAST

One of the most delightful introductions to the charms of Sydney is to walk around Circular Quay from the Rocks to Mrs Macquarie's Chair. The harbour sparkles and the city soars.

S ydney is a typical modern city of freeways and skyscrapers. Most of the modern development has occurred since the 1960s. Prior to that the city was characterised by three and four-storey Victorian and Edwardian buildings of considerable grace and solidity. Today it is hard to imagine that only two hundred years ago Captain Arthur Phillip brought a group of convicts to Sydney Cove and established a tent colony which was to grow into modern-day Sydney. Little of that original colony is left but a walk from The Rocks around the Quay to the Opera House, through the Royal Botanic Gardens, around to Mrs Macquarie's Chair and the Art Gallery, then up Macquarie St is a pleasant walk through the city's 19th-century history.

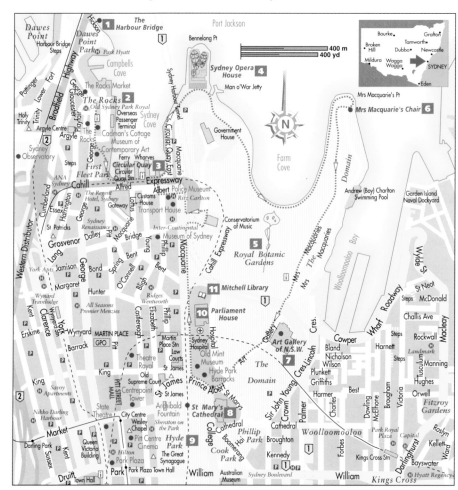

■ THE HARBOUR BRIDGE

No visit to Sydney can be considered complete without a leisurely walk across Sydney Harbour Bridge. Entry to the pedestrian walkway is via the south-east pylon which is reached by walking up Argyle Street in The Rocks, ascending the Argyle Steps, crossing Cumberland Street and following the signs marked 'Bridge Stairs'. The view is spectacular at any time of the day but is particularly impressive in the early morning or late afternoon.

The bridge took nine years to build, weighs 60 000 tonnes and, at its highest point, is 134m above the harbour. From 1932 until 1967 it was Australia's largest building and when it was originally constructed it was the second largest bridge of its kind in the world with a main span of 503m. It is still listed in the *Guinness Book of Records* as the widest steel arch bridge in

the world with eight traffic lanes, two railway lines, a cycleway and footway all being located on a deck that is 49m wide.

■ THE ROCKS

Walk from the Harbour Bridge Steps down to the Argyle Cut, a tunnel carved from solid stone.

In the 18th and 19th century, this was the centre of the city's wild military and convict night life. A map dating from July 1788, only six months after the arrival of the First

Fleet, has one completed building—the hospital—and two proposed buildings—a church and storehouses. Today The Rocks remains Sydney's most concentrated area of historic significance. The Sydney Cove Authority recognises 20 important 19th-century buildings in the area bound by the Cahill Expressway, Sydney Cove and Cumberland Street.

A sensible walk through The Rocks starts at the Argyle Cut and runs back through Playfair Street to The Rocks Square. This walk would include the old police station (1882) on the western side of George Street; the Museum of Contemporary Art (well worth a visit, it has travelling exhibitions as well as an excellent permanent collection of important international contemporary art works); and Sydney's oldest building, John Cadman's cottage (a stone cottage built in 1816 by the superintendent of boats) next door to The Rocks Visitors Centre, which is located in the old Sailors Home.

Further north is Campbells Storehouse (1839–1861), now converted into a number

The graceful sails of the Opera House.

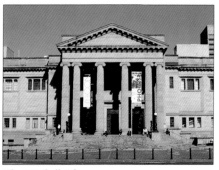

The Mitchell Library.

of tourist-orientated restaurants. Lying at anchor in Campbells Cove is the tall ship *Bounty*, a faithful replica of Captain Bligh's 18th-century vessel that was built for the Mel Gibson film *Mutiny on the Bounty*.

3 CIRCULAR QUAY

From the Visitors Centre walk along the foreshore of Sydney Cove. There are excellent views of the Opera House from this side of the cove. After about 300m you will reach the small First Fleet Park. Turn east and head across to the Opera House via the ferry terminal.

Circular Quay is the hub of Sydney. It is the ciy's emotional heart. In the earliest days it was known as Sydney Cove and it was here that Governor Arthur Phillip moored the First Fleet and set the convicts to work building a penal colony of barracks and tents. The reasons for its choice seem to lie in its beauty although the real reason—good, reliable fresh water from the Tank Stream—has long been hidden under concrete and asphalt.

Circular Quay is a major transport node. Today it provides a wide range of ferry services to Manly, Taronga Zoo Park, Cremorne Point, Mosman, Neutral Bay, Darling Harbour, Balmain and a number of other destinations.

4 OPERA HOUSE

Continue to walk around the Quay until you reach the Opera House.

The design for the Sydney Opera House was determined by a competition that was announced in 1955. There were over 230 entries from 32 countries. The prize of £5000 was awarded to 38-year-old Danish architect Joern Utzon. The construction took 14 years and cost over $100 million. The project was funded by a state lottery.

The Sydney Opera House's famous 'wings' or 'shells' required extraordinary engineering skills. Three huge cranes were imported to Sydney from France to help install 2194 precast concrete ribs. The ribs were held together by epoxy resin and 300km of tensioned cable. All this was surfaced by ceramic tiles made in Sweden.

The Opera House has five theatres—a concert hall, opera theatre, drama theatre, cinema and recording hall—as well as two restaurants, a number of bars, six lounges, a library, five rehearsal studios and 65 dressing rooms.

5 BOTANIC GARDENS

Continue east from the Opera House. After about 150m you will enter the gates to the Domain and the Royal Botanic Gardens. There is a pleasant walk around the foreshores to Mrs Macquarie's Chair.

Sydney's Royal Botanic Gardens had their genesis when Governor Arthur Phillip collected seeds at Rio de Janeiro and Cape Town on his journey to Australia. In 1788 he set the land apart as a farm and named it Farm Cove. It became a botanic garden in 1816 when Governor Lachlan Macquarie had a road constructed to Mrs Macquarie's Chair and appointed Charles Fraser as the superintendent of the gardens.

The diversity of plants is remarkable. The gardens have over 4000 trees and plants from around the world. There are specialist collections in the herbarium and the pyramid glasshouse where the heat and humidity support an outstanding mixture of tropical and subtropical plants.

6 MRS MACQUARIE'S CHAIR

Continue around the foreshore for about 600m until you reach Mrs Macquarie's Point which offers excellent views across the harbour and back towards the Opera House.

Mrs Macquarie's Chair (often called Lady Macquarie's Chair) is where the wife of Governor Lachlan Macquarie would sit to enjoy the view across the harbour. A road was built from the governor's residence to the headland in 1816. For over 150 years it has been one of the most popular of all the harbour vantage points with excellent views across to the island of Fort Denison. The construction of the Sydney Opera House and the Sydney Harbour Bridge have meant that the westerly view produces the dramatic effect of having both buildings silhouetted against the setting sun.

7 ART GALLERY OF NEW SOUTH WALES

There are two roads serving the one-way system from Mrs Macquarie's Chair south to the city. From here it is a pleasant 1km walk to the Art Gallery.

The Art Gallery of New South Wales contains representative examples of art works ranging from a substantial Aboriginal collection to modern Australian masters, and excellent examples of the country's finest colonial artists are all on display. Of particular interest are the works of Conrad Martens and the huge, sensuous works of contemporary artists Lloyd Rees and Brett Whiteley. The gallery also contains works by European masters, including Picasso and Rembrandt. Admission to the gallery is free.

8 ST MARY'S CATHEDRAL

Continue south for 400m from the Art Gallery and you will see the back entrance to St Mary's Cathedral, the city's premier place of worship for its Catholic community.

St Mary's Cathedral is still incomplete although the foundation stone was laid in 1868. If you stand out the front and look at the cathedral's twin spires you will notice they come to an abrupt halt. The spires will not be completed until June 2000. The location has been used by Sydney's Catholic community for more than 170 years. In 1821 a stone was laid on this site and the original Church of the Blessed Virgin Mary was built. It was destroyed by fire in 1865 and three years later the foundation stone of the present cathedral was laid. The building is classically Gothic in design.

9 HYDE PARK

Cross the road from St Mary's Cathedral and you are in Hyde Park. If you continue to walk south you will reach the War Memorial. By walking a short distance north you will reach the Archibald Fountain.

Hyde Park is the city's central open space. Originally the site, in the early 19th century, of the city's first racecourse, it was established

as Hyde Park in the early years of the 20th century. Spread over 16ha, the park is divided by Park Street. The dominant feature of the southern section is the New South Wales War Memorial and the dominant feature of the northern part is the Archibald Fountain.

10 PARLIAMENT HOUSE

About 100m down Macquarie St is the New South Wales Parliament House, a famous and prominent landmark in the city.

Built in 1810, Parliament House, situated in Macquarie Street, is one of the city's most elegant historic buildings. The Legislative Assembly (the lower house) is known to Sydneysiders as the bearpit because of the no-holds-barred approach to debate. When parliament is in session, it is possible to visit the Public Gallery and watch the state politicians 'debating' legislation.

11 MITCHELL LIBRARY

Continue to walk down the east side of Macquarie St. On the corner, with the Cahill Expressway arching around it, is the Mitchell Library.

Known locally as the Mitchell Library, the State Library of New South Wales is the state's major repository of historic documents, sketches and information. The centrepiece of this interesting combination of old and new buildings is the Mitchell Library, the largest collection of colonial Australiana in the world. The core of the collection—the initial 61 000 volumes—was donated by David Scott Mitchell, an avid bibliophile who was one of the first 24 students at Sydney University, from where he graduated in 1859. He left both the books and a substantial legacy so that the collection could be housed and well-protected. Mitchell once paid £7000 for an entire collection that contained the diaries of Joseph Banks, the botanist who accompanied Captain Cook up the eastern coast of Australia.

The Art Gallery of New South Wales.

2 SYDNEY'S EASTERN SUBURBS

■ DRIVING TOUR ■ 16KM ■ 1 DAY ■ BEACHES, BAYS AND HEADLANDS

World-famous Bondi Beach, home of sun, sand and good surf, is the great drawcard which attracts holiday-makers to Sydney's Eastern Suburbs.

Sydney's eastern suburbs are an area of extraordinary diversity. For over a century the foreshores of the harbour have been home to the city's elite, the harbour beaches have been popular retreats for sunlovers and the ocean beaches, particularly Bondi Beach, have become symbols of Sydney's outdoor lifestyle. This tour heads to Watsons Bay via New South Head Road then crosses over the rugged headlands of Watsons Bay and Dover Heights and drops down to Bondi Beach.

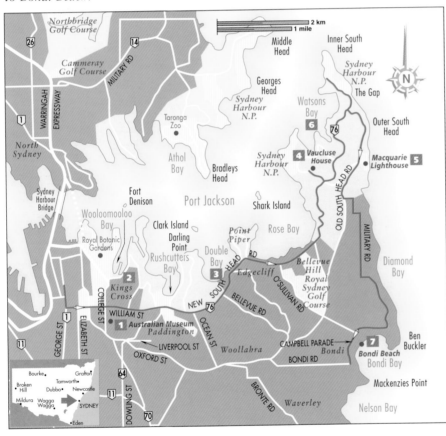

1 AUSTRALIAN MUSEUM

The Australian Museum, the nation's oldest and largest natural history museum, is located at 6 College Street near Hyde Park at the city end of William Street. Its displays of Australian flora and fauna are considered the finest in the country and some experts have rated it as one of the world's top natural history museums. This is hardly surprising given that it is now the repository for over eight million pieces.

Of particular interest to the visitor are the permanent exhibitions on Aboriginal Australia, local mammals, birds and insects. There is also an excellent, and hugely popular, dinosaur display. The museum has particularly impressive exhibits on Australia's delicate ecology (called Dream-time to Dust) and a hands-on exhibit called Discovery Space.

2 KINGS CROSS

Head east along William St and before you reach the underpass turn left and head off into Kings Cross.

The most famous, or infamous, of all the inner city areas is Kings Cross, Sydney's equivalent to London's Soho. In the 1930s Kings Cross was the centre of the city's bohemian community. This continued until the 1960s when the Cross, as it was affectionately known, was still a strange and wonderful mixture of high-class hotels, bohemians, prostitutes, strip clubs, classy nightclubs and quality restaurants.

Most Sydneysiders feel the demise of the Cross can be dated to the arrival of US servicemen on rest and recreation leave from Vietnam in the mid-1960s. They injected huge amounts of cash into the suburb's economy and this inevitably

changed the area's 'charm' into something more overtly commercial.

Today the Cross is still a tourist attraction with many excellent hotels and fine restaurants; however, it has acquired a reputation as a centre of hardcore pornography, drugs and crime. If Sydney has a violent heartland then the Cross is it. The only advice to the visitor is to be careful.

Having offered that warning, it is important to remember that Kings Cross is truly schizophrenic—a Dr Jekyll by day and Mr Hyde by night. In the daytime the leafy parks and tree-lined streets, the smell of coffee from the numerous excellent coffee lounges and eateries and the attractiveness of the El Alamein fountain are all magnets. Victoria Street to the south of the Kings Cross tunnel has some outstanding places to eat and its cafes offer the best coffee in Sydney.

Perhaps the greatest attraction is just sitting in a cafe and watching the world go by. Watching the *demi monde* emerge around lunchtime, with their dark glasses and world-weary demeanour, is a fascinating pastime.

3 DOUBLE BAY

Return to New South Head Rd. Continue through Rushcutters Bay, up the hill to Edgecliff and down into Double Bay.

No visit to Sydney would be complete without a trip to Double Bay, one of Sydney's eastern suburbs noted for its self-conscious sophistication and overtly European ambience. The suburb's style is largely a result of large numbers of eastern Europeans moving into the area from the 1950s onwards. The suburb, and the surrounding suburbs of Bellevue Hill, Vaucluse and Point Piper, had always been an area where members of the city's elite lived but the arrival of wealthy eastern Europeans saw the development of a distinctive cafe society with many of the hotels and restaurants offering outdoor, on-street tables.

Double Bay is a shopping centre noted for its designer clothes shops, bookshops, antique dealers and interior decorators and its excellent

Waves breaking on Bondi Beach.

Doyles famous fish restaurant at Watsons Bay.

local cinema which commonly shows popular art movies. In recent times it has tried, successfully, to maintain a village atmosphere.

Although harbour swimming has declined in the past 20 years (largely because of pollution) there are two excellent swimming areas near Double Bay—Seven Shillings Beach and Redleaf Pool.

A particularly pleasant way to experience the suburb is to go to the ferry wharf and catch the ferry back to Circular Quay. This offers excellent views of the many large homes that line the foreshores from Double Bay to Woolloomooloo.

4 VAUCLUSE HOUSE

Leave Double Bay on New South Head Rd. Continue on up to Bellevue Hill then down to Rose Bay. From Rose Bay drive up the hill and turn left into Vaucluse Rd which winds around to Vaucluse House located 10km from the city centre.

Set in gracious grounds, the original house was built in the 19th century by Sir Thomas Henry Brown Hayes, a larger-than-life character transported to Australia for kidnapping the woman he loved, the daughter of a wealthy Irish banker.

The house was taken over by Captain John Piper (after whom Point Piper was named) in 1822. In 1827 it was purchased by the explorer William Charles Wentworth, one of the trio of men who first crossed the Blue Mountains. Wentworth carried out extensive renovations and modifications and lived in the house until 1853. It is likely that the first cabinet meeting of the newly enfranchised government of New South Wales was held at Vaucluse House in 1856.

The house is much more than a link to the early history of Sydney. It is a beautifully preserved Sydney colonial residence. The rooms are furnished with superb pieces from the period. Visitors can experience the luxury of the house and its grounds and walk through the gardens to the edge of the harbour. The Vaucluse House Tea Rooms offer fine food and are often used for weddings which are held in the gardens.

The grounds are open from 8.00am–5.00pm daily and the house is open from 10.00am–4.45pm. This is a rare opportunity to experience what life in Sydney's eastern suburbs was like for the colony's elite in the middle of the 19th century.

5 MACQUARIE LIGHTHOUSE

Return to New South Head Rd. At the top of the hill is the Macquarie Lighthouse, one of Sydney's most famous and prominent landmarks.

The first signal station on the headland, known as South Head, was established as early as 1790 to indicate that the new settlement had moved from Botany Bay north to Port Phillip. By 1794 there was an iron basket on the headland which could be lit if ships approached at night-time. In 1818 the first lighthouse, designed by convict architect Francis Greenway, was completed. It remained in service until 1873 when colonial architect James Barnet, who designed the Customs Office and the General Post Office, designed the present Macquarie Lighthouse. It was completed and opened a decade later, in 1883.

6 WATSONS BAY

Leave Macquarie Lighthouse and continue until you descend to Watsons Bay.

This is the furthest the public can drive towards the South Head headland. It is also one of the most interesting areas in Sydney's eastern suburbs. The central point is Robertson Park, where the buses from the city centre terminate. This delightful park runs down to the water's edge. There are a couple of restaurants, a hotel and a takeaway all within close proximity. The most famous of the restaurants is Doyles, which is internationally known as one of Sydney's finest seafood eateries. There can be few more pleasant experiences than to sit at Doyles at sunset and gaze across the harbour while eating fresh lobster. If you want a cheaper option, with food that is nearly as good as the restaurant's, the takeaway at the wharf offers a wide range of fresh seafood which is ideal for a picnic on the beach or in the park.

Walk up the hill to The Gap, where the distance between the harbour and the Pacific Ocean is only a few hundred metres. For years The Gap had a macabre reputation as a popular place to commit suicide. More recently, it has become a popular place for walking. Nearby is the anchor from the sailing ship *Dunbar* which, on 20 August 1857, mistook The Gap for the entrance to Sydney Harbour and was wrecked on the rocks with only one of the 121 passengers and crew surviving.

7 BONDI BEACH

Leave Watsons Bay and travel back on New South Head Rd. Instead of taking the route back to Vaucluse House, take the left-hand route on Old South Head Rd and turn left into Military Rd which winds around the coast until it drops down to North Bondi and joins Campbell Pde.

Sydney's most famous beach, Bondi has come to symbolise the Australian way of life. The image of a bronzed Aussie standing on a golden beach or a woman wearing a bikini sunbaking on the beach is synonymous with Bondi. The reality is that Bondi, which lies 7km east of the city, was the city's most popular beach from the 1890s until the 1950s because it was well-serviced by trams and it was the most readily accessible beach for people living in the inner city areas.

Early images of Bondi are decidedly European in flavour. In the 1890s, the beach had a huge aquarium as a tourist attraction. In the 1930s there were deckchairs spread from one end of the beach to the other and, on weekends, it was packed with holiday-makers and sunlovers.

By the 1960s, however, Bondi was in decline. The old seafront buildings were fading and access to the less crowded beaches north of Manly was such that they offered a better destination.

In recent times the beachfront has gone through a metamorphosis. Bondi is once again a fashionable address. The apartments and home units that characterise much of the suburb have been occupied by young people who enjoy the inner city feel of the suburb. The promenade area along Campbell Parade now offers a sophisticated cafe atmosphere where fast food outlets mix with good quality restaurants.

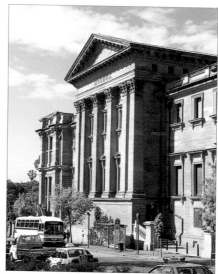

Australian Museum in College Street.

3 TARONGA ZOO, BRADLEYS HEAD AND CLIFTON GARDENS

■ FERRY AND WALKING TOUR ■ 10KM ■ 1 DAY ■ A DAY AT THE ZOO AND ON THE FORESHORE

Sydney's Middle Harbour still has large tracts of unspoilt bushland ideal for walking and exploring while Taronga Zoo boasts some of the best views of the harbour.

Sydney can boast one of the most scenically located zoos. Running from the ridge to the shoreline, *Taronga Zoo* is an excellent zoo with an array of animals and superb views over the city. From *Taronga Zoo* it is possible to walk around the foreshores to *Bradleys Head* and *Clifton Gardens*.

1 CIRCULAR QUAY AND FORT DENISON

From Circular Quay catch the ferry across the harbour to Taronga Zoo. This is a short and delightful trip which offers excellent opportunities to see the Opera House, the city skyline, the Royal Botanic Gardens and Fort Denison from the water. The ferry leaves from Wharf Two, and the journey takes about 12 minutes.

Although the ferry does not stop at Fort Denison (it is possible to catch a separate ferry there), as you pass the island try to imagine what this crag of rock was like on 11 February 1788 (in the middle of summer) when the convict Thomas Hill was sentenced to be 'sent and confined in Irons for the space of one Week on Bread and Water on the small white rocky Island adjacent to this Cove'. At the time it was called Rock Island, measured only one-fifth of a hectare, and stood 25m above the high tidemark at its highest point. In 1796 the convict Francis

Morgan was hanged on the island, and his body was allowed to rot and his bones to bleach for the next four years.

In 1841, over concern about Sydney Town's lack of protection, it was decided that the island would be quarried to sea level

and a fort built. The fort was completed in 1857 with its distinctive martello tower and three 8in, 32lb guns hoisted to the top of the tower. The guns and the fort were never used to defend the city, however. The views of the city centre and the Opera House from Fort Denison are worth a separate journey there.

2 TARONGA ZOO

The ferry arrives at Athol Wharf and there are three ways of exploring the zoo. The most sensible is to catch the gondola from the wharf to the top of the zoo and then walk back to the wharf through the zoo. You can also catch a bus to the main gate or you can enter the zoo from the wharf area and walk up the hill exploring the exhibitions.

Taronga Zoo was opened in 1916. On 24 September, the first ferry from Circular Quay to the zoo carried an elephant named Jessie. She stayed at the zoo until her death in 1939. Soon after Jessie's arrival, a regular passenger ferry service was established.

Voted the best international zoo in 1992, Taronga Zoo has superb views over Sydney Harbour and a substantial collection of Australian native fauna. The zoo is open from 9.00am–5.00pm every day and the displays include echidnas, dingoes, wombats, kangaroos and wallabies, plus Australian snakes and spiders. The koala walkabout and platypus exhibit offer exceptional opportunities to study these creatures which few Australians have seen in the wild.

The impressive main gates at Taronga Zoo in Mosman.

There is also a comprehensive display of animals from all around the world with the monkeys and apes being particular favourites. The animals are fed at various times of the day. The aim is to structure the activities in such a manner that people can make their way progressively down the hill. In recent years the zoo has successfully sought sponsorship, so among the exhibits is the McDonald's Orangutan Rainforest, the Coca-Cola Bottlers Chimpanzee Park, the SC Johnson Wax Platypus exhibition and the Sydney Water Macquarie Island display. The zoo prides itself in being an example of modern zoological best practice and consequently the old cage system has slowly given way to a more animal-friendly environment.

3 ATHOL WHARF TO BRADLEYS HEAD

Return to Athol Wharf (the zoo wharf) and start walking back up the hill until you reach what is known as the zoo's lower gate, 250m from the ferry. From this point (it is 4km from here to Clifton Gardens) the track winds around the shoreline of Athol Bay. There are excellent views across the harbour. The walk to Bradleys Head is about 25 minutes.

Bradleys Head, according to enthusiasts, offers the best view of Sydney Harbour. It was named after William Bradley, the first lieutenant on HMS *Sirius*, one of the ships in the First Fleet. The fortifications at the top of the headland (which once looked straight out to the Heads but are now surrounded by trees) were first constructed in the 1840s as part of the defence program which also saw the construction of Fort Denison. The program was a result of two American men'o'war that simply sailed through Sydney Heads one night and anchored off Sydney Cove. Not surprisingly, the citizens of Sydney Town were somewhat alarmed when they woke in the morning to see two warships in the bay. They realised that in the event of war, they were inadequately protected.

Some fortifications were built on the headland but they were not completed at that time. It wasn't until the 1870s, when there was fear that the war in Europe might spill over to Australia, that the guns which now stand in the fortifications were unloaded at North Sydney and moved along a poorly made bush track. The track eventually became known as Military Road, the name it still has today. The guns and the fortifications are great fun for children, with the underground passageways and the huge guns that can be clambered over.

4 THE MAST OF HMAS *SYDNEY*

Continue from the old fortifications down the hill to the water's edge, taking in the beautiful harbour views on the way. The delightful park at the base of the hill is ideal for picnics. You will soon notice the mast from HMAS Sydney.

HMAS *Sydney* looms large in the naval history of Australia. On 9 November 1914 it sank the German ship *Emden* near the Keeling Islands in the Indian Ocean. The mast was placed at Bradleys Head as a celebration of the ship's famous victory.

5 CHOWDER BAY

Return up the hill to the fortifications. There is a set of steps beside the toilets. Continue along the road until you reach the track which will take you around the headland to Chowder Bay and Clifton Gardens.

The walk passes through some particularly delightful bushland with black wattle and tree ferns. It also provides endless, excellent views across the harbour. On the way to Clifton Gardens take the turn-off to Chowder Bay. This pleasant bay is surrounded by bushland. Like everywhere else on this walk, the bay offers beautiful views over the harbour.

6 CLIFTON GARDENS

Return to the main track. Clifton Gardens is now only 500m away down the hillside.

It is one of the happy accidents of Sydney Harbour that this entire area is protected by nearly 20km of foreshore and it has always been illegal to build any residence closer than 30m from the shoreline. The area was granted for land use about 1831. It was around this time that Thomas Graham, who worked at the Botanic Gardens, began developing a garden on the low-lying flats beside the harbour. He planted an orchard, grew a variety of vegetables in his garden and, as was typical of the early settlers, planted a number of European trees to remind him of his native England.

Clifton Gardens is a peaceful retreat from the hurly-burly of the city. During the week it is very quiet and on the weekends it attracts numbers of people but, as a general principle, only those people who know its charms. It is not a common destination for those simply looking for a good picnic spot.

There was a time when Clifton Gardens did attract undesirables. In fact in the 1890s it was a popular weekend retreat for inner city gangs who would fight each other and cause mayhem among the more sedate holiday-makers. In her book *The Companion Guide to Sydney*, Ruth Park quotes a contemporary

Aerial view of Bradley's Head.

description of the leader of the louts whose clothes were ornamented

> ... coster fashion with pearl buttons. He had red parrakeet boots all silk and embroidery, and decorated with rows of silver bells which jangled as he walked. He had his photo inlaid on the toe of one boot, and his donah's [girlfriend's] picture on the other. His queer little hat was sacred. To knock it off was to challenge him to war. Formidable fighter as he was, his donah was yet more feared. When she got properly going, no one, not even a policeman, would attempt to quieten her.

As you make your way up the hill from Clifton Gardens you will marvel at the size and graciousness of the homes. The district has some of the finest Queen Anne mansions in Sydney. The buildings are set mostly in huge grounds. In the days when they were built it was common to have grand tennis courts, wide entrances and gracious gardens. Many of these have disappeared as the large holdings have been subdivided.

Once at the top of Thompson St it is possible to catch a bus back to Athol Wharf or to walk down Bradleys Head Rd to the wharf. The walk from Clifton Gardens via David St and Thompson St back to the upper gates of the zoo is 2.3km.

Fort Denison was an isolated prison for the most dangerous convicts.

4 THE NORTHERN BEACHES AND PITTWATER
■ DRIVING TOUR ■ 31KM ■ 1 DAY ■ A DAY EXPLORING THE BEACHES FROM MANLY TO PALM BEACH

Elegant crescents of yellow sand arc between rocky cliffs and offer Sydneysiders outstanding surfing and leisure beaches from Manly to Palm Beach.

Sydney's northern beaches stretch like a string of pearls from Manly Beach (located on a narrow isthmus of land north of North Head) to Palm Beach, which lies south of the mouth to the Hawkesbury River. The beaches are a playground in the summer with people flocking to their favourite destinations. A driving trip through this area is essentially about stopping to enjoy the views and, if the journey is made in summertime, an opportunity to swim or surf at the many excellent beaches along the way.

1 MANLY

It is easy to spend an entire day at Manly. The suburb is a classic seaside destination with three good surf beaches (in reality it is only one, broken up into Manly, North Steyne and Queenscliff), a mall that stretches from the ocean to the harbour, many holiday attractions and fast food outlets, and a pleasant harbourside where the ferries from Circular Quay arrive and depart.

Rumour has it that the suburb got its name when Governor Arthur Phillip, visiting the area in January 1788, noted the strength and masculinity of the local Aborigines and decided to name the place Manly Cove. The area was settled by Europeans as early as 1810 but development didn't occur until 1853, when Henry Gilbert Smith purchased 100ac for £1000. Smith was the true father of the suburb, establishing a ferry service the following year and naming the main street

from the harbour to the ocean The Corso after a street he remembered in Rome. In 1855, Smith subdivided the area and began selling plots of land. He is also credited with the planting of the Norfolk pines that characterise the suburb and offer shade on both sides of the isthmus.

By the 1860s, although there was a ban on daylight bathing, the beaches were being used for sunbathing and there were bathing boxes which were wheeled into the water so that people could bath in private. By the turn of the century this ban on daylight bathing was being challenged.

One brave swimmer, William Gocher, editor of a Manly newspaper, decided the laws were stupid and needed to be changed. He went for a swim at Manly Beach on 8 September 1902. In his book *Lifesaver*, Peter James recalls:

Through the pages of his paper, he announced his intention of bathing at mid-day on the following Sunday from Manly's ocean beach. A large crowd gathered to see Gocher hauled off to gaol in a horse-drawn paddy wagon, but the police did not appear. The following day, Gocher went to the Police Commissioner asking for clarification of the legal situation regarding sea bathing during daylight hours. The Commissioner informed him that no police action would be taken against citizens if they bathed during the day, providing they were suitably clad.

While in Manly you should walk along The Corso from the harbourside to the ocean front, then turn southwards and make your way up Darley Road which is in the middle of The Corso (this can be done by car if you don't want to spend a couple of hours walking around the suburb). You will first pass St Patrick's College (now a hotel management college) which was built in 1884 to train young Catholic priests. From here, continue along North Head Scenic Drive. This will take you to some of the best and most impressive views over the harbour as well as the fascinating old buildings of the Old Quarantine Station where passengers from overseas who were suspected of carrying disease were housed prior to their arrival in Sydney.

2 MANLY TO NEWPORT

Return to your car. If you have driven to North Head, return along the route (3.8km) you have taken and turn into Belgrave St at the harbourside end of The Corso. After 500m Belgrave St becomes Pittwater Rd, which winds up the coast towards Newport, Pittwater and Palm Beach.

South Steyne, one of Manly's beaches.

Each one of the beaches along the way has its own appeal and it is part of the pleasure of the trip to turn off and enjoy the views or to walk along the beaches. At Dee Why (the name probably comes from the Aboriginal word *diwai*, which was used to describe a bird that lived in the lagoon) turn into Howard Avenue, which will take you to the beach and the pleasant saltwater baths. At Long Reef–Collaroy, drive past the golf course (beautifully located on the headland) and turn seaward on Anzac Avenue. There are views from the headland which has a number of fine examples of fossils embedded in the rock platform and is now part of the Long Reef Aquatic Reserve. Just a little further along the coast (which can be accessed by turning north into Beach Road off Anzac Avenue) is

Manly's busy mall—The Corso.

Boats moored near the Palm Beach wharf.

Collaroy Beach and Collaroy's excellent rock pool. The beach has a reputation for a strong undertow so stay between the flags if you decide to go for a swim.

The road then turns slightly away from the coast and passes through Narrabeen, with its large lake, and Mona Vale (the main road here becomes Barrenjoey Road while Pittwater Road heads off to the left) before swinging back and rising over the headland and dropping down to Newport.

3 PITTWATER

After 17km the road from Manly enters the small village suburb of Newport. Turn west in Newport and explore Pittwater. Along the shoreline you will find the famous Newport Arms, the Royal Motor Yacht Club and the Royal Prince Alfred Yacht Club as well the baths at Salt Pan Cove.

Pittwater is a glorious expanse of water. It was discovered by Governor Phillip in 1788 who, naming it after William Pitt the Younger, declared it to be 'the finest piece of water which I ever saw ... it would contain the navy of Great Britain'. Governor Phillip would be amazed that the place he imagined containing the navy of Great Britain today contains only small pleasure craft and numerous windsurfers. Pittwater is an area of natural beauty and a pleasant retreat from the city, offering ferry trips, easy access to beaches, well-protected swimming areas and quietness unlike the more populated ocean beaches, and various local bushwalks.

4 PALM BEACH

Return to Newport Shopping Centre. The journey to Palm Beach is 9km along Barrenjoey Rd. The road rises above the coast and then drops down to Avalon before winding around Pittwater.

Of special interest are the views afforded from the ridge that runs up the coast. This ridge becomes particularly impressive along the peninsula, where the wonders of modern architecture and engineering find houses perched on the edges of cliffs. Palm Beach is one of Sydney's most attractive weekend retreats, noted for its sailing boats and its ferry service across to The Basin.

In theory, although most of the locals would disagree, Palm Beach and Pittwater are part of Sydney. In reality, the people who live on the Peninsula (as they call the area) think of themselves as being distanced from what goes on far to the south. Certainly, a trip to Palm Beach is not like visiting a beach in the Sydney metropolitan area.

There is a variety of attractions awaiting the visitor at Palm Beach. The ferry trip across to The Basin (the ferry leaves from the Palm Beach public wharf at Snapperman Beach) is a good way to start, and from The Basin there are a number of interesting walks around the shoreline of the Ku-ring-gai National Park. On the Palm Beach side of Pittwater at Snapperman Beach are a number of good restaurants and fish and chips shops. The walk along the isthmus, either along the beach or east of the golf course,

and up to the lighthouse is well worth the effort. The lighthouse was designed by James Barnet, the colonial architect who designed the Sydney GPO, the Customs House at Circular Quay and the lighthouse at South Head. It was built in 1881 and for many years operated as an important beacon for the traffic that plied the Hawkesbury River and the waters of Broken Bay. The view from Barrenjoey across to Lion Island and north to the Central Coast justifies the walk. But for the highly regarded Sydney writer Ruth Park, the reason for visiting Palm Beach was simply 'to join the bodies lying motionless on the singularly golden sand, stupefied with sun, staring through their eyelids at the sky'.

5 WHALE BEACH

When you reach the main surfing area of Palm Beach, take the road up the hill. This is Florida Rd and, as it winds around the coastline, it becomes Whale Beach Rd.

One of the highlights of the journey to Palm Beach is the round trip. By following the winding Florida Road and Whale Beach Road back along the coast every turn brings another spectacular view and another million dollar mansion into view.

The whole area is worth exploring. Over the years millionaires, film stars and musicians have settled on the Peninsula. The houses they have built at Palm Beach and Whale Beach are dramatic exercises in cliff perching. The views are superb. It is easy to imagine the lifestyle that goes on inside these opulent residences matches the view.

Whale Beach itself is a well-kept secret. Difficult to access, the land wasn't sold as residential blocks until the 1920s and it wasn't until 1927 that the first house was built. No-one knows exactly how the area got its name. Some argue that a whale was washed onto the beach in the early years of this century while others insist that Little Head (the headland at the north of the beach) looks like a whale.

Whale Beach Rd winds down toward Barrenjoey Rd and from there it is 38km back to the centre of Sydney.

Sailing yachts and fishing cruises moored in Pittwater.

5 KU-RING-GAI CHASE AND WEST HEAD

■ DRIVING TOUR ■ 126KM ■ 1 DAY ■ A DAY IN KU-RING-GAI CHASE

On the northern edge of the Sydney basin is the Ku-ring-gai National Park, an area of wild bushland and beautiful, isolated beaches.

The Ku-ring-gai Chase National Park is the city's northerly barrier. Suburban development reaches to the borders of the park and then leaps across the Hawkesbury River and Broken Bay to start again on the Central Coast. The national park is an escape from the city. It is close and yet, when you start wandering along the bush tracks or clambering around the rocky headlands and small beaches, you feel as though you are in bushland that hasn't changed for thousands of years and the city is an infinite distance away. The park is notable for three major activities: bush-walking (the paths are easy to follow and offer excellent variety), picnics and barbecues (there are parks on the water's edge and, if you are in a boat, wonderful, isolated beaches) and boating. The beaches and foreshores of the park are designed to cater for all kinds of boats.

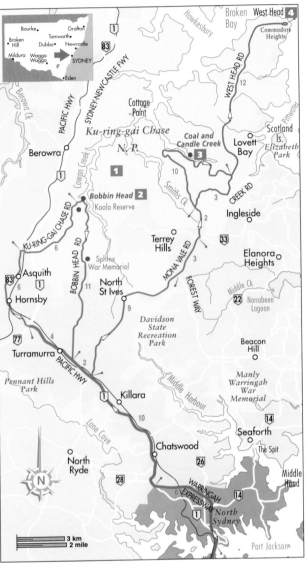

1 KU-RING-GAI CHASE NATIONAL PARK

Drive north along the Pacific Hwy for 18km from Sydney to Pymble. About 2km beyond Pymble shopping centre turn right into Bobbin Head Rd and continue for 6km until you reach the entrance to the national park.

Covering 14 658ha and situated about 24km from the centre of Sydney, the Ku-ring-gai Chase National Park is located on the sandstones and shales of the Sydney basin. The geological history of the park is that about 200 million years ago the sea level rose to cover the swamps, deltas and coastal channels of the east coast. Inevitably, sand was laid down by the ocean. About 50 million years later, the rocks that had been formed by these deep deposits of sand were uplifted and, as they rose, the creeks and rivers running to the ocean cut deep valleys. When the ice melted after the last ice age (about 6000 years ago) the valleys were drowned, forming Broken Bay and the subsidiary valley systems of Pittwater, Coal and Candle Creek, Smiths Creek, Cowan Creek and Berowra Waters.

The result is Sydney sandstone covered by typically thin, sandy soils that produce a kind of heathland on the plateau and eucalypts in the valleys. It seems extraordinary, given the poorness of the soils, but

Ku-ring-gai Chase has over 900 native species of flora and, although the larger animals have long gone, it has a surprising diversity of fauna.

The range of eucalypts—the Sydney red gum and scribbly gum are in abundance—the angophoras, the varieties of coastal banksia, the wattles and the wildflower displays, make any walk through the park a discovery of the variety of plants that once existed across the entire Sydney basin. In the gullies the enthusiast will find coachwood, water gums and turpentine.

The winter and spring wildflower displays in the park are truly magnificent. The dramatic red of the waratah is matched by purple and pink boronias, yellow pea flowers, and the pink and white heath make it a native flower wonderland. There are few places on the eastern coast, and particularly so close to

Sydney, where such displays are so readily accessible to keen bushwalkers.

There is much argument about the name Ku-ring-gai. Some sources claim that it is a corruption of 'Gurringai', the name of a group of Aborigines who lived in the area. Other sources claim the name was 'Garingal', while others claim the word means 'the home and hunting ground of the Kuring people'. Whatever the case, the Dhurag people lived in the area before European settlement and the park is one of the richest sources of Aboriginal art and culture in the Sydney basin.

Ku-ring-gai Chase National Park is a monument to the forethought of a small group of people who, in the 1890s, decided that 'in the interest of this rapidly increasing neighbourhood, of the inhabitants of the

The bridge over Cowan Water at Bobbin Head.

Boating on Coal and Candle Creek.

Aerial view of Lion Island at the mouth of Broken Bay.

North Shore generally' an area around the Cowan Creek should be set aside 'as a National Park for North Sydney'. The government was receptive to the idea and in 1894 the park was declared.

At this edge of the park is the famous Lady Davidson Rehabilitation Hospital, where for decades the victims of the gassings on the western front during World War I stayed and recuperated. It has been a long-term hospital for the war wounded and it is a comment on the life of these men and women (many of whom had a normal life taken from them by war) that just within the gates of the national park is the Sphinx War Memorial (turn right after entering the park), which was carved out of the Hawkesbury sandstone by diggers recuperating at the hospital. The Sphinx is a strange memento of the fact that so many Anzacs stopped in Egypt before being shipped across the Mediterranean to Gallipoli.

Near the Sphinx War Memorial is the start of the Bobbin Head Track, which winds through the bush to the wharves at Bobbin Head. The Sphinx Track, which starts behind the memorial, goes down to Cowan Creek and follows it to Bobbin Head. This is a pleasant, but quite lengthy, walk which takes a couple of hours. It should only be attempted if you are not intending to complete the rest of this tour. The Sphinx Track is an excellent introduction to the variety of flora in the national park and the park at the end of the walk is ideal for picnics and barbecues.

2 BOBBIN HEAD

Continue down the hill from the Sphinx for 3.6km and you will reach the parks and waterfront at Bobbin Head. Bobbin Head is the most developed area of the park with the famous Halvorsen Boat Sheds plus a variety of other nautical organisations offering cruisers for hire. There is a large picnic area with extensive parking and good barbecue facilities.

Visitors interested in the diversity of fauna and flora in the park will find the Kalkari Visitors Centre (about 1.5km west of Bobbin Head on the Ku-ring-gai Chase Road) an ideal starting point. The Visitors Centre has detailed displays of the flora and fauna in the park, plus maps and information for bushwalkers. There is a great variety of walks in the park, ranging from short, easy walks around the picnic areas to major walks such as the one from West Head to The Basin and beyond. The park provides easy-to-understand maps and, in many instances, the walks are defined by coloured and numbered signs.

3 COAL AND CANDLE CREEK

Leave the Kalkari Visitors Centre and drive 4.5km west along Ku-ring-gai Chase Rd until you reach the T-intersection at Belmont Pde. Turn right and left to cross the railway line and head south on the old Pacific Hwy for 11.5km until you reach the major intersection of the Pacific Hwy with Mona Vale Rd. Turn east into Mona Vale Rd and continue for 9.5km until, having passed through Terrey Hills, you see McCarrs Creek Rd which becomes West Head Rd. Follow this road for a further 7km until you reach the edges of Coal and Candle Creek.

The Coal and Candle Creek journey passes through bushland before tumbling down to the edges of Broken Bay. In her book *The Companion Guide to Sydney*, the highly regarded Australian author Ruth Park advises visitors to Coal and Candle Creek to 'stop the car and poke around the rocks, disturbing perhaps a tree goanna, flattened on a warm stone, striped toes splayed, or a tawny frogmouth, seemingly made of bark, but with an expression like an old vicar'.

Regardless of whether you see owls or goannas, this is an area for picnicking and exploring. That is the great thing about Ku-ring-gai Chase. All you have to do is explore. If you're lazy you can lie in the picnic grounds, fall asleep after a huge lunch, and let the rest of the family go off and explore. Like Bobbin Head, Coal and Candle Creek is a retreat from the rush and bustle of the city.

4 WEST HEAD

From Coal and Candle Creek continue along General San Martin Drv for a further 5km until you reach West Head Rd, turn left and continue for 14m until you reach the parking area at Commodore Heights which is also known as West Head.

A favourite sightseeing location in the Ku-ring-gai Chase National Park is the lookout at West Head, sometimes known as Commodore Heights. This superb view of the mouth of the drowned Hawkesbury River, known at this point as Broken Bay, has views across to Lion Island (so named because from various angles it looks like a crouching lion), across to Patonga and to the narrow isthmus of sand that separates Palm Beach from the Barrenjoey headland. There can be few views in the Sydney area to compare with the wonderful diversity and beauty of this vista. It is possible from this point to walk down to Pittwater, where the beaches below are ideal locations for picnics—the path is located to the south of the viewing area. For those who are keen it is possible to walk around to The Basin (a marvellous expanse of water protected from Pittwater by a narrow channel) and catch the ferry across to Palm Beach. Such a journey presumes that there is someone in the party who is happy to drive to Palm Beach to collect the walkers. The ferries from The Basin arrive and depart from the wharf near Snapperman Beach.

From West Head return to Sydney either by driving directly to Terrey Hills or taking the turn to Newport and returning via the city's northern beaches. The journey from West Head via Terrey Hills is 43.5km from the centre of the city.

Smiths Creek in the Ku-ring-gai Chase National Park.

6 THE LOWER BLUE MOUNTAINS

■ DRIVING TOUR ■ 50KM ■ 1 DAY ■ FROM CONVICT HISTORY TO ARTISTIC RETREAT

Convict-built bridges, quiet lakes and excellent bushwalks characterise the gentle slopes at the eastern edge of the Blue Mountains.

The Blue Mountains to the west of Sydney are one of the most popular destinations in New South Wales. Within easy reach of Sydney (the Nepean River at the eastern base of the mountains is only 57km from the city centre), the Blue Mountains are a fascinating combination of spectacular views, interesting convict history, chic restaurants and holiday destinations, and small artistic retreats. The lower Blue Mountains (from Glenbrook to Springwood) seem like an extension of suburban Sydney but they have a number of excellent attractions including some very fine convict-built roads and bridges and, most notably, the beautiful sandstone house in which the famous Australian artist Norman Lindsay lived for many years.

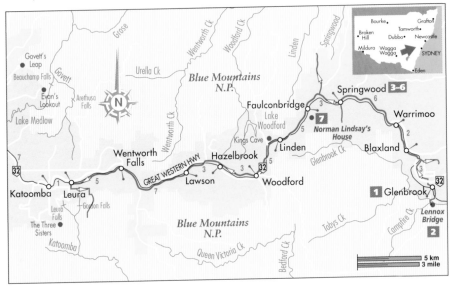

1 GLENBROOK

Turn right off the Great Western Hwy just after the Tourist Information Centre (in Hare St) and then turn left into Levy St. Turn right when you reach Glenbrook Rd and you will reach the Glenbrook Lagoon, about 1.5km from the tourist information centre.

Glenbrook is an obvious starting point for any exploration of the Blue Mountains. There is an excellent tourist information centre located on the Great Western Highway which provides travellers with bushwalking maps and brochures, as well as details of how to get to the main sights.

Glenbrook was first mentioned by Europeans when Blaxland, Lawson and Wentworth, while crossing the Blue Mountains, passed the Glenbrook Lagoon on 12 May 1813. They described it as 'a large lagoon of good water full of very coarse rushes'. It later became a notable landmark when William Cox, who built the first road over the mountains, erected a storeroom near the lagoon. Subsequently, Governor Lachlan Macquarie placed a military depot on the road near the lagoon to monitor movements over the mountains.

In *Fourteen Journeys over the Blue Mountains*, Major Henry Antill described the settlement at Glenbrook in 1815 as

… a good log hut with two rooms, one of which answers as a store. It is placed about 100 yards on the right of the road, near a small lagoon of fresh water. The soldiers have enclosed a small piece of ground for a garden, and one of them had displayed some taste in laying it out in little arbours and seats formed from the surrounding shrubbery.

The small township of Glenbrook really came into existence in 1874, with the construction of the zigzag railway up the Lapstone monocline to a place called Wascoes Siding, named after a nearby inn. On completion, water from Glenbrook lagoon was piped to the trains. Today the lagoon is a pleasant retreat with reeds around its edges and numerous birds, particularly ducks and mallards, using its foreshores.

2 LENNOX BRIDGE

Continue along Glenbrook Rd until you reach Mitchells Pass Rd which, if you turn east, offers access to Lennox

Bridge, the Quarry, Knapsack Gully Creek and Elizabeth Lookout. Continue down the road, back towards the base of the mountains, for 2.5km until you reach Lennox Bridge.

Lennox Bridge was built by David Lennox (1788–1873), a Scottish master mason who had worked with the famous British bridge builder Thomas Telford before emigrating to Australia. The bridge is the second oldest stone arch bridge in Australia.

The bridge was Lennox's first job after his appointment as Superintendent of Bridges. Assisted by 20 convicts, he began work in November 1832 and the bridge was completed in July 1833. The bridge is held up on a 3m radius stone arch and is about 10m above the gully floor. On the keystones were carved 'David Lennox' (now difficult to see) and 'AD 1833'. The bridge remained in continuous use from 1833 until 1926, and was open until 1964.

3 SPRINGWOOD

The road from Lennox Bridge is one way. To return to Glenbrook you have to drive down Mitchells Pass Rd for 2km to Emu Plains, turn left and drive 500m until you once again join the Great Western Hwy. Drive 5.5km back up the hill and you will reach the Glenbrook Tourist Information Centre. From here it is 13km to Springwood. To enter Springwood you have to turn left into Macquarie Rd off the Great Western Hwy.

Like all the settlements in the Blue Mountains, Springwood really started to

Lennox Bridge near Glenbrook.

develop after the arrival of the railway in 1867. The township had been named by Governor Macquarie when he first crossed the mountains in 1815. He noted a 'pretty wooded Plain near a Spring of very good fresh Water' and named it 'Spring-Wood'.

Most of the interesting buildings are in Macquarie Street, which runs along the southern side of the railway line. Braemar, in Macquarie Road, was built in 1892 and is now owned by the Blue Mountains City Council. It is a typical colonial cottage of the period.

Further along Macquarie Road is the Frazer Memorial Presbyterian Church. The church was built from local stone in 1895, after John Frazer, a politician who had built a large mansion in Springwood, bequeathed £5000 to the church.

The Springwood Railway Station in Macquarie Road was built on the railway platform in 1884 and, because it has become an essential part of the Springwood townscape and is an interesting example of railway architecture of the period, it is now classified by the National Trust.

4 FAIRY DELL

Continue west along Macquarie Rd for approximately 1km and turn left into Raymond St. Take the first turn to the right into Springwood Ave and follow the signs to the Fairy Dell Reserve.

One of the attractions of Springwood for bushwalkers is the Fairy Dell, which is located no more than 10 minutes from the railway station. The walk, which heads from Springwood Avenue behind the car park on the south side of the railway line, can last for 40 minutes and come out at Picnic Point or continue for an hour and reach Lawsons Lookout. The ferns, native plants and peaceful bush settings are delightful, a point that was not lost on the writers of *The Pictorial Guide to the Blue Mountains of New South Wales* who, in 1882, observed, 'Going through the grounds at the back of the "Royal", a beautiful secluded gully will be found with several stretches of flat land, where the thoughtful owner of the hotel has had seats placed, and on hot days this cool retreat is very enjoyable.'

5 HENRY PARKES' GRAVE AND THE CORRIDOR OF OAKS

Return to Springwood Ave and turn right into Homedale St and then left into Macquarie Rd. Continue for about 2.5km and the grave of Sir Henry Parkes is clearly marked on the left-hand side of the road.

One of the earliest residents was Sir Henry Parkes, who moved to the area in 1877. It is said that the original railway platform at Faulconbridge was specifically built to serve his residence which was known as Faulconbridge House.

Sir Henry Parkes' grave is in Faulconbridge Cemetery. On the railing surrounding his grave is a plaque that describes his role in Australian history:

Sir Henry Parkes, Father of Australian Federation, five times Prime Minister of New South Wales, arrived in Australia July 25, 1839, worked as station-hand,

Braemer, built in 1892 in Springwood.

Customs Officer, bone and ivory turner. In 1850 became proprietor of Empire Newspaper. Member of New South Wales Parliament from 1854–1894, Sir Henry Parkes is especially remembered for his efforts to develop New South Wales Education and Railways and his work for Federation earned him his title Father of Federation.

6 PRIME MINISTERS AVENUE

You have already passed the Avenue of Oaks. Turn the car around and return along Macquarie Rd for about 500m until you reach a small park that is signposted on your left. The Avenue of Oaks lies between the road and the railway line.

The Prime Ministers Avenue of Oaks is located in Jackson Park. Joseph Jackson, a New South Wales Member of Parliament, gave the park to the local council in 1933 with the explicit intention of having every Australian Prime Minister, or a nearest surviving relative, plant an oak tree. Jackson was a huge admirer of Henry Parkes and believed that his Avenue of Oaks was a suitable monument to the man most responsible for the federation of Australian states.

7 NORMAN LINDSAY'S HOUSE

At the western end of the Avenue of Oaks cross back onto the Great Western Hwy and turn towards the east. About 700m from the turn-off take the Grose Rd to your left and travel north for 600m until you reach Chapman Pde. About 1.3km along Chapman Pde is Norman Lindsay Cres, which offers parking for visitors.

Norman Lindsay moved to Leura in 1911. In 1912, after seeing the property while riding down a wood-cutters' track, he bought 17ha of land and the stone house at 128 Chapman Pde, Faulconbridge, for £500. Over the years Lindsay made the house a centre for artists and writers and it became a popular retreat.

The house and gardens are now owned by the National Trust, which has preserved the gardens (they are particularly beautiful when the wisteria is in full bloom) and presented an excellent display of Lindsay's model ships, paintings and illustrations.

By any measure, local or international, Lindsay was a prodigious and highly original talent. His artistic skills ranged from cartoons through paintings (both watercolours and oils) to statues, model-ship building, etchings, pen drawings, pencil drawings, novel and children's fiction writing, book illustration, furniture and pottery decoration.

Apart from short periods in Sydney, Lindsay spent the rest of his life in Faulcon-

The gardens of Norman Lindsay's house.

bridge. When he died in 1969 (having spent nearly 60 years in the Blue Mountains) he left 16 watercolours, 17 oil paintings, nine pen drawings and a good sample of his pencil drawings, ship models and sculptures to the National Trust on the understanding that it would purchase the house at Faulconbridge and display the bequest.

The gallery is a delight. Lindsay's fleshy nudes and leering satyrs, his acerbic commentaries on the foibles and inhibitions of the bourgeoisie, his superb use of light, his wonderful sense of 'naughty' humour, give all his paintings and pen sketches a continuing relevance. In style they don't belong to the 20th century but in subject matter they are truly timeless.

For most Australians their major contact with the work of Norman Lindsay is through *The Magic Pudding* (1917), which has become a classic of children's literature. The gallery features illustrations from the book.

The gallery's display of Lindsay's ship models (it owns eight from a known production of 14) is perhaps its most important asset. The ships are extraordinary in their detail and craftsmanship.

Drive 2km back to the Great Western Hwy and then 14.5km back to Glenbrook.

Frazer Memorial Presbyterian Church.

7 THE UPPER BLUE MOUNTAINS

■ DRIVING TOUR ■ 23KM ■ 6 HOURS ■ SPECTACULAR SCENERY AND MOUNTAIN RETREATS

Sheer sandstone cliffs, spectacular views and dense bushland make the Upper Blue Mountains one of the premier tourist attractions in New South Wales.

The Blue Mountains between Leura and Mount Victoria is the true heart of this spectacularly beautiful area. This is the area with the most famous views (the Three Sisters at Katoomba and Govett's Leap at Blackheath), the most historic and opulent hotels, the best springtime gardens and the most chic villages. In winter the area is brushed occasionally by snow. In summer it is a delightful retreat from the oppressive humidity of the Sydney basin. This is Sydney's answer to the famous hill stations of India—an elegant retreat for the wealthy.

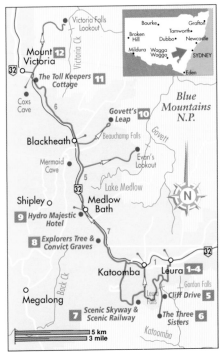

1 LEURA

The journey starts from the Mall, the main shopping street in the village of Leura.

Leura is the most urbane and sophisticated of all the villages in the Blue Mountains. Its Mall is full of chic coffee houses and eateries; its streets are tree-lined and elegant; its houses are attractive and commonly surrounded by English and European-style gardens.

The first Europeans in the area were Blaxland, Lawson and Wentworth in 1813, who reputedly spent a night camped near today's Leura Railway Station. The railway station was constructed in 1891. In the 1920s the area was a popular holiday destination for Sydneysiders eager to escape the heat and humidity of the city. By the 1970s it had become popular with Sydney's artistic community as a weekend escape destination. An appropriate start to any visit in this area is to walk the length of the Mall, choose one of the many coffee shops and have a cup of coffee.

2 SUBLIME POINT LOOKOUT

Drive down the Mall. At the bottom of the Mall turn left into Megalong St and continue until you reach Gladstone Rd. Turn right and continue to the Fitzroy St T-intersection. Turn left and follow the road until you reach Sublime Point Rd. Follow it to the end.

Sublime Point Lookout is regarded by many as the finest of all the lookouts in the Blue Mountains. It has views across the Jamison Valley towards the Three Sisters at Katoomba and, particularly on warm days, it is common to see the blueness that rises from the gum trees that cover the valleys and the hilltops.

3 EVERGLADES

Return up Sublime Point Rd until you reach Fitzroy St. Instead of turning right into Gladstone Rd, continue straight ahead to Everglades Ave. Turn left and you reach Everglades Gardens.

Everglades is a National Trust property with 5ha of gardens that contain native bushland mixed with displays of bluebells, daffodils, rhododendrons and azaleas. The gardens were created in the 1930s by Danish-born landscape designer Paul Sorenson who was working, sometimes with as many as 60

assistants, for Henri Van de Velde, a wealthy Sydney businessman. Everglades is open from 9.00am daily.

4 LEURALLA

Drive up Everglades Ave until you reach Craigend St. Turn left and continue until you reach the Leura Mall road, turn left again and continue down Leura Mall to Olympian Pde. Leuralla is located on the left-hand side of the road.

Located at the bottom of the Leura Mall road (near Olympian Parade), Leuralla is open on weekends. This impressive Art Deco mansion houses the Dr H.V. Evatt Memorial Museum as well as a substantial art collection. Across the road is a little amphitheatre with excellent views across the Jamison Valley.

5 CLIFF DRIVE

Continue around Olympian Drv, into Lone Pine Ave and then Gordon Rd which, heading west, becomes Cliff Drv.

The Cliff Drive between Leura and Katoomba is a highlight of any visit to the area. The views across the Megalong and Jamison valleys, the different angles on the

Three Sisters, the Ruined Castle and Mount Solitary, the variety of excellent picnic spots and the range of lookouts make this a must for anyone wanting to experience the full beauty of the area.

6 THE THREE SISTERS

Continue along Cliff Drv until you reach Echo Point Rd. Turn left and park in the Echo Point car park.

The Katoomba area became hugely popular

The Three Sisters viewed from Echo Point, Katoomba.

Hydro Majestic Hotel, Medlow Bath.

with the establishment of a railway station in 1876. It quickly became a favourite holiday resort providing excellent bushwalking, delightful views over the valleys and gracious hotels. Any visit to Katoomba should start at Echo Point. Not only does the point offer superb views but the Blue Mountains Tourist Centre will provide you with all the maps and information you can possibly require. Echo Point offers exceptional views of the Three Sisters, Mount Solitary, the Ruined Castle and the vast Jamison Valley.

7 SCENIC SKYWAY AND SCENIC RAILWAY

Continue around the edges of the cliffs by driving up Echo Point Rd, turning into Panorama Drv and winding around Cliff Drv until you reach the signs to the Skyway and Scenic Railway. Parking is available in the large car park that adjoins the attractions.

You can cross the Jamison Valley in the Katoomba Scenic Skyway. This is not for the faint-hearted. The aerial cable car floats across the valley some 275m above the valley floor and offers views of Katoomba Falls and Orphan Rock. The Skyway, the first horizontal passenger-carrying ropeway in the southern hemisphere, was completed in 1958 and, combined with the Scenic Railway, has become one of Katoomba's top tourist attractions.

Nearby is the Scenic Railway. Built in the 1880s to bring coal from the valley floor to the top of the cliffs, it is claimed to be the steepest railway in the world. It drops 230m into the Jamison Valley in a cable car that was once used by coalminers.

8 EXPLORERS TREE AND CONVICT GRAVES

Continue west along Cliff Drv until it becomes Narrow Neck Rd. Narrow Neck Rd will take you back to the Great Western Hwy. About 2km west of Medlow Bath is a sign on the left-hand side of the road indicating the Explorers Tree.

The Explorers Tree is nothing more than the stump of a dead tree which has been preserved under a roof and surrounded by a fence. The tree is said to have been inscribed with the initials of Blaxland, Wentworth and Lawson when they passed this way in May 1813, although the famous marks are no longer evident.

About 100m from the tree is a collection of six unmarked graves (no names, just headstones cut out of rock) of convicts who died while working on the construction of the original Coxs Road across the mountains. It is worthwhile pausing to reflect on the hardships of these anonymous labourers who died so far from Britain.

9 HYDRO MAJESTIC HOTEL

Return to the Great Western Hwy and drive 3km west to Medlow Bath. On the left-hand side of the road is the famous Hydro Majestic Hotel.

The fame of Medlow Bath hinges on the Hydro Majestic. In keeping with the medicinal qualities of the mountains, this remarkable hotel was built as a 'hydropathic establishment' in the late 19th century by Sydney businessman Mark Foy. Originally conceived as a health resort, Foy established a reputation for a strict regime of therapies. He had fresh produce delivered from the Megalong Valley via a specially built flying fox. Today, the Hydro Majestic has an old-world gentility.

10 GOVETT'S LEAP

Continue west along the Great Western Hwy for 5km until you reach the township of Blackheath. At the railway station turn right into Govett's Leap Rd and continue 2.5km until you reach Govett's Leap Lookout.

The story of Govett and his 'leap' belongs more to mythology than to fact. It is claimed that the bushranger Govett, when chased by police, spurred his horse on and rode over the waterfall which drops 450m into the Grose Valley rather than surrender. It is more likely that Govett's Leap was named after William

Romaine Govett, a young surveyor who spent many years surveying the Blue Mountains and the Hawkesbury area.

The evidence for the leap being named after the surveyor is that in 1835 William Govett wrote, 'The most remarkable of these cascades is the one near the Weatherboarded Hut (Wentworth Falls) and that which falls into the head of the Grose River; which the surveyor general named "Govett's leap" from the circumstance of my first having come upon the spot when surveying with Mr Rusden.'

11 THE TOLL KEEPERS COTTAGE

Drive 2.5km back to the Great Western Hwy, turn right (west) and drive 4km until you reach a bridge over the railway line. Directly across the bridge is the Toll Keepers Cottage.

Known variously as the Toll Bar or Toll Keepers Cottage, this historic building was completed in 1849 and is a reminder of a time when travellers along the road had to pay a toll. The toll house was used between 1849 and 1876; each coach with springs that travelled the road was required to pay one shilling and sixpence. Heavy vehicles were not charged because it was believed they helped to crush the loose stones.

12 MOUNT VICTORIA

Continue 1km west along the Great Western Hwy until you reach Mount Victoria.

Mount Victoria is a small and charming settlement. By the late 19th century it was a popular 'hill station' retreat for wealthy Sydney families who would take the train and stay either in the large guesthouses or in the mansions they built for themselves. Today it is a pleasant township with a large number of impressive and substantial historic buildings, including the Mount Victoria Historical Museum which is located in the old refreshment rooms at the now defunct railway station. The museum contains an interesting collection of documents, photographs and artefacts from the local area.

There are a large number of important historic buildings in Mount Victoria: the old Bank Building (1855) at 22 Station Street; the Mount Victoria Police Station (1887) at 32 Station Street; the library (1875) at 30 Station Street; the gracious Victoria and Albert Guesthouse or Hotel Mount Victoria; and the impressive and ornate Imperial Hotel (1878). These are minor attractions, however, when compared to Westwood Lodge in Montgomery Street (1876), which was built as a summer retreat by John Fairfax.

Main street of Leura.

8 BELLS LINE OF ROAD

■ DRIVING TOUR ■ 100KM ■ 5 HOURS ■ A JOURNEY THROUGH THE NORTHERN BLUE MOUNTAINS

Rising gently from the Hawkesbury–Nepean floodplain, Bells Line of Road passes through rich apple-growing areas to the beautiful garden areas of Mount Tomah and Mount Wilson.

Today Richmond is a modern town notable as a popular weekend, day-trip destination. Located 57km from Sydney (about an hour from the Central Business District), Richmond is an ideal starting point for people wanting to explore the northern side of the Blue Mountains, an area characterised by apple orchards, beautiful cold-climate gardens, and outstanding views south across to the rugged cliffs around Blackheath. This is a journey quite different from one through the main Blue Mountains.

1 KURRAJONG

Leave Richmond on Smith St and travel west, across the Nepean River and through Kurmond. The road from Richmond crosses the Nepean River at North Richmond. The bridge, although it seems so far above the level of the river has, in recent times, been flooded and damaged by logs and debris. Beyond the bridge, the road rises to the small township of North Richmond and then begins the long ascent through Kurmond to Kurrajong Heights. After 11km you will reach the small village of Kurrajong.

This is an area like no other in the Blue Mountains. The land has been cleared, leaving gently undulating foothills. The local people have planted European cold-climate trees and bushes, and commercial fruit crops—apples, pears, peaches, apricots, nectarines, walnuts and cherries—fill the roadside stalls with cheap, high-quality produce that makes any trip a fruit-shopping bonanza.

The first European into the area was Captain Watkin Tench who, with his party, seems to have reached Knights Hill. Certainly in his diary he recorded that he explored to 'the elevation which bounded our research we gave the name of Knight Hill, in honour of the trusty serjeant who had been the faithful and indefatigable companion of all our travels'.

Archibald Bell Jnr was aged 19 when he passed through the area and crossed the mountains along what was to become Bells Line of Road in 1823. His was not a solitary achievement. Sensibly, Bell used the knowledge of the local Aborigines who had been crossing the mountains for tens of thousands of years. Although the mountains had been crossed at Katoomba a decade earlier, there was still no satisfactory route through them from Richmond. Bell reached Mount Tomah on his first attempt. On his second attempt he followed the ridge across to the present site of Bell and from there made his way down into Hartley Vale where he joined up with Coxs Road.

2 BELLBIRD HILL LOOKOUT

Return to Bells Line of Road and continue to Kurrajong Heights pausing, at every opportunity, to look back across the Sydney basin. About 2km further on is Bellbird Hill Lookout, which is an excellent viewing point over the Sydney basin.

No wonder this route has been a popular drive for Sydneysiders. From various points on the road, on a clear day, you can see across Sydney. It is possible to make out the outline of the major buildings in the Central Business District. Some people claim they have seen Sydney Harbour Bridge.

3 KURRAJONG HEIGHTS

Drive another 2km and follow the signs to Kurrajong Heights village.

Kurrajong Heights village is a mixture of the historic and the tourist-tempting. There are art galleries, antique and gift shops as well as St James' Church of England (a building dating from 1889), St David's Presbyterian Church (1886) and the post office, which is a rarity having been prefabricated in England and shipped out to Australia.

Lochiel House, with its hand-hewn hardwood and sandstone floor, is one of the oldest buildings in the district and is now used as a craft shop. The house was built by Joseph Douglass, who was granted the land at Kurrajong in 1825. Like so many early buildings, the house has changed its usage

Front of Withycombe from the gardens, Mount Wilson.

The views from Mount Tomah Botanic Garden are spectacular.

over the years. In the early days Douglass used it as a residence. By the 1850s it was a popular accommodation spot known as Ivy Lodge and offering meals and 'stabling and fodder for a horse'. When it was purchased by the Cameron brothers they changed its name to Lochiel House. The building subsequently became a post office before becoming a craft shop.

4 BILPIN

Drive back to Bells Line of Road and continue west for another 10km until you reach the tiny township of Bilpin which is famous for its apples.

Bilpin—the name is synonymous with apples in the mind of most residents of New South Wales—is a small town on Bells Line of Road. For most travellers Bilpin is the place where they stop at the Fruit Bowl to buy apples or apple juice. Outside is one of Australia's distinctive 'bigs'—the Big Fruit Bowl.

Bilpin was originally named Belpin after Archibald Bell Jnr, who also gave his name to Mount Bell, Bell Range, the town of Bell, and Bells Line of Road

5 MOUNT TOMAH BOTANIC GARDEN

Continue along Bells Line of Road for another 14km until you reach Mount Tomah. Turn right and park in the grounds of the Mount Tomah Botanic Garden.

Archibald Bell Jnr reached Mount Tomah on his first attempt to cross the Blue Mountains. In his diary he reported the richness of the soil in the Bilpin area (which inevitably led to the arrival of settlers eager to grow fruit trees) and the rainforest and huge tree ferns around Mount Tomah. The Mount Tomah Botanic Garden (now a Blue Mountains section of Sydney's Royal Botanic Gardens) was established in 1935 when the French horticulturist Alfred Brunet purchased the site. Brunet developed the area as a cut flower farm until the 1970s when he offered it to the Royal Botanic Gardens.

In 1988, as part of the Bicentennial year, considerable work was undertaken at the garden. The result is a beautiful 31ha garden that features an excellent collection of cool-climate plants from around the world. One-third of the site is devoted to southern hemisphere species, including a cool temperature eucalypt forest and rainforest areas. Some of the original Brunet Garden remains. The grassy park-like glade is ideal for picnics, there is a superb residence and formal gardens, and an extensive terraced rock garden in front of the visitors centre.

The balcony of the visitors centre offers one of the most spectacular views in New South Wales. It would be easy to spend a day at these gardens.

6 THE LOOKOUTS

Drive 7km west of Mount Tomah until you reach the Mount Banks Picnic Area.

There are a number of lookouts on the road from Mount Tomah to Mount Wilson. Each one of them is worth diverting to. They offer excellent views across the Grose Valley to the cliffs that lie to the north of Blackheath and Wentworth Falls.

7 MOUNT WILSON

Drive another 2km west and you will reach the Pierces Pass Picnic Area, which offers excellent views. About 1km further west turn left to Mount Wilson and continue for 8km until you reach the township.

Mount Wilson is a charming and gracious village with many beautiful cold-climate gardens nestled in the Australian bush. This small village is famous today for the fact that between 1912 and 1937 Australian novelist Patrick White's parents lived in a house called Withycombe. The house still stands and is located on the corner of The Avenue and Church Avenue. In his book *Flaws in the Glass*, White recalled his time at Mount Wilson in terms of 'gullies crackling with smoky silence, rocks threatening to explode, pools so cold that the breath was cut off inside your ribs as you hung suspended like the corpse of a pale frog'.

Archibald Bell Jnr passed through the area in 1823 and nine years later, in 1832, William Romaine Govett (of Govett's Leap fame) climbed Mount Wilson and subsequently described it as a 'high mass of range of the richest soil covered with almost impenetrable scrub'. It was surveyed in 1868, subdivided into 62 portions, and named after the Minister for Lands, John Bowie Wilson. The railway arrived in 1875 and by 1880 there were eight houses in the village. Over the years Mount Wilson became a village for the wealthy. It was the perfect hill station. A cool, misty area with soils and a climate that were ideal for the re-creation of England in a foreign land.

In her cooking/history book on the town, *Mount Wilson: A Potted History*, Audrey O'Ferrall notes, 'Around the original houses built by 1880 were planted gardens which contained oaks, elms, beeches and pines from Britain, rhododendrons, magnolias, cedars and spruces from the Himalayas and red oaks, tulip trees and conifers from North America'. It is this diversity of flora which makes Mount Wilson one of the most unusual and beautiful villages in the Blue Mountains. The best way to explore the gardens is to get out of the car and start walking. The experience of the town is the experience of its gardens, its avenues of trees, its lookouts, walking trails and picnic areas. The time to visit Mount Wilson is either spring or autumn, when many of the locals open their gardens—some of which are over a century old—to the public. Of particular note are Church Avenue, Queens Avenue and The Avenue with their rows of plane trees, limes, elms, liquidambars, beeches and pink cherries.

Walks to Wynnes Rocks Lookout, the Cathedral of Ferns and the Waterfalls Picnic Ground all offer excellent views and pleasant picnic locations. Wynnes Rocks Lookout can be reached via Queens Avenue and Wynnes Rocks Road. The Cathedral of Ferns is a delightful section of rainforest along Mount Irvine Road. There is a 'giant tree' as well as huge tree ferns, sassafras, a wide range of eucalypts and coachwood trees.

After exploring Mount Wilson, drive the 8km back to Bells Line of Road. The tiny, virtually non-existent town of Bell is a further 7km away and it is 16km down the far side of the mountains to the town of Lithgow.

Autumn in Mount Wilson.

27

9 THE MACQUARIE TOWNS

■ DRIVING TOUR ■ 156KM ■ 1 DAY ■ A JOURNEY THROUGH AUSTRALIA'S EARLY EUROPEAN HISTORY

A series of historic towns on the Hawkesbury River are a reminder of Sydney Town's early need to develop local agriculture.

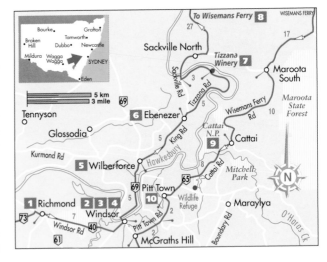

In 1810 Governor Lachlan Macquarie established the five Macquarie towns in the Hawkesbury Valley—Windsor, Richmond, Castlereagh, Wilberforce and Pitt Town. He specifically located the townships on a ridge above the Hawkesbury River which, when it had flooded in 1809, had devastated the farms in the area. Macquarie then exhorted all the settlers in the area to 'move to these places of safety and security', and it was on this basis that the towns began to grow. Today Windsor and Richmond have grown into modern, prosperous towns that still retain considerable old-world charm, and Wilberforce and Pitt Town, which are much smaller, have many delightful historic buildings.

1 RICHMOND

To get to Richmond from the centre of Sydney take the M4 west to Penrith (a distance of 52km) then turn north on Hwy 9, the Northern Rd, and follow the signs to Richmond for 23km. The Northern Rd becomes Londonderry Rd. Continue on Londonderry Rd, turn right into Bosworth St and one block north you are in Windsor St.

Richmond was first settled by Europeans in 1794 and quickly became the granary for the colony. Throughout the 19th century the town grew because of the rich agricultural lands that surrounded it. The appeal of Richmond is restricted to its main street (Windsor Street) and March and Francis streets, which run parallel on either side of Windsor Street.

At 122 Windsor Street is a house built around 1850 by Andrew Town, who became the largest breeder of pedigree horses in the world in the 1880s. Behind the house are extensive stables. A few houses further down is Benson House, built in the 1840s, and across the road is Toxana (1841) which, when it was first built, occupied the entire block.

Further up, beyond Richmond Park which is an ideal place for a picnic, are St Andrew's Uniting Church (originally a Presbyterian church built in 1845) and the Old Butcher Shop. Opposite the ambulance station is Bowman House, which remains largely unaltered from the original building John Bowman constructed in 1821.

If you turn either left or right at Chapel Street you can inspect the historic houses in Francis Street (which include Josieville, built by Joseph Onus in the late 1830s, and Clear Oaks farmhouse which dates possibly from 1820) and March Street where Rutherglen, built in the 1830s, stands in excellent repair and is still used as a private dwelling.

2 WINDSOR—ST MATTHEW'S ANGLICAN CHURCH

Leave Richmond heading east along Windsor St. About 6km from Richmond turn left into Moses St and continue, left again, into Clairmont Crescent, which brings you to the front of St Matthew's Anglican Church.

St Matthew's Anglican Church is known affectionately as the Cathedral of the Hawkesbury. It is widely acknowledged as one of the best works of the great convict architect Francis Greenway. Built by convicts between 1817 and 1820, the site was chosen by Governor Macquarie.

The church's gravestones offer a fascinating insight into the early life of the town. No gravestone is more interesting than that of Andrew Thompson who died in 1810. Thompson was a convict who arrived in Australia in 1792 after being transported for 14 years for stealing cloth worth £10. He subsequently became the first emancipist appointed as a magistrate and was the first person buried in the cemetery at St Matthew's.

3 HAWKESBURY MUSEUM

Continue north along Moses St and turn right into Tebbutt St and left into George St. Continue along George St and turn left into Johnson St, which becomes The Terrace. Turn right into Thompson St.

The Hawkesbury Museum and Tourist Centre is located at 7 Thompson Square. It has an excellent range of material about all the Macquarie towns as well as maps and descriptive walks around Windsor and Richmond. Take time to have a careful look at the museum's displays, which include Aboriginal artefacts as well as chronicling the European settlement of the area from earliest times (including a 1794 plan for

The bend in the Hawkesbury River at Wisemans Ferry.

some farms) through the development of the town after 1810 to the river economy of the 19th century and the creation of the RAAF base at Richmond.

4 JOHN TEBBUTT OBSERVATORY

Leave the museum and turn left into George St and continue across the main road until you reach Palmer St. Turn right into Palmer St and continue until you reach the John Tebbutt Observatory.

Tebbutt, a gentleman farmer and talented amateur astronomer, was born in Windsor in 1834. In 1845 his father built the house in Palmer Street, which John inherited in 1870. In 1879 he built the substantial brick observatory. Both the wooden and the brick observatory stand today, and the house, built in 1845, has remained in the Tebbutt family. Tebbutt achieved particular fame in 1984 when it was decided to include his portrait on the $100 note. The observatories are open for inspection.

5 WILBERFORCE

Return to Windsor on Palmer St and George St. Turn right into Bridge St and cross the Hawkesbury River. Continue on the road for 6km until you reach Wilberforce. Turn right onto Buttworth Lne and left to enter the Hawkesbury Heritage Farm.

Wilberforce, which was named by Governor Macquarie to honour the great British philanthropist William Wilberforce, was established as one of Macquarie's five towns in 1810. Its main place of interest is the Hawkesbury Heritage Farm, which is a successful attempt to recapture what life must have been like along the Hawkesbury in the early 1800s. The centrepiece of the village is Rose Cottage which, built around 1810, is the oldest timber building in Australia. Other interesting buildings at the Hawkesbury Heritage Farm include an Anglican church built from huon pine in 1860, a blacksmith's shop from the 1860s, a slab cottage (1840s) and the Riverstone Police Station (1850s).

6 EBENEZER

Leave Hawkesbury Heritage Farm, turn right into Wilberforce Rd and right again (after three blocks) into King Rd which becomes Sackville Rd. Continue for 5km until you reach Tizzana Rd. Turn right into Tizzana Rd and keep deviating to the right until you enter Coromandel Rd which, after 1km, will bring you to Ebenezer Presbyterian Church.

Ebenezer is an early 19th-century village which can claim to have the oldest standing Presbyterian Church in Australia and the

Hawkesbury Museum and Tourist Centre.

oldest existing school building in Australia. The church was built in 1808–1809 by Scottish farmers and looks more like a crofter's cottage than a church. The area was settled in 1806 by a number of free settlers who sailed to Australia on the *Coromandel* in 1802. One of their number, James Mein, was an elder of Galashiel's kirk and he started holding informal services in his house at Portland. Out of these meetings grew the desire to build the church at Ebenezer.

7 TIZZANA WINERY

Drive back up Coromandel Rd and take the turns to the right until you are heading north on Tizzana Rd. After 5km you will reach Tizzana Winery which is a large stone building on the right-hand side of the road.

The winery promotes itself as 'a touch of Tuscany on the banks of the Hawkesbury River'. Tizzana was built in 1887 by Dr Thomas Henry Fiaschi who emigrated to Australia from Florence in 1875. Fiaschi was a strong advocate of the judicious use of wine. The Tizzana Winery is open for tastings and local wines, as well as wines from other small vineyards, can be purchased.

8 WISEMANS FERRY

Continue for another 3km until you reach Sackville Rd. Turn right and wait for the ferry to take you across the Hawkesbury River. Continue on the Sackville Rd and follow the signs for 27km until you reach Wisemans Ferry.

Wisemans Ferry was named after the convict Solomon Wiseman, a journeyman lighterman, who arrived in Sydney on 20 August 1806. In 1817 he was granted 200ac on the banks of the Hawkesbury River where by 1821 he had established the Sign of the Packet inn.

During this time the main land route from Sydney to Newcastle was via Windsor, along to Wisemans Ferry and up the Putty Road to Singleton. In 1826 a new route via Castle Hill gained popularity and, as a result of this, Solomon Wiseman built a punt and was granted a seven-year lease on the rights to transport goods and travellers across the Hawkesbury River. Located on the Old Northern Road before the ferry is the Wisemans Ferry Inn (the building has been altered over time but much of the original still remains) where, in 1826, Solomon Wiseman built himself a handsome two-storey residence, Cobham Hall, which he later turned into the Branch Inn hostelry.

9 CATTAI NATIONAL PARK

Return from Wisemans Ferry along Old Northern Rd and turn onto the Wisemans Ferry Rd. After 27km there is a road running off to the left which is the entrance to Cattai National Park. Continue for 1km along this road, pass through the park entrance and then turn left and continue until you see the historic homestead on a small hill on your right-hand side.

Officially opened on Australia Day 1983, Cattai State Recreation Area is a 223.5ha park on the banks of the Hawkesbury River. The park includes a 'convict lagoon', excellent walking and bicycling tracks and the historic Caddie Park homestead. The

handsome sandstock homestead was built by convicts in 1821. It has sweeping views across the Hawkesbury River and is notable for its three dormer windows. The east wing is a recent (1938) addition. About 60m north of Caddie Park homestead are some stone foundations of a tiny dwelling which is believed to date from 1799.

10 PITT TOWN

Return to Wisemans Ferry Rd and continue west for 7km to Pitt Town.

Pitt Town was planned in 1810 and named after William Pitt the Elder, the famous 18th-century British statesman and prime minister. Strolling throughout this delightful village may take as long as it does to walk Windsor because its buildings are widely distributed.

Of particular interest is the former Maid of Australia Inn, a typical street corner inn located at 87 Bathurst Street which operated between the 1850s and 1890s. At 104 Bathurst Street are the remnants of the Blighton Arms, which dates from the earliest years of the town. The original owner, Henry Fleming, lost his licence in 1819 but reopened in 1830, calling the building the Macquarie Arms. Adjacent is Mulgrave Place, a house built in 1823 with a more modern verandah (about 1860) and north wing (1913).

Further along the street are the town's two churches, St James' Anglican and Scots Presbyterian Church. St James' was designed by Edmund Blacket and built by Thomas Collison for £1050 in 1857–1858. Blacket also designed the 24 pews, pulpit, reading desk and communion rail. Scots Church, a much simpler building than St James', was built and dedicated in 1862.

Continue on Pitt Town Rd until it joins up with Windsor Rd, which will return you either to Windsor (if you turn right) or Sydney (if you turn left).

Old graves at St Matthew's Church, Windsor.

An historic homestead at Pitt Town.

10 THE OLD HUME HIGHWAY

■ DRIVING TOUR ■ 150KM ■ 6 HOURS ■ EXPLORING THE HISTORIC TOWNS ON THE SOUTH-WESTERN EDGE OF SYDNEY

The Hume Highway now by-passes the historic coaching stops of Camden, Campbelltown, Picton and Thirlmere on the south-west outskirts of Sydney.

Sydney sprawls to the south-west, and Campbelltown, once an historic village, is now part of the city's furthest suburbs. Beyond lie the historic townships of Camden and Picton. All have become part of the city's commuter belt but their interesting old buildings remain, surrounded by modern shopping centres. This is the edge of the city before it gives way to the dense eucalypt forests of the Southern Highlands.

1 CAMPBELLTOWN

Leave Sydney via Canterbury Rd and follow the signs to the South Western Motorway. Campbelltown is located 55km south-west of the GPO. Turn off St Andrews Rd onto Campbelltown Rd.

Campbelltown has a number of older buildings in town and around the district which remind us that it was the first district to be settled outside of Sydney. By 1806 it had become the central thoroughfare for those headed on to the south-west grazing plains. Governor Lachlan Macquarie named the town after his wife, Elizabeth Campbell.

In 1826, the ex-convict Frederick Fisher disappeared. The following year another ex-convict, George Worrall, was arrested, tried and convicted of Fisher's murder. According to folklore, a respectable local named John Farley claimed to have seen Fisher's ghost sitting on a fence when he was returning home after a few drinks at a nearby inn. The ghost apparently pointed to the location of the body. Fisher's Ghost is Campbelltown's most famous spectre.

2 CAMPBELLTOWN JAPANESE GARDENS

Follow Campbelltown Rd south through the city and just past the Camden Rd traffic lights there is a minor turn-off on the right into Art Gallery Rd.

The gardens and tea house, based on a 16th-century design, were set up by Campbelltown's sister city of Koshigaya to mark the Bicentenary. The meticulous landscaping is exquisite and there are koi in the stream.

3 HISTORIC CAMPBELLTOWN

Walk across the road from the Japanese Gardens towards the town centre.

The first building you will notice is historic Emily Cottage (*c.*1840), a small quaint stone house with a gabled roof thought to have originally operated as a toll house. Across Camden Road is the southernmost end of Queen Street and what now remains of Fishers Ghost Creek.

At 320 Queen Street is the Campbelltown Art and Craft Society. This building was licensed as the Farriers Arms Inn in 1843 and was owned by blacksmith Edward Fitzgerald. Next door is Kendalls Millhouse, now Fishers Ghost Restaurant. It was erected next to Campbelltown's first steam-driven flour mill in 1844. Virtually opposite is the Campbelltown Community Centre, originally a produce store and bakery (*c.*1853).

Walk up Queen Street to the mall. The old town hall stands at no. 315, on the site of George Worrall's farm. It was constructed around the old Temperance Hall. These buildings are used by the Campbelltown Theatre Group.

The buildings from 284 to 298 Queen Street form an 'historic precinct' within the city mall. These two-storey colonial houses of brick or sandstone all date from the mid-19th century and all feature some fine work on the balustrades, columns, windows and doors: 298 Queen Street (*c.*1858) is said to have been a staging post for Cobb & Co; 294 was Bursill's shop (*c.*1842); 292 was Legacy House (*c.*1844); 288–290 is the Old Railway Hotel (*c.*1840), converted to a music hall in the 1850s.

The Old Railway Hotel, Queen Street, Campbelltown.

4 MOUNT ANNAN BOTANIC GARDEN

From the corner of Queen St and Camden St follow the Camden Rd west to its end and turn right into Narellan Rd. After 4km turn left into Mount Annan Drv. Another 1.4km further along there is a roundabout. Turn left into the gardens.

Mount Annan Botanic Garden is Australia's largest botanic garden. Within its 400ha you will find 20km of walking trails, a loop road, two ornamental lakes with lakeside picnic areas, an education centre, nursery and arboretum, an abundance of birdlife, most of Australia's known native plant species and some introduced species. The flora is featured in a variety of settings— a terrace garden, bottlebrush garden, wattle garden, banksia garden and a western garden. There are also woodland and lakeside plant communities. From the hill it is possible to see Campbelltown, the Sydney skyline to the north-east, and to the south-west, the Menangle district and the Razorback Range. There are picnic facilities, bike tracks and bicycles for hire. Don't miss the human sundial, a sculptural feature made of basalt columns that allows you to tell the time by raising your hands in the air.

5 CAMDEN

Return along Mount Annan Drv to Narellan Rd and turn left. After 3.6km you will reach the end of the road. Turn left into Camden Valley Way. Continue 3.8km to Camden.

Camden is famous in the early history of Australia because, in 1795, a herd of over 40 cattle were found grazing by the river where the town of Camden now stands. Governor Macquarie named the district Cowpasture Plains. Shortly afterwards, John Macarthur and Walter Davidson selected land west of the Nepean. Macarthur named his property Camden Park Estate in honour of Lord Camden, then the colonial secretary.

Most of Camden's historical buildings are located in John Street. They form an impressive streetscape sweeping up to St John's Church on the hillside at the end of the road. To the left is St Paul's Catholic Church, a Gothic Revival structure of brick

The Rail Transport Museum at Thirlmere.

with stone dressings. The foundation stone was laid in 1859. On the right are a group of old brick buildings including the 1857 courthouse and the 1878 police station and residence. Both were built on land that was provided by the Macarthurs who also donated £100 towards building costs.

The two-storey brick cottage Macaria at 37 John Street is an outstanding example of Gothic Revival architecture and was built in the late 1840s for Henry Thompson who built the first flour mill. Macaria now serves as the council chambers. Next door is Camden Cottage (*c.*1830), a small Georgian residence, thought to be the first built in Camden.

On the corner of John Street and Argyle Street is the Victorian Classical Revival CBC Bank building which opened in 1878. The intricate wrought-iron work on the balconies is original, as are the medallions of Queen Victoria in the gates.

At 40 John Street is the Camden Historical Museum, located in what was once the School of Arts (1866). The museum contains clothes, photographs, household implements, uniforms, musical instruments, booklets, maps, furniture, coins, guns and badges.

St John's Church, built on elevated land chosen by John Macarthur, is an outstanding example of Gothic Revival architecture. It was built from 386 000 locally made red sandstock bricks. The structure is dominated by a large tower topped by an enormous needle spire. There is a stone-flagged floor, beautiful Gothic stone tracery in the windows and an unusual ceiling.

6 RAZORBACK MOUNTAIN AND LOOKOUT

Follow Menangle Rd south to the T-intersection and turn left into Broughton St and continue for 1km to the next T-intersection. Turn right onto the old Hume Hwy and follow it for about 12km to the intersection with Mount Hercules.

Razorback Lookout offers excellent views of Menangle, Camden and the Sydney skyline beyond. The Razorback Range was named after a type of wild pig that has serrated bristles on its back. The first road over the range was cut in 1825 by convict gangs. The current route was cleared in 1830 and, until the establishment of the freeway, was part of the main road from Sydney to Melbourne.

7 PICTON

Continue south for 8km to Picton.

Picton was once a thriving township servicing the traffic between Sydney and Melbourne. In 1845 the small settlement was named Picton after Sir Thomas Picton, who had been one of the Duke of Wellington's generals at the Battle of Waterloo. Picton has a number of notable historic sites. Just south of the intersection of Argyle Street and Margaret Street, at the bottom of Vault Hill, is the old courthouse, built in 1864. The classic Victorian post office (*c.* 1892), on the corner of Argyle and Menangle streets, with its impressive clock tower, is a typical, prominent late 19th-century building built of stone.

St Helen's Park House at Campbelltown.

Opposite is the CBC Bank (now the National Australia Bank) built in 1885. It is notable for its pointed Gothic arch windows, its cast-iron railing and the original coach house and barn behind the building. The coach house has been converted into a local historical museum.

Across Stonecutter Creek, to the left, is the George IV Inn, one of the oldest hotels in the country. Said to have been built in 1819 but not licensed until 1839, it is a large and rambling building in Argyle Street on the southern side of Stonecutter Creek. The inn's verandah, stables and courtyard capture an earlier time when the journey from Sydney was a long and uncomfortable coach ride.

8 PICTON TUNNEL

Go through the underpass. The road bends to the left. Around the corner, to the right, is the Anglican rectory. Just past the rectory a dirt track heads off to the right. At the fork, take the left branch to the original Picton Tunnel.

Picton Tunnel was opened on 28 February 1867 and used for over 50 years until the double track was constructed. It was used for a time as a mushroom farm. Return to Argyle Street and turn right. On your left is the old gatehouse erected in 1867 for the keeper of the level crossing when the railway was extended from Picton to Mittagong.

9 THE VIADUCT

Continue south along Argyle St. Turn left into Prince St and continue until you turn left into Menangle St and turn left again into Webster St.

The viaduct consists of five massive arches made of stone quarried from 200m downstream. Measuring 83m in length, it is now the oldest stone archway over water in New South Wales. The viaduct has been in continuous use since it was opened in 1863.

10 THIRLMERE RAIL TRANSPORT MUSEUM

Follow Argyle St southwards for 3km. Turn right across the railway line into Thirlmere and then left after about 100m. Continue for 1km until you reach the Rail Transport Museum.

The Rail Transport Museum in Barbour Rd is the largest and oldest such museum in the country, with 60 locomotives—steam, diesel and electric—and 100 carriages. There are picnic and barbecue facilities, and on Sunday there are rides to Buxton along the old single-track Picton–Mittagong Loop Line.

Continue south on Thirlmere Rd for 21km and turn onto the Hume Hwy. Mittagong is 5km away.

11 THE ROYAL NATIONAL PARK

■ DRIVING AND WALKING TOUR ■ 133KM ■ ONE DAY ■ A DRIVE AND WALK IN THE ROYAL NATIONAL PARK

The Royal National Park south of Sydney is a wonderland of quiet beaches, dramatic clifftop paths, bushwalks and ideal picnic destinations.

*I*n 1879 the first Australian National Park (it was only the second national park in the world—Yellowstone in the United States was the first) was established on a modest 7200 hectares of land south of Port Hacking. It was dedicated by the government as an area specifically for rest and recreation, a purpose that has not changed for over 100 years. Today it is a beautiful and accessible retreat from the city characterised by the delightful Audley Weir with its boats; the excellent run of isolated beaches along the eastern edge of the park; and the interesting bushwalks, including the major walk along the coast and around the edge of the cliffs.

1 THE ROYAL NATIONAL PARK

The journey from Sydney to the Royal National Park is 31km. The easiest route is to follow George St from the GPO turning into City Rd at Broadway then continuing along as it becomes King St in Newtown and the Princes Hwy. After 31km, and it is clearly signposted, the visitor turns left into Farnell Ave to enter the park.

The Royal National Park spreads from the beaches of Wattamolla and Garie, through the coastal wilderness to the quiet waters of the Hacking River and on to the windswept low open woodlands on the western edges of the park. The 14 969ha of glorious and diverse national park are less than 40km from the centre of Sydney. That so much reserve land exists so close to Australia's largest city is a monument to the foresight of the New South Wales government and specifically to Sir John Robertson, who first suggested the idea of a national park.

It is probable that the original idea was to create a large, open space for the future residents of Sydney. Certainly, when it was dedicated in 1879, it was observed that the park should be 'a sanctuary for the pale-faced Sydneyites fleeing the pollution— physical, mental and social—of that closely packed city'.

In 1880 the land was doubled to 14 500ha and in 1934 New South Wales conservationist Myles Dunphy persuaded the government to add a further 520ha of land around Garawarra. The park was converted from a national park to a 'royal' national park (a change that seemed very important at the time) after Queen Elizabeth II travelled through the park on her way to Wollongong in 1954.

2 AUDLEY WEIR

Drive 3.2km from the Princes Hwy on Farnell Ave which turns into Audley Rd. At the bottom of the hill the road crosses Audley Weir.

One of the most popular picnic spots in the park is the grassy area to the south of the Audley Weir. Here, beside the dammed Hacking River, is a pleasant area of parkland where boats can be hired and where picnics can be enjoyed under the willow trees and beside the cool waters of the river. Picnickers and sightseers stop at Audley and spend the day playing games and relaxing. The more adventurous cross the weir and continue on to the beaches.

3 THE COAST TRACK

Continue along the main road through the park for another 10km until you reach the turn-off (the road at this point is known as Sir Bertram Stevens Drv) into Bundeena Drv. After a further 10.5km you will reach the small township of Bundeena.

For people wanting to explore the coastline in the Royal National Park there is the Coast Track, a marvellous 30km walk from Bundeena to Otford. This track runs the

The rugged coastline is evident throughout the Royal National Park.

Beautiful Garie Beach.

length of the park's coastline passing through Little Marley and Marley Beach, Wattamolla, Burning Palms and Garie. Unless you are fit, fast and/or foolish, the walk is too long to attempt in one day. Enthusiasts tend to complete the walk in two days while daytrippers, happy to do the first section, walk for two hours, reach Little Marley and Marley Beach, and then return to Bundeena.

Of all the trails in the park the Coast Track is the most spectacular. The walk follows the sandstone cliff line which affords beautiful, panoramic views over the Pacific Ocean. In winter and spring the low scrubland and heath is alive with magnificent displays of wildflowers.

The smell of the wildflowers, the tang of the winds blowing up from the ocean, the sculptured sandstone of the headlands and caves, the sandy beaches, and the sounds of the birds, all contribute to make the Coast Walk an unforgettable experience.

Day walkers should recognise that Marley Beach is dangerous for swimming but Little Marley Beach, further south, is a popular swimming and fishing spot. Little Marley also offers a camping area and a freshwater stream. The walker can then take the track up onto the plateau and head back to Bundeena.

All walkers in the national park should pay particular attention to the park's rich diversity of fauna and flora. The park has six major vegetation regions. Spread throughout the park are substantial pockets of rainforest. Rainforest most commonly occurs in the valleys of the Hacking River and along the coast south of Garie and is easily identified by the stands of cabbage tree palms, coachwood and sassafras as well as wonga-wonga vines, wombat berry, settlers flax and shiny fan ferns.

Along the beaches, in the sand dunes and on the rocky cliff faces, walkers will find hairy spinifex, guinea flower, and coast rosemary, and, on the back dunes, the ubiquitous coastal tea-tree.

Beyond the rainforest and coastal areas are stands of blackbutt and Sydney blue gum surrounded by hopbush and a twining creeper with dark red flowers called dusky coral-pea.

Further from the coast is an area of grassy eucalypt woodland which characterises the slopes of the national park. This area is notable for its red bloodwood (a gum with a very distinctive urn-shaped gumnut), gnarled and twisted scribbly gums, and the distinctive grass trees with their spear-like flower spikes

and leaves that splay out at the base of the plant like a grass dress. Other unusual plants in the grassy eucalypt areas include false sarsaparilla (its deep purple flowers add to the colour of the park between August and December), hairy spider flowers and the eggs and bacon shrubs (characterised by yellow flowers with red centres).

At the edges of the plateau is a feast of wildflowers. The black ash is the dominant tree in this area but bushwalkers marvel at the range of banksias and the paperbark, dwarf apple, shrub oak and Port Jackson mallee.

On the plateau, an area that at first sight seems inhospitable, walkers brush past the mountain devil shrub with its red tubular flowers, cone sticks, drumsticks, the finger hakea with its clusters of white flowers and its egg-shaped fruit that splits to release winged seeds, and stands of black she-oak.

Walkers who pass the freshwater swamps in the park will see Christmas bells with their red and yellow flowers (they appear between December and February), needle bush, bottlebrush, pink swamp-heath, coral-heath and paperbark shrub.

Just as the park offers walkers a rich diversity of flora, so does it also offer birdwatchers and animal lovers an unusual combination of native and introduced species of fauna. On the coast the silver gull (an aggressive scavenger that always hangs around when you are having a picnic) is everywhere. More rare are the white breasted sea-eagle, the crested tern, the black cormorant and the white-faced heron.

In the forests and woodlands the alert birdwatcher can see wedge-tailed eagles, black-shouldered kites, white-naped honeyeaters, crimson rosellas, peewees, red wattlebirds, sulphur-crested cockatoos and bronzewings. People who are very lucky, or very patient, can see satin bower-birds and lyrebirds in the rainforests. Around the swamps and lagoons the azure kingfisher, welcome swallow, New Holland honeyeater and black duck can be observed.

Native mammals in the park include black rats, bush rats, a range of gliders, bandicoots, ringtail possums, dunnarts, lizards and goannas. There are also a number of snakes in the park. Summer walkers should be careful as many of them are poisonous. It is unlikely that day visitors will make contact with any of these animals since they are either shy, nocturnal, or both.

4 THE BEACHES

Return from Bundeena 10.5km to Sir Bertram Stevens Drv. Turn left and continue for 5km until you reach the sign for Garie Beach. The beach is 2.8km from the turn-off.

While any national park offers the greatest rewards to bushwalkers and people who want to explore the natural beauties, it is true that the Royal National Park offers much more than flora, fauna and landscape. The beaches at Garie, Burning Palms and Wattamolla are places of exceptional beauty. Burning Palms, a hideout for fishermen since the turn of the century, has a number of

small cottages that have been tolerated by the park authorities. The difficulty of building and maintaining the cottages is obvious. Every piece of timber, and all food supplies, had to be carried by hand down the steep slopes to the cottages.

The entire 19km of coastline which forms the eastern boundary of the park is noted for its excellent fishing. Apart from the hardy fishermen who are lucky enough to have shacks at Burning Palms there are regular day fishermen who find spots at the base of the cliffs where they catch a variety of fish from the rock ledges and beaches.

5 BURNING PALMS

There are two ways to reach Burning Palms. You can walk south along the coastline from Garie Beach (the walk is approximately 4km) or you can return 2.8km from Garie Beach to Sir Bertram Stevens Drv and take the immediate left turn into Garrawarra Farm Rd. It is a gravel road. At the end you are only 1km from the beach.

Burning Palms is one of the many delightful isolated beaches in the park and is well worth visiting. It is quiet and peaceful and an ideal location for anglers.

6 STANWELL TOPS

A further 19.5km south the visitor reaches Stanwell Tops. Perhaps the greatest reward of all awaits those who travel right through the Royal National Park and, passing through Otford, arrive at Stanwell Tops. The view from Stanwell Tops is worth travelling all day for. On a clear day you can see down the coast to Wollongong. The jutting headlands of Coalcliff, Scarborough and Clifton make this ruggedly beautiful stretch of coastline one of the scenic jewels of Australia's east coast.

Return to Sydney either by driving back through the Royal National Park or continuing 3.8km west until you reach the old Princes Highway. Turn right and continue 21km until you reach the entrance to the park. From here you can return to Sydney.

Looking south from Stanwell Tops.

CHAPTER 2
THE SOUTH COAST

12 WALKING WOLLONGONG

■ WALKING AND DRIVING TOUR ■ 8KM ■ 5 HOURS ■ A WALK AND DRIVE AROUND WOLLONGONG

Known throughout the country as a steel town, Wollongong is, in fact, a beautiful coastal city with an attractive harbour, excellent Botanic Gardens and many interesting historic buildings.

Wollongong is the third largest city in New South Wales after Sydney and Newcastle. It has a population in excess of 250 000 and Greater Wollongong effectively stretches from the edges of the Royal National Park in the north to Shellharbour in the south. Historically, Wollongong is a city which was driven by the vast deposits of coal in the area. In turn this resulted in the construction of one of Australia's largest steel mills at Port Kembla, south of the city. In spite of this industrial base, the city is located on the coast and consequently is characterised by many beautiful beaches and edged by attractive holiday destinations.

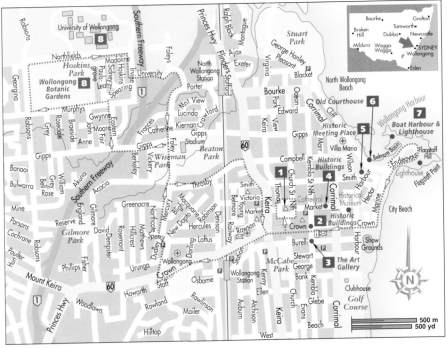

1 WOLLONGONG

Wollongong is the tenth largest city in Australia. There is a perception about the city that bears no relation to the delights of its remarkable charm and beauty. It is hard to pinpoint when people started thinking of it as big, industrial, smelly, smoky and ugly. Wollongong is a great place to go for a day out or a holiday. It offers the traveller a sophisticated shopping area, excellent beaches, some of the most spectacular scenery on the state's coast, sites of great natural beauty and ideal fishing spots. The port and Wollongong Harbour are

Wollongong from Sublime Point.

both interesting places to visit and the town's history, particularly its coalmining background, is fascinating.

If it hadn't been for a heavy surf Captain Cook would have made his first landing in New South Wales within the Illawarra, and he noted in his logbook the attractive appearance of the shore and the presence of Aborigines—the Wodi Wodi tribe, who had been in the area for at least 20 000 years. The first Europeans to meet the Aborigines of the Illawarra were explorers George Bass and Matthew Flinders and their servant William Martin in 1796. Sailing south in *Tom Thumb*, their tiny boat was overturned at Towradgi Point. In search of fresh water they stopped at what is now Port Kembla where they were approached by two Aborigines who led them to Lake Illawarra. There numerous others gathered on the shore, and during an encounter Flinders gave a number of the locals a shave in an attempt to play for time and defuse hostilities.

The following year the survivors of the wreck on Sydney Cove walked through the

area and noted evidence of coal. As a result of this, George Bass found coal at Coalcliff and by 1805 timber cutters were in the area cutting down the huge stands of cedar.

The town plan was gazetted in 1834 and the first regular steamship service to Sydney began that year. Convict labour was used to cut a path down Mount Keira in 1835–1836 and to carve a safe harbour out between 1837 and 1844 so that passengers could step rather than wade ashore.

The region's first coalmine commenced operations at Mount Keira in 1849. By 1880 there were 10 mines along the Illawarra escarpment, giving birth to a string of mining villages that now constitute the northern suburbs of the City of Greater Wollongong.

2 HISTORIC BUILDINGS IN CROWN STREET

Wollongong's main street is Crown St. Between Keira St and Kembla St it has been converted into a pedestrian-only shopping mall. Go to the eastern or ocean end of the mall and cross over Kembla St. Adjacent to the fountain, at Crown and Kembla sts, is the Tourist Information Centre.

Near the Information Centre is the post office (1892) and next door to that, at 87 Crown Street, is a terrace shop with decorative facade and verandah, one of Wollongong's last remaining commercial structures dating from the 19th century.

3 THE ART GALLERY

Return to the corner of Crown and Kembla Sts and turn left. One block south at Kembla and Burelli Sts is the Art Gallery.

The Wollongong City Art Gallery is the largest regional art museum in Australia. It features changing exhibitions that showcase local, national and international artwork. With 27 panels along its curved facade it is also the only public art museum in Australia with a major exhibiting gallery facing the street.

4 HISTORIC BUILDINGS IN MARKET STREET

Return to Kembla and Crown sts and turn left, heading west through the mall. To the right is Wollongong Uniting Church (1882). When you reach the amphitheatre turn right, heading north up Church St. At the top of the hill is St Michael's Cathedral.

One of Wollongong's more notable buildings, St Michael's Cathedral was designed by Edmund Blacket, perhaps Australia's best-known 19th-century architect. The building incorporates sandstone from an older church that was completed in 1847.

From the church it is possible to gaze eastwards straight down Market Street to the ocean. At the top of Market Street, diagonally

The picturesque lake in the Botanic Gardens.

opposite the church, is the Italianate Courthouse, built in 1886 and designed by colonial architect James Barnet with a turret clock added in 1890. Extensions were completed in 1951 and, in 1970, the original courtroom was restored.

Walk east down Market Street. Cross over Kembla Street and to the right is one of the oldest surviving buildings in the Illawarra, the Congregational Church. Dating back to 1857, this church counted John Fairfax and David Jones among its original benefactors.

Continue along Market Street. Cross over Corrimal Street and, to the right, at the Queens Parade corner, is a building which served as an earlier post and telegraph office (1876–1892). The second storey was added in 1882. It is now the Illawarra Museum and features re-creations of 19th-century domestic, working and educational spaces complete with pioneering artefacts. There is also a display on the Mount Kembla mining disaster.

5 HISTORIC MEETING PLACE

Continue to the end of Market St, turn left into Harbour St and follow it to the Smith St intersection.
A small bronze plaque, at Smith and Harbour streets, commemorates a meeting that took place on 2 December 1816 between the first European settlers and John Oxley. Oxley had been sent by Governor Lachlan Macquarie to survey the area and to negotiate free land grants with the graziers who had ventured into the area after Charles Throsby had introduced the first cattle in 1815. This site was chosen as the meeting place because Throsby's stockmen had built their hut here.

6 OLD COURTHOUSE

Continue on to the T-intersection where Harbour St meets Cliff Rd.
At this corner is a distinguished sandstone building (1858) that served as a courthouse until the Market St premises were opened. It is now the naval cadet headquarters.

7 THE BOAT HARBOUR AND LIGHTHOUSE

Opposite this intersection is Belmore Basin.
Wollongong's harbour was once the centre of all activity in the Illawarra. It is hard to imagine that until the railway arrived and Port Kembla was developed, most of the wealth of the Illawarra was shipped from this modest harbour. Remnants from its heyday include the concrete base of a crane, which juts from the waters of the outer harbour, and the first lighthouse. Made of cast iron and riveted boiler plates, the lighthouse was erected in 1871–1872 after numerous wrecks on offshore reefs. Its gas lamp was replaced with electricity in 1916.

The second lighthouse is situated on Flagstaff Hill, the headland that encloses one side of the harbour. The hill was named after a flagstaff placed on top of a stockade in the 1830s to warn incoming ships of harbour conditions. The concrete lighthouse was built in 1936. You can walk or drive to the crest of the headland via Endeavour Drive. Belmore Basin, with its small fishing fleet and flotilla of pleasure craft, is part of the character and appeal of Wollongong. It is a delightful place for a picnic. There is a restaurant and a fishing co-operative that supplies fish from the local fishing fleet.

If you walk northwards a short distance along Cliff Road, you can see (or walk through) a cutting that has been gouged out of the cliff adjacent the Olympic pool. Now a pedestrian track, the cutting was originally part of the tramline route from Mount Pleasant Mine to the harbour.

Set 1km north of Belmore Basin, along Cliff Road, are the cannon and underground fortifications of Battery Park Fort, which was established in the 1890s to guard the approaches to the harbour. The fort closed a decade later. Earlier fortifications were situated on Flagstaff Hill. Also buried at Battery Park are some coke ovens. Built in 1875, the ovens were among the area's first industrial enterprises.

8 THE UNIVERSITY, GLENIFFER BRAE AND THE BOTANIC GARDENS

Return to the corner of Smith and Keira sts and drive north along the Princes Hwy. After 1.5km you will cross a bridge and find yourself at a major intersection. Turn left onto the Southern Freeway but stay in the left lane and turn off immediately into the exit ramp on the left. At the T-intersection turn left and then turn left immediately onto the overpass. At the T-junction turn right, drive to the end of the road and turn left, then turn right at the next T-junction into Murphys Ave. On the right, after 300m, is the car park of the Botanic Gardens.
Wollongong is proud of its 19ha Botanic Gardens. The land was first granted to James Spearing in 1825. His Paulsgrove estate was, for a time, the largest population centre in the Illawarra, with 43 people. The property was subdivided and later became dairying land. In 1928 it was purchased by Sidney Hoskins, a founding director of Australian Iron and Steel, who donated the land to the local council to use as a garden, the development of which began in 1964.

There are pamphlets at the entrance with outlined walks through exotic, subtropical and Illawarra rainforest, eucalypt forest, an azalea bank, a pathway out to a rotunda in the middle of the picturesque lake where ducks and other birds abound, a fountain, beautiful secluded rose garden, woodland garden at its best in winter, and a glasshouse for tropical plants. Paths, small creeks, open grassy areas and pleasant shaded spaces make the gardens an ideal place for a picnic. The gardens are open from 7.00am–4.45pm on weekdays and 10.00am–4.45pm on weekends with hours extended to 6.45pm with summertime daylight saving. Conducted walking tours are held on the first Sunday of each month by the Friends of the Botanic Gardens.

People interested in architecture should walk up the hill to Gleniffer Brae (now the Wollongong Conservatorium of Music), completed in 1939 for the Hoskins family. The chimneys alone are worth the walk. Nearby are the beautiful grounds of Wollongong University.
From Gleniffer Brae return to the centre of the city by retracing the route you took to the university.

Looking north from Wollongong harbour.

13 THE COASTAL TOWNS

■ DRIVING TOUR ■ 32KM ■ 4 HOURS ■ FROM STANWELL PARK TO BULLI

They were once small mining communities. Today the villages from Stanwell Park to Bulli are delightful communities nestled between the Pacific Ocean and the cliffs of the escarpment.

From the southern edge of the Royal National Park to the centre of Wollongong are a run of beaches and headlands that form one of the finest stretches of coastline in Australia. This is an area of spectacular cliffs, secluded and intimate beaches with rock pools, and small villages, many of them having their roots in the coalmining of the area's early European settlement. To drive through the area is to experience the history as well as the physical beauty of a stretch of coastline that is often neglected by holiday-makers heading further south.

1 STANWELL PARK

Stanwell Park is famous for its connections with the early history of human flight. This beach resort was once the home of Lawrence Hargrave, the inventor of the box kite and one of the founding fathers of modern aviation. Hargrave moved to Hillcrest House in 1893. The house is located on the road up to the Stanwell Park Railway Station.

Hargrave carried out many of his experiments, particularly those with box kites, on Bald Hill, above Hillcrest House. Sharing with Hargrave an understanding of the impressive aeronautical potential of the area, the hang-gliding fraternity today use the hill as a launching point for their spectacular flights out over the Pacific Ocean and back onto the beach far below. Across the road from the Hargrave Memorial is Intabane, an unusual

mansion with a witch's hat roof which was used as an army lookout in World War II.

2 THE COASTAL DRIVE

From Stanwell Park, Lawrence Hargrave Drv snakes its way along the coastline, passing through the well-named Coalcliff where a narrow winding section of road is sandwiched between sheer cliffs and a precipitous drop into the ocean.

It is with a feeling of some relief that the land soon opens up on both sides of the road at Clifton—the first of several small, picturesque villages with beautiful sandy beaches and rock pools at the eastern edge of rocky cliff faces. Surfers, swimmers, anglers, sunbathers and beachwalkers are all attracted to this stretch of coast.

Although these coastal 'villages'—Coalcliff, Clifton, Scarborough, Wombarra, Coledale, Austinmer, Thirroul and Bulli—now form a continuous residential strip, they were originally separate coalmining settlements that developed in the mid-19th century and they retain a sense of integrity and beauty. The houses huddle together along the coastline but they also continue up the escarpment. In the past decade the region has become increasingly desirable, and expensive, for people commuting from Sydney. Clifton and Scarborough retain modest and popular pubs that hang over the cliffs.

3 THIRROUL

At the southern end of Lawrence Hargrave Drv is Thirroul, 15km from Stanwell Park.

The name comes from the Aboriginal word Thurrural, said to mean the 'Valley of the Cabbage Tree Palms'. Thirroul has long

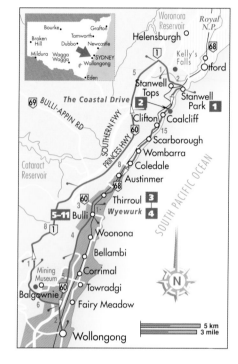

been a beach resort, although as the major train stop of the Illawarra's outer northern suburbs it has become a focal point for the growing number of people who commute to Sydney.

4 WYEWURK—D.H. LAWRENCE'S HOME

As you reach Thirroul shopping centre on Lawrence Hargrave Drv, turn left at the first set of traffic lights. At the first T-intersection turn left, at the next turn right, at the third turn left then take the first right into Craig St. Wyewurk is the second house along, to the left. It is a private house and is not open to the public.

Thirroul's greatest claim to historical fame is that from May to August 1922 the novelist D.H. Lawrence lived and worked at 3 Craig Street in the Californian-style mission bungalow Wyewurk. It was here that Lawrence wrote most of the novel *Kangaroo*, in which the town based on Wollongong was called Wollona.

Seen from the street, the visitor gets no idea of the magnificence of the view from the front garden. There is a small park at the southern end of the street, however. Steps at the edge of the park allow visitors an opportunity to appreciate the view and, like Lawrence, to walk on one of Thirroul's most charming beaches and around the rocks directly below the house. Lawrence's description of this location is powerful and evocative:

He liked the sea, the pale sea of green glass that fell in such cold foam. Ice-fiery, fish-burning. He went out on

A steam train outside the Black Diamond Heritage Centre at Bulli.

Wyewurk, the home of D.H. Lawrence in 1922.

to the low flat rocks at low tide, skirting the deep pock-holes that were full of brilliantly clear water and delicately-coloured shells and tiny, crimson anemones. Strangely sea-scooped sharp sea-bitter rock floor, all wet and sea-savage.

5 BULLI

Return to Lawrence Hargrave Drv and continue south-wards, passing over the railway line and through the second set of lights. At the end of Lawrence Hargrave Drv turn left onto the Princes Hwy at the bottom of Bulli Pass. The road curves around a hill and then lev-els out, passing under a railway overpass that bears a sign declaring your entry into the 'Black Diamond Township' of Bulli.

The name Bulli derives from an Aboriginal word thought to signify 'two mountains'. It was used from 1815 to describe the area from Bulli south to Mount Keira. That year, Charles Throsby opened up the Illawarra to settlement when he hacked a path down the slopes of the Bulli mountain in search of pasture for his cattle.

Cedar-getters had been in the Illawarra since 1812 and were to be found in the Bulli area by 1815. They cut the timber where it fell and carted it to the beach or hauled it up the Bulli pass for transportation by bullock train to Parramatta.

The first permanent settler was Cornelius O'Brien, who established a farm in 1823. In 1837 O'Brien sold his land to Captain Robert Westmacott who extended the property, bred racehorses, founded a brick-works (an industry still operative today), co-founded a steamship company that trav-elled to and from Sydney, cut a superior path down Bulli Mountain which is still in use today as the Bulli Pass, helped organise the first local agricultural society and estab-lished the first coalmine in the region.

A mine was opened in 1862. Miners' cottages were built and a tight-knit community developed with a hotel, a Wesleyan church and shops. The mine was closed down in 1987 after 125 years of operation. A number of old timber cottages, shops and other buildings survive from the 19th century.

6 BULLI MINER'S COTTAGE

Just beyond the railway overpass, to the right, at no. 200, is the Bulli Miner's Cottage.

The Bulli Miner's Cottage was built about 1870. Remarkably, eight children lived together at one time in this small structure. It has been described as 'a very rare sub-stantially intact survivor of a building style

common to Bulli in the mid to late nine-teenth century'.

The cottage is of a rough-hewn slab construction with pit-sawn plank walls of hardwood timber. The roof, once shingled, probably with ironbark, is now of corrugated iron. There are a number of mining artefacts and furnishings and, behind the cottage, the memorial wall recalls the 541 men who have lost their lives in the region's mines from 1887 to the present.

7 BULLI FAMILY HOTEL

Continue along the highway to the traffic lights (500m). Just beyond them, to the right, is the Bulli Family Hotel.

The most impressive building in the district is the Bulli Family Hotel. Opened in 1889, this huge Victorian public house is one of the township's most prominent landmarks. Customers have included two governors-general and noted politician Henry Parkes, who addressed a public meeting here in 1893. Classified by the National Trust in 1977, the Bulli Family Hotel remains largely in its original condition. The beautiful cast-iron balcony, fluted iron columns, elaborate moulded trim and frosted bar windows have been preserved and the 'Bulli bricks' with which it was built are still intact.

8 BLACK DIAMOND HERITAGE CENTRE

Continue past the hotel and take the first right into Railway St. Drive to its end and turn right again, cross over the short railway bridge and take the immediate right into Franklin Ave. On the right-hand side of the road is the railway station.

The Black Diamond Heritage Centre is located in the building on the eastern platform of Bulli Railway Station. The centre was built in 1887 and saved from demolition in 1989 by the community. It provides an interesting history of the local area.

9 BULLI PASS

Return to the highway and turn right, heading north. Instead of turning right, back into Lawrence

Hargrave Drv, follow the steep course of the highway up Bulli Pass.

It is hard to imagine how slow and precipitous Bulli Pass once was. One point that can be appreciated as you rise above the coastal plain is the beauty and density of the subtropical rainforest which stood densely on either side of the original track. The views from the pass are magnificent.

10 BULLI PASS SCENIC RESERVE

When you reach the top of the pass, take the second right, signposted for Helensburgh, Campbelltown and Bulli Pass Scenic Reserve. Take the branch to your left, which is also signposted. This road curves under the Appin Rd and through a cutting. At the end of the cutting a sign directs you to turn right to Bulli Pass Scenic Reserve.

The scenic reserve has a cafe and a lookout perched on the edge of the escarpment offer-ing spectacular views over the Illawarra coastline. It was here, on 19 October 1920, that a ceremony was held to officially name the new coast road from Sydney to Melbourne the Princes Highway, after the Prince of Wales. A 2km bushwalking track leads to Sublime Point Lookout.

11 SUBLIME POINT

Return along the driveway and turn right, heading north along the old Princes Hwy. After 1.5km there is a signposted turn-off on the right to Sublime Point.

From this stunning vantage point you can see a massive sweep of coastline with the Illawarra stretching out below on the flat lands between the mountain and the deep blue of the sea. Few places on Australia's east coast can match this scenery.

There is a kiosk, toilets, picnic and barbecue facilities and two walking tracks at the southern edge of the clearing that lead down the escarpment or back to Bulli Pass Scenic Reserve.

Return to the old Princes Hwy and drive north for 10km until you reach Lawrence Hargrave Drv, which will return you to Stanwell Tops.

The impressive Bulli Family Hotel.

14 SEASIDE RESORTS AND PLEASANT VALLEYS

■ DRIVING TOUR ■ 34KM ■ 1 DAY ■ BLOWHOLES, RAINFORESTS AND COASTAL VIEWS

Between the Escarpment and the Pacific Ocean, the green hills are dotted with dairy and beef cattle and the beaches offer easy day access from Sydney.

*L*ocated only 118km south of Sydney, Kiama is a popular day-tripper destination. The town is known throughout Australia for its famous blowhole, a fissure in the rocks which, when the sea and wind are in the right direction, hurls huge plumes of seaspray into the air. Behind Kiama, the rich and fertile Jamberoo Valley is home to the dairy industry and the escarpment offers superb views over the coast and impressive remnants of rainforest, with waterfalls and pleasant, cool bushwalks.

1 KIAMA

Kiama is a popular seaside resort characterised by dramatic rocky coastline, sandy beaches and an attractive harbour. The land behind the town is dominated by lush green dairy pastures, and rolling hills that were once clad in dense subtropical forests.

An abundance of cedar drew the first Europeans to the area and, by 1815, timber was being shipped from Kiama's main beach, Black Beach. By the 1820s Kiama was supplying nine-tenths of the Sydney cedar market.

In 1819 surveyor James Meehan surveyed the district by land and Surveyor General Oxley explored the area, which he called Kiarami. Seven years later he reserved the land adjacent to the harbour for the development of a township. Kiama developed as a shipping and service centre for the local industries. In the 1840s chains were affixed to the rocks on either side of Black Beach to provide secure moorings. The iron post that functioned as an anchor pin for the securing chain is Kiama's oldest surviving historic artefact. It can be seen, still driven into the rocks with some chain remnants, from the concrete walkway on the north-western side of the harbour.

The development of the harbour, which was completed in 1876, contributed to the development of the basalt-quarrying industry in Kiama. The first quarry was established in 1855. The gravel was transported to Black Beach by horse and dray where, before the wharf was constructed, it was floated out to waiting ships by barge.

Another input into the local economy came from Sydneysiders who were drawn by the ocean views, local scenery and mild climate as early as the 1880s. The establishment of a direct link to Sydney, the improvement of the roads, and the additions of boating and surfing enhanced Kiama's attractiveness as a tourist destination.

2 THE BLOWHOLE AND THE LIGHTHOUSE

The main street in Kiama is Terralong St. As you head east along Terralong St you reach a roundabout at the post office. Drive through this roundabout and take the turn to the left which leads up the hill to the lighthouse. This is where the blowhole is located.

The town's greatest attraction, this sea-cliff cavern offers spectacular 'blows' only when the wind and water are coming rather precisely from the south-east. On those occasions waves roar through a hole in the cave roof, sending spray up as high as 60m. The site is floodlit until 9.30pm.

Near the blowhole is the 15m lighthouse, opened in 1887 on George Bass Point. It was converted to electricity in 1969 and extends its beams to a distance of 27km. Once attended by a keeper, the lighthouse has long been automated.

Kiama's famous blowhole.

3 THE ROCK POOLS

Depart from the blowhole car park. Turn north and head down the hill. About 100m down the hill, on the right-hand side, is the Kiama rock pool.

On either side of the harbour are two attractive rock pools. The one on the northern side was built in 1888. Its location was determined by indecency laws which forbade bathing in public. The southern rock pool can be spectacular when the sea is rough.

4 STORM BAY AND CHRIST CHURCH

From the rock pools continue down the loop road past the harbour and turn right at the T-intersection. The small rocky bay to the left is known as Storm Bay. Turn left into Terralong St. Less than 100m up the slight hill is Christ Church.

Christ Church was built in 1858 of local basalt and red cedar. Based on a design by Edmund Blacket, the church is in the Gothic Revival style. An interesting timber ceiling of local cedar in the form of an inverted ship's hull was added in 1872. The nautical motif was reiterated in the blue windows above the altar and the ensign of HMS *Kiama*. The grave of John Gowen (*c*.1763–1837), a marine from the First Fleet, can be found in the small graveyard behind the church.

5 KIAMA TERRACES

Head back into the main section of town past the post office. Turn right at the Collins St roundabout. On the right-hand side of the road are the Kiama Terraces.

Dating from 1886, these buildings were designed to house quarry workers and their families. The only weatherboard terraces left in New South Wales, they were in a state of disrepair by the 1960s and came close to being demolished. Classified by the National Trust and placed under a permanent conservation order, the terraces have now have been restored and are a major tourist attraction with everything from restaurants to bookshops and shops selling crafts and seashells.

6 SADDLEBACK LOOKOUT

Return along Collins St to the roundabout and turn right into Terralong St. Continue north, under the Princes Hwy overpass, and west on Jamberoo Rd. About 6km from the overpass turn left into Fountaindale Rd which is signposted for Saddleback Lookout. When you reach the top of the road you have to make a sharp right and head further up the hill to reach the lookout.

Saddleback Mountain Lookout is open 8.00am–4.00pm daily. There is one lonely table for picnickers and a concrete slab noting distances and directions to other locales. The reserve itself is modest but the mountain, which marks the point where the escarpment turns into a series of foothills that run down to the sea, offers one of the most dramatic and interesting views on the entire south coast. From Saddleback you can see north to the steelworks of Wollongong, south to Jervis Bay and inland to the edges of both the Jamberoo and Kangaroo valleys.

7 JAMBEROO

Return the way you came, down Fountaindale Rd to Jamberoo Rd, and turn left. It is 2km from here to the outskirts of Jamberoo.

Jamberoo is a small and charming village situated in lush green dairy pastures surrounded by coastal escarpments and rolling hills. The area was first settled by cedar-getters, who took the wood to Kiama for shipment to Sydney. The clearing of the land enabled the establishment of grazing runs and the area was settled in the 1820s. The township developed on the private land of the Hyam Estate.

Although there has been considerable development on the outskirts of the town, time seems to have stood still in Jamberoo. This historic village has an English feel which is accentuated by the dry stone walls that separate some of the farms in the area. These stone fences were erected from the 1850s by Thomas Newing of Kent, who brought the craft with him from England. He died in 1927.

8 MINNAMURRA FALLS RESERVE

Head north out of Jamberoo and turn west onto the Jamberoo Mountain Rd. Follow it for 2km and you will see a sign on your right directing you to a surviving remnant of subtropical rainforest (400ha) at Minnamurra Falls Reserve.

Minnamurra Falls Reserve was declared in 1903 and the first trails were established during the Depression by people on relief payments. Located in Budderoo National

The fertile Jamberoo Valley is ideal for dairy cattle.

Park, the reserve is open 9.00am– 5.00pm daily (except on Christmas Day). On the right at the entrance is Kellys Cottage (1853). There is a rainforest education centre, with a display of rare rainforest plants and information about the site. There are 90 different species of ferns (two-thirds of the fern types in the state) and 80 species of native trees in the reserve.

The walking track, in its entirety, is 4.2km long and takes about two hours to complete. There are two parts to this walk: the Rainforest Loop Walk (1.6km) and the Falls Walk (an additional 2.6km). To see the falls the entire 4.2km walk must be undertaken.

The reserve has two falls, one a 50m and the other a 25m drop into a narrow rainforest gorge. There is a raised wooden pathway along the route, which protects the environment and makes the track wheelchair accessible. The gradient is suitable for children and the elderly.

Trees in the reserve include the sandpaper fig, used by Aborigines to sand their wooden tools; the Illawarra fig tree; a giant stinging tree, its leaves covered in fine hairs saturated with concentrated acids for self-protection; red cedar; cabbage tree palms; and bush cherry.

Platypus and lyrebirds live in the reserve and, occasionally, an eastern water dragon can be seen basking on the rocks.

9 BARREN GROUNDS BIRD OBSERVATORY AND NATURE RESERVE

Return along Minnamurra Falls Rd and turn right into Jamberoo Mountain Rd. Continue up the escarpment for 5km until you reach the signpost on the left-hand side of the road directing you to Barren Grounds Bird Observatory and Nature Reserve.

Barren Grounds Bird Observatory and Nature Reserve is situated on a sandstone plateau 610m above sea level. With approximately 120 species, this 1962ha reserve is a bird-watcher's paradise. The rare ground parrot and eastern bristle bird are located in the park. In fact, their presence was the reason the reserve was declared in 1956. There are also

grey currawong, crimson rosellas, emu wrens, gang-gang cockatoos, honeyeaters and the occasional lyrebird. The mammals are generally nocturnal, although swamp wallabies and echidna are sometimes spotted. The flora consists essentially of heathland, which becomes carpeted by wildflowers in spring, and dry sclerophyll woodland. Ferns cover the ground in places and there are orchids on the rock ledges that grow atop other plants.

There are several walking tracks that depart from the Visitors Centre. Griffiths Trail is a circular 9km track through a range of vegetation communities. The Cooks Nose Track (3.2km) leads to a cliff-top lookout over Kangaroo Valley. The walk to Drawing Room Rocks is along flat ground and offers magnificent southerly views.

Return to Barren Grounds Observatory. Drive back to Jamberoo and continue on to Kiama.

Jamberoo's mock Tudor pub.

Beach fishing near Kiama.

15 BERRY AND KANGAROO VALLEY

■ DRIVING TOUR ■ 93KM ■ 1 DAY ■ VILLAGES AND VALLEYS

Seven Mile Beach stretches in a gracious white arc of sand and behind it the undulating countryside, home to dairy cattle and vineyards, gives way to the steep, timber-covered escarpment.

In recent times Berry has become very fashionable as Sydneysiders, particularly those living in the southern and eastern suburbs, have found its pleasant rolling hills an ideal location for weekend retreats. Over the past decade, from the humble beginnings of the alternative lifestyle cafe, the Berry Bazaar, Berry has grown to a town awash with gift and craft shops, coffee lounges and antique shops. It should be pointed out, however, that the town's famous donut shop (a caravan on the main street) has remained unchanged. Nearby, and part of the attractions of the local area, are the historic village of Coolangatta (the first European settlement in the district) and the beautiful Kangaroo Valley.

ing of the whole Australian Gothic-Revival'. Next door, the post office (1886) is also of historic interest. It was built on the land sold for this purpose by David Berry, the brother of Alexander Berry, who was present at the opening.

2 THE COURTHOUSE

To find the courthouse, continue along Queen St for two blocks and turn left into Albany St. Take the second right into Victoria St. The courthouse is on the left before the next intersection.

The Courthouse (1891) is an elegant Victorian Classical Revival building designed by colonial architect James Barnet, who was involved in the construction of a number of notable public buildings in Sydney, including the General Post Office, Customs House and the Macquarie Lighthouse at South Head.

3 KANGAROO VALLEY

Leave Berry heading south on the Princes Hwy. Before you reach the end of the town the Kangaroo Valley road is to the right. This road winds up the escarpment and over into Kangaroo Valley, 15km west of Berry.

The patchwork quilt of farms, the rainforest clinging to the steep slopes of the valley, the prettiness of the river, the facilities for the traveller, the small creeks that cross the valley, all make Kangaroo Valley a very special and particularly attractive place. Most people who travel to Kangaroo Valley are happy to picnic beside the Kangaroo River, walk across the Hampden Suspension Bridge, hire a canoe and go for a row on the river, and visit the craft shops, food shops and tea rooms in the village.

In 1840 the Reverend W.B. Clarke observed that the valley 'takes its name from the kangaroos which formerly abounded here but are now extinct'. The township grew with the improvement of roads in the late 1870s, the opening of a bridge over the river in 1879, the introduction of the cream separator in 1881, the connecting of telephones in 1884, improvements in local banking in the 1880s and the building of butter factories from 1888.

1 BERRY

For most of the past century, Berry has been a quiet rural service town meeting the needs of the surrounding farming district. The local Chamber of Commerce named it 'The Town of Trees' in 1975 because, towards the end of the last century, the local settlers planted extensive stands of English oaks, elms and beech trees. Many of these still stand today, giving the town a distinctly English feel.

Berry was originally called Broughton Creek, but the name was changed in 1890 in honour of the entrepreneurial Scotsman Alexander Berry who took up a run on the Shoalhaven River in 1822. By 1863 Berry owned more than 40 000ac and had set up his headquarters at the foot of Mount Coolangatta.

Today, Berry has a number of significant historical buildings. As you enter the town from the north you will notice the old National Bank (1889) and the former English Scottish & Australian Chartered

Bank (1886) at 135 Queen Street, which is now a local history museum. The building is unusual with its asymmetrical stepped facade and interesting casement windows. It is believed to be the only survivor of about six country banks built by William Wardell (1823–1899) who designed the ES&A Bank head office in Melbourne, acclaimed as 'the most distinguished build-

Hampden Suspension Bridge, Kangaroo Valley.

Kingsford Smith's Southern Cross at Gerroa.

4 HAMPDEN SUSPENSION BRIDGE

Drive through the town and continue for 1km until you reach Hampden Suspension Bridge. Cross over the bridge and park on the far side.

Built in 1898, the Hampden Suspension Bridge is reputedly the oldest surviving suspension bridge in the country. Noted for the castellated towers at either end, which resemble the turrets of a medieval castle, the bridge was named after the state's governor, Lord Hampden. There are picnic and barbecue facilities on both sides of the river.

The river below the bridge is a popular swimming and canoeing spot. Canoes can be hired adjacent to the bridge at Kangaroo Valley Tourist Park.

5 CAMBEWARRA LOOKOUT

Drive back from Kangaroo Valley on the Berry Rd making sure you take all the turns to the right. About 3km out of Kangaroo Valley township the road turns right and heads up the mountains. Follow the signs to the Cambewarra Lookout, which is 11km from Kangaroo Valley.

Cambewarra Lookout is 678m above sea level and offers excellent views across Nowra and the Shoalhaven Valley. This is one of the most spectacular panoramas along the South Coast escarpment.

6 COOLANGATTA HISTORIC VILLAGE

From Cambewarra Lookout continue 7km down the mountain until you reach the Princes Hwy. Continue south for 2km until you reach Bomaderry. Turn left into Bolong Rd and continue for 12km. Coolangatta Historic Village is clearly signposted. It stands on a hill above the road.

Many of the original buildings from the Coolangatta estate remain, including the homestead with maids' quarters and laundry (one wing survives after a fire devastated the original building in 1946), a large mid-Victorian cottage, the stables and coachman's quarters (*c*.1823), the tinsmith's shop, two coach houses (one *c*.1832), a billiards room, the blacksmith's shop, convict cottage (*c*.1840) and estate office, the community hall (*c*.1840), the cemetery and a monument to David Berry. A pottery craft centre is located in the original schoolhouse (established in 1861) and the old library was transported to Shoalhaven Heads where it became St Peter's Church. It currently offers accommodation in the historic buildings.

7 GERROA

Leave Coolangatta Historic Village and head north—the road is now called Crooked River Rd—for 13km until you reach the township of Gerroa.

Gerroa is a quiet and popular holiday destination at the northern end of Seven Mile Beach. The explorer George Bass sailed alongside Seven Mile Beach and crossed the shoals at the entrance to the Crookhaven River which he named the Shoalhaven. The beach became a venue for horseracing as early as the 1860s and later for car and bike races. It was the site upon which the speed of 100m/ph was first attained, on land, in Australia.

Gerroa lies at the northern end of Seven Mile Beach National Park, an area of spinifex, coast wattle, tea-tree, coast banksia, and a hinterland forest of she-oaks, bangalay, saw banksia, southern mahogany and burrawangs. There is a large bird population in the district, including honeyeaters, currawongs, crimson rosellas, thornbills, kookaburras, ravens, grey fantails, eastern whipbirds and white-throated treecreepers, and the occasional white-breasted sea eagle.

8 KINGSFORD SMITH MEMORIAL PARK

Continue along Crooked River Rd until you reach the Kingsford Smith Memorial Lookout, located at the intersection of Crooked River Rd and Headlands Drv.

In 1933, Seven Mile Beach was used by Sir Charles Kingsford Smith as the runway for the first commercial flight between Australia and New Zealand. Flares were lit upon the beach to mark out the runway and several thousand people came from Sydney and the local area to witness the 2.30am take-off, turning on their car headlights to provide the aviator with extra illumination.

The historic flight is commemorated by the Kingsford Smith memorial and lookout at the top of the hill. The memorial consists of a one-dimensional concrete rendering of Kingsford Smith's aeroplane, the *Southern Cross*. The lookout offers panoramic views over Seven Mile National Park.

9 BLACK POINT

Continue east for about 2km along Headlands Drv. Eventually you will reach the Black Point car park.

This is a popular and well-established site for geography and geology excursions. It has one of the best displays of fossils on the coast. Breaking or removing the rocks is forbidden. All you need do is lower your eyes and know what you're looking for to see the exposed fossils. The rock platform is said to be ideal for catching tuna, kingfish, snapper, drummer, trevally, salmon, tailor and groper. But be careful, because the waves can be dangerous.

10 GERRINGONG BOAT HARBOUR

Drive 2km along Headlands Drv to Crooked River Rd. Turn right and continue for 4km until you reach the edge of Gerringong. Turn east into Jupiter St which will take you to the boat harbour.

Gerringong Boat Harbour was once a major port where the produce of the local area was shipped to Sydney. Cedar-getters began to use the site in the 1840s. Looking at the harbour today it is hard to imagine that a 400ft jetty once extended out from where the boat ramp now stands and that sailing ships regularly arrived bringing stores and supplies from Sydney and taking away local produce. A government grant saw the erection of a 200ft jetty in 1880. Boats could still only approach it at high tide, however, because they hit bottom at low tide. Consequently, another grant in 1882 saw its extension to 400ft. A cyclone tore the structure apart a few years later.

There is a pool at the boat harbour, a boat ramp and a small park with children's swings. Tuna, kingfish, mulloway, snapper, flathead, morwong and even marlin can be caught in the offshore waters.

11 GERRINGONG

Return up Jupiter St and turn right and continue for 500m to the centre of Gerringong.

Gerringong was once a rural dairying village in one of the richest dairy farming areas in New South Wales. Since the 1980s the town has become a popular retirement and holiday destination.

In recent times Gerringong has enjoyed a reputation as a source of major sporting figures. From a pool of talent across many fields, the town has consistently thrown up numerous state competitors. Several have progressed to national representation, particularly in Rugby League, a local forte since 1912 when Gerringong won the first season of the South Coast Rugby League competition. Rod Wishart and Michael Cronin are the most famous local products. The town oval has been named in Cronin's honour.

Turn back towards Gerroa and turn right into Belinda St. You will pass Mick Cronin's Hotel as you head back to the Princes Hwy. Berry is 18km away.

The Silos Restaurant outside Berry.

16 EXPLORING JERVIS BAY

■ DRIVING TOUR ■ 170KM ■ 1 DAY ■ ON THE SHORES OF THE NATION'S HARBOUR

The beaches are impossibly white. The foreshores are peaceful. The bushwalks are full of interest. Jervis Bay is a hidden treasure on the South Coast.

Jervis Bay is both an inlet and a uniquely beautiful national parkland and holiday destination. At approximately 15km long and 10km wide, the spacious natural harbour is sheltered by headlands of forest and heathland. With a depth of 27m, the bay is thought to be the deepest sheltered harbour in Australia. The waters are remarkably beautiful and range in hue from aquamarine to a deep blue. The fauna and the flora are diverse, and include eucalypt forest, woodland, swamps, dunes, mangrove, rainforest relics, coastal scrub, grassland and a heathland rich in wildflowers. There are lakes and estuaries, historic sites, high sandy ridges, a coastline of coves, majestic cliffs up to 135m in height, and beaches noted for the remarkable whiteness of their sands.

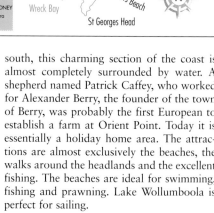

1 NOWRA

Nowra is the commercial centre of the Shoalhaven District on the south coast of New South Wales. The survivors of the wreck of the *Sydney Cove* walked through the area in 1797 and George Bass explored it later that same year. He followed Seven Mile Beach and crossed the shoals at the entrance to the river. Unimpressed with the shallowness of the river mouth, Bass named it Shoals Haven. In 1805, the coastline was mapped from the land by Lieutenant Kent and Assistant Surveyor General James Meehan. They explored the area, noting the dense rainforest and stands of solid timber. Cedar-getters were operating in the area by 1811. They floated and towed the logs down the river to Greenwell Point, where they were loaded aboard waiting steamers.

2 MEROOGAL

From the Princes Hwy bridge over the Shoalhaven River head south and turn right into Worrigee St. Drive to the intersection with West St at the end of this road.
Meroogal is an historic, timber, Gothic-style house managed by the Historic Houses Trust of New South Wales. Built in 1885, the dwelling contains original household contents collected by four generations of women in the Thorburn and McGregor families.

View of the beach at Huskisson.

3 SHOALHAVEN HISTORICAL MUSEUM

Head south along West St for one block and turn left into Plunkett St. Head east for four blocks to Kinghorne St.
The Shoalhaven Historical Museum is located in the old police premises (1900) and is open Saturdays, Sundays and public holidays from 1.00pm–4.00pm. The museum is a good introduction to the history of the local area with exhibitions on the nautical and cedar-cutting industries in the local area.

4 GREENWELL POINT

Leave the museum and head back to the Princes Hwy. Turn right and, at the next block turn into Kalandar St which becomes Greenwell Point Rd. Greenwell Point is 14km away.
Greenwell Point is a fishing village named after the Aboriginal doctor Greenwell, noted for his treatment of snakebites and toothaches. In 1883, George Haiser started the oyster cultivation for which the area is now known. There are concrete boat ramps off West Street (turn left as you enter the town) and Greenwell Point Road (follow it to its end), and a natural ramp for light boats off Haiser Road (turn right off Greenwell Point Road just past the school and follow the waterline).

5 ORIENT POINT

Return along Greenwell Point Rd for about 4km and head south towards Culburra and Currarong. After 5km turn left to Culburra and continue for another 5km. Turn left off the main road into Prince Edward Ave and, after 2km, turn left into Park Rd.
With the Crookhaven to the west, the Tasman Sea to the east and Lake Wollumboola to the south, this charming section of the coast is almost completely surrounded by water. A shepherd named Patrick Caffey, who worked for Alexander Berry, the founder of the town of Berry, was probably the first European to establish a farm at Orient Point. Today it is essentially a holiday home area. The attractions are almost exclusively the beaches, the walks around the headlands and the excellent fishing. The beaches are ideal for swimming, fishing and prawning. Lake Wollumboola is perfect for sailing.

6 CROOKHAVEN HEADS

Return along Park Rd to Prince Edward Ave. Turn left and follow the road for 1km.
At Crookhaven Heads there are a number of very pleasant coastal bushwalks (of little more than 50 minutes in any direction). Clear directions are offered from the headland near the old Crookhaven Heads lighthouse. The views are impressive, with the rock formations being the result of the way the bedding has been twisted.

7 CURRARONG

Return along Prince Edward Ave for 3km and turn right, heading west for 5km. Turn left and proceed

The ruins of the old lighthouse at Jervis Bay.

southwards for 4km and turn left again. It is a further 12km to Currarong.

Currarong, in Crookhaven Bight at the northernmost point of the Beecroft peninsula, has a beautiful beach. There is also safe swimming for children at Currarong Creek. The fishing is reputedly excellent and there are two boat ramps.

The Beecroft peninsula is an attractive and historic area with a diverse array of native flowers and wildlife. Bushwalking, fishing and camping are available at Honeymoon Bay on the western perimeter of the promontory. Unfortunately, the peninsula is also used as a weapons range and so is subject to closure at short notice. There is a lookout with spectacular views at the Point Perpendicular lighthouse, where the sheer cliffs are 90m high. On the headland are two walking tracks. The Wreck Walk (1 hour) takes you to what's left of SS *Merimbula*, wrecked at Beecroft Head in March 1927.

8 LADY DENMAN MUSEUM

Return 29km to Nowra. Turn left onto the Princes Hwy and head south for 12km to Klimpton. Turn left into Jervis Bay Rd and after 8km turn left onto the Tomerong–Huskisson Rd. It is 3km to Huskisson. As you enter the town, turn left into Dent St.

The Lady Denman Museum deals with the history of wooden shipbuilding at Huskisson, and the Museum of Jervis Bay Science and the Sea has a broader collection of maritime history. Adjacent to a stand of spotted gums is a boat-building shed, fish feeding, the Beaufort Memorial propeller, a mangrove boardwalk, and picnic facilities.

9 HUSKISSON

Return to Tomerong St. Take the first right into Sydney St and the second left into Owen St. This is the main street of Huskisson. Continue east to the water's edge. There is a parking lot across the road from the hotel.

Huskisson is a typical sleepy holiday resort and fishing port. The main street has takeaway food shops, a coffee shop, a dive shop and a huge beachfront hotel—the Husky Pub—which provides drinkers with delightful views across the bay. Here you can sit in the beer garden and enjoy a meal.

The town was named after William Huskisson, secretary of the colonies and leader of the House of Commons from 1827 to 1828. Huskisson had the misfortune to be run over by a locomotive while talking to the Duke of Wellington at the opening of the Liverpool and Manchester railway in 1830. George Dent established the local shipbuilding industry in 1864. The availability of local timber encouraged the growth of the industry which was thriving by the 1880s and continued until 1966. One boat made locally in 1912, the *Lady Denman* ferry, which operated in Sydney Harbour, was towed back to Huskisson in 1981 to serve as a maritime museum.

10 VINCENTIA

From the Huskisson hotel proceed south along Hawke St until you reach a T-intersection. Turn left into Keppel St which becomes Burrill St. Cross the bridge and proceed along Elizabeth Drv.

Vincentia was originally called South Huskisson but was renamed in 1952 after John Jervis (after whom Jervis Bay was named), who was also the Earl of St Vincent. Vincentia is a holiday town. There are holiday facilities, long beaches and the waters are good for fishing, windsurfing, and diving. The first left off Elizabeth Drive is Holden Street, which will take you out to the bay and

Lady Denman Museum in Huskisson.

a concrete boat ramp. If you continue along Elizabeth Drive, Plantation Point Parade branches off to the left and leads to a natural ramp for catamarans and skiffs.

11 JERVIS BAY

Return to the roundabout at Elizabeth Drv and head west on Wool Rd. After 2km turn left into Jervis Bay Rd. The Jervis Bay Visitor Information Centre is 8km along the road.

In 1901, after Federation, plans were set in motion to create a national capital. The subsequent *Seat of Government Act* (1908) declared that access to the sea was imperative. Accordingly, 7400ha of land at the southern end of Jervis Bay were officially handed over by New South Wales to the Commonwealth government to be developed as a port and naval base. Work began in 1913 and, in 1915, the Royal Australian Naval College opened at Captain Point under federal administration as HMAS *Creswell*. The college no longer exists but some officer training still occurs at Jervis Bay.

12 HMAS CRESWELL

Past the Visitors Centre is the road to HMAS Creswell.

Access to HMAS *Creswell* is restricted. Visits of 20 minutes' duration are permitted on weekends and most public holidays. In the grounds is the Royal Australian Naval College Historical Collection, containing artefacts relating to the college and the Jervis Bay area and an extensive collection of model sailing ships. The main buildings around the quadrangle—the Clock Tower, the Dining Hall, the College Hospital (now the sailors' mess) and the two-storey timber Commandant's House—have all been listed for preservation by the National Trust. All the original buildings are of weatherboard cladding with red-tiled roofs.

13 GREEN PATCH

Return to Jervis Bay Rd and continue east for 3km until you reach Green Patch.

Green Patch has a popular and beautiful camping ground that accommodates caravans as well as tents. There are picnic tables, good barbecue facilities, toilets, hot showers (but no power), an excellent sheltered beach and hundreds of tame rosellas. The birdlife here is prolific and the flora is diverse. Dolphins and penguins are commonly seen in the bay and kangaroos often visit the camping ground.

Return along Jervis Bay Rd for 25km and turn right onto the Princes Hwy. It is a 12km drive back to Nowra.

View across Jervis Bay.

17 MILTON TO NAROOMA

■ DRIVING TOUR ■ 129KM ■ 1 DAY ■ A DRIVE DOWN THE SOUTH COAST

Through undulating dairy and beef country the South Coast road winds. Too often the traveller needs to head east to catch a glimpse of the Pacific Ocean.

The New South Wales south coast is one of the state's best-kept secrets. The natural tendency of holiday-makers is to head north and consequently, the charming beaches and undulating dairy country that stretches from Milton and Ulladulla through Batemans Bay to Narooma is often overlooked. Interestingly, the area has not escaped holiday-makers from Canberra who know that the trip through Bungendore and Braidwood to Batemans Bay is the quickest access to the coast.

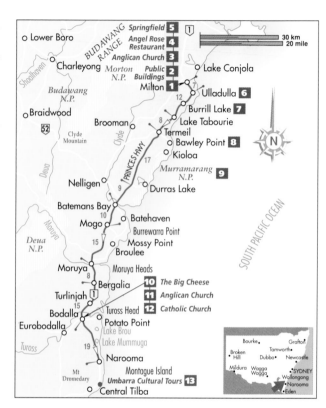

1 MILTON

Milton is a rural centre linked to Ulladulla (in the next decade the short rural strip between the two towns will, inevitably, be filled by suburban development) and a series of small coastal holiday resorts. The first land grant in the area was issued in 1827 to Reverend Thomas Kendall (1778–1832). Kendall settled to the north of the present township of Milton and called his property Kendall Dale. There he ran cattle and felled timber utilising ticket-of-leave men for labour. An area known as The Settlement, upon the site of present-day Milton, was soon occupied by farmers. Creeks, rivers, gorges, mountains, lakes and swamps made access by land difficult so the settlers turned to the harbour, imaginatively known as Boat Harbour, for the shipment of produce. There were no breakwaters nor any jetty, just a chain by which ships were secured.

2 MILTON'S PUBLIC BUILDINGS

As you enter Milton from the north, along the Princes Hwy, there are several public buildings on either side of the road which make a contribution to the streetscape.
The post office (1880), extended in 1894 and 1904, was originally a single-storey struc-ture. Beside it are the police station and the unusual, asymmetrical courthouse (some sources date it at 1877, others from the 1890s) with turned timber columns. Opposite is the old town hall building (1871) with its interesting facade of quoins. It is now the library. Next to it is a courtyard, where a public mural of Milton and its environs can be seen, and the Milton Cultural Centre.

3 ANGLICAN CHURCH OF ST PETER AND ST PAUL

Continue along the highway to the Church St intersection.
On the south-western corner is the Anglican Church of St Peter and St Paul. The church was built in a Gothic style and completed in 1860, although it was not consecrated for many years because of debts. It has been argued that the Chinese Elm tree on the grounds is the oldest in Australia, and was planted by Alice Kendall (grand-daughter of the Reverend Thomas

Kendall) when she returned from missionary work in China in 1920.

4 ANGEL ROSE RESTAURANT

Continue along the highway, cross over Gordon St, and proceed to the next intersection where the high-way meets Croobyar Rd.
To the right is Colleen English Candlemaker's Cottage, thought to be one of the oldest structures in the area; and to the left is the Angel Rose Restaurant, a two-storey struc-ture that was originally a store (*c.*1887). The balcony was added at a later date.

5 SPRINGFIELD

Continue south along the Princes Hwy for about 2km.
On the western side of the highway is Springfield, an attractive 11-roomed house with elaborate iron lacework about the verandah. Considered distinct in its architec-tural features, the house was built in the 1860s by Ephraim Mison, who owned a timber mill above the wharf at Ulladulla.

6 ULLADULLA

Proceed south for about 4km along the highway to Ulladulla. At the southern end of town, turn left off the highway into Deering St.
The Coomie Nulunga Cultural Trail com-mences opposite the Lighthouse Oval car park in Deering Street, just past the 4m

The Big Cheese at Bodalla.

Boats moored at Ulladulla harbour.

Aboriginal figure of Bulan. This delightful walk was created by the local Aboriginal Land Council from a land grant. The first stage of 700m takes you through low scrub down to Renny Beach; the last section of the walk winds in the manner of the Rainbow Serpent, the creator in Aboriginal Dreamtime. Along the way are detailed handpainted and carved information posts that incorporate the names of local plants and animals. There is a small bridge across a creek and a viewing platform facing the sea. The best times for the walk are dawn and dusk, when the animal life is at its most active. Visitors are requested to stay on the main trail for the protection of the flora and fauna.

At the end of Deering Street is Warden Head Lighthouse, built in Ulladulla in 1873 and re-erected at the present site in 1889. Made of iron and designed by a colonial architect, the original optical apparatus is intact and still in operation. Fishing off the nearby rocks is excellent and there are good views of the harbour and surrounds.

7 BURRILL LAKE

About 5km south of Ulladulla, the Princes Hwy crosses the inlet which leads into Burrill Lake.

The shores of Burrill Lake are lined with natural bushland. There are fine views to be had from Dolphin Point. Simply cross the bridge and take the first left into Dolphin Point Road. This will lead you past Bungalow Park Caravan and Camping Park, where there is a bird sanctuary. Burrill Lake has a number of boat ramps, including a concrete launch on the northern side of Burrill Inlet off Kendall Crescent and a natural ramp for catamarans and skiffs.

8 BAWLEY POINT

Head south from Burrill Lake, along the Princes Hwy, for 17km. Just south of Termeil, turn left into Bawley Point Rd. Bawley Point is 6km away.

Bawley Point is a beautiful seaside village where coastal steamships were once built. Timber was the main industry here and an initial sawpit was replaced by a sawmill in 1881. The mill constructed in 1910 was reputedly the largest in the southern hemisphere at the time.

About a kilometre east of the highway is Mimosa Hill Wildflowers and Holiday Cottages, with native and South African species. A further kilometre east is Protea Grove, specialising in proteas, Australian natives and dried flowers. There are quiet beaches and headlands to the south and north of Bawley Point, and lagoons to the north and west where the prawning is good in season.

About 3km south of Bawley Point, along the coast road, is the car park for the Murramarang Aboriginal Reserve which contains a midden and has provided considerable insight into the early inhabitants of the area. The lagoon to the north of the headland is traditionally associated with beliefs about the creation of the land. A self-guided walking track with explanatory signs commences at the car park.

9 MURRAMARANG NATIONAL PARK

From Bawley Point it is possible to continue driving south past the Murramarang Aboriginal Reserve into the northern section of Murramarang National Park. Alternatively, return to the highway and continue south towards Batemans Bay. South of Termeil, heading east from the highway, are Bucks Rd, Dam Rd, Mount Agony Rd, Livingstone Creek Rd, Pebbly Beach Rd and Durras Rd—all of which lead to different areas of the national park. Take the turn-off to Durras. It is 25km from Bawley Point to the Durras turn-off and a further 5km to Durras and Murramarang National Park.

The great attraction of Murramarang National Park is that it is possible to see kangaroos on the beach. The park covers about 27km of beautiful coastline and forest scenery. No more than 2km across at its widest point, it features a variety of landforms, including sandy and shingle beaches, rugged headlands, tombolos, cliffs, rock stacks, wave-cut platforms, fossil-bearing rocks and four offshore islands.

The wildlife is fairly typical of the coast: eastern grey kangaroos, swamp wallabies, red-necked wallabies and other mammals. The varied birdlife, including parrots, finches, honeyeaters, eagles, hawks, terns, thrushes, oystercatchers, wrens, muttonbirds, albatrosses and fantails. Kangaroos commonly feed near the beaches.

The park offers swimming, surfing, fishing, picnicking, beachwalking, bushwalking and nature study.

10 THE BIG CHEESE

Return 5km to the intersection of Durras Rd and the Princes Hwy. From here it is 9km to Batemans Bay, a further 28km to Moruya and then 23km to Bodalla.

As you enter Bodalla from the north you will find, on your left, the Big Cheese, a tourist complex offering cheese and honey sales, a modest luncheon, a gift shop and an ice-cream parlour.

11 ALL SAINTS ANGLICAN CHURCH

Continue south along the highway for a short distance and you will see the Anglican Church to your left.

The merchant Thomas Mort died before he could build a church for the Bodalla community and so his family built the All Saints Anglican Church as a memorial to Mort and his first wife, Theresa. His second wife laid the foundation stone in 1880. The church was designed by Edmund Blacket in Gothic Revival style and bears a memorial tablet. The minister was the Reverend W.H. Walsh, Blacket's earliest patron, who came to Bodalla to retire and served virtually as private chaplain to the Mort family. Built of grey granite quarried on the estate, the church features a large tower and spire at the south-western corner, a large rose window at the west end, oak woodwork and furnishings, and a pipe organ from England.

12 ST EDMUND'S AND OUR LADY OF THE ASSUMPTION CATHOLIC CHURCH

Continue along the Princes Hwy to the southern outskirts of Bodalla.

Laidley Mort, the son of T.S. Mort's first marriage, had the Catholic Church built in 1886 for his wife, Mary. She named the church St Edmund's and Our Lady of the Assumption Catholic Church. Mary received her education at Bruges, in Belgium, and she is said to have asked the architect John Horbury Hunt to base his design on Bruges Cathedral.

13 UMBARRA CULTURAL TOURS

Proceed south along the highway for 18km to Narooma. From Narooma, continue south for 19km before turning left into Bermagui Rd and following it for a few kilometres to the Umbarra Cultural Centre.

A most interesting way to see Mount Dromedary (known by the Yuin people as Gulaga), Mystery Bay, Camel Rock, Mumbulla Mountain and Fairhaven Point is to take a guided four-hour, four-wheel-drive tour with the Yuin people of Wallaga Lake at the Umbarra Cultural Centre. The centre provides information about local Aboriginal culture in the area, and there are Dreamtime stories, bark-hut building, spear and boomerang throwing, bush medicine and bush tucker. Also available are cruises of the lake, its birdlife and midden sites with a full commentary on their cultural significance.

Return from Umbarra to Narooma (22km) then continue north on the Princes Hwy to Milton.

18 TILBA TILBA TO TATHRA

■ DRIVING TOUR ■ 77KM ■ 6 HOURS ■ FROM WOODEN TOWNS TO WOODEN WHARVES

Head to the coast through the national parks and you will find a wonderland of unspoilt and peaceful beaches edged by dramatic rocky headlands.

From Tilba Tilba to Tathra is a trip through the European and Aboriginal history of the South Coast. It is a journey from a delightful timber town that has become a pleasant tourist destination of gift shops and eateries to the beautiful Aboriginal coastal haunts of Wallaga Lake and Mimosa Rocks and then on to Tathra where once the South Coast ferry brought supplies and collected the local dairy produce. Tathra is the last of the South Coast wharves and a reminder of the region's pre-eminent form of transport until the 1940s.

1 CENTRAL TILBA AND TILBA TILBA

Central Tilba and Tilba Tilba are two historic villages incorporated in the Dromedary Conservation Area. Captain Cook named Cape Dromedary and Mount Dromedary, the highest point on the South Coast, in April 1770. A gold find was reported in 1853 and, after reef gold was uncovered in 1860, prospectors rushed to the district. The Dromedary Gold Mining Company continued operations until the beginning of this century. Some of the prospectors settled at Tilba Tilba, where a post office was opened in 1873 with Richard Bate employed as the postmaster.

The Bate family became prominent in the area. Henry Bate moved to the town after taking up land on the slopes of Mount Dromedary in 1864, where he built Mountain View homestead. Until a church was erected in 1881, Henry Bate provided a room for church services. The family increased its holdings throughout the 1880s, by which time the town possessed two stores and a hotel. In 1891, Samuel Bate became one of the founders of the ABC Cheese Factory in what was to become Central Tilba. The factory closed in the 1960s with a downturn in the local dairy industry but re-opened as a result of a tourism boost. Bates General Store was opened there in 1894 (it includes the post office) and, the following year, the township sprang up on land sold by Samuel Bate.

Because the town was so rapidly established all the buildings are homogeneous, and are built from timber. Since the town failed to develop after goldmining died in the area, it has remained untouched. The entire village is now classified by the National Trust as the Central Tilba Conservation Area.

2 THE TILBAS SCENIC ROUTE

Drive 2km south (the road departs from the general store in Central Tilba) to Tilba Tilba, which is little more than a few houses.

Both Tilbas are located on a road that forms a loop off the Princes Highway just north of the Bermagui turn-off. Those keen on a scenic drive (of about 15km) can take the unsealed road north out of Central Tilba, which then heads east and south back to the highway just south of Corunna Lake. It is a signposted tourist drive.

3 WALLAGA LAKE NATIONAL PARK

Continue on through Tilba Tilba to the Princes Hwy. About 1km south there is a turn to your left which is the coastal road to Regatta Point and Bermagui. Continue on this road for 4km until you reach Regatta Point.

On the eastern shore of Wallaga Lake is Wallaga Lake National Park, a beautiful open forest. Camel Rock, on the shoreline, is an unusual rock formation. The park is generally hilly with steep gullies and so is best explored by boat (available for hire from Regatta Point and Beauty Point, on the eastern shore). The location is perfect for fishing, swimming and boating. There are few beaches but a number of shallow bays and sheltered inlets. The fauna in the area includes potoroos, koalas, bandicoots and swamp wallabies.

Wallaga Lake was formed when two river valleys were flooded at the end of the ice age and the river mouths were blocked by a large sandbar. It was used by Aborigines for thousands of years and there are many ancient relics, including a number of middens on the foreshores. Access to Merriman Island, in the middle of the lake, is forbidden because of its important significance for indigenous communities. The island was the first place to be gazetted as an Aboriginal site. A focus of tribal culture, the island is associated with the story of King Merriman, widely known among the Aborigines of the South Coast.

According to legend, King Merriman lived on the island while his people lived on the shores of the lake. His power derived from his ability to understand a black duck, his *moojingarl*, that forewarned him of forthcoming dangers. One day the duck told him of a group of warriors coming from the far south to do battle. King Merriman remained on the island while the other men took the women and children to a place of safety and then hid in the reeds. The first to sight the approaching warriors, the King warned his men who fought a fierce battle but lost. The opposing tribesmen then set out for the

Mimosa Rocks National Park.

island. King Merriman threw powerful spears, and a boomerang that severed the arms and heads of his opponents before returning to him, but it was not enough. He then turned himself into a whirlwind and flew off. He passed over the fierce Kiola tribe and their wise men correctly divined his presence and that it meant the defeat of the Wallaga people and the advance of another tribe. King Merriman journeyed on to the Shoalhaven tribe to warn them but the Kiola tribe defeated the invaders and the King, whose power was finished, stayed for a time at the Shoalhaven then travelled away.

4 BERMAGUI

Continue along the coast road for another 5km until you reach Bermagui.

Bermagui is an attractive fishing port located on the estuary of the Bermagui River. In spring the warm currents bring marlin and yellowfin tuna close to the coast and charter boats take divers, deep-sea and big-game fishers out to sea. One of the most notable figures to fish at Bermagui was the American author of westerns, Zane Grey, who wrote of his experiences in *An American Angler in Australia* (1937) and his posthumously published novel, *Wilderness Fresh*. The town park is named after him and the local hotel has photographs of his stay.

5 HORSESHOE BAY AND BLUE POOL

On entering Bermagui, head south along Coluga St and cross the Bermagui River. The road becomes Bridge St and curves east to become Cutajo St. Turn right into Scenic Drv. Blue Pool is signposted on your left.

Horseshoe Bay and Blue Pool are situated on the headland to the east of the town centre. Horseshoe Bay is on the northern side of the promontory and Blue Pool, with its large saltwater pool, lies off Scenic Drive on the southern side. The Bermagui headlands are a popular rock-fishing location.

6 MIMOSA ROCKS NATIONAL PARK

Return to Scenic Drv and continue south. After approximately 1km Scenic Drv joins the main road out of Bermagui heading south. Continue for 17km until you see a sign on the left to Mimosa Rocks National Park. The route is a narrow dirt road that leads to a number of car parks near the ocean. Follow the signs to Aragunna.

Mimosa Rocks National Park stretches south of Bermagui for 17km in a strip of coastal beaches, caves, cliffs, rocky coves, massive offshore rock stacks, headlands, lagoons, coastal lakes and a heavily wooded hinterland, including patches of rainforest. The park supports a rich and diverse range of birdlife, including cormorants, great egrets, sea eagles, goshawks, crested terns, silver gulls, pied oystercatchers, hooded plovers, topknot pigeons and brown cuckoo-doves. There are also sugar gliders, ringtail possums, brushtail possums, bandicoots, wallabies, echidnas and goannas. Snorkelling, surfing, rock and beach fishing, swimming and bushwalking, coastal bird-watching and foreshore fossicking are all popular pastimes.

Tathra Wharf, now a museum and coffee shop.

The highlight of any visit is the Aragunnu site, which is one of the most interesting and well-presented Aboriginal sites on the Australian coast. The National Parks and Wildlife Service has constructed a series of boardwalks that take the visitor past a huge and ancient midden near a freshwater creek to a point where there are excellent views across a rocky beach to Mimosa Rocks.

Heading south, the approach to the Picnic Point site along Wapengo Lake Road and through banksia and stringybark forest is impressive. Middle Beach is popular with surfers. Nelson Lagoon is beautiful in the spring with its birdlife and blooming wattles. Moon Bay, 250m from the car park at the south of the national park, near Tathra, is particularly popular with surfers.

7 TATHRA AND TATHRA WHARF

Return to the main road and turn left. Continue 22km south to Tathra. Drive through the town and follow the signs to Tathra Wharf. This involves following Andy Poole Drv and turning left into Wharf Rd.

Tathra is a small coastal township situated high on the bluff above its wharf. The area west of what is now Tathra was first settled by Europeans when pastoralists began illegally squatting on crown land in the 1820s and 1830s. Following an inquiry into the transport facilities in the Bega district in 1851, the Illawarra and South Coast Steam Navigation Company was formed.

Tathra came into existence as a small jetty that served as a shipping outlet for a group of local farmers led by Daniel Gowing, who had offered financial reward to anyone willing to ship produce to a point further north. The jetty was replaced in 1861–1862 by a wharf that was erected out of funds donated by local farmers and the Illawarra Company. The wharf was built of turpentine driven into solid rock. The site was chosen because of the shelter it offered from southerly winds and because it was the best site available between Merimbula and Bermagui.

The Illawarra Company built a cargo shed in 1866 and growing usage led to the enlargement of the wharf in 1873, 1878, 1886, 1889, 1903 and 1912. Among other changes, a cattle yard was built in 1901, the existing two-storey shed was constructed in 1907 and a crane added in 1912. The absence of a railway line and poor roads made the steamer service crucial.

The Princes Highway from Batemans Bay to the Victorian border was still gravel in 1940. South Coast shipping finally disappeared in 1956. The wharf's deterioration led to an order for its demolition in 1973 but local action from the National Trust saw its preservation. It is the only remaining coastal steamer wharf in New South Wales and one of six historic timber wharves listed on the Register of the National Estate.

The Tathra wharf site also features a maritime museum with displays on Tathra's place in steam-shipping history and its popularity as a tourist destination earlier this century.

Boats moored in Bermagui harbour.

The Two Story B&B at Central Tilba.

19 EDEN AND THE BEN BOYD NATIONAL PARK

■ DRIVING TOUR ■ 92KM ■ 1 DAY ■ AUSTRALIA'S WHALING PAST

Famous as a whaling port in the 19th century, Eden and the coast of Ben Boyd National Park are now rugged, windswept and dramatic.

The far south coast of New South Wales is an area of small fishing townships, tiny hinterland villages and vast areas of largely unspoilt and rugged forest lands. The early settlers in the region were whalers, timber-cutters and farmers who eked a simple life from an isolated land. The winds of the southern Pacific blow storms into the bays and the forests can be dark and intimidating. Still, there is great beauty here for anglers, bushwalkers and those who love dramatic, untouched countryside.

The ruins of Boyds Tower.

1 EDEN

Eden is the last town of any significance before crossing the border into north-eastern Victoria. It is situated on a point that juts out into Twofold Bay and is bounded to the north and south by national park and by woodland to the west.

The early history of the bay is closely tied to the whaling industry. The first whales were killed in 1791. The migration of these animals (mostly right whales) to and from the Antarctic waters took them past Twofold Bay between May and November of each year. Commercial exploitation commenced in the early years of the 19th century, when whaling ships took shelter in the bay from inclement weather, subsequently using it as a base for operations.

The original white settlement was made by John Raine in 1828 when he established the first shore whaling station on mainland Australia. A particular group of killer whales visited the area each year, over a very long period of time, using the south of the bay as their base for the season. Locals, recognising them by distinctive markings, assigned them individual names and found them to be a great help in hunting and bringing whales into the bay.

The killer whales hunted in packs, driving the whales into shallow water, preventing their escape to deeper waters and attempting to frustrate their attempts to take in air. Apparently the killer whales, when they detected whales about, would travel to the whaling station, make a great deal of noise to attract the whalers, wait for the boats to launch and then lead them to the whales. The combination increased the success of a hunt, ensuring a meal for the killer whales. They fed almost exclusively on the lips and tongue of the whales, leaving the rest of the carcass for the whalers.

One of Twofold Bay's famous killer whales, Tom, was found dead in the bay in 1930. His skeleton has been preserved in the Killer Whale Museum at the corner of Imlay Street and Cocora Street. The building contains other items of interest, details and booklets about this aspect of local history and takes bookings for water cruises. The museum also offers fine views of the bay from the gallery.

2 BOYDTOWN

Head south along the Princes Hwy for 8km then turn left at the gates into Boydtown Park Rd. Follow the road for 500m to the car park of the Seahorse Inn.

Boydtown is really little more than a ghost town. It was originally a substantial township that was built by the famous whaling entrepreneur Benjamin Boyd, a wealthy London stockbroker who came to Australia to seek his fortune. Boyd had a scheme to enter into shipping and pastoral enterprises, arguing that large steamships were required to serve the needs of the south coast, where settlers were reliant upon sea travel. He persuaded many British investors to participate financially.

Boyd arrived in 1842 and established a coastal steamship service. He quickly put the paddle-steamer *Seahorse* into operation. It covered the southern route from Sydney to Twofold Bay and Hobart. Within two years

of his arrival Boyd had become one of the largest landholders in the colony, owning nearly two and a half million acres in the Riverina and Monaro regions. Boyd decided that Twofold Bay would serve as the port for his enterprises in the Monaro hinterland. Grandiose plans were made for the establishment of a township, and the construction of Boydtown commenced in 1843. Shore whaling and the related oil extraction process had been established on the bay for 15 years and Boyd added both to his other enterprises, undertaking the settlement of East Boyd for this purpose.

Boyd was a firm believer in low wages for his employees and had difficulty finding recruits for his various enterprises. To make matters worse, *Seahorse* was irreparably damaged after striking a rock. In 1849, the liquidators were called in. All operations at Twofold Bay ceased with most of the construction still incomplete. Boyd's entire colonial endeavour was a spectacular failure. Boyd left for the California goldfields in 1849. He disappeared at Guadalcanal, in the Solomon Islands, in 1851.

The principal relic of Boyd's adventures is the Sea Horse Inn. Symbolic of Boydtown itself, the hotel was built of convict labour and never fully completed. For the first 30 years of this century it was left vacant, reduced to a mere shell from vandalism and deterioration. The inn was renovated by the Whiter brothers who purchased it in 1936, later adding a second storey. Full restoration occurred in the 1980s.

The inn is situated amid attractive gardens and was constructed on the shores overlooking Twofold Bay. Mostly Elizabethan in its conception, it has Tudor and Georgian elements, with hand-carved doors, stained-glass ornamentation, winding staircases, large open grates, Gothic arches and attic bedrooms. Although the foundation was made of sandstone from Pyrmont in Sydney, lugged from the shore to the site by bullock wagon, the rest of the hotel was constructed of local stone, thousands of red bricks (from clay quarried nearby) and pit-sawn hardwood, with cedar and oak fittings from England. Perched on a ridge near the inn are the ruins of a church, which was never completed or used.

3 DAVIDSON WHALING STATION

Return to the Princes Hwy and continue south for another 10km then turn left into Edrom Rd. Look for the sign to Green Cape Lighthouse. After 11km turn left into Boyd Rd. The Davidson Whaling Station is 4km further along the road.

At the mouth of the Towamba River is Kiah Inlet and the Davidson Whaling Station, proclaimed an historic site in 1986 under the authority of the National Parks and Wildlife Service, which restored the existing materials and developed visitor facilities. Alexander Davidson was a carpenter who worked for Benjamin Boyd in the 1840s. He opened the whaling station in the 1860s and it became a family concern, utilising traditional bay whaling procedures, until the death of the industry in the 1920s.

Little of the station remains today but the site is worth a visit as there is sufficient interpretive and explanatory text, illustration and photographs to help the visitor imagine

The harbour at Eden.

what the area must have been like when the station was in operation.

4 BOYDS TOWER

Return to Edrom Rd and turn left. Continue north towards Twofold Bay. Near the end of the road (about 4km further on) turn right onto a gravel road at a sign marked Ben Boyd National Park.

At the extremity of the promontory that forms the southern shore of Twofold Bay is the monolithic stone structure known as Boyds Tower, built of Pyrmont sandstone from Sydney. The tower was intended as a whaling lookout and a lighthouse as well as a landmark to reflect upon Boyd's good name. The structure was never completed and permission for its use as a lighthouse was refused. It did serve as a whale-spotting site, however. Although the walls and the stone-work at the crest of the tower were finished, lightning has dislodged some of the latter. The letters B-O-Y-D are clearly chiselled into the stones at the top of the tower. The woodwork of the internal staircase has been destroyed.

The tower was designed by Oswald Brierly, an English artist and student of naval architecture, who accompanied Benjamin Boyd to Australia. Brierly lived at Twofold Bay for some five years and acted as manager of the whaling site at East Boyd.

An old cottage at Davidson Whaling Station.

5 SALTWATER CREEK

Return to Edrom Rd and head south-west back towards the Princes Hwy. After 9km there is a left turn onto Green Cape Rd, a good quality gravel road. Continue for 8km to a T-intersection and turn left. Follow the road for 4km to another T-intersection. Turn right and it is 4km to Saltwater Bay.

Saltwater Creek is a fine swimming and fishing location. A 9km walking track begins here, running south along the coast through high heaths, rugged cliffs, rock platforms and beaches to Bittangabee Bay, another quality fishing and swimming location. There are campsites with picnic areas, fireplaces, pit toilets and some tank water at both Salt-water and Bittangabee. Bittangabee can also be reached by road.

6 BITTANGABEE BAY

If you ignore the Saltwater Bay turn-off and continue south on Green Cape Rd, after 4km you will reach Disaster Bay Lookout, which offers good views over Disaster Bay, Wonboyn Lake and Nadgee Nature Reserve. Just past the lookout, on the left, is another turn-off which will take you out to Bittangabee Bay.

Bittangabee Bay, a base for the whaling operations of the Imlay brothers, was taken over by Benjamin Boyd in 1848. The stone ruins of an old house set amid a garden area, probably started by the Imlay brothers but never completed, can be found adjacent to the Bittangabee camping area. There are interpretive signs. The beaches at Bittanga-bee, Green Glades, Jane Spiers and Newtons are all good spots for swimming, fishing and picnicking.

7 GREEN CAPE LIGHTHOUSE

Return to Green Cape Rd and continue towards the east. You will pass a turn-off on the left to Pool Pit Rock and one on the right to City Rock. At the end of the road is Green Cape itself, at the south-eastern tip of the park.

The view from the promontory is outstanding. Here is an historic cemetery for the 71 people who lost their lives in the wreck of *Ly-ee-Moon*, one of many ships that sank in the appropriately named Disaster Bay in the 19th century. Hence it is also the site of a lighthouse, originally kerosene-powered, built in 1881 on the rocky headland. This spot is popular with scuba divers and affords impressive views of the area. Pulpit Rocks is considered one of the best locations for land-based fishing, especially if you are after kingfish or yellowfin tuna.

Return to the Princes Hwy and then return to Eden.

View across Twofold Bay from Eden.

CHAPTER 3
SOUTH BEHIND
THE GREAT
DIVIDING RANGE

20 THE SOUTHERN HIGHLANDS ESCARPMENT

■ DRIVING TOUR ■ 43.5KM ■ 5 HOURS ■ FITZROY FALLS, ROBERTSON AND BURRAWANG

Behind the South Coast the escarpment rises steeply to the rolling hills and rich soils of the Southern Highlands.

Beyond the South Coast lies the rugged escarpment of the Great Dividing Range, which runs down the east coast of Australia. If there is an area in New South Wales that contains distinctively Australian eucalypt forests while evoking the rolling green hills of England, this is it. This was the location for the movie *Babe.* It is one of the finest potato-growing areas in the country and is characterised by rich red soils and good, reliable rainfall. And, equally, it has particularly beautiful and spectacular waterfalls where the rolling hills meet the sheer walls of the Illawarra escarpment.

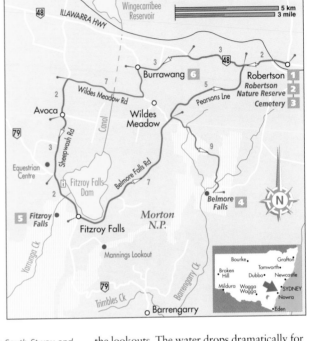

1 ROBERTSON

Robertson is a small, quiet village on the Illawarra Highway just west of the Illawarra escarpment and Macquarie Pass, which functions as a link between the South Coast and the highlands. There are a number of places around the town where lookouts provide spectacular views across the coastal plain to the Pacific Ocean.

The town is noted for its distinctive red volcanic basalt soil which is known as Robertson soil. The combination of this soil, a good rainfall and cool winters has made the town the centre of the largest potato-growing area in New South Wales. Robertson is also the centre of a dairy industry, with an old dairy factory at the eastern end of the town.

2 ROBERTSON NATURE RESERVE

Turn south off the Illawarra Hwy, just past the County Inn at Robertson and cross the railway line. Turn left again at the T-intersection into South St and proceed about 100m to the car park on the right.

The Robertson Nature Reserve is ideal for bushwalking. It is an exceptional 5ha remnant of temperate rainforest south-east of the town which provides a good idea of how the plateau once looked. There is a pleasant 600m circular walking track around the reserve with interpretive signs and disabled access.

3 CEMETERY

Continue east along South St for approximately 2km until you reach a gravel road. This is Missingham Pde. Continue along it until you reach the cemetery.

The cemetery offers an excellent view over the dairy lands of the area, which have a distinctively English feel about them. Charles Throsby, passing south from the Moss Vale area to Kangaroo Valley in 1818, en route to Jervis Bay, sent his servant Joseph Wild off with the local Aborigines to have a look at the area east of Moss Vale which became known as the Yarrawa Brush.

Surveyor Robert Hoddle and a gang of convicts cut a bridle path down the slopes in 1830 as part of a track intended to join the Cowpastures (Camden) to Kiama and Gerringong. He described the Yarrawa Brush as 'the most formidable brush I have ever seen. The vines so thickly entwined around the huge trees and small as to render the sun obscure at the time it shone with great brilliancy.'

4 BELMORE FALLS

Return in a westerly direction along South St you and make a left turn into Belmore Falls Rd. About ten minutes along the partially tarred road there is a sign-posted left turn to Hindmarsh Lookout which offers spectacular views over Belmore Falls into Morton National Park and Kangaroo Valley.

Belmore Falls were named after the Earl of Belmore, the Governor of New South Wales. This isolated and undeveloped site has been popular as a tourist destination since a road was established in 1887. The Fitzroy Falls Visitors Centre, on the road opposite the falls, has a pamphlet on the history of the area and the lookouts. The water drops dramatically for over 100m from two of the falls into the Barrengarry Creek Valley to join the Kangaroo Creek and become part of the upper reaches of the Shoalhaven River catchment area. This is an ideal place for a bush picnic.

5 FITZROY FALLS

Return to Belmore Falls Rd and turn left. There is another lookout point along here. Pull over to the left and walk through the bush. It is a further 5km drive to the T-intersection. A left turn will take you towards Fitzroy Falls.

Belmore Falls, the edge of the escarpment.

Fitzroy Falls was originally called Throsby's Waterfall, after Charles Throsby, who was one of the first explorers and settlers of the Southern Highlands. He passed near the falls in 1818, en route to Jervis Bay. They were renamed in 1850 during a visit by Sir Charles FitzRoy, Governor of New South Wales (1846–1851) and Governor-General of the colonies (1851–1855).

The area around the falls is characterised by rugged sandstone cliffs, deep and well-forested valleys, and the Clyde, Shoalhaven, Endrick and Kangaroo rivers. There is a diversity of flora and fauna. Wildflowers are in abundance on the plateaus, giant turpentine trees below the major cliffs, coachwood and black ash are numerous and provide true rainforest canopy where the soil is richest.

The park has many birds of prey, including hawks, wedge-tailed and other eagles, parrots, honeyeaters, lorikeets, crimson rosellas, cuckoos, cormorants, grebes, lyrebirds and two threatened species—the swamp parrot and eastern bristle bird. There are also macropods, bandicoots, possums the dunnart, echidnas and dingoes, plus the marsupial mice, snakes and lizards upon which the predators feed.

The Fitzroy Falls Information Centre is located at Fitzroy Falls and there are cafe, picnic and barbecue facilities beside Yarrunga Creek. The stillness of the stream and the attractiveness of the setting make this an ideal place to eat before heading off on one of the two excellent walking paths that run along the ridge on either side of the Yarrunga Creek Valley. Before you start either walk, go to the lookout. The falls tumble 82m to the floor of the ravine and the view, on a clear day, is both dramatic and beautiful.

The East Rim Walking Track is 3.5km long and, while an easy walk, takes about two hours to complete. It's about three hours to Valley View Lookout and back.

A dramatic sunset between Robertson and Fitzroy Falls.

There are plenty of good vantage points along the track. Perhaps the easiest and most interesting of the walks is the first section of the West Rim Walking Track. An easy walk of 15 minutes from the falls is the Jersey Lookout, which offers an excellent view back on the falls and the dense rainforest that grows around the creek below. This is the view shown in of most of the photographs taken of the falls.

The track continues north-west to the fire trail, which it follows for 20m, before branching to the west to Twin Falls. The walk takes about 12–15 minutes. The two lookouts on the eastern side of Twin Falls offer good views of Yarrunga Creek, Twin Falls and, further south, the lower Grotto Falls. On the western side of the stream, Paines Lookout allows walkers an excellent close view of Twin Falls. The track then continues to Starkeys Lookout, an ideal vantage point for viewing the Lady Hordern Falls, which cascade 76m to the foot of the crevasse.

6 BURRAWANG

Continue west and north from Fitzroy Falls along Sheepwash Rd for 7km. Turn right into Wildes Meadow Rd and continue for 3km until you reach a T-intersection. Turn left and follow the road for 2km until you reach the village of Burrawang.

Most visitors to the Southern Highlands spend time in Bowral, Moss Vale, Berrima and Mittagong. It is rare for people to make a special trip to Burrawang. Yet this tiny village, with its wonderfully antiquated general store, its important collection of historic buildings, impressive church, and its atmosphere of an English hamlet dropped in Australia, is a real gem.

European settlement began when people began to move up from the Illawarra in the early 1860s. The first land grant in the area was at Wildes Meadow, in 1859. Two of the earliest settlers, John and Elizabeth McGrath, apparently walked from Jamberoo when Elizabeth was seven months pregnant.

A post office was established in 1865. It was named after the Burrawang Palm, then plentiful in the area. The first inn was licensed in 1866. The first school (Anglican) was

established in the late 1860s, to be replaced by a public school in 1876. Religious services transferred from a makeshift location to proper church buildings in 1875 (Catholic), Anglican (1886) and Presbyterian (1888). Burrawang was also home to one of the earliest newspapers in the district, the *Burrawang Herald*, established in 1883. A School of Arts building was erected (c.1889). Social life centred on the Burrawang and Wildes Meadow Bachelors' Club, which conducted two balls each year. The Burrawang and West Camden Farmers' Club was established in 1879 and held its first show at Burrawang in 1880. The show was later moved to Robertson.

The village developed as a service centre to the rich pastoral land around it. A sawmill and flour mill were in operation by 1880 and, along with dairying, potatoes and other vegetables, they were the economic mainstays of the area. The isolation of the town, because of the poor roads, meant that Burrawang could not take advantage of the rail link at Moss Vale to send milk to Sydney. Instead, the local farmers relied on butter production.

The appeal of this small township is its antiquity and the fact that is has remained relatively untouched. The greatest pleasure is to simply walk around and soak up the atmosphere. The General Store (c.1875) in Hoddle Street has traded continuously for 135 years. Inside, the shelves are stocked with antiquated products, labels, tins and bottles. The Burrawang Village Hotel is an attractive and pleasant English village pub.

There is an antique store in the Old School House. The old School of Arts building has been restored and is currently home to a theatre group. Scarletts Fruit and Vegetable Shop on Hoddle Street is also of interest. The town's three churches—St Peter's Catholic Church, St David's Anglican Church and the Presbyterian Church—are all worth a look and many of the residences are of historic interest.

Leave Burrawang heading east. After 3km you will reach an intersection with the Illawarra Hwy. It is 5km drive back to Robertson.

The main street of Robertson.

Rolling hills behind the Robertson cemetery.

21 AROUND BOWRAL AND BERRIMA

■ DRIVING AND WALKING TOUR ■ 54KM ■ 1 DAY ■ ELEGANT BOWRAL AND HISTORIC BERRIMA

Historic townships nestle between rolling hills in an area known for its outstanding gardens and gracious homesteads.

The weather can be very hot and humid in Sydney in the summer months after the Christmas and New Year festivities. Consequently, as early as the 1880s, wealthy Sydney families left the city for their cooler hill retreats in the Blue Mountains and the Southern Highlands. The townships that grew up along the Hume Highway and the southern railway line—notably Berrima, Mittagong, Bowral and Moss Vale—became elegant retreats, and to this day they retain a degree of that old-world charm.

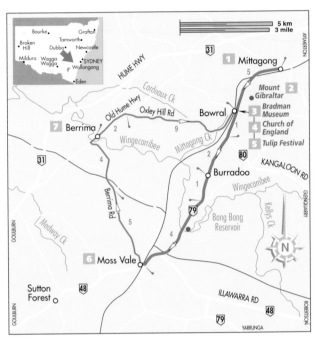

1 MITTAGONG

Mittagong is known as the Gateway to the Highlands. The town is located in the Nattai River Valley between Mount Gibraltar, known locally as The Gib, and Mount Alexandra. The first European settler in the area was William Charker, who was grazing his cattle there as early as 1821. In 1827, George Cutler built the Kangaroo Inn. The area was virtually deserted until the new road through Berrima was completed in the 1830s. John Charker set up the Woolpack Inn at the southern end of what is now Mittagong, and George Cutler built a new Kangaroo Inn at the northern end. Ann Cutler built the Fitzroy Inn in 1845. Today it operates as the Oaklands Guesthouse. Other inns followed, including the Prince Albert Hotel built by Bartholomew Rush in 1845. It is now the motel Poplars to the north of Mittagong.

A good starting point is the Southern Highland Visitor Centre at 62–70 Main Street. Just past it, on the left, is St Stephen's Church of England (1876–1878), a Gothic stone church designed by Edmund Blacket, although his original design was for a larger, more ambitious project which was rejected by his clients.

2 MOUNT GIBRALTAR (THE GIB)

Just beyond the church is a major intersection. Proceed along Bowral Rd and take the second left into Bessemer St. Pass under the railway line and follow the road to the left and then turn right into Oxley Drv. After a winding 3.5km drive there is a sharp right turn up to Mount Gibraltar. It is another 500m to the Mittagong Lookout.

The old sign at Bowral's famous Bradman Oval.

Mount Gibraltar (at 863m) is the highest point between the Illawarra coast and the Great Dividing Range. It has four scenic lookouts. The Mittagong Lookout faces north and north-east over Mittagong (240m below). Next is Jellore Lookout, facing west and northwest to Mount Jellore. In the distance are the Blue Mountains. The Oxley View overlooks one of the first European land grants, Wingecarribee, which was issued to explorer John Oxley. The Bowral Lookout looks over Bowral (180m below) with Wingecarribee Dam, Moss Vale and the Cuckbundoon Range near Goulburn in the distance. The 1.2km Rim Track (distinctly marked by yellow posts) connects all four lookouts.

3 BRADMAN OVAL AND BRADMAN MUSEUM

Oxley Drv reaches a T-intersection with Bong Bong St 3.5km beyond Mittagong Lookout. Turn left into Bong Bong St, then take the fifth left into Boolwey St and in the Glebe Park is Bradman Oval and the Bradman Museum.

Bowral's most famous son is cricketing legend Sir Donald Bradman. The Bradman Museum takes a comprehensive look at the history of cricket, particularly in its early days, and has an interesting display of Bradman memorabilia, including the bat he used to score 304 at Headingley in 1934. Other items include an oak bat dating back to the 1750s.

The museum was opened by the Don with much ceremony in 1989. There is a tea shop and admission charge, and you can obtain a leaflet to guide you through the Bradman Walk which takes in the Bradman history, including the two family residences.

Bradman arrived in Bowral as a child, scored a century for the local school at the age of 12 and lived for three years at 20 Glebe Road, opposite the oval. People interested in Bradman's early history should travel two blocks east to the family home at 52 Shepherd Street. It was here, in the backyard, that the young Bradman developed his batting skill by hitting a golf ball with a cricket stump against a water tank and continually volleying the rebounds.

4 ST JUDE'S CHURCH OF ENGLAND

From Glebe Park return along Boolwey St for two blocks and turn left into Bendooley St.

The original St Jude's, consecrated in 1874, was designed by the famous architect Edmund Blacket (the designer of Sydney University's quadrangle). The church was thought too small, though snobbery played its part. The prevailing view was that Norman churches were only appropriate for 'primitive' societies. Consequently, a new church was built in 1886–1887 and only the bell turret, the western end of the vestry, the font, communion rails and the stone beneath the communion table remain from the original building. The gracious rectory was built in 1880.

5 TULIP FESTIVAL

Head north along Bendooley St for two blocks to the Merringang St corner.

The town's famous Tulip Festival, held during the September school holidays, offers spectacular floral displays and a rare opportunity to wander through the sumptuous English gardens of the town's larger private homes. The centrepiece of the festival is the beautiful Corbett Gardens.

6 MOSS VALE

Turn left into Merrigang St and then left into Bong Bong St. After 900m there is a roundabout. Ignore the extreme left exit and proceed ahead. It is 8km to Moss Vale.

Moss Vale is the service and administrative centre of Wingecarribee Shire. Like many towns in the Southern Highlands, the climate and the planting of European trees combine to create an English village feel.

In 1817, Charles Throsby, Hamilton Hume, Joseph Wild and others explored the country west of Sutton Forest. A site for the establishment of a village to be called Bong Bong was surveyed in 1821. It became the first European settlement in the Southern Highlands.

The town centre has a pleasant park and gardens with a band rotunda. This is an agreeable place for a picnic. In spring and autumn the trees in the park are spectacular. Further up the main street is the old Dominican convent—an impressive building with a row of elm trees leading to the front portal, which looks as though it has been lifted out of rural France and placed in the middle of Moss Vale.

7 BERRIMA

Just past the convent, turn right into Waite St which becomes Berrima Rd. It is 7km to Berrima.

Berrima was meant to be the administrative, commercial and manufacturing centre of the land between the Cowpastures (Camden) and Goulburn. Situated on the main road, the town benefited from the through traffic, but despite the healthy sale of town lots, few houses were erected. The first two inns were built in 1834. The railway, when it arrived in the 1860s, bypassed Berrima, following a route to the east through Mittagong and Bowral to Moss Vale. As though forgotten, Berrima has remained relatively unchanged since 1890.

The main gates at Berrima's historic gaol.

The town is very manageable and is easy to explore on foot. The Courthouse Museum is a good place to start, particularly as it doubles as the local information centre. Built between 1835–1838, it was the site of the colony's first trial by jury in April 1841. This impressive sandstone building, with its solid stone columns, fine masonry and cedar joinery consists of a courtroom flanked by jury rooms and cells. Used as a court of assizes until 1848, it ceased to operate as a courthouse altogether in 1889. The museum contains special displays relating to crime and punishment in the district, including life-size models depicting the 1843 trial of Lucretia Dunkley, who conspired with her lover to murder her husband with an axe.

Opposite the courthouse, over Wilshire Street, is Australia's oldest surviving gaol. It was built of local sandstone between 1834 and 1839 by convicts in chains, although the present gateway and walls were constructed in 1863–1868. The internal buildings were demolished and rebuilt in 1945. On either side of the gaol are the superintendent's and deputy superintendent's houses (both built in the 1880s). The deputy superintendent's house is on the corner of Argyle and Wilshire streets. The northern wall has a fine cast-iron moulding, the Bulls Head Fountain (1877), which channelled water from the roof into a water trough for the horses of those attending the courthouse.

Walk north along Argyle Street to the next corner (Oxley Street). The Finlayson Memorial Church was built in 1867. Turn left into Oxley Street. On the right is Bellevue House, a two-storey sandstone colonial home built about 1850. Return the way you came along Oxley St, cross Argyle St and turn left into Wilkinson Street. A short distance along, on the right, overlooking the town, is Harpers Mansion (1834), a two-storey Georgian sandstock brick house with a stone-

Corbett Gardens in springtime, Bowral.

flagged verandah, sandstone quoins and cedar joinery. It was bought by the Catholic Church in 1856 which used it as a presbytery and then as a convent. A little further east along Oxley Street is the public school, part of which dates back to 1869. The well on the grounds was built by convict labour.

Return west along Oxley St to the old highway and turn left. On the corner is one of the town's few remaining weatherboard buildings, Bramber Cottage (*c.*1860), which once housed an early post office.

Proceed south along the highway. Not far from Wingecarribee Street is a two-storey Georgian building with red brickwork, a verandah and stone lintels, which currently houses the Berrima Galleries. It was originally the Taylors Crown Inn (*c.*1834). Almost opposite is Old Breens Restaurant, which was built about 1840 as Breens Commercial Hotel. It has shuttered French windows and a stone-flagged timber verandah.

Proceed south along the old highway. The next road to the left is Wingecarribee St. On the south-eastern corner is the Old Bakery Tea Rooms, housed in a three-storey building originally used as a bakehouse. The old ovens are still there to be seen, plus a small collection of historical material. At one time the front section was occupied by the Commercial Bank of Sydney.

Cross over the highway to the Surveyor General Inn, named after Surveyor General Thomas Mitchell. Continue south along the old highway. Jellore Street, Bryan Street and Market Street enclose the village common, which is bordered by tall pines and now divided by the old highway. Just across Jellore Street, in the north-eastern corner of the common, is an oak tree planted in 1890 by Sir Henry Parkes, the Father of Federation.

Head north out of town on the old Hume Hwy for 2km, then turn right onto Oxleys Hill Rd. It is 9km to the T-intersection in Bowral. Turn left into Kirkham Rd. Cross over the railway line and continue towards Mittagong which is 3km away.

22 GOULBURN TO WOMBEYAN CAVES

■ DRIVING TOUR ■ 270KM ■ 1 DAY ■ SHEEP, COUNTRY TOWNS AND CAVES

Beyond the Southern Highlands lie the rich wool growing pasturelands of the Southern Tablelands where Goulburn's Big Merino symbolises the regional prosperity.

Goulburn is a handsome and prosperous city at the edge of the Southern Highlands. Surrounded by rich sheep country and boasting the Big Merino, the area extends to both Crookwell and Taralga in the north. Beyond this point, the countryside becomes increasingly rugged as it enters the southern reaches of the Blue Mountains. It is here, nestled in an isolated valley, that the beautiful Wombeyan Caves are hidden. This is an area of diversity and great rural and bushland beauty.

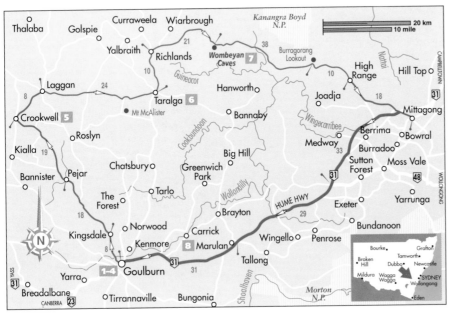

1 GOULBURN GAOL

Drive into the centre of Goulburn on Sydney Rd.

As the visitor from Sydney approaches Goulburn, they will immediately notice the large and forbidding walls of Goulburn Gaol on the right-hand side of the road and across a small valley. The town had a lock-up as early as 1830 and a gallows and flogging post in 1832. Goulburn was once a centre for police parties hunting bushrangers, who frequented the area until the arrival of the railway.

A major stockade for chain-bound convicts and men working on the construction of the Great South Road was built at Towrang,

Autumn poplars along the streets of Taralga.

15km north-east of Goulburn, about 1836–1842. The stockade became the principal penal establishment in the southern district and was renown for its harsh discipline. Goulburn was gazetted as a municipality in 1859 and became the first inland Australian city in 1863. A new gaol at North Goulburn was completed in 1884. Today it operates as a maximum-security prison.

2 BELMORE PARK AND THE COURTHOUSE

Continue into town along Lagoon St which becomes Auburn St, the main street of the city. About 2km from the first set of traffic lights you will notice Belmore Park on your left-hand side.

Belmore Park is located on the site of the town's original marketplace and was named Belmore Square in 1869 when Lord Belmore opened the railway and Lady Belmore planted the oak tree at the centre of the park. Belmore Park has a band rotunda (1897), numerous civic monuments and shady picnic areas. On the Montague Street side of the park is the town's third courthouse (1887), a Classical Revival polychrome brick structure which reflects

the town's importance in the late 19th century. It was designed by colonial architect James Barnet and features a copper dome, colonnaded facade and richly decorated interior.

3 ROCKY HILL WAR MEMORIAL

Continue down Montague St until you reach Sloane St. Turn right and continue past the railway station until, after two blocks, you come to Blackshaw Rd on your left. Turn left and pass under the railway line, and turn right into Park Rd. Continue on Park Rd which becomes Hetherington St, and turn left into Memorial Drv. After 200m you will reach the Goulburn War Memorial.

Rocky Hill War Memorial, a stocky 20m tower in Memorial Drive, was built by public subscription in 1923 to honour locals who fought and died in World War I. Floodlit at night by a rotating beacon, the memorial can be seen from any approach to the city. Rocky Hill itself is a good vantage point, offering views over the city. The lookout is open daily from dawn until dusk.

4 THE BIG MERINO

Return to Sloane St via Memorial Drv, Hetherington St, Park Rd and Blackshaw Rd. Turn left and continue to Mundy St. Turn right and continue to Cowper St. At Cowper St turn left and continue for 800m and you will see the Big Merino on your right.

The Big Merino, a replica sheep 15m high and 21m long, is on Hume St. It is the focal point of a complex that showcases the area's wool industry. Crafts and other produce made from wool are on sale. There are also souvenirs, a display on the production of wool, a lookout area over Goulburn, a restaurant and a tavern.

5 CROOKWELL

Make your way back to the centre of Goulburn via Hume St, Cowper St, turning right into Clinton St and left into Auburn St, and continuing out of town until you reach Goldsmith St. Turn left into Goldsmith St, then right into Fitzroy Rd which becomes Crookwell Rd. Crookwell is 43km to the north.

Crookwell is a picturesque town of fine gardens and tree-lined streets which functions as a service centre to the surrounding rich agricultural and pastoral district. The district is one of the state's major producers of seed potatoes, and wool, fat lambs, beef cattle, oats, hay, dairy produce and cold-climate fruits are also produced.

Settlers were in the district by 1828. Some wheat and potatoes were grown from 1840 and several inns were built at road junctions. Two of the world's longest cattle treks departed from Crookwell in the 19th century and the first branch of the Country Women's Association (CWA) was formed here in 1922.

There are a number of historic buildings in town. In the main street (Goulburn St) are the courthouse (1891), the police station (1878), the Royal Hotel (1862), the old Bank of New South Wales (now Westpac) (1875), the Crookwell Hotel (1884), the former Methodist Church (now Uniting) and the Commercial Hotel (1874). Behind the Commercial Hotel is the old stone flour mill, opened in 1871 by town pioneer William Stephenson. A good place for a picnic is Kiamma Creek Park in Roberts Street, which has many mature poplar and willow trees.

6 TARALGA

Follow the signs to Taralga. You will pass through Laggan, 8km to the north, from where Taralga is a further 28km to the east.

Taralga is a delightful and historic country town with some fine old stone buildings. The first European to pass through Taralga was the explorer Charles Throsby who, in 1819, journeyed from Cowpastures (Camden) in search of new grazing lands. John Macarthur, who owned all the land around Taralga, rewarded Throsby with 1000 acres and by 1824 Macarthur's son James and his nephew Hannibal had established themselves in the Taralga region, where they helped to pioneer Australia's wool industry. A private village was established on land donated by James Macarthur and cleared by convicts in order to house and service members of the Macarthur family and their employees.

Orchard St is the town's main thoroughfare. Start at the southern end of the street, at the intersection with Bannaby Street, where you will find the Hotel Taralga, built for Martin Tynan in 1876 as the Richlands Hotel. It later became a post office and is now a private residence.

On the other side of the road is the courthouse and former police office (1878), now a youth centre and play group centre. Heading north from this point are the post office (1897), which has a new facade;

Coolabah Meats, located in an old saddlery shop; and the Goodhew Centre, which was built in 1880 as a store.

7 WOMBEYAN CAVES

Leave Taralga on the Wombeyan Caves Rd. After about 4km the road becomes gravel. The journey is 32km from Taralga on a winding road through pretty and sometimes dramatic scenery.

Wombeyan Caves—a network of over 230 caverns—have a well-deserved reputation as one of the country's most attractive cave systems. The caves are under the management of the Tourism Commission of New South Wales, and the camping and recreation areas, with their rows of poplar and willow trees growing along the banks of the Wombeyan Creek, offer dozens of shady spots for picnickers and campers.

Wombeyan Caves were discovered in 1828 by a party led by the explorer John Oxley and pastoralist John Macarthur. The party camped near the site of the present kiosk. During the night the horses strayed downstream and the subsequent search led the party to the Victoria Arch entrance to the Fig Tree Cave. The journals of the journey make no mention of the explorers entering the cave. It wasn't until 1865, with the appointment of Charles Chalker as first caretaker, that the system was explored in any detail.

Chalker discovered nine major caves, many of which are closed to the public for reasons of preservation. There are guided tours of four caves available between 10.00am–4.00pm daily. The Wollondilly Cave (discovered by Chalker in 1865 and opened to the public in 1885) is regarded by many as the best of the caves. A guided tour of Wollondilly takes about one and a half hours. The Kooringa (Aboriginal for 'king') Cave was also discovered by Chalker in 1865 and opened to the public in 1875. Although only a small cave—the tour takes one hour—its shawls and stalagmites are outstanding. The Mulwaree Cave (discovered in 1865 and opened in 1885) has spectacular

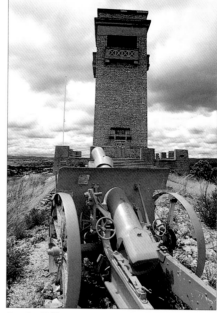

Rocky Hill War Memorial, Goulburn.

stalactites close to the pathways, which have led the guides to call it the Connoisseurs Cave. The Junction Cave (discovered by T.M. Chalker in 1897 and opened in 1906) is 1.2km from the kiosk. This cave takes one and a half hours to inspect and the formations called Chalkers Blanket, The Rapids and the Grand Column are regarded as the cave's highlights.

8 MARULAN

The journey from Wombeyan Caves to Berrima is 65km. It is a very windy, if picturesque, drive on a narrow dirt road. At various points the road offers an excellent view of the Burragorang Valley, passes through a lengthy sandstone tunnel and crosses the Wollondilly River. From Berrima it is 53km to Marulan. Follow the road south from Berrima until it connects with the Hume Hwy. At Marulan, take the exit that leaves the freeway and enters the town.

Although many of the buildings in Marulan are now closed and boarded up, it is still interesting to walk down the main street and look at the houses and shops that were built during the boom after the arrival of the railway.

The railway station and the stationmaster's residence were completed in 1868. They are both examples of Victorian public architecture. If you walk back to the main street you will notice a fine Georgian-style police station which was completed a few years later. On the other side of the road is the tiny St Stephen's Uniting Church (1875). On the same side of the road, a couple of doors down, is the Coronation Store (now closed), a good example of a 19th-century shop with an attached residence. Over the road is the Marulan Post Office, and next to the service station in the centre of town is Wattle Glen cottage. The Royal Hotel (also closed and boarded up) was built and expanded in 1870–1880. It is a fine example of a Victorian hotel.

Return to the Hume Hwy and continue back to Goulburn.

The electricity-generating windmills near Crookwell.

23 MOSS VALE TO MARULAN

■ DRIVING TOUR ■ 60KM ■ 5 HOURS ■ A DRIVE THROUGH THE SOUTHERN HIGHLANDS

The villages of the Southern Highlands are characterised by gracious gardens, green paddocks where cattle graze, and interesting historic buildings.

Although Bowral, Moss Vale and Mittagong were the main Southern Highlands 'hill stations', there were many other smaller settlements which attracted people eager to escape the heat of the Sydney summer. From Moss Vale, the road heads through the rolling countryside to the small villages of Sutton Forest, Exeter, Bundanoon, Penrose, Wingelo, Tallong and Marulan. These villages are quiet retreats accessible to Sydney while offering rural and bush escapes.

1 MOSS VALE

Like many Southern Highlands towns, the climate and the planting of European trees have combined to give Moss Vale a distinctly English village feel. In 1817 the first European party arrived in the district. The group comprised Charles Throsby, Hamilton Hume, Joseph Wild and others, who explored the country west of Sutton Forest. Governor Lachlan Macquarie awarded Throsby 1000ac and made him superintendent over the construction of a road from Picton to the Goulburn Plains.

In 1853, a visitor to the future site of Moss Vale observed there were five slab and bark structures and wheat was being grown. At the time, the only inhabitant in the area was Jeremy ('Jemmy') Moss, one of Charles Throsby's herdsmen. It was from him that the town's name was derived.

The village prospered in the late 1870s and 1880s partly because, like other Southern Highlands' towns, it became a popular holiday resort when the construction of the railway line enabled wealthy Sydneysiders to discover the beautiful scenery and healthy climate.

2 THROSBY PARK

To reach Throsby Park head north on Argyle Rd (the main road in Moss Vale), turn right at the roundabout into Robertson Rd (this is the Illawarra Hwy) and after 1.5km (past the local showground) turn left onto Throsby Park Rd.

Throsby Park is now administered by the New South Wales National Parks and Wildlife Service. It is an impressive colonial Georgian residence set on land granted to Dr Charles Throsby in 1819 in recognition of his pioneering work exploring and opening up the South Coast and the Southern Highlands.

Throsby built a cottage on the land in 1823 for his nephew Charles as he preferred to remain at his home in Glenfield and had no children of his own. The nephew and his wife Elizabeth built Throsby Park in 1834. Elizabeth was only 16 when she married Charles. She bore him 17 children and died at the age of eighty-three. Her great-great-granddaughter still lives in the rear section of the residence and runs Throsby Park Riding School.

Throsby Park is largely unchanged and retains much of the original furniture, cedar joinery and fittings. It is a huge, single-storey, 27-room house built of locally quarried stone. Wings extend from the main block to form a courtyard enclosed by a separate kitchen. There are cellars, servants' attics, cedar doors, marble and stone fireplaces, as well as a grand drawing room and dining room. The 1823 cottage is still standing as are the farm buildings, including the sandstock-brick barn (*c.*1828), which was formerly used as a shearing shed and is now a private residence.

3 SUTTON FOREST

Head back towards Moss Vale on Robertson Rd (the Illawarra Hwy) for 1.5km. Drive through Moss Vale shopping centre and continue on the Illawarra Hwy for 5.5km until you reach the small town of Sutton Forest.

Sutton Forest is little more than a pub, a few buildings, a couple of antique and gift shops, a riding school and a church. The early history of the village is much more impressive than its current size would suggest. In 1817, Hamilton Hume and Charles Throsby explored the country west of Sutton Forest. Throsby named the Sutton Forest area Cooloorigan. Governor Macquarie was much impressed with the beauty of the area and the quality of the soil. He named the settlement after Charles Manners Sutton, the speaker of the British House of Commons, on 2 November 1820.

Buildings began to slowly accumulate around an Anglican chapel erected in 1829. At the time, it was the only church south of

Moss Vale's main park in spring.

the Cowpastures (the Camden area). A Church of England school was established as early as 1826. A small township began to grow up around the three inns that lined the road—the Talbot (1833, renamed the Royal in 1866), the Red Cow and the Hart (also 1834). The first store appeared some time in the 1830s.

Despite the laying of the foundation stone in 1837, it wasn't until 1861 that the All Saints Church of England, designed by Edmund Blacket, replaced the 1829 building. A visitor in March 1832 described Sutton Forest as:

> ... a most luxurious spot ... There is as much of the English village in miniature about this township as any I know of— a homeliness of scenery that strikes the attention, and induces a second pause to look again at the neat cottages, the snug little church, the light timber with its umbrageous foliage, and the refreshing lagoons on the roadside which incite the weary horse, or bullock to slake his thirst on a sultry summer's day.

4 ALL SAINTS CHURCH OF ENGLAND

Continue through Sutton Forest on the Illawarra Hwy for about 1km. The Church of England is on your left.

All Saints Church of England was erected in 1861. Designed by Edmund Blacket, the church was consecrated by Bishop Barker. The cemetery bears testimony to the existence of the earlier church. It became the resting place for many soldiers who were stationed at Berrima. The visiting governors worshipped here.

5 EXETER

Return about 1km to the Scottish corner store on the Illawarra Hwy and turn right onto the Highlands Way. Continue for 5km until you reach Exeter.

Exeter is a quiet highlands settlement known as 'Little England' because of its trees, private gardens and climate. The first European

All Saints Church at Marulan.

settler in the area was James Badgery, in 1821, and the town was established in 1889. Today it is a pleasant spot for a stroll. St Aiden's Church of England (1895, enlarged in 1903) has some fine stained-glass windows. There are also a couple of gracious houses set well back from the road and approached by gravel driveways behind handsome entrance gates.

6 BUNDANOON

From Exeter head south out of town along Ringwood Rd to Bundanoon. The journey on the Highland Way is 6.7km long.

Bundanoon is known for its delightful avenues of English trees. Because of its impressive hotel and the excellent bush-walking in the Morton National Park, the town has enjoyed continuing prosperity.

The village began to emerge in the late 1860s and early 1870s. An early post office was established in 1872. Coalmining commenced in 1867. Timber-getting became important to the local economy in the 1870s and there were two sawmills operating by 1881, as well as a sandstone quarry, two stores and two churches (Methodist and Anglican) and a butcher's shop.

Bundanoon started to attract tourists in the late 1880s because of its proximity to impressive natural scenery. Guesthouses began to appear and pathways to the scenic sights were constructed.

7 GLOW WORM GLEN

As you enter Bundanoon from Exeter there is a turn-off on the left before the shopping centre. It is signposted as William St and Glow Worm Glen. Continue on for two blocks and you will reach the start of the bushwalk.

There is a short and easy 25-minute walk to the sandstone grotto known as Glow Worm Glen, although the blue luminescence of the larvae can only be seen at dusk and in the evenings. Carry a torch for the return walk to your vehicle.

8 PENROSE

Return to the Highlands Way and continue 9.5km south-west to Penrose.

Penrose came into existence in the late 1860s when the railway between Sydney and Goulburn was being constructed. The town thrived until the 1930s and then slowly declined when the trains no longer stopped at the station.

Today, Penrose is on the edge of oblivion. Nearly every house and every business in the town is either for sale or boarded up. This is a far cry from the romantic image of the tiny, quiet village 'nestled amidst towering pine trees, fringed by the State Forest, deep gullies and gorges' depicted in *A Village Called Penrose* by Lesley Day, in 1987.

The railway with its two stations, Kareela and Cables Siding—where the railway crossings at the northern and southern ends of town are now located—arrived in 1868. People began to settle beside the track in 1870. One of the first properties belonged to Philip Rush, who occupied the land now known as Sylvan Glen in 1870.

The Old Garage in Sutton Forest.

By the 1890s the town had grown large enough to have its own Methodist Church (previously used in Bowral and re-erected in Penrose in 1893), post office and police station. It was surveyed in 1895 and plans were made for a village, named after Penrose in Cornwall.

By the 1920s the town was on the edge of the boom created by the fashion of holidaying in the Southern Highlands. Edenholme, with views across to Jervis Bay, was opened as a guesthouse and Mrs Teudt, who ran the guesthouse, gained a reputation as a superb cook. Edenholme was destroyed by fire in the early 1950s.

In the 1910s orchards were planted in the district. During World War I the two sidings were closed and Penrose Railway Station was opened. By the 1930s, more guest-houses—notably Cherry Hinton and Sylvan Glen—were opened and the fresh country air attracted visitors from Sydney.

9 MARULAN

Follow the Highland Way south-west for another 22km, through the tiny historic settlements of Wingello and Tallong, until you reach the T-intersection with the Hume Hwy. Turn left and it is 1km to Marulan.

Marulan has been bypassed three times. The original township was situated at the junction of Bungonia Road and the Great Southern Road and was known as Mooroowoolen. It was laid out and settled as a private township. This township was notable for its unusual characters. Bob Fitzsimmons, a famous bare knuckle prize-fighter, owned the local blacksmith's shop. Joseph Peters, one of the first ticket-of-leave men to be granted land in the district, settled on land between Marulan and Goulburn and opened an inn.

Mooroowoolen did not last long. When Major Mitchell surveyed the area and laid out a new street plan, the town was moved. Joseph Peters, realising that his inn would be valueless if the whole town moved, managed to hold up the development until he moved his inn to a new site.

In the 1860s, when the railway line was being built through the area, the town became a railway camp. The town was moved again at this time, and developed on its present site around the railway station. On 1 September 1878, the name of the town was changed from Mooroowoolen to Marulan.

The return trip to Moss Vale along the Hume and Illawarra highways is 42km.

24 CANBERRA TO THE COAST

■ DRIVING TOUR ■ 157KM ■ 1 DAY ■ CANBERRA'S SEASIDE JOURNEY

The villages to the east of Canberra came into existence during the nineteenth-century gold rushes. Today they offer friendly resting places for people rushing from the national capital to the coast.

*I*n the 1960s, when the Commonwealth government was attempting to persuade Sydney and Melbourne-based public servants to move to Canberra, the government insisted that Canberra was only a few hours from the beach and that the South Coast around Batemans Bay would eventually become Canberra-by-the-sea. They were right. Today, thousands of Canberra residents head off for the coast each weekend and, as they travel, they pass through the picturesque towns of Bungendore and Braidwood. The trip to the sea has become a trip through beautiful countryside and country towns full of gift shops and good restaurants.

Willows beside the river in Queanbeyan.

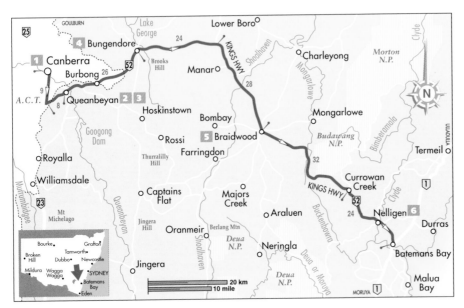

The Cook waterjet on Lake Burley Griffin.

1 LAKE BURLEY GRIFFIN AND THE COOK WATERJET

Canberra, the national capital, is a carefully designed city of circuits and long, elegant roads. In the middle of the city is the artificial Lake Burley Griffin, named after the city's town planner. The lake is surrounded by important buildings such as the High Court and the National Library. One of the highlights of the lake is the Cook waterjet which, on most days, shoots water high above the lake.

2 QUEANBEYAN

Leave Civic (the heart of Canberra) and travel across Lake Burley Griffin towards Parliament House. Follow the signs to Queanbeyan, which is 16km away. You enter Queanbeyan on Canberra Ave which, as it approaches the city centre, becomes Farrer Pl. On the right-hand side, on the corner of Farrer and Lowe sts, is the Queanbeyan Tourist Information Centre.

The city of Queanbeyan is a located on the Queanbeyan River. Once occupied by the Ngarigu people, the first Europeans in the vicinity were the exploratory party of Charles Throsby. While searching for the Murrumbidgee River in 1820, they found and followed the Queanbeyan River into a valley at the eastern end of the Limestone Plains. By 1841 there were three brick and seven timber buildings at Queanbeyan. By 1885, when it was declared a municipality, there were eight hotels, four churches, two flour mills, a tannery and a lemonade factory, as well as dwellings and shops.

Queanbeyan Tourist Information Centre is housed in the former council chambers (1925). On the front lawn is a sundial dating from 1860 and, to the rear, the showgrounds where the entrance gates, grandstand and shearers' bar are of historical interest.

Over the road from the Information Centre is the Queanbeyan Museum, housed within the old police sergeant's residence (1876). There is a medical exhibit, machinery shed, a period bedroom, a clothing collection, kitchenware exhibit and blacksmith's display.

3 QUEANBEYAN RIVER AND COLLETT STREET

Continue down the main street to the bridge over the Queanbeyan River. Drive across the bridge and park on the left-hand side. Walk across the bridge, turn right and walk up Collett St.

Queen Elizabeth Park was originally the town's market reserve when Queanbeyan was gazetted in 1838. There are barbecues, toilets and a children's playground. The willow trees along the riverbank allegedly began as cuttings from Napoleon's grave on St Helena. The town's first police magistrate collapsed and died in the park while playing cricket in 1856.

On the corner of Collett and Morrisett streets is Queanbeyan Books and Prints, a second-hand book emporium located in the old mill house (1883). It was built as the residence for Martin Byrne, who built the adjacent flour mill, Byrnes Mill (now a restaurant), in 1883. He was also the licensee of the original Royal Hotel (1850).

4 BUNGENDORE

Return to your car and continue out of town on the Bungendore Rd. After 34km you will reach the historic town of Bungendore.

Bungendore is a small town with numerous specialty shops and old stone, brick and timber buildings. The village began about 1835 and mail started arriving as part of the Queanbeyan route in 1836. The town site was proclaimed in 1837. The following year a lock-up was built, and the Harp Inn was established as the settlement became an important crossroads. The first post office was built in 1840, an Anglican Church (c.1843) and the Bungendore Inn in 1847, which became a Cobb & Co staging post.

The railway arrived in 1885 and the town remained a railhead until the line reached Queanbeyan in 1887.

The ideal way to see Bungendore is to go for a walk. Start your walk at the south-western corner of Molonglo Street and Gibraltar Street. This building was erected in the 1870s as the Oriental Bank, and was used in the filming of *Ned Kelly* in 1969 with Mick Jagger in the leading role. Note the stables and the tiny cottage built for the boy who tended the bank manager's horses. Opposite the old bank is the former Beehive Hotel (1859). The old stables to the rear are now a residence.

Walk north along Molonglo Street for a short distance. To the right is Deniston Cottage Antiques, situated in a stone cottage built in 1860. Continue to the far end of town and turn right at Majara Street. To the left, set back from the road, is the Gothic Revival architecture of the gatekeeper's house, stationmaster's cottage and single-storey railway station (1884–1885). The station was closed in 1987.

On the corner of Majara and Gibraltar streets is the old public school (1879). An Anglican school had existed on this site since 1862. The next building is the post office (1882) and adjacent is the police residence (1902). The renovated rear section was originally the lock-up and the whole doubled as a police station until 1980. Next door is the attractive stone courthouse (1864), now the police station. On the other side of Butmaroo Street is the Gothic Revival St Philip's Anglican Church (1864). The elm trees are over a century old.

5 BRAIDWOOD

Return to the Kings Hwy and continue east for 28km until you reach Braidwood.

The first Europeans into the Braidwood area were William Kearns, William Packer and Henry Marsh, who travelled through the district in the summer of 1822. They described the land as suitable for settlement and in the next two years a number of people moved into the district. The town grew dramatically with the discovery of gold in the Braidwood–Araluen district in 1851–1852. The largest gold discovery in Braidwood was a huge 350lb (170kg) nugget that was 67 per cent pure gold, found in November 1869.

Inevitably, the gold rushes brought with them the bushrangers. The area around Braidwood became one of the wildest and the most infamous of all the goldrush areas, with the Clarke family and Ben Hall regularly holding up gold consignments out of Braidwood and Araluen. Today, Braidwood is a charming historic township with a large number of significant and important historic buildings.

The first stop for anyone wanting to explore Braidwood is the museum, located at the northern end of Wallace Street. This museum has excellent brochures and books on Braidwood and the surrounding area. The best way to explore Braidwood's historic

buildings is to start on the corner of McKellar and Wallace streets, proceed south to Lascelles Street and then head east to Elrington Street. Complete the circuit by coming up Elrington and back to McKellar Street.

The former council chambers are located at 185 Wallace Street. This sandstone and brick building with its gabled roof was constructed in 1835. Located directly over the road is the Braidwood Historical Society Museum building, which was built by surveyor James Larmer in the 1840s. It was initially used as the Royal Hotel. The Commercial Hotel is a handsome Victorian, three-storey rendered brick building characterised by impressive cast-iron columns and decorative lacework on the second-storey balcony. Next door, set in mature gardens, are two red-brick single-storey police residences dating from about 1880. They have hipped roofs of corrugated iron and their windows are topped with flat brick arches.

Braidwood's first courthouse was constructed in 1837 by Dr Wilson. The current courthouse, built in 1900, is a classic example of a Federation single-storey brick building. St Bede's Roman Catholic Church was built between 1856 and 1870 out of local granite. This impressive building is noted for its huge bell which, according to some, can be heard ringing 15km away. The church is located on the corner of Wallace and Lascelles streets. The town's other main church is St Andrew's Church of England, located in Elrington Street. It was designed by Edmund Blacket, the architect responsible for the quadrangle at the University of Sydney.

6 NELLIGEN

Leave Braidwood and continue east for 45km until you reach the small township of Nelligen. The discovery of gold at Araluen, Majors Creek, Captains Flat and Braidwood in the early 1850s ensured the future of Nelligen, and by 1853 a steamship was plying the Clyde River. That same year saw the commencement of

Historic buildings in the main street of Braidwood.

a road from Braidwood, which was completed in 1856. The town was gazetted in 1854. Nelligen became a thriving port for gold, travellers, sheep, cattle and various kinds of produce. Gold was loaded onto boats headed for Sydney.

The district's history has been well recorded on a variety of plaques located around the town. In the park by the riverbank is a large map of the original town (*c.* 1854), which lists and locates 24 sites of historic interest, including the site of the original ferry service across the river (in operation from 1895–1964) and the location of the first school (1865). Nearby is the Bushranger's Tree. Also in the park is a plaque marking the site of the Illawarra Steam Navigation Company's storehouse and offices. This huge building, originally a double timber structure over 40m long and 15m wide, was in use until 1952, before it fell into disrepair and was finally demolished in 1965. Just to the south is the old Mechanics Institute, and further south along the shoreline is a boat ramp.

At the end of Braidwood Road is the old Steampacket Hotel (1860s), which was rebuilt in 1925 after a fire destroyed the original building. At 7 Braidwood Street is the Old Nelligen Post Office Guesthouse, built in 1900 and now fully restored in keeping with the original character of the building.

Continue for 10km on the Kings Hwy until you reach a T-intersection with the Princes Hwy. Batemans Bay is 1km south of this turn-off.

Parliament House, Canberra.

25 THE SNOWY MOUNTAINS

■ DRIVING TOUR ■ 373KM ■ 2 DAYS ■ IN THE HIGH COUNTRY

A snowy playground in wintertime, the Snowy Mountains are now one of the state's major tourist attractions with fishing, craft shops and bushwalking in the summer months.

In the winter months the Snowy Mountains (known as The Snowies) are Australia's skiing playground. Thousands of enthusiastic skiers head off from Sydney and Canberra to the winter resort destinations of Thredbo, Perisher Valley and Guthega. Too few people realise that the mountains are just as interesting, and much less crowded, in the summer months. It is then that the wildflowers bloom and it is possible, even if you are not terribly fit, to walk to the top of Mount Kosciuszko, Australia's highest mountain. It is equally possible to explore the fascinating gold diggings at Kiandra and to go trout fishing at Adaminaby. This is an area that offers much more than skiing.

1 COOMA

Cooma is the main town in the Snowy Mountain region. The area was first explored by Europeans in 1823 when an expedition led by Captain Currie and Major Ovens moved south from Lake George searching for good grazing land. Gold was discovered near Kiandra in 1859, which resulted in over 15 000 people passing through the town in less than a year.

The arrival of the railway in 1889 ensured easy access to the snowfields and made Cooma the centre of a winter tourist industry which continues to boom to this day. Then, in 1949, Cooma became the headquarters for the huge Snowy Mountains Hydro-Electric Scheme, which was to bring workmen from 27 nations to the town.

Historically, the most interesting area of Cooma is that known as the Lambie Town Walk. The walk starts in Massie Street and passes the post office (1877), Solomons Store (1862) and the Cooma Hotel (also 1862), across to the impressive courthouse (1889) with its shuttered French windows and gracious front verandah, and the old prison (1870s), which is still in use today.

The walk then passes Nijong Reserve and enters Lambie Street—surely one of the finest domestic streetscapes in rural New South Wales. The street has a total of 11 listings in the National Trust Register, including a beautiful pair of late Victorian semi-detached cottages at 39–41 Lambie Street,

Lake Jindabyne.

an early coursed stone terrace dating to 1850 with five bays and a rolled-iron roof at 55 Lambie Street, and a gracious two-storey Victorian house (1880) which now spreads across 51–53 Lambie Street. The Lord Raglan Hotel at 11 Lambie Street (1854), the oldest inn in the district, became a bank in 1860 and is now a gallery. At the end of the street is the Royal Hotel (1858) and its outbuildings. The hotel has a cast-iron verandah and an hipped roof.

2 THE SNOWY MOUNTAINS AUTHORITY INFORMATION CENTRE

Head north along the main road in the direction of Canberra for about 2.7km and on the left-hand side of the road, clearly marked, is the Information Centre.
The Snowy Mountains Authority (SMA) Information Centre is open seven days a week and provides an excellent relief model of the region. Documentaries are shown of the Snowy Mountains Hydro-Electric Scheme, one of Australia's greatest engineering projects.

3 BERRIDALE

Return along the main road, past the Tourist Information Centre and follow the main street of Cooma south-west out of town for 7km. Take the left-hand road towards Jindabyne and follow it for 26km to Berridale.
The tiny settlement of Berridale calls itself the Crossroads of the Snowy. Each winter Berridale becomes a stopover point for the thousands of people heading to the snowfields. As a wit in Jindabyne observed, 'Berridale is the sort of town where if you blink you'll miss it but if you roar through you'll remember it forever because you'll probably get booked for exceeding the speed limit'.

One of the chief attractions of the town is the poplar drive (on the Jindabyne side of

town) which, in autumn, boasts one of the finest stands of yellowing poplar trees anywhere in the Snowy Mountains.

4 SNOWY RIVER WINERY

Turn off the main road into Rock Well Rd, which heads south towards Dalgety. The turn-off is clearly marked with a large sign indicating that this is the route to the Snowy River Winery. After 11km turn to the right. The winery is a further 3km.
The Snowy River Winery is actually located on the Snowy River and represents the highest vineyards in Australia. It specialises in cold-climate white wines which can be bought at the cellar or drunk in the delightful restaurant overlooking the Snowy River. The winery is open 10.00am–5.00pm daily.

5 JINDABYNE

Return to Berridale and turn left and head towards Jindabyne, which is 29km from the turn-off.
Jindabyne is a new town created after the original settlement was drowned by the Snowy Mountains Hydro-Electricity Authority in the late 1960s. Nestled at the end of Lake Jindabyne, modern-day Jindabyne owes its continuing existence to its proximity to the major ski resorts in the Snowy Mountains and the superb facilities it offers for trout fishing. The town lies below the snowline but is close to the Perisher–Blue Cow ski runs.

Beside Lake Jindabyne, the Australian Polish community have built a huge statue of Sir Paul Strzelecki, who explored the wilderness of the Snowy Mountains and named Australia's highest mountain. The plaque on the statue notes that 'While exploring in the Snowy Mountains region he discovered and climbed Mount Kosciuszko which he named in honour of the Polish leader and patriot Tadeusz Kosciuszko'.

6 THREDBO VILLAGE

Head west along the Alpine Way. After 33km turn right onto the loop road. Thredbo Village is 2km further on.

Thredbo Village is an all-year resort. The chalets, the narrow winding streets, the skiing and bracing mountain walks all contribute to a feeling that Thredbo is like no other town in Australia. Thredbo has a reputation as a ski resort, although the local businesses have made a concerted effort to make the summer attractions as interesting as the winter ones. The village boasts a golf course, tennis courts, mountain bicycling facilities, horseriding, and for the really adventurous, paragliding from Crackenback Mountain. From here you can walk to the top of Mount Kosciuszko.

7 KHANCOBAN–MURRAY 1 POWER STATION

Continue along the loop road through Thredbo Village and back onto the Alpine Way. Head west for 67km. This road is gravel and windy and is therefore not suitable for caravans and trailers. After 67km there is a sign to the Murray 1 Power Station.

The Murray 1 Power Station has good interactive displays relating to the history of hydro-electricity in the area. The power station, which has a capacity of 950 000kW (the second largest in the Snowy Mountains), came into operation in 1966. It was followed by Murray 2 in 1969, with a capacity of 550 000kW, the third largest station.

8 KHANCOBAN

Return to the Alpine Way and continue north for 10km to Khancoban.

The road from Jindabyne to Khancoban, known as the Alpine Way, was constructed in 1956 as a direct result of the needs of the

Snowy Mountains Authority. Prior to that there was a track that had been opened in the early 1930s and which supposedly followed the route the Aborigines took when making their annual pilgrimage to the bogong moth country. Unfortunately, the track was so steep (it rose 1800m in every 10km) that even cattle had difficulty using it.

The valley turns a myriad of dramatic colours in the autumn as the willows, poplars and other deciduous trees change colour.

9 CABRAMURRA

Travel north from Khancoban along the Alpine Way for 65km to Cabramurra.

Cabramurra rejoices in its title of the highest settlement in Australia. The village is actually a construction camp which came into existence in 1951 and was known variously as Ghent's Camp and Saddle Camp before the name Cabramurra was finally settled on. Cabramurra is now totally owned and operated by the Snowy Mountains Authority.

Cabramurra began as a rough-and-tumble construction town during the building of the dams and power stations. In those days the accommodation was basic. Today, Cabramurra is a model construction settlement with new brick houses (all of which boast an interesting roof design to ensure that the snow doesn't settle on them), neat little streets, undercover shopping and amenities designed to keep the workers happy.

10 KIANDRA

From Cabramurra, drive north-east for 18km until you come to a T-intersection with the Snowy Mountains Hwy and turn right. Approximately 300m up the road is Kiandra.

In its heyday, Kiandra was a true goldrush town which rose and fell in less than a year. At its peak it attracted over 10 000 men, women and children and saw the construction of banks, hotels and the usual services required by such a large population. Within 12 months, most of the gold was gone and the population was reduced to less than 300 people. Now, 140 years later, Kiandra is a

The Past Times Craft Shop near Cooma.

ghost town standing forlornly on plains that, even in summertime, look lonely, glaciated and cold. Kiandra's moment of glory occurred in a few months in 1859–1860. The rush broke out after payable gold was discovered by David and James Pollock in what became known as Pollocks Gully in November 1859.

The most interesting thing about Kiandra is its Heritage Trail. Starting at the courthouse, the visitor is led through the marshy grasslands to the site of the Church of the Ascension, the post and telegraph office, Matthew's Cottage (which is still standing), the Alpine Hotel, the School of Arts, Yan's Store (now a ruin), the Kiandra Hotel, the teacher's residence, dance hall, school, Kiandra Pioneer Ski Club and the Wolgal Club. The walk is pleasant and easy with detailed and informative plaques.

11 ADAMINABY

Head south along the Snowy Mountains Hwy for 39km to Adaminaby.

The original town of Adaminaby (which is now under the waters of Lake Eucumbene) came into existence in 1885, although pastoralists had been in the area since the early 1830s. It wasn't until the discovery of gold along the Eucumbene River in 1859–1860 that people began to move into the area in significant numbers.

The Snowy Mountains Authority moved the town to its present site in 1956–1957 to make way for the rising waters of Lake Eucumbene. So complete was the removal that the old churches—perhaps the most interesting buildings in town—were also moved. Of the more interesting are St John's Anglican Church (on the hill behind the shopping centre), which was originally built in 1906 and moved in 1956, and the Uniting Church, previously the Presbyterian Church, built in 1886.

Continue along the Snowy Mountains Hwy for 50km and you will return to Cooma.

Autumn colours at Khancoban.

26 ON THE EDGE OF THE SNOWY MOUNTAINS

■ DRIVING TOUR ■ 222KM ■ 1 DAY ■ QUIET TOWNS ON THE SLOPES

The towns on the edge of the Snowy Mountains—Tumut, Tumbarumba, Batlow, Gundagai—are ablaze with colour in autumn and are verdant in spring.

Some of the prettiest towns in New South Wales lie on the edge of the Snowy Mountains. Tumut, with its beautiful, tree-lined river and its green rolling hills; Gundagai, on the banks of the wide Murrumbidgee; sleepy and peaceful Tumbarumba and Batlow, where the hills are covered with orchards. This is an area of special beauty and peacefulness, where time has stood still and old country values still exist.

1 TUMUT

By any measure, Tumut is an exceptionally pretty country town. The Tumut River, which runs for 145km before joining the Murrumbidgee River at Gundagai, flows along the edge of the town. The plains spread out on either side of the river and the foothills of the Snowy Mountains rise on all sides. The early settlers planted poplar and willow trees, resulting in spectacular displays in summer and autumn. The rainfall ensures that apart from times of drought, the valley is characteristically green and fertile.

The first Europeans into the area were the explorers Hume and Hovell who, travelling down the Murrumbidgee River in 1824, came across the Tumut River. They subsequently entered the Tumut Valley.

By 1860, the town had grown to a point where the local newspaper eagerly reported that the cricket club was holding annual meetings and the cricket played on the town's racecourse was so popular that three publicans' booths were provided to quench the thirst of the players and spectators. After the game the players headed for the Woolpack Hotel for more drinking.

Tumut has a large number of historic buildings, notably its collection of hotels, the courthouse and the very fine Anglican Church designed by Edmund Blacket. The best way to see the town is to start at the bottom of Wynyard Street (the main street) and work your way to the top of Telegraph Hill, which offers the visitor an excellent view over the entire town.

Poplars and willows edge the Tumut River.

At the bottom you can see one of the town's most distinctive features—the row of Lombardy poplars that lie across the Tumut River from the Anglican Church. The trees were planted in 1861 and form a distinctive wall that is quite impressive in summer and autumn. On the other side of the river is All Saints Anglican Church and further up the street are the historic courthouse, a number of beautifully preserved old hotels, and at the top of Telegraph Hill is a view across the valley.

2 BATLOW

Continue over the hill on Wynyard St and turn right into Fairway Drv, which is the boundary for the local golf course. This road eventually joins up with Adelong Rd (the Snowy Mountains Hwy). Continue for 8km and then turn left for Batlow, which is a further 25km away.
Batlow is surrounded by orchards and in recent years has become famous as one of Australia's premier producers of apples, pears, cherries, numerous varieties of berries and stone fruits. The discovery of gold in the early 1850s at Adelong and in the Batlow valley led to the establishment of a small settlement at Reedy Creek in 1854. The town was named after a Mr Batlow, the surveyor who laid out the town's street plan. The primary function of the settlement was to service the surrounding goldmining area. Out of this settlement grew the town of Batlow.

The goldmining era was short-lived and by 1855 the first orchards had been planted. By 1900 more than 5000 trees, both for orchards and for timber milling, had been planted in the district. The area continued to prosper through the 1930s with the introduction of cider manufacturing. After the outbreak of World War II the Batlow Packing Company provided both American and Australian forces with dehydrated fruit and vegetables. Today, Batlow is at the centre of the most important apple-growing area in New South Wales. It is surrounded by more than 350 000 apple trees, and the packing and processing plants are the town's main employers.

3 WEEMALA LOOKOUT AND FLORA AND FAUNA RESERVE

Take the road out of Batlow towards Tumbarumba and turn west into Cherry Lane to reach Weemala Lookout. This lookout offers outstanding views over the township. It is also an excellent vantage point for a panoramic view across the northern end of the Snowy Mountains.

4 TUMBARUMBA

Return to the road to Tumbarumba and continue south for 38km until you reach Tumbarumba.
Tumbarumba is a delightful, sleepy little country town largely untouched by the modern world. The town has been bypassed by the major road and rail routes between Sydney and Melbourne and consequently has an old-style charm, plus a number of beautifully preserved old buildings, all of which makes Tumbarumba an attractive destination.

This was part of the Wiradjuri country before European settlement, and it is from the Wiradjuri language that the word tumbarumba, probably meaning 'sounding ground', is derived. It has been suggested that there are places in the district where the ground makes a hollow sound when struck.

The first Europeans into the area were Hume and Hovell, in 1824. They were followed by settlers, who moved into the area in the 1830s. Gold was discovered in the Tumbarumba district in 1855 and the Tumbarumba Gold Field was proclaimed in 1866. The discovery of gold attracted large numbers of Chinese, who worked the gold fields and established elaborate sluices and water races to assist their labours.

Tumbarumba's major attractions are the courthouse and police residence, which are located at 66 Winton Street. These two single-storey buildings were constructed in the 1880s. Their age is evident in the VR (Victoria Regina) embossed into the cast-iron lacework. The outbuildings are gabled and the courtroom has a double height ceiling. To enjoy a good overview of Tumbarumba's more interesting buildings continue up Bridge Street, turn right into Murray Street, pass the churches and turn right into Regent Street and head back towards the historic Tumbarumba Hotel. The hotel stands on the hill above the Tumbarumba Creek and welcomes visitors arriving from Wagga and Jingellic.

5 GUNDAGAI

From Tumbarumba head north-west to the Hume Hwy, which is 62km from the town. Turn north on the high-way and the town of Gundagai 70km away .

Gundagai, forever associated with the dog on the tuckerbox in Australian folklore, is situated on the Murrumbidgee River. More than any other Australian town, Gundagai has proved an irresistible subject to writers of popular verse. This perhaps relates to the fact that Five Mile Creek, to the north of the town, was a popular meeting place with teamsters, drovers, shearers and bush travellers. 'Lazy Harry', 'On the Road to Gundagai' and 'Flash Jack from Gundagai' are three anonymous poems relating to the town. Banjo Paterson wrote a ballad

entitled 'The Road to Gundagai' and Jack O'Hagan wrote 'Along the Road to Gundagai' which, in 1922, became an international success and the signature tune for the popular radio show 'Dad and Dave'.

A village developed in the 1830s on the road to Melbourne. Despite warnings by local Aborigines, a town plan was approved in 1838 on the low-lying alluvial flats on the northern side of the Murrumbidgee. The first flood hit the town in 1844. Gundagai was finally moved to higher ground after a flood virtually destroyed the settlement in 1852, killing 83 of the 250 residents and destroying 71 buildings. The railway arrived at Gundagai in 1886 and the town became a municipality in 1889.

The Gundagai Tourist Information Centre is located in Carberry Park, Sheridan Street. It features the 'Marble Masterpiece'—an elaborately detailed Baroque Italian palace in miniature (1.2m high) set within a formal square. The entire construction consists of 20 948 pieces of 20 different varieties of marble collected throughout New South Wales. Each piece has been cut, turned and polished by hand. The palace was created by distinguished Gundagai mason Frank Rusconi, who worked on it in the evenings for 28 years in 1910–1938. The centre also has a gemstone collection and a Flood Inundation Display. A National Trust Guide to the town's historic buildings is available for a small charge and the centre has its own Two Foot Tour of the town's history and architecture.

Opposite the Information Centre is the Services Club. The dining room was originally part of a flour mill (1870). Note the thick slate walls. There is a display of historic photographs in the foyer.

Head east along Sheridan Street, over Otway Street, and turn left into Kitchener Street. At the south-western corner of Kitchener Street and First Avenue is the former Literary Institute, a two-storey Italianate building with decorative facade built in 1870 as a single-storey structure.

The Dog on the Tuckerbox near Gundagai.

The Tumut Valley in spring.

Return along Kitchener Street and turn left back into Sheridan Street. Walk past the Art Deco theatre (1929) to the Family Hotel (1858). In the early days, when it was the Fry's Hotel, the premises were shared by a Cobb & Co booking agency and the Commercial Bank. Note the typical country-town verandah.

Adjacent is the National Bank, built as the CBC Bank in 1877. The Chan Kong Chinese Restaurant nearby was built as a doctor's residence in 1875.

A little further along is the Gabriel Gallery. Among its collection are Henry Lawson's walking stick, dictionary and chair, and his letters to Grace McManus, who cared for him in 1920 at Coolac. The main exhibit is a photographic collection of works by Dr Charles Louis Gabriel, a resident of Gundagai from 1887 until his death in 1927. Photographs that capture Gundagai at the turn of the century line the walls.

Turn left into Byron Street. On the left are the police station and gaol. The first stage of the gaol was built as a watch-house in the 1860s. Until the 1920s the police station (also built in the 1860s) was occupied by mounted troopers who escorted the mail coach and fought bushrangers such as Ben Hall, Johnny Gilbert and Captain Moonlite.

Return along Byron Street and turn left back into Sheridan Street. On the left is a prominent feature of the town's streetscape, the courthouse (1859). This was one of the first stone buildings to be erected after the 1852 flood and was the site for the trial of Captain Moonlite. Make sure you continue to the end of town and walk across the famous Gundagai Bridge, built between 1896 and 1899.

In your vehicle, return to Sheridan St and follow it across the floodplain. The road rises up to the edge of the pedestrian bridge. Once over the Murrumbidgee River, turn left and continue through Brungle and back to Tumut. The distance is 35km.

Tumbarumba's Courthouse.

27 ON THE BORDER

■ WALKING AND DRIVING TOUR ■ 316KM ■ 1 DAY ■ BORDER TOWNS AND RIVER VALLEYS

Beyond the Snowy Mountains the western slopes give way to the vastness of the Riverina plains which are drained by the mighty Murray and Murrumbidgee Rivers.

Albury is a thriving and prosperous city situated on the border of New South Wales and Victoria. It is also located on the Murray River, which receives the snow-fed waters from the Snowy Mountains. This is rich pasture land on the edge of the Great Dividing Range.

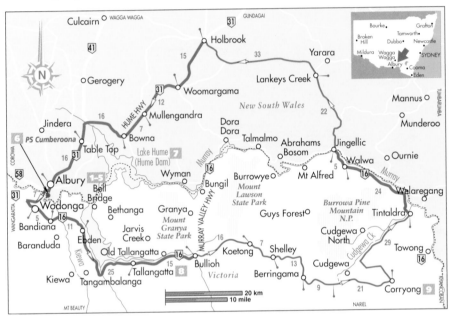

1 ALBURY

The twin towns of Albury and Wodonga, although they are 7km apart and on opposite sides of the Murray River, form a large urban area that is the border between New South Wales and Victoria. The area around the Murray was once inhabited by the Wiradjuri people. In 1824 the explorers Hume and Hovell reached the future site of Albury, carved their remarks into the trunks of two trees, and crossed the river, which they called the Hume. It was later renamed the Murray. Squatters followed the explorers and the first land in the area was taken up in 1835. Albury grew because it was located at a spot where the river was fordable.

After Victoria separated from New South Wales in 1851, the two towns became customs posts. Goods tended to be cheaper in New South Wales so Victorians would swim their stock across the river and women bought their clothes and groceries over the border, wearing several layers of clothing home past the customs point. While flour and bread were taxed in New South Wales dough was not, so Victorian bakers set up dough houses in New South Wales and ferried it back across the Murray to be baked into bread.

The paddle-steamer on the Albury coat-of-arms is a reminder of the role that river transport played in local development after the first river steamer, *Albury*, arrived in 1855. Albury–Wodonga benefited from a political commitment to decentralisation in the 1970s. Wodonga was proclaimed the first 'rural city' in Australia in 1973.

2 HISTORIC BUILDINGS

This is a walking tour of central Albury. It starts on the corner of Dean and Olive sts.

The growing prosperity of Albury from the 1850s can be seen in the impressive Victorian civic buildings on Dean Street between Kiewa and Olive streets. The Classical Revival court-house (1860) is one of the few remaining buildings designed by colonial architect Alexander Dawson. The large two-storey post office (1875), at the corner of Dean and Kiewa streets, features arch work buttressed by a colonnade and a clock tower with cupola and weathervane that was added in the 1920s. The largely unaltered Classical building that houses the technical college was formerly the telegraph office (1885). The CML building has a five-storey clock tower with curved copper roof. The ANZ Bank (*c.*1915) is a large Edwardian bank with a terracotta tiled roof. By contrast, the T&G Building, dating from the mid-1930s, features a more modern design, the highlight of which is a five-storey tower with extremely long, thin vertical window recesses and a ziggurat summit.

The Albury Regional Art Centre is inside the splendid, ornate and virtually unaltered Edwardian town hall (1907) with cupolas and extravagant stucco. The centre has an impressive collection of works by one-time resident Sir Russell Drysdale.

From the post office, head north along Kiewa Street. A few doors along, at 514 Kiewa Street, is St Matthew's Anglican Church, built of local stone. The foundation stone of the church was laid in 1857. The original Norman design, by noted architect Edmund Blacket, was never completed. While the nave, choir, vestry and campanile are his, the contrasting Gothic elements—notably the chancel, vestries and transepts—were designed by J. Boles and added in the mid-1870s. The pipe organ was added in 1876.

3 MONUMENT HILL LOOKOUT

In your vehicle, head west along Dean St. Turn right into Thurgoona St, left into Pemberton St and take the fifth left into Roper St.

Monument Hill is named after the 30m war cenotaph there. Rising 90m above the city, the hill offers views as far as Dean Street. To the south lie Wodonga and, on the horizon, the Victorian Alps.

Directly below the hill is Mungabareena Reserve. Here the Aboriginal tribes from the high plains met for centuries to celebrate the coming of spring. They laid aside their weapons and their tribal differences to celebrate, then travelled north to Mount Beauty and Mount Buffalo to feast on the nutritious bogong moth.

Albury from the Monument Hill Lookout.

A paddle-steamer on the Murray River.

4 BOTANICAL GARDENS

Return along Roper, Pemberton and Thurgoona sts, turn left into Dean St, then take the first right into Wodonga Pl. On the right are the Botanical Gardens.

The highlights of the Botanical Gardens include a 30m Queensland kauri, several river red gums grown from seeds of the Hovell Tree and a pine that grew from a seed taken from Lone Pine in Gallipoli. Also in the gardens is the Hume Monument, which was built in America and erected in place of the destroyed Hume Tree in the late 1850s. In 1884 the monument was moved to the gardens from its original site by the riverbank where it was being misused as a mooring point by riverboats. The bandstand was built in 1890.

5 ALBURY RAILWAY STATION

From Wodonga Place turn right into Smollett St. Follow it to cross over Young St into Railway Place.

The Italianate red-and-white brick railway station (1881) has a 22m clock tower, original cedar joinery and a cast-iron platform with fluted columns. It is the third longest platform in Australia and the longest in New South Wales, owing to its role as changeover point. The stationmaster's residence is also worth a look and is set in attractive gardens.

6 PS CUMBEROONA

Leave the railway station and turn left into Young St. Follow the Hume Hwy through town until you reach the parks on the left-hand side of Wodonga Rd. Take the road to your left at Hovell St and continue around until you reach the banks of the Murray River.

The PS *Cumberoona*, a replica of an 1886 paddle-steamer that once regularly visited Albury, offers one-hour tours of the Murray every day in season. Near its mooring point in Noreuil Park, a reproduction Cobb & Co coach will take you for a ride on weekends.

7 THE HUME DAM

Return to the railway station and continue for 1km to Borella Rd, which is the Riverina Hwy. After 13km you will reach Lake Hume.

About 16km west of town, the Hume Dam, built between the end of World War I and 1936, arose out of the River Murray Agreement. At the time of completion it was the largest dam in the southern hemisphere and one of the largest in the world. The dam's surface area measures 20 190ha, total length is 1.6km, capacity is nearly 3 million megalitres and it has 343km of shoreline. There are 29 regulating gates, each 6m by 8m, and a hydro-electric station has been established to best utilise the volume of water.

Spanned by Bethangra Bridge, Lake Hume is used for swimming, sailing, waterskiing, paragliding, fishing, sailboarding, jetskiing and canoeing. There are picnic, barbecue and children's play facilities, a spectacular dam wall, scenic countryside, swimming beaches, boat ramps, stores, canoe hire, camping and a holiday resort that boasts a giant waterslide.

8 TALLANGATTA

Continue along the Riverina Hwy for about 6km until you reach the Murray Valley Hwy. Turn left and after 28km take the signposted turn-off to Tallangatta. Drive through the town and continue on for 7km until you each the plaque that marks the location of old Tallangatta.

Tallangatta was physically removed from the Murray River Valley when the Hume Reservoir was built in the 1950s. There is a plaque on the side of the Murray Valley Highway which reads:

> The township of Tallangatta was originally situated in the valley immediately below this point on land subject to inundation by waters of the Hume Reservoir. The transfer of the township by the State Rivers and Waters Supply Commission to the new site five miles to the west was completed on 29 June 1956.

In 1997, when the Hume Reservoir reached an unprecedented low level, it was possible to make out the streets and the remnants of the old buildings in the water. The foundations of the Bank of New South Wales that once stood on one of the town's street corners were visible, as were Towong Street and the former Murray Valley Highway.

9 CORRYONG

Continue along the Murray Valley Hwy for 76km to the town of Corryong.

Small metal silhouettes of the Man from Snowy River stand beside the road at both ends of Corryong, declaring that this is Man from Snowy River Country. Not only is Corryong the Victorian gateway to both the Snowy Mountains and Kosciuszko National Park, but it is generally accepted that a local named Jack Riley was the inspiration for Banjo Paterson's famous poem 'The Man from Snowy River' (1890).

Explorer Paul Edmund de Strzelecki passed through the area on his way to Gippsland in 1840. The district was opened up for selection in the 1860s and a township slowly emerged to cater to the needs of the small landowners.

The town's pretty hillside cemetery is located at the top of Pioneer Avenue (signposted from the main road). It contains the simple grave of Jack Riley. In contrast to Paterson's ballad epic, the tombstone laconically declares: 'In memory of The Man from Snowy River, Jack Riley, buried here 16th July 1914'.

The Man from Snowy River Museum is located at the corner of McKay and Hanson streets in the old shire offices. It is essentially a local history museum with an eclectic collection that includes an old lock-up, a slab timber hut set up as an old-fashioned dairy, wooden skis dating back to the 1870s (including a pram on skis owned by Olympic skiers Thomas and Elyne Mitchell), some lovely Victorian costumes and an unusual flying jacket handmade of bits and pieces by a World War II prisoner of war.

Return to Albury via the scenic route, which involves following the Tintaldra Rd to Towong (13km) and then heading north to Tintaldra (11km). Head west towards Wodonga and, 31km from Tintaldra, turn to Jingellic. After 55km you will reach the town of Holbrook. Head south on the Hume Hwy to Albury, which is 66km away.

Civic gardens in the centre of Albury.

CHAPTER 4
SOUTH WEST

28 ALBURY TO ECHUCA

■ DRIVING TOUR ■ 267KM ■ 1 DAY ■ RIVERBANKS AND PADDLE-STEAMERS

The muddy Murray flows slowly towards the sea through flat wetlands. The riverbanks are covered with distinctive Murray river gums and beaches characterise the bends in the river.

Other countries have rivers that loom large in their consciousness—the Danube, the Mississippi, the Amazon. In contrast, Australia, because it is such a dry and flat country, does not possess a truly great river. At any point along its length, a swimmer of moderate ability could make it across the Murray River. At Albury, and even at Echuca, the Murray is relatively narrow and characterised by muddy banks and endless stands of gum trees. Still, a journey along the Murray is a journey into Australia's history.

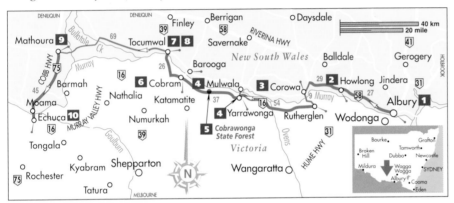

1 ALBURY

The paddle-steamer on the Albury coat-of-arms is a reminder of the role river transport played in local development after the first river steamer, *Albury*, arrived in 1855. On the northern bank of the Murray, off Wodonga Place, is a series of parklands: Oddies Creek Park, Noreuil Park, Hovell Tree Park, the sportsground, the Botanic Gardens, Mates Park and Padman Park. Within the parklands is a 19th-century iron waterwheel from the Tallandoon goldfield, where it powered a stamp battery. The waterwheel is very rare as most were made of wood and hence have rotted away. It was purchased by the Harper brothers, local farmers who used it until 1948 to power farm equipment. The wheel has a 5m diameter with capacity for 60 attached buckets. Also there is the PS *Cumberoona*, a replica of an 1886 paddle-steamer that once regularly visited Albury. *Cumberoona* offers one-hour tours of the Murray every day in season.

2 HOWLONG

Head north along Wodonga Pl and turn left into Smollett St and left again into Padman Drv (the Riverina Hwy). Continue west for 30km to Howlong.

Howlong is an attractive riverside town on the New South Wales–Victoria border. The first European in the area was New South Wales Surveyor General Major Thomas Mitchell, who crossed the Murray at the location of the present townsite in 1836. A monument to Mitchell stands on the Victorian side of the river.

Isaac Rudd took up a run called Hoolong, or Oolong, in the early 1840s, after an Aboriginal place name meaning 'beginning of the plains'. The town was laid out in 1854. There was, at one time, an upper and lower Howlong, which were located some distance apart.

The riverside location makes Howlong an ideal spot for walking, horseriding, photography, fishing, boating and swimming. There is also an attractive golf course.

3 COROWA

Continue west along the Riverina Hwy for 22km to the turn-off to Corowa, which is 4km further on.

Corowa is a typical Australian country service centre in a prosperous district devoted mainly to the cultivation of wool, cereals, wine grapes and fat stock. The town is supported by a huge piggery, an abattoir, timber-milling and winemaking.

Charles Sturt explored the Murray River area in 1829–1830. In 1838, John Foord and John Crisp saw the land and subsequently took up the 30 000ac run known as Wahgunyah, which included land on both sides of the Murray. Foord bought a steamer, built a flour mill, subdivided his holdings and established the private township of Wahgunyah on the southern bank of the Murray in 1857, which served as a river port and an important site for stock crossings. He also purchased a punt that was used by many diggers to cross the river on their way to the Beechworth goldfields.

Corowa is known as the Birthplace of Federation. Federation Museum in Queen Street, opposite the Presbyterian Church, contains documents and mementos relating to the struggle for Federation, as well as sketches, photographs, books, agricultural implements, horse-drawn vehicles, Aboriginal artefacts and other displays relating to local history.

The town is considered to have one of the finest collections of intact Federation-style buildings in Australia. Much of the main thoroughfare, Sanger Street, is under the protection of the National Trust. The Globe Hotel started as a Cobb & Co inn. The railway station and stationmaster's house are the original early 1890s structures and the former, in John Street, now houses the information centre (from where you can obtain a pamphlet that outlines a walking tour of the town). St Andrew's Presbyterian Church (at 204 Federation Avenue) is an attractive building situated adjacent to an older church.

4 MULWALA AND YARRAWONGA

Drive west from Corowa for 41km, following the signs for Yarrawonga.

Yarrawonga is located at the south-western corner of Lake Mulwala. Mulwala is on the western shore of the lake and Yarrawonga is over the river in Victoria. The two settlements are linked by a bridge over the mouth of the lake and virtually constitute a continuous settlement.

The Mulla Walla people are said to have occupied the area before the first white settlers arrived in 1842. The major

Cobram Hotel in Cobram.

The Cobb & Co. Royal Mail coach, Echuca.

development in the town's history has been the construction of the Yarrawonga Weir and Lake Mulwala in the late 1930s as part of the Murray–Darling Irrigation Scheme. The reservoir covers 6000ha and is a popular tourist attraction. Picnicking at the foreshore parks, birdwatching, fishing, sailboarding, waterskiing, swimming, canoeing, sailing, boating and guided paddleboat cruises are all popular on the lake. Pelican Island is a breeding ground for pelicans and there are several ibis rookeries. Thousands of partially submerged trees poke eerily out from the water.

5 COBRAWONGA STATE FOREST

Continue west from Yarrawonga towards Cobram. The journey is 36km and on the way you pass through the Cobrawonga State Forest.

The southern bank of the Murray River between Yarrawonga and Cobram is bordered by the Cobrawonga State Forest, comprising 2500ha of fauna-rich river red gum forest. There are a number of possible destinations for those who wish to see the river and forest. Slightly west of Yarrawonga, Cullens–Breans Road heads off the Murray Valley Highway to Yarrawonga Common where there are picnic tables. Further west are the billabongs and beaches of Bruces Bend and Nevins Bend (both have fireplaces and picnic tables), the beaches and islets of Bourkes Bend (fireplaces and picnic facilities), and Cobrawonga Island (beaches and walking tracks).

6 COBRAM

The Cobram–Barooga Visitor Information Centre is located in a 1910 grain shed at the corner of Station Street, which was the town's commercial centre prior to 1900, and Punt Road. Opposite the centre is a log cabin that was originally erected in the Yarrawonga district as a home for the Toms family about 1875. The cabin was moved to the present site in 1977. The Masonic lodge, by the south-eastern corner of Main and Station streets, was built in 1888 as a store. On the south-western corner is the Cobram Hotel (1892). Adjacent to the highway, opposite

Station Street, is a memorial to explorer Charles Sturt, the leader of the first European party to pass through the area in 1838.

The Murray, with its towering river red gums and sandy beaches, is one of the town's greatest attractions. The most popular and readily accessible beach is Thompsons, which is located near the bridge at the north-eastern edge of town, off Boorin Street. To the east of town are Scotts Beach, Horseshoe Lagoon and Twin Knobs Beach. To access this area, head east along Morakii Street towards the bridge then turn right onto River Road, passing orchards to the right and red gum forest to the left.

7 TOCUMWAL

From Cobram take the bridge over the Murray River into Barooga and then follow the signs to Tocumwal, 19km to the north-west.

Tocumwal derives its name from *Tucumiva*, an Aboriginal term said to mean 'deep hole'; a reference to what is now known as The Blowhole, a bogey some 25m deep at its lowest point which is said to be sacred to the Ulupna and Bangarang people. According to legend, a giant Murray cod living in the waterhole was prone to eat any young child who fell in. Hence the giant fibreglass Murray cod in the town square at Tocumwal.

The first runs in the area opened up in the 1840s. In 1860, Edward Hillson purchased 5000ac from Patrick Hennessey and it was on this land that the town was built. A postal service commenced the following year. The village was recognised in 1872, the same year a punt was established, which encouraged through traffic and in turn led to further development.

8 TOCUMWAL'S RIVER BEACHES

A track leads from the shopping centre, at the bottom of Deniliquin St, to the town beach.

The sandy town beach is one of many along the Murray, where river red gums provide a pleasant backdrop. The area is well suited to those interested in camping, canoeing, waterskiing, swimming, river cruises, fishing, horseriding, four-wheel-drive trips, bushwalking and golfing.

Swimming in the Murray River, Corowa.

9 MATHOURA

Head west on Deniliquin Rd for 38km, to the signpost to Mathoura. Continue for 25km to a T-intersection and turn right. Mathoura is 5km away.

Mathoura is the gateway to the world's largest river red gum forest. Mathoura Forest covers 53 000ac and abounds with flora and fauna. The plentiful supply of game and water was an irresistible combination for the Aborigines who once dwelt here. Trees scraped of bark for the construction of canoes and burial mounds can still be seen in the district.

The red gum requires a plentiful supply of water to regenerate and local rainfall is insufficient. Thus the forest owes its existence to the annual spring floods when the snow melts on the Snowy Mountains. There are numerous beautiful driving trails that wind through the forest, where some of the trees rise to a height of 40m.

10 ECHUCA

Head south from Mathoura on the Cobb Hwy. Echuca is 45km away.

At one time Echuca was the largest inland river port in Victoria. It is this aspect of the town's past that has become the theme of its redevelopment. Paddle-steamers now travel the local waters. The survival of many original buildings and the port area's authentic appearance attracted the makers of *All the Rivers Run*, who used it as the setting for their mini-series on the riverboat era.

The old port area is under the supervision of the Port of Echuca, which has its headquarters at 101 Murray Esplanade. It is open from 9.00am to 5.00pm daily and is responsible for the Wharf Museum Tour which explores the port area, including the old wharf, paddle-steamers and barges, and historic buildings such as the Bridge and Star hotels. There are currently six riverboats operating out of Echuca, which offer cruises of various sorts along the Murray.

To continue this journey see Tour 29.

Historic paddle-steamer on the bank of the Murray River, Echuca.

29 ECHUCA TO MILDURA

■ DRIVING TOUR ■ 525KM ■ 2 DAYS ■ MORE RIVERBANKS AND PADDLE-STEAMERS

Sandy beaches, stands of red river gums and old townships which once were ports for the riverboats. This is the Murray between the riverports of Echuca and Mildura.

This tour continues from Tour 28, however, the tour can also be taken on its own. From Cohuna to Mildura, dairy farms, citrus orchards, vegetable farms and vineyards sweep across the landscape. Swan Hill makes the changeover to sheep, cattle and wheat country and the hard lives of the early settlers is evident. Still around the Murray, the magic of the river, magnificent river red gums and a huge array of bird life can be enjoyed.

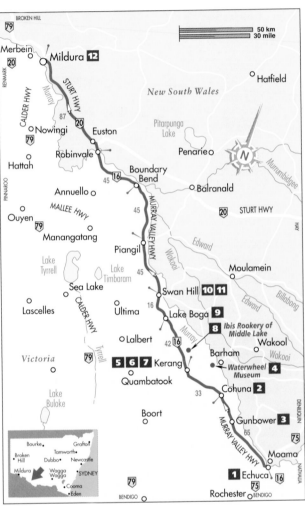

1 ECHUCA AND THE TORRUMBARRY WEIR

Head north-west from Echuca along the Murray Valley Hwy for about 27km to the signposted turn-off to Torrumbarry Weir, which is about 4km past the tiny settlement of Torrumbarry.

Torrumbarry Weir is a very pretty location within a bushland setting with birdlife, fishing, barbecues, playground equipment and a caravan park.

2 COHUNA

Return to the Murray Valley Hwy and continue along the highway to Cohuna, which is 66km from Echuca and 35km from Torrumbarry.

Cohuna is a peaceful little town on the Murray Valley Highway. Opposite the main road is a portion of Gunbower Creek, a branch of the Murray River. The area is thought to have been occupied by the Baraparapa people long before white settlement and prehistoric burials of world importance were found locally in 1925 and in the late 1960s. Major Thomas Mitchell passed through the area on his 1836 exploration of the area. The first settlers came to the district from the north in 1835 or 1836.

The former Scots Presbyterian Church has become the display centre for the Cohuna and District Historical Society. There are household items and memorabilia of the district, including a portion of a tree marked by Thomas Mitchell in 1836 on what was the first exploratory journey by Europeans into this part of the country. The museum is located in Sampson Street.

3 GUNBOWER ISLAND

Cohuna Island Rd heads off the highway at the roundabout in town. It leads directly over the creek, which runs adjacent to the highway, onto Gunbower Island.

Gunbower Island is sandwiched between the Murray River and its branch, Gunbower Creek. At 50km long, Gunbower is reputedly Australia's largest inland island, extending from Koondrook to Torrumbarry Weir. The island is characterised by swamps, enormous river red gums and, on the higher ground, box forest. The beautiful red gums make excellent timber and have been milled since the 1870s.

Gunbower supports a diversity of native animals, including kangaroos, emus, goannas, possums and snakes, plus 160 bird species. Still in its natural state, the island is ideal for bushwalking, camping, birdwatching and canoeing.

4 WATERWHEEL MUSEUM

Follow the Murray Valley Hwy west towards Kerang for about 5km, turn right onto Carwardines Rd, just before Barr Bridge, then turn left onto Brays Rd when you come to the church.

Mathers Waterwheel Museum houses a well-laid out collection of memorabilia. There is also an aviary of native birds.

5 KERANG

Return to the Murray Valley Hwy and continue north-west for 30km to Kerang.

Kerang's symbol is a flying ibis. This is a reference to the fact that the area around Kerang, with its 50 or so small lakes, contains the most populous ibis rookeries in the world with an estimated 200 000 ibis using the area for breeding purposes each year. The lakes are also home to thousands of other waterbirds and are popular recreational destinations.

The town's information centre is located in the Lester Smith Lookout Tower, an old water storage tower built in 1883 which has a display of local and exotic gemstones. The tower also offers excellent views of the area. The tower stands at the corner of the Murray Valley Highway (Wellington Street) and Shadforth Street.

6 KERANG HISTORIC MUSEUM

From the information centre, walk west along Wellington St and take the first left into Riverwood Drv. Just beyond the tennis courts is the entry to the Kerang Historical Museum.

Kerang Historical Museum is located in the former Franklin homestead. The museum features displays relating to local history, including farm machinery, cars and material on town founder Woodford Patchell, who pioneered the use of irrigation in the district.

7 KERANG WETLANDS SYSTEM

There are about 50 small lakes, swamps and lagoons around Kerang. Each spring as many as 200 000 straw-necked, white and glossy ibis breed in the reedbeds of the local lakes, making them the world's most populous ibis rookeries. The added advantage of this natural phenomenon is that the birds eat at least 5 tonnes of insects a day, mostly from surrounding paddocks, thereby helping to protect the crops in the district from infestation. Interestingly, these waterbirds breed only with the onset of floodwaters and will abandon their nests if the water recedes.

The wetlands are also home to thousands of other waterbirds, including egrets, spoon-

Historic bridge on the Murray River, Swan Hill.

The Big Murray Cod, Swan Hill.

bills, kites, harriers, sea eagles, grebes and heron. The main lakes are adjacent to or just off the Murray Valley Highway to the north-west of town and, as they are so readily accessible, they are very popular spots for recreational activities.

8 IBIS ROOKERY OF MIDDLE LAKE

Head out of Kerang along the Murray Valley Hwy for 8km to Reedy Lake. Continue along the highway for another 2km where a sign will direct you to the Ibis Rookery of Middle Lake.

This is the principal breeding ground of the ibis. The viewing tower is best visited at dawn and dusk, when the sky is black with tens of thousands of ibis leaving or returning to their nests.

9 LAKE BOGA

Continue along the highway for another 45km to the settlement on the edge of Lake Boga.

Lake Boga is a popular spot for swimming, fishing, picnicking and sailing. On the highway beside the lake is a restored Cannie Ridge Steam Pump used for pumping water into irrigation channels from 1904 to 1952. At Jacaranda Crescent in Lake Boga township, a well-restored Catalina flying boat marks the site of the museum which is located in an old World War II bunker. The museum recalls the occasion in the war when a flying boat repair depot operated at Lake Boga.

10 SWAN HILL

Continue north-west along the Murray Valley Hwy for 19km to Swan Hill.

Swan Hill is a well-laid-out city with a pleasant, garden-like main street. Here the Murray River meets the Little Murray River and, as the town's Giant Murray Cod indicates, the river provides good opportunities for fishing, as well as boating and water sports. In 1853, Francis Cadell made his famous steamer voyage along the Murray, starting from the mouth of the river and making his way as far as Swan Hill. Despite popular claim, it was not the first such voyage, but it did herald the start of the inland river trade and Swan Hill became the first major inland port. A wharf was built and remained in use until the 1920s—the remnants can still be seen on the riverbank along with a photograph and plaque.

McCallum Street is the main thorough-fare. At its eastern end is the bridge (1896) over the Murray, which takes you into New South Wales. The bridge was the first lift-span bridge on the Murray—note the large counterbalancing weights. The central section was designed to raise so that paddle-steamers could pass through underneath.

11 SWAN HILL PIONEER SETTLEMENT

Continue south along Monash Drv. Just past the railway station, at Horseshoe Bend, is the Swan Hill Pioneer Settlement.

The Pioneer Settlement is an open-air historical museum that covers 4ha of land on the banks of the Little Murray. Australia's first such display, the settlement re-creates a 19th-century river port town. All employees are dressed in period attire. Kangaroos and peacocks stroll around the complex while sheep and goats are tethered. There are several picnic areas, including one at Pental Island, reached by a small bridge.

Authentic streets and buildings have been re-created in the Horseshoe Bend Township. The Stereoscopic Theatre (1895) was an entertainment venue in the late 19th century. It creates a three-dimensional impression when pictures within the large cylindrical chamber are viewed through special binoculars. There is a Masonic hall displaying the arcana of Masonic rituals; a replica coach-house (*c.*1860) with shingle roof, stub floor and drop-log walls; a drop-log post office which is still in use; a general store; an old-time photographic studio; a newspaper office and printery from Ballarat that is still

functioning; and one of the country's first prefabricated iron houses (1854), shipped to Australia when the gold rushes led to a population surge. Towanninie homestead's outbuildings include a mallee-stump stable, a mud-brick kitchen and log cabin.

Equipment at the settlement includes vintage cars, an old locomotive, carriages, trucks and buggies and there are free horse-drawn wagon rides. Activities such as baking, blacksmithing, pottery, woodturning, printing, damper-making, saddlery and chaff-cutting are all carried out in the traditional manner with traditional equipment.

12 MILDURA

Continue north-west along the Murray Valley Hwy for 146km until you reach the Sturt Hwy. Mildura is an 80km drive along the Sturt Hwy, which will bring you into the town from the north. As you cross the river, turn right into Seventh St then right again into Madden Ave. Pass under the railway bridge and proceed to Mildura Wharf.

The streets of Mildura provide a clue about the economic basis of the area, having such names as Orange, Lemon, Lime, Avocado, Cherry, Muscat, Vineyard, Olive and Walnut. The district supplies 80 per cent of Australia's dried fruit, 15 per cent of its citrus fruit, 85 per cent of the state's winemaking grapes and boasts the second- and third-largest packing companies in the world.

Old paddle-steamers and showboats ply the waters at the wharf, recalling the colonial days before the railways when the inland river trade was a major means of intra-national transport. The *Melbourne* (1912) is still run by steam power and you can watch the original boiler being stoked. Among its services, *Rothbury* (1881) makes weekly trips to Golden Zoo Park and Trentham Winery. The showboat *Avoca* (1877) offers night-time cruises with dinner, music and dancing while *Coonawarra* (1894) undertakes cruises of three to five nights with accommodation.

PS Gem Adelaide *paddle-steamer near the Pioneer Settlement, Swan Hill.*

30 HISTORIC RIVERINA

■ DRIVING TOUR ■ 432KM ■ 1 DAY ■ FLATLANDS AND BUSHRANGERS

Beyond the southern slopes the rich plains of the Riverina stretch westward until New South Wales slowly disappears into the vast western desert.

Here are the great flat lands of interior Australia. They stretch from Wagga Wagga and the foothills of the Snowy Mountains all the way to the border with South Australia. These are the great grasslands where sheep graze on vast properties and where, in years when it doesn't rain, the entire area turns into a dustbowl. In the flatlands the distance of 100km means nothing more than a one-hour drive because there is nothing on the roads to stop you or slow you down.

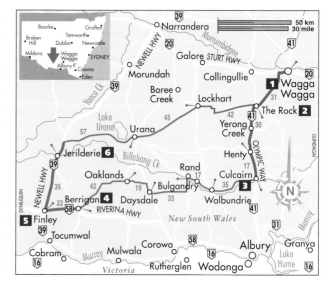

1 WAGGA WAGGA

Wagga Wagga is one of Australia's largest inland cities and is considered the capital of the Riverina area of New South Wales. Wagga, as it is commonly known, is a town of fine buildings, tree-lined streets, parks and gardens.

The first inhabitants of the area were the Wiradjuri people. There was some early pastoral settlement in the 1820s but it was the 1829 exploration of the river system by Charles Sturt that opened up the area to white settlers. The site became an important river crossing, situated as it was at the intersection of the north–south track between New South Wales and Victoria, and the east–west track along the Murrumbidgee River.

The visitors centre at the corner of Tarcutta and Morrow streets will provide you with a pamphlet outlining a walk that takes in some of the town's historic buildings. In Cross Street is St Andrew's Presbyterian Church and manse (c.1890). Turn into Church Street and on your right is St John's Church of England, begun in 1876. On the other side of the road is St Michael's

Cathedral. Highlights include the Gothic arches, beautifully crafted marble in the altar and the Edwardian presbytery, the Bishop's House (1910) which has impressive timber detailing around the verandahs, bay windows and gables.

Turn right into Johnston Street and then take the path to Wagga Beach and Cabarita Park. Follow the footpath along the levee bank to Sturt Street, where you will find the red-brick police station (1880s and 1927) and the Sturt Monument, which commemorates the completion of the flood levee banks in 1960.

Turn left into Fitzmaurice Street where, on your left, is the outstanding Edwardian courthouse complex (1900) with its massive square clock tower, belltower, cupolas, decorative ironwork and cedar joinery and fittings. The courthouse is considered one of the finest of its type in Australia. The National Bank building (1885) and post office (1886–1888) are two fine buildings in

the Classical Revival style which make significant contributions to the cityscape.

Turn right into Johnston Street and walk to its end passing, along the way, the ANZ Bank and lovely old homes that have been converted into offices. When you reach the T-intersection, return up Johnston Street to Trail Street and turn right over the lagoon bridge to enter the Victory Memorial Gardens (1928) on the banks of the Wollundry Lagoon. Within the memorial gardens are an avenue of poplar trees, a life-sized copper sculpture of the Jolly Swagman boiling his billy, the Pioneer Memorial Sundial, a sunken garden, a senses garden for the blind, a children's play area, picnic facilities, swans, duck, geese, waterfowl, fish and tortoises.

2 THE ROCK

From the centre of Wagga, in Baylis St, head west along Edward St and at the outskirts of town turn left into Olympic Way (signposted for Albury). After 26km take the signposted turn-off for The Rock, which is located just off the highway.

The Rock was named after a local geological feature, a craggy outcrop that dominates the immediate landscape. Initially known as Kengal, the town soon became known as Hanging Rock because of a spectacular overhang on the east face of the hill. However, a major rock fall in 1874 changed the shape of the overhang.

The summit of Hanging Rock Hill can be reached via the Yerrong trail, which leads from the picnic area at the foot of the hill. The track passes through the 365ha nature reserve that surrounds The Rock and within which can be found several relic plants, including a species of groundsel thought to be unique to

Wagga's historic railway station.

the area. The walk takes about three hours but the view is worthwhile. On a clear day it is possible to see Mount Kosciuszko on the horizon to the south-east. To the west is Galore Hill and beyond that, the rolling plains of western New South Wales.

3 CULCAIRN

Return to the Olympic Way and continue south for 49km to Culcairn.

Culcairn is a small township with beautiful tree-lined streets. The town's main claim to historical fame concerns the career of bushranger Dan 'Mad Dog' Morgan, who terrorised the district in 1862–1865.

In June 1864, national newspapers carried stories of Morgan's antics at Round Hill station, then leased by Edward Henty, where Mad Dog Morgan rounded everybody up and forced them to drink alcohol. He was about to depart when, according to one account, he fell into a rage because manager Sam Watson claimed that Morgan's stirrups were stolen. Another version has it that Morgan thought he'd been fired upon when his own gun accidentally went off. The result was that Morgan shot and wounded Watson, ran around firing indiscriminately, shot John Heriott, the son of a neighbouring grazier, chased another individual and then returned to Heriott, placing a gun to his temple.

When Watson said, 'For God's sake, Morgan, don't kill anyone', Morgan became compassionate, swore he would kill everyone who did not come to Heriott's assistance, carried him to a bed and agreed that overseer John McLean should go to Walla Walla to fetch a doctor.

When Heriott's condition improved, Morgan headed for Ten Mile Creek, found McLean and shot him and then returned him to Round Hill. He left just before the police arrived. McLean died just after a week of suffering. With a £1000 reward on his head, Morgan was killed in an ambush the following year. From hearing these events it is easy to see how Mad Dog got his nickname.

The original Round Hill homestead (1848) is 2.3km east of Culcairn on the right-hand side of the road to Morven and Holbrook. The grave of the overseer John McLean has been moved from its initial site to the roadside and is clearly signposted. It lies 800m east of the homestead, on the same side of the road.

4 BERRIGAN

Head west from Culcairn to Walbundrie, which is 32km away. Continue for another 121km through the tiny towns of Rand and Oaklands to Berrigan.

Berrigan is a traditional small country town that grew up around the Berrigan Hotel, which opened in 1888. A commercial and service centre for the local farmers, the village was proclaimed in 1890. The railway arrived in 1896. The Mulwala Canal was dug in 1935–1942, from Lake Mulwala to Berrigan Shire, which led to the development of cattle, sheep and cereal production, pigs, goat milk, Angora wool, dairying, citrus fruit, tomatoes, potatoes and grapes.

Berrigan has a number of substantial old buildings. It is best to simply wander around

The Murrumbidgee River near Wagga Wagga.

town, and the highlights include the brick post office (on the corner of Carter and Jerilderie streets) and, in Chanter Street, the Federal Hotel with its Dutch gables. Across the road is Memorial Hall with its arches and gables. The lead window at St Aidan's Anglican Church commemorates the European pioneers.

5 FINLEY

Head west on the Riverina Hwy for 21km to Finley.

Finley is a service centre for the Berriquin Irrigation Area that surrounds it. Squatters from the Port Phillip district moved into the southern and western Riverina in the early 1840s. The first building on the future town-site was a shepherd's dwelling known as the Murray Hut. It was located at a midpoint between Jerilderie and Tocumwal at the junction of two stock routes adjacent to a swamp (now Finley Lake).

The main street of Finley crosses Mulwala Canal, at 155km the largest irrigation channel in Australia. At the northern approach to town is the Wheels of Prosperity display, intended as a symbol of water's importance to the town and district. The landscaped foreshores of artificially constructed Finley Lake make for a pleasant picnic or barbecue. There is also a wharf, a boat ramp, a pool, a gardens area and children's play facilities, including a replica sailing ship.

Mary Lawson Wayside Rest, at the south end of town, also has playground equipment. Nearby is a log cabin replica of a pioneer home run by the historical society with a display of local historical material, including antiquated pumping equipment and machinery.

6 JERILDERIE

Head north on the Newell Hwy for 35km to Jerilderie.

The name Jerilderie comes from the language of the Jeithi people—Djirrildhuray is thought to mean 'with reeds' or 'reedy place', probably referring to the town's location on the banks of Billabong Creek.

Jerilderie is best known as the site of one of the most infamous and daring raids of bushranger Ned Kelly. At the time of their Jerilderie raid, the Kelly gang had a £1000 reward on their heads for the deaths of three policemen and for a major bank robbery. Ned and Dan Kelly, with Steve Hart and Joe Byrne, arrived at the Woolshed Inn on Saturday, 8 February 1879. Late in the evening they moved on to the police station.

The Wagga Council Chambers in Bayliss Street.

Ned Kelly called out that there had been a murder at the Woolshed Inn and Sergeant Devine and Constable Richards emerged, to be taken captive and imprisoned. Dan Kelly helped Mrs Devine prepare the courthouse, over the road, for Sunday mass.

The gang spent Sunday quietly at the police station, though two of them, dressed in the policemen's uniforms, snuck into town for a look around. At midday on Monday the four (two again dressed in police uniform) rode into town. They went to the Royal Mail Hotel, one end of which was rented by the Bank of New South Wales. There they herded everyone into the building, about 30 people in all, at gunpoint.

Byrne entered the bank and bailed up the clerk and teller. Kelly emptied the available cash (£690) into a sack. Kelly obtained a counter-key to the 'treasure drawer' from the manager, who was discovered in his bath, and there found another £1450. Having accumulated £2140 they headed south into the bush.

Today the original post and telegraph office remains largely unchanged and at the same location in Powell Street. Next door is an information centre and museum known as The Willows, an historic home (1878) built to serve as the residence for a water-powered stone-grind flour mill that was relocated in 1884.

From Jerilderie drive back to Wagga Wagga. The distance via Urana and Lockhart is 168km.

The War Memorial at The Rock.

31 THE MURRUMBIDGEE IRRIGATION AREA

■ DRIVING TOUR ■ 233KM ■ 1 DAY ■ FLAT LANDS AND CANALS

Once nothing more than dry, flat plains, the Murrumbidgee Irrigation Area is now one of the richest fruit- and grape-growing areas in Australia.

The Murrumbidgee Irrigation Scheme was one of Australia's great experiments. Rich lands without adequate water, rivers that ran full with melting waters from the Snowy Mountains. The aim was to get the summer waters from the Murrumbidgee to irrigate the rich dark soils of the Riverina. The result was a land crisscrossed by canals with paddocks rich with produce and once-brown fields that are now permanently green.

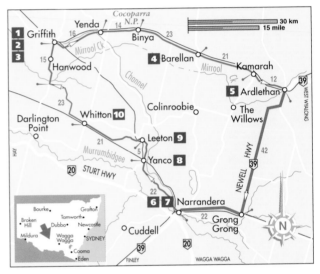

1 GRIFFITH

Griffith came into existence as a result of the construction of the Murrumbidgee Irrigation Area (MIA) early this century. The area developed when, in 1906, Samuel McCaughey developed an irrigation system at Yanco and convinced the government to undertake the construction of the MIA. The scheme transformed the barren plains into a fertile oasis, now the richest agricultural country in Australia.

Local settlement started with makeshift accommodation for the men who were building the canal 5km south-east of the present townsite. Griffith was designed in 1914 by American architect Walter Burley Griffin according to a radial design, with wide, tree-lined streets, ring roads and parks, although the plan was not strictly adhered to. Today, the surrounding wineries produce 80 per cent of New South Wales' and 20 per cent of Australia's wine grapes. Citrus fruit is the other major local product with valencia oranges the largest crop. Stone fruits, vegetables, wheat, cotton, sheep, wool, eggs and canola are also produced in quantity.

The main feature of Griffith is the enormous roundabout at the western end of Banna Avenue. Start east of this point, at the corner of Banna and Jondaryan avenues, where you will see, on a tall column, a Fairy Firefly fighter bomber. The plane stands as a tribute to those of the district who served in World War II. The nearby Dethridge Wheel is a memorial to the MIA pioneers. If you head west along Banna Avenue to the central hub you will pass, on your right, the Regional Art Gallery, CWA Park, and then, at the roundabout, the attractive courthouse (1928). The courthouse is in Memorial Park, which is also the site of the Griffith War Memorial.

2 PIONEER MEMORIAL VILLAGE

At the inner roundabout, turn left into Benerembah St and left again into Kooringal Ave. At its end, turn left into Animoo Ave. Take the second left into Wyangan Ave then the fourth right into Noorilla St. At the end of Noorilla St, the road veers left as Remembrance Drv. Follow Remembrance Drv and, just past this intersection, to the right, are Scenic Hill and Pioneer Memorial Village.

Pioneer Memorial Village, situated on 18ha of pleasant bushland, consists of about 40 old and replica buildings from the Riverina area. The souvenir shop is housed within the former Bynya Homestead (1879), with largely original timbers. There is an old school, church and shearing shed, large collections of horse-drawn vehicles, steam-powered machines and antiquated examples of working engines, farm machinery and newspaper printing machines. There is also a drop-log saddler's shop, Fairview cottage (1880) with its home-made nails and timbers dressed with broad axe and adze, Griffith's first hospital, Goolgowi railway station, Aboriginal canoe trees, a miniature lake and a picnic area.

3 SIR DUDLEY DECHAIR'S LOOKOUT

Return a short distance along Remembrance Drv and make a left turn into Scenic Drv.

Immediately to your right is Rotary Lookout. Further along Scenic Drive is Sir Dudley DeChair's Lookout, a natural rock formation which affords an interesting bird's-eye view of the way agriculture has developed around the town. Griffith is totally surrounded by orchards and vineyards. From here, or via the Narinari Loop Walking Track from Scenic Hill, it is possible to visit the fascinating Hermits Cave. The cave was built by Valerio Recitti, an Italian migrant who cleared and decorated the caves, creating massive stone galleries and pathways, cliffside gardens and floral painted rock walls. In order to remain unseen, Recitti worked at night and early in the morning, moving hundreds of tonnes of rock.

Yanco Agricultural High School.

4 BARELLAN

Return along Scenic Drv, turn right into Remembrance Drv and take the first left into Mallinson St. At its end turn left into Macarthur St, then turn left at the round-about into Wakaden St, which heads westwards to Barellan, 55km away.

Barellan is a quiet Riverina wheat town. It is a typical service centre supplying agricultural equipment and food for the surrounding area. The most distinctive building in town is the Commercial Hotel (1924), a large and gracious hotel with an impressive upper verandah.

The town's major claim to fame is that it is the birthplace of the famous Australian tennis player Evonne Cawley (nee Goolagong). Evonne attended Barellan Primary School before moving to Sydney, where she developed her world-class tennis-playing skills.

5 ARDLETHAN

Continue east from Barellan for 33km to Ardlethan.

Ardlethan is a small service town in the heart of the Riverina. It is claimed that its name is the Gaelic word for 'hilly'. The town came into existence when gold was discovered in the 19th century. Goldmining in the area was short-lived but the subsequent discovery of tin resulted in the establishment of a tin mine which, in its heyday, was the largest in the state. As mining declined the town became a service centre for the surrounding wheat and fat lamb properties. The town contends that it is the birthplace of the Australian kelpie breed of sheep dog. This fact is marked by a bronze memorial in Stewart Park.

6 NARRANDERA

Follow the Newell Hwy south for 42km and then west for another 22km to Narrandera.

The streets of Narrandera are lined with beautiful white cedar trees. The town has been declared an urban conservation area by the National Trust. As you enter town along the Newell Highway (Whitton Street), you will pass the railway station and stationmaster's residence (*c*.1885) on your right. Very close by, at the corner of Whitton and Arthur streets, is the former Railway Hotel which was built to take advantage of the through traffic at the station. The present building was erected in 1916 and is now a guesthouse.

7 NARRANDERA PARK

Follow the highway along Whitton St and turn left into Cadell St. After three blocks you will see Narrandera Park to your right.

Narrandera Park is fronted by the Big Playable Guitar, at nearly 6m. The guitar contains the local tourist information centre, the miniature zoo, Aboriginal canoe trees, Queensland bottle trees, playground equipment, electric barbecues, toilets and the Tiger Moth Memorial. The latter is an actual Tiger Moth aeroplane which serves as a tribute to the World War II trainee pilots who received elementary instruction on these planes in Narrandera between 1940 and 1945. A pamphlet outlining a walk that takes in the town's heritage buildings is available from the information centre.

Opposite the park, at the corner of Cadell and Twynam streets, is the Parkside Cottage Museum which is housed in a century-old building. Features include the Macarthur opera cloak, made in 1816 from the first bale of wool ever sent to England by the Macarthur family. There are also items from Scott's Antarctic Expedition.

8 YANCO

Drive south along Cadell St and turn right into Audley St. Take the fourth right into Hay St, which is sign-posted for Leeton. Yanco is 18km along this road.

Samuel McCaughey, who created the MIA, built a magnificent red-brick and sandstone mansion at North Yanco. At his bequest, the homestead and 400ac became the Yanco Agricultural High School. Situated 3km south of Yanco is a small lake with water birds and impressive gardens. Yanco Powerhouse was built in 1913 to drive McCaughey's irrigation scheme. Prior to its connection with the state power grid in 1950, the powerhouse used 10 000 tonnes of coal annually. Also in Yanco are McCaughey Aquatic Park—3.6ha of parkland with small lakes, bridges and a playground—and Waring Park in Main Street. Just east of Yanco is the main canal of the MIA at its widest point.

9 LEETON

Continue north for 5km to Leeton.

Following Walter Burley Griffin's design, Leeton is an orderly town with a concentration of Art Deco buildings, shady and tree-lined streets and 102ha of public recreation parks and reserves.

Today, Leeton is one of the largest fruit and vegetable growing regions in Australia. Sunburst Foods, the largest citrus producer in New South Wales, was formed at Leeton in 1974 when eight local citrus-growing families, unable to successfully market their fruit, combined to establish a juicing operation at Leeton. Tours of local plants can be organised through the visitors centre. Sunburst Juice Factory, on Brady Way, processes 40 000 tonnes of fruit a year and offers tours of the plant at 10:45am each weekday.

Leeton has 21 buildings listed with the NSW Art Deco Society Register. These are to be found along Kurrajong and Pine avenues. The buildings have rendered and elaborately sculptured parapets, suspended awnings with ornate ceilings, recessed doorways to shopfronts which feature curved display windows complete with leadlight glazing, and decorative ceramic tiling around front walls and entry porches. At the intersection of Kurrajong and Pine avenues is the war memorial and one of the town's most striking structures, the Roxy Theatre (1930). The Roxy numbers among the few remaining rural Australian movie palaces of the 1920s and is the town's finest example of Art Deco architecture.

Walk south along Wade Avenue until it terminates in Church Street. Standing

Empty shops in the main street of Barellan.

opposite the southern end of Wade Avenue is the courthouse (1924). Nearby, in Ash Street, is St Mary's convent (also 1924), opened by Melbourne's Archbishop Daniel Mannix in 1927.

10 WHITTON

Head west along the road to Griffith for 24km to reach Whitton.

Whitton is the oldest town in the Murrumbidgee Irrigation Area. It developed on one of the main routes used by teamsters moving people and goods into the south-west of the state. In 1881 a railway arrived and the town became a railhead. Four years later it was gazetted as Whitton after the first engineer of the New South Wales Railways. The courthouse and gaol museum is in Gogeldrie Street. The courthouse building dates from 1890 and houses early farming and irrigation equipment, photographs and other exhibits of local history. There is a lovely old steam-driven traction engine out the front. Other buildings of historical interest are the post office, with its original counters and safes; the McGaw Presbyterian Church (1900); and St John's Anglican Church (early 1890s).

At the northern outskirts of Whitton, take the left turn signposted for Griffith. Continue for 22km until the T-intersection. Turn right onto Olympic Way and it is 15km to the centre of Griffith.

The Fairy Firefly fighter bomber in Griffith.

CHAPTER 5
WAY OUT WEST

32 UP THE DARLING

■ DRIVING TOUR ■ 440KM ■ 1 DAY ■ DESERTS AND ANCIENT LAKES

Western New South Wales is part of Australia's vast central desert region. Here the rainfall is less than 250mm per year and the 'great grey plain' stretches to the horizon.

The inhabitants of New South Wales rarely acknowledge that nearly half of their state is, at best, marginal land and, at worst, desert. The far west of New South Wales is flat, scrubby land characterised by blistering hot summers and huge daily temperature ranges. Here, the Darling River carries the tropical rains from north Queensland down to water this inhospitable land.

1 WENTWORTH

Wentworth is an attractive old town whose history is inseparable from its position where the Murray and Darling rivers meet. The world's fourth largest river system, the Darling drains one-fifth of Australia. Explorer Charles Sturt arrived at the river junction in 1830 and identified the Darling as 'a new and beautiful stream coming apparently from the north'. He weighed anchor opposite a tree, which he marked. Sturt's Tree is located by the riverbank in Willow Bend Caravan Park, at the southern end of Darling Street.

The first houses at present-day Wentworth appeared about 1851. The future of the town was determined when William Randell's river steamer *Mary Ann* sailed from Mannum near Adelaide down the Murray past the Darling junction. He was pursued and overtaken by Francis Cadell's *Lady Augusta*. Randell and his wife moved to Wentworth and opened a small general store in 1856, and Cadell opened a trading store at the junction later that year.

The town soon became an important and commercially influential river port at the centre of the New South Wales, Victorian and South Australian river trade. Much of the wool clip of south-western New South Wales found its way via bullock, donkey and camel wagon to Wentworth. A wharf was erected by 1860. By the time Wentworth was declared a municipality in 1879, it was the busiest inland port in Australia. In 1895, 485 vessels were recorded as passing through the customs house with a record 31 in one week alone.

2 WENTWORTH GAOL AND WENTWORTH MUSEUM

Start from the corner of Francis and Beverley sts.
The old Wentworth Gaol is considered the state's best example of a small Victorian gaol. It was built in 1879–1891 of one million locally made bricks with bluestone

trim from Victoria and slate brought from Wales as ship's ballast. Wentworth Gaol was a small but notoriously harsh prison with 45cm thick walls, lookout towers, a stretching rack, a whipping stool, stocks, and shackles set into a boulder in the unshaded centre of the courtyard. The gaol closed down in 1929. Today it houses the Morrison collection of antique bottles, gemstones, minerals and Australiana and a statue of Harry Nanya, his partner and their child. Harry Nanya, who died about 1880, was one of the last full-blooded, free-roaming Aborigines of the local tribe.

On the other side of Beverley Street is the Wentworth Museum with exhibits of 3000 items, including fossil remnants found at Perry Sandhills of extinct Australian megafauna. Of special interest are the diprotodon—a sort of giant wombat—and a giant kangaroo.

3 LOCK NUMBER 10

Head south on Beverley St to the T-intersection. Turn right into Cadell St and drive to its end.
Lock Number 10 and Weir was built in 1929. There is also a boat ramp here. Opposite is the town cemetery. The river system is ideal for powerboating, fishing, rowing, waterskiing and houseboats.

4 THE PADDLE-STEAMER *RUBY*

Return along Cadell St. Turn left, back into Beverley St and then right, back into Sandwych St. Proceed across the bridge over the Darling River to Fotherby Park.
Located in Fotherby Park are the old court-house building (a slab cottage) and the dry-docked paddle-steamer *Ruby*, near the

junction of the Darling River and Tuckers Creek. One of the last steamboats engaged in the passenger and cargo trade, *Ruby* is currently being restored and will be moved to a position alongside the new wharf.

5 MUNGO NATIONAL PARK

Travel east on the Silver City Hwy for about 25km. Just before you reach the outskirts of Buronga, turn left

The Menindee pub.

The great grey plain between Wilcannia and Menindee.

into Arumpo Rd, which is unsealed, and follow the signposts for 103km.

Mungo National Park is a 14 000ha archaeological site of world importance. Lake Mungo is one of 17 dry lakes that constitute the Willandra Lakes World Heritage Area, declared in 1981. The desolate and sometimes eerie landscape of sand, sparse but resurgent vegetation, and the spiny, hard, pitted, crinkled and fluted dunes and ridges can look more like a moonscape.

About 25 000 to 45 000 years ago, the lake was one of a series of freshwater lakes along Willandra Creek. The lakes dried up about 14 000 years ago and are an extraordinarily rich source of fossils. The remains of extinct creatures—Tasmanian tigers; giant, short-faced kangaroos; and a strange oxen-sized animal called a Zygomaturus—have been found. Carbon dating has indicated that Aborigines inhabited the area 40 000 years ago, making it the site of the oldest known human occupation in Australia. From the lake they gathered mussels, Murray cod and golden perch. They also hunted wallabies and rat kangaroos and collected emu eggs. A 26 000-year-old grave contains the earliest known human example of cremation. After the ritual incineration the bones were smashed and deposited in a hole by the pyre.

Today, the pre-European vegetation is returning. Birdlife is increasing, particularly pink cockatoos and chats and the striking mulga parrot. There are also kangaroos, emus and lizards. The visitors centre, open every day, is located near the park entrance. It contains extensive displays of local Aboriginal culture and the area's geomorphology and archaeology, plus an audio-visual room. There is a 65km, self-drive tour through the park which is easily managed by family cars. The drive includes 15 stops, each with signposted information. It will take you to the Mungo woolshed, the Walls of China, the Grand Canyon, Belah campground, an old squatter's hut, the remnants of Cobb & Co coach tracks at Vigars Wells where the teams stopped for water, the viewing area at Lake Leaghur and the ruins of Zanci station.

6 POONCARIE

From the park there is a road that heads due west, via Top Hut, for 54km. At the T-intersection turn right, and it is 29km to Pooncarie.

Pooncarie has been known as The Port by locals since the days when it was a staging place for the river steamers that began plying the Darling River in 1858 en route for Menindee and Wilcannia. Today there is only a hotel, a store, the post office and several dozen inhabitants. However, Pooncarie still hosts what is thought of as one of the better race meetings in the region every October.

7 MENINDEE

Continue north along the good-quality unsealed road for 123km to Menindee.

Menindee is a tiny settlement surrounded by citrus orchards, vegetable cultivation and some 20 lakes fed by the Darling River. It is a strange experience to drive through such marginal land that you wonder whether it ever rains and to suddenly come across vast freshwater lakes full of dead trees and surrounded by sand, saltbush and inhospitable red soils.

The lakes were previously an unreliable source of water, spreading out during flood periods and disappearing when the river level dropped. Now that the flow is controlled by a water storage scheme, the current storage capacity is 1 794 000 megalitres, three and a half times the volume of Sydney Harbour and covering eight times its area. The purpose of the scheme is the provision of regulated flows for water supply and irrigation. A pipeline running from Menindee provides Broken Hill with a regular supply of water.

Captain Francis Cadell, who pioneered the operation of river steamers along the Murray, established a store near the hotel at Menindee in 1856. It was named Wurtindelly after the Aboriginal word for the sand ridges on which it was built. These two buildings became the nucleus around which the town grew.

8 KINCHEGA NATIONAL PARK

Drive north for 1km to the signposted turn-off on the left to Kinchega National Park.

The 44 000ha national park extends westwards from the Darling River. It includes river red gum forests, blacksoil flood plains along the Darling River where kangaroos and emu flocks are frequently seen, the varied and colourful vegetation of the red sandhills and sand plains, and a series of tall lunettes (crescent-shaped dunes) on the eastern side of the lakes created by a combination of westerly winds and waves. The lakes are home to a variety of waterbirds, including pelicans, spoonbills, egrets, cormorants and swans. The best time to see the wildlife is at dawn or dusk.

Kinchega woolshed is still standing. Here, 6 million sheep were shorn over the course of a century. At its peak in the 1880s, the woolshed had stands for 26 blade shearers. The remains of the homestead and cemetery are nearby.

9 WILCANNIA

Continue north-west towards Broken Hill for 16km. To your right is a signposted dirt road which will take you north-east to Wilcannia, 138km away.

Wilcannia experiences an average annual rainfall of 252mm. The settlement of the area by Victorian pastoralists began in the 1850s, and by 27 January 1859 the steamer *Albury* had made its way up the river to Wilcannia. The township reached its height in the 1880s when it boasted 13 hotels and a population of 3000 inhabitants. If you take the road down to the river's edge you will have an excellent view of the old centre-lift bridge which was built in 1896 and is now classified by the National Trust. The wharf, dating from the 1870s, can be seen from the bridge.

Turn south into Reid Street just near the bridge and you will notice the beautiful post office (1880) and its attached residence which continue to serve the local community. The Club Hotel on the other side of Reid Street dates from 1879 and is built on the site of the town's first hotel after it burnt down. On the other side of the highway is the Knox and Downs Store (1899) and, further east along Reid Street, on the river side of the road, is the Athenaeum Library (1883), now a museum. Just on the other side of Byrnes Street is the London Bank building (1890), now used as the Central Darling Shire Offices. At the western end of Reid Street is the Courthouse Hotel (1879) and, alongside, the old warehouse (1878) which backed onto the river. Across the road is the impressive courthouse (1880), next to the old maximum security prison, now the police station (1881), and the police residence (1880), all built of locally quarried sandstone and designed by colonial architect James Barnet.

The journey finishes in Wilcannia.

33 BROKEN HILL, SILVERTON AND THE BREAKERS

■ WALKING AND DRIVING TOUR ■ 72KM ■ 6 HOURS ■ MINES, MOVIES AND DESERT COUNTRY

Mining towns surrounded by desert are typical of the north-west corner of New South Wales. Here, on the edge of the desert, mineral riches are found and processed.

Broken Hill is a remarkable and unusual township on the edge of the desert. Known as the Silver City, it has been Australia's great silver, lead and zinc mining town. Like mining towns the world over, Broken Hill is characterised by a rough-and-tumble charm. The city has elegant buildings amid the pits and slag heaps. Only a few kilometres from Broken Hill, the great grey plains of western New South Wales give way to desert. The location has been a popular one for movies, where the outback provides a character of its own making.

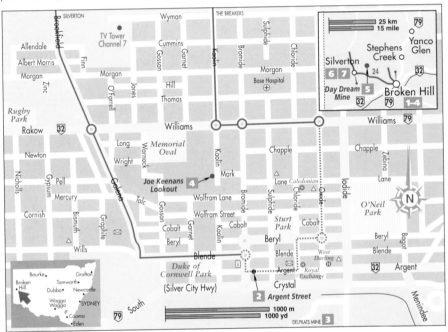

1 BROKEN HILL

Broken Hill, or the Silver City as it is sometimes called, has always been associated with silver, lead and zinc mining. Many of the streets are named after metals, minerals and compounds. The town is also the centre of the 16-million ha West Darling pastoral industry, which has 1.75 million wool-producing merino sheep.

The earliest known inhabitants of the area are said to be the Willyama people, although, with no permanent water supply in the area, their presence was only intermittent. The first Europeans to see the Barrier Range were the explorer Charles Sturt and his party in 1844. Sturt was endeavouring to determine the existence of an inland sea. Pastoralists followed in the wake of Sturt in the 1850s, and much local land was taken up in 1864. Goods were shipped up the Darling via river steamer and then hauled overland by bullock teams.

It wasn't until 1883, after the discovery of silver in the area, that Charles Rasp, a boundary rider at Mount Gipps station, discovered what he thought were tin deposits at the 'broken hill'. The samples he took contained silver chloride. A syndicate of seven was set up with the object of purchasing the surrounding land to prevent a rush from other miners. In January 1885, the syndicate hit a rich vein of silver in what turned out to be one of the world's largest known silver-lead-zinc lodes. The ore body was a continuous arc 7km long and 220m wide. Later that year they decided to form and float shares in the Broken Hill Proprietary Company (BHP), which was to become Australia's biggest and most powerful public company.

2 ARGENT STREET

Argent St is Broken Hill's main thoroughfare. From the corner of Argent and Bromide sts, proceed north for one block to the roundabout at the corner of Bromide and Blende sts, where the information centre is located. The information centre will provide a map and pamphlet to accompany a signposted heritage walking tour that takes in the many outstanding heritage buildings now listed by the National Trust. Most of the notable buildings are in Argent Street.

Return along Bromide Street to Argent Street and then turn left into Sulphide Street. The most impressive of Broken Hill's historic hotels is the large, three-storey Palace Hotel (1889) with its lengthy verandahs and elaborate cast-iron balustrades. It was used in the Australian movie *Priscilla, Queen of the Desert*. Diagonally opposite is the unpretentious courthouse (1889), designed by colonial architect James Barnet. In the grounds is a sculptured bronze war memorial made by noted artist Charles Webb who died one week before its public unveiling in 1925.

Next door, in Argent Street, is the Federation-style technical college (1900–1901) with its large, arched windows and ornamented entrance. Built to meet the needs of the mining industry, the college now also houses a museum. Adjacent to the college is the modest police station (1890). It replaced an earlier tin shed in which the prisoners were chained to the flooring joists, although if a female prisoner was being held they were chained to the station fence outside. The next building, as you continue along Argent Street, is the town's architectural

Peter Brown's Bush Artist Gallery in Silverton.

Pro Hart's gigantic ant at Broken Hill.

highlight, the extraordinarily ornate town hall (1890–1891).

Adjacent, at the corner with Chloride Street, is the red-brick post office (1890–1892), again designed by James Barnet, with its massive turret capped by a decorative mansard roof and enveloped by a footpath verandah and corner balcony.

3 DELPRATS UNDERGROUND TOURIST MINE

Return to the information centre. Drive along to Argent St, heading east, past the post office, to the corner of Argent and Iodide sts. Turn right, cross over the railway line and turn right following the signs to Delprats Underground Tourist Mine.

The town's mining history can be experienced first-hand at Delprats Underground Tourist Mine. This two-hour tour will take you deep inside one of BHP's old mines in a cage with miner's hat and light. The tours are held at 10.30am on weekdays and at 2.00pm on Saturdays.

4 JOE KEENANS LOOKOUT

Return along Iodide St, turn left into Argent St and then right into Bromide St. Continue north for 1km and turn left into Marks St, where you will find Joe Keenans Lookout.

There is a fine view of the town and the mine dumps plus information boards on the town's history at Joe Keenans Lookout. This is the best place in Broken Hill to get an overview of the town and the mine. The information board explains what the mining operation looked like at its zenith.

5 DAY DREAM MINE

At the end of Marks St, turn right into Kaolin St and then left at the roundabout into Williams St. After five blocks turn right into Brookfield Ave, which becomes the Silverton Rd. About 20km from Broken Hill is a signposted right turn. From here it is 13km to Day Dream Mine.

It is possible to experience a sense of what life was like for the miners of the late 19th century at the old Day Dream Mine, which opened in 1882. The tour takes one hour. You can make a booking at the visitors centre or simply turn up any time between 10.00am and 3.30pm, seven days a week.

6 SILVERTON

Return to the Silverton Rd and turn right, continuing on for 3km to Silverton.

Silverton is a fascinating place. Once a thriving mining centre with a population of 3000 inhabitants, it is now a virtual ghost town with a number of historic buildings, several art galleries, museums and a pub.

Prospectors began working in the area in 1867 after a false report of a gold find by a local station hand. In 1875, two men hit a lode of silver while drilling a well on Thackaringa station, south of present-day Silverton. In 1881, John Stokie established the Umberumberka claim. Miners and prospectors began to arrive, especially from the declining copper fields of South Australia. A settlement, initially known as Umberumberka, emerged 2km south-west of

View across Broken Hill from Joe Keenans Lookout.

the present township. It consisted of a store, a hotel and two boarding houses to cater for a population of 150. The town centre gradually shifted and was named Silverton in 1883 when a survey took place. Slap-dash huts of iron and canvas began to proliferate. In 1884, 6000 tonnes of ore were extracted, three-quarters of it being sent to South Australia for processing.

Silverton's geographic isolation was an added expense. The Day Dream Mine, to the north-west, opened in 1883 and a settlement of 400–500 people formed around that site. The discovery of a huge lode at Broken Hill soon began to draw the population away. By 1888, Silverton was down to 1700 people and dwindled to 286 by 1901. Umberumberka Mine closed in 1892, Day Dream was abandoned in the 1890s and Thackaringa Mine closed in 1897. Today, fewer than 100 people remain in Silverton and most of them cater to tourism.

7 SILVERTON HERITAGE TRAIL

As you drive into Silverton from Broken Hill, you will cross Blackhill Creek and enter Burke St. Take the second left into Loftus St and proceed up the hill.

To the left is the old school building which served as an educational centre between 1885 and 1970. At the top of the hill is the Catholic Church (1886), which is now an artists' studio. Return along Loftus Street a short distance and turn left into Canopus Street To the left is the old masonic lodge (1885). The construction was paid for by Charles Rasp, one of first lodge members.

Continue along Canopus Street, turn right into Layard Street and proceed to Sturt Street. Sturt Street is the route along which the now dismantled railway ran. On the corner is the only person in Australia who has a licence to deface the currency. Andy is a coin carver who fashions money into interesting pieces of jewellery.

Turn right, into Sturt Street. On the right is the old Methodist Church, built as a Presbyterian Church in 1885. As the Wesleyans greatly outnumbered the Presbyterians, the Presbyterians sold their church

to them when the Wesleyan Church was destroyed by a tempest in 1891.

Return to Layard Street and continue to the Silverton Hotel at the Burke Street corner. Silverton has recently become a haven for film-makers looking to capture the spirit of the outback. The town has been the setting for *Wake in Fright*, *Mad Max 2*, *A Town Like Alice*, *Hostage*, *Razorback*, *Journey into Darkness* and *Golden Soak*, as well as many commercials and documentaries. One prominent feature in these films is the Silverton Hotel (1885), built to house the town's postal service which was established in 1883. A photographic collection bears witness to the hotel's place in Australia's film history. This is a pub with lots of character and a wry humour typical of Australia.

Turn right into Burke Street. To your right is the Silverton Pioneer Museum. Open daily, the museum features an outdoor display of farm equipment, including carts, wagons, engines, tools and machinery from the old sheep stations, all located in a garden setting. The indoor collection contains minerals, shells and Aboriginal rock carvings. The building is also home to an opal shop. Over the road are the old municipal chambers (1889).

At the corner of Burke and Loftus streets is the town's second gaol. The original gaol was a timber and iron building. When New South Wales Chief Justice Sir Frederick Darley visited Silverton in 1888, he was appalled at the conditions the inmates had to endure. Twenty-two men were crammed into four small cells and secured at night in leg irons, regardless of whether or not they had been tried. The present gaol was erected in 1889 but was soon superseded by facilities at Broken Hill. It became an overnight lock-up in 1892, a boys' reformatory in the 1930s and was closed altogether in 1943.

Broken Hill and Silverton are also home to a substantial artistic community and there are several galleries in town, all open on a daily basis.

Return along Silverton Rd to Broken Hill (23km).

34 THE DESERT CIRCUIT

■ DRIVING TOUR ■ 619KM ■ 2 DAYS ■ OUTBACK DESERT AND SCRUB

Arguably the best and total Australian experience is this desert circuit which includes the underground mines at White Cliffs, the desert lakes at Menindee, the Darling River port of Wilcannia and the starkness of Mootwingee National Park.

There is an argument that anyone wanting to experience the full range of magic and beauty of the Australian outback would have trouble improving on the circuit from Broken Hill which takes in the inland lakes around Menindee, the 19th-century river port at Wilcannia, the unusual opal-mining town of White Cliffs and the great desert national park at Mootwingee. Within this circuit are all the elements of the outback, and they are all within relatively easy reach of Broken Hill.

1 SUNSET STRIP

From Broken Hill, turn off Argent St into Menindee Rd and head south-east for about 87km to the signposted right turn to Sunset Strip (2km).

The Menindee lake system has become a tourist attraction and recreational facility for the people of Broken Hill, who drive nearly 100km to gaze out upon a muddy lake full of dead trees in a rather odd version of a waterfront resort. Instead of the 'luxury villas' of the coastal resorts, here are inexpensive, kit-type holiday homes where corrugated iron is more common than brick. While the well-irrigated gardens are attractive, the exteriors of the houses are ordinary.

2 COPI HOLLOW

Return to the Menindee Rd and continue south for about 7km. Just after you cross the interconnecting channel between Lake Menindee and Pamamaroo Lake there is a signposted left turn on an all-weather road which leads to Copi Hollow.

Copi Hollow, between Menindee Lake and Pamamaroo Lake, is an artificially con-structed interconnection developed for speedboats, sailing, swimming and water-skiing. The inland speed championships are held here each year in mid-May. There is a well-shaded shoreline park with picnic and barbecue facilities, amenities block and a caravan park.

3 PAMAMAROO LAKE

Return to the Menindee Rd. About 5km from the Copi Hollow turn-off is another signposted turn-off on the left to Pamamaroo Lake and the main weir.

Recreational facilities are available at Lake Pamamaroo and at the main weir, where a plaque on a tree indicates the location of the Burke and Wills campsite. The water in Menindee Lake can get very cold and wind squalls can produce dangerous waves. The extensive waterways around Menindee make the area one of the finest freshwater fishing locations in New South Wales.

4 MENINDEE

Return to the main road and continue south for 8km to Menindee.

Menindee is a tiny settlement surrounded by citrus orchards, vegetable cultivation and some 20 lakes fed by the Darling River. It is a strange experience to drive through such marginal land that you wonder whether it ever rains and to suddenly come across vast fresh-water lakes full of dead trees and surrounded by sand, saltbush and inhospitable red soils.

The first settler and hence the effective founder of Menindee was Tom Pain and his family, who arrived in 1852, determined to establish a home and business on the river. He opened the Menindee Hotel the following year. With numerous additions the hotel has remained open and is considered the second-oldest hotel still in continuous operation in New South Wales. It is now known as Maidens Menindee Hotel for the simple reason that it was owned in 1896–1979, by the Maiden family. Burke and Wills stayed at the Maidens Hotel, where you can still see the arrow the explorers carved in the doorpost to indicate the direction their journey would pursue.

One of the people who waited at Cooper Creek while Burke and Wills attempted to

Menindee Lake at sunset.

get to the north coast of the continent was Dost Mahomet, an Afghan camel driver. After losing an arm in a camel-related accident Mahomet settled in Menindee and worked in the bakery of William Ah Chung, who established one of the first market gardens in town. Mahomet's grave is located about 1km out of town on the road towards Broken Hill. Ah Chung's bakehouse (c.1880), is still standing in Menindee Street. It currently houses an art gallery.

5 WILCANNIA

Continue north-west towards Broken Hill for 16km. To your right is a signposted dirt road which will take you north-east to Wilcannia, 138km away.

Wilcannia experiences an average annual rainfall of 252mm. The settlement of the area by Victorian pastoralists began in the 1850s, and by 27 January 1859 the steamer *Albury* had made its way up the river to Wilcannia. The township reached its height in the 1880s when it boasted 13 hotels and a population of 3000 inhabitants. If you take the road down to the river's edge you will get an excellent view of the old centre-lift bridge which was built in 1896 and is now classified by the National Trust. The wharf, dating from the 1870s, can be seen from the bridge.

Turn south into Reid Street just near the bridge and you will notice the beautiful post office (1889) and its attached residence which continue to serve the local community. The Club Hotel on the other side of Reid Street dates from 1879 and is built on the site of the town's first hotel after it burnt down. On the other side of the highway is the Knox and Downs Store (1899) and, further east along Reid Street, on the river side of the road, is the Athenaeum Library (1883), now a museum. Just on the other side of Byrnes Street is the London Bank building (1890), now used as the Central Darling Shire offices. At the western end of Reid Street is the Courthouse Hotel (1879) and, alongside, the old warehouse (1878) which backed onto the river. Across the road is the impressive courthouse (1880), next to the old maximum security prison, now the police station (1881), and the police residence (1880), all built of locally quarried sandstone and designed by colonial architect James Barnet.

6 WHITE CLIFFS

From Wilcannia, take the signposted turn-off north to White Cliffs, 93km away.

White Cliffs has an average annual rainfall of 234mm. Arriving in White Cliffs is like arriving in any opal-mining settlement. It is immediately obvious that every regular activity comes a bad last to the one thing that drives the town—seeking a fortune. The pub is dusty and lonely, the general store is small and simple, the roads are rough and unsealed, the settlement is spread in every direction, and the attempts at civilisation are crude and simplistic.

Opals were found in the area as early as 1884, but it wasn't until 1889 that any real

Wilcannia's historic Post Office.

interest was shown. The year 1889 was one of drought and four kangaroo shooters were hired to reduce their numbers on the Momba Pastoral Company station. The roo shooters found opals and, realising their potential value, sent them off to Adelaide for valuation. William Johnstone arrived in 1892 and set up the first store and hotel.

The real growth of the town did not occur until 1893, when news of some good finds drew miners to the area. By 1897, the population of White Cliffs had grown to about 1000 people. Building materials were scarce and expensive, however, and the heat in summer was oppressive. Consequently, about 1894, miners started converting their old shafts into homes. As the hills were solid sandstone rather than earth, the dugouts were in no danger of collapsing and the temperature inside was constant. Today, the town's population is around 200 and this number rises to about 500 in winter when gem-seekers come from the south. In 1987, the production of opals from the White Cliffs fields was valued at $150 million.

A heritage trail has been created to direct you to a dozen significant sites around town. The trail includes the Bill O'Reilly Oval (turn right at the pub), which is nothing but hard red dirt. It must be one of the easiest ovals in Australia on which to score a boundary. Bill O'Reilly's father was the town's first schoolteacher and the great cricketer is the town's most famous son. St Mary's Anglican Church standing forlornly on a dusty back road behind the general store. It is common in the late afternoon to see kangaroos standing opposite the church. The White Cliffs Dug-Out is a superbly appointed underground motel that will never get the star rating it deserves because it has communal toilet and shower facilities.

7 MOOTWINGEE NATIONAL PARK

Head west from White Cliffs on the unsealed dry-weather road for 42km and then turn left and head south-west towards Broken Hill. After 86km there is a signposted left turn to Mootwingee National Park and the park office.

Mootwingee National Park is located on a rocky, cypress pine and mulga-clad red-sandstone range. The wildlife includes falcons and wedge-tailed eagles, euros, skinks, frogs, snakes, emus, kangaroos and lizards. There are numerous self-guided walks of varying length and difficulty through shaded gullies, open ridges, dry sandy creek beds, historic Aboriginal and European sites, pleasant rock pools and some truly splendid scenery.

The park's 5-million-year-old quartzite and sandstone gorges have acted as water catchments and provide a reliable source of water. Consequently, the reserve contains Aboriginal material dating back some 40 000 years, including paintings, stone arrangements and other artefacts. Mootwingee Historic Site has some particularly impressive rock engravings and ochre stencils—created by blowing mouthfuls of pigment over the hand—together with explanations of relevant aspects of Aboriginal mythology. Access to this site is by guided tour only, of about two and a half hours duration, on Wednesday and Saturday mornings from April to November at 11.00am. There is a small fee associated with this tour, which also takes in the Mootwingee Cultural Resource Centre. Alternatively, you can follow the self-guided Homestead Creek Track which also takes in significant Aboriginal sites.

The Old Coach Road Drive (10km long) takes in the ruins of Rockholes Hotel, Gnalta Lookout and some amazing rock formations. The Thaaklatjika Mingkana Walk includes Wrights Cave, named after William Wright, the one-time manager of Kinchega station, who was hired as part of the Burke and Wills expedition at Menindee because of his knowledge of the local area. The cave contains Aboriginal artwork as well as a blue triangle painted by Wright with his initials inside.

Return to the main road and continue south-west towards Broken Hill. It is 68km until you reach a T-intersection with the Silver City Hwy. Turn left and follow the highway for 53km reach Broken Hill.

CHAPTER 6
THE CENTRAL COAST

35 AROUND BROKEN BAY

■ DRIVING TOUR ■ 155KM ■ 1 DAY ■ QUIET BEACHES AND SLEEPY WEEKEND RETREATS

To the north of Sydney lies Broken Bay which is edged by a series of attractive and peaceful holiday beach resort villages.

No matter which way you head from Sydney, you will always find holiday attractions, bushwalks and plenty of accommodation catering for the unceasing desire to escape from the city. The area to the north of the city has particular appeal because, since the 1940s, it has been a popular retirement destination. Consequently, the combination of quiet waters and attractive beaches sees tens of thousands of Sydneysiders heading north every weekend. They are greeted by attractions and destinations designed for relaxation.

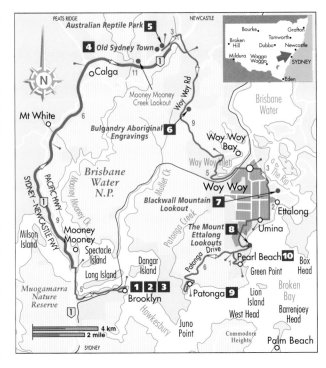

1 BROOKLYN

From Hornsby, follow the old Pacific Hwy north for 22km and turn right onto the Brooklyn Rd just before you cross the Peats Ferry Bridge over the Hawkesbury. If you're on the freeway, cross over the bridge and take the Brooklyn/Mooney Mooney Exit on your left. Turn right at the T-intersection and double back across the bridge to the southern side, and turn left into Brooklyn Rd.

Brooklyn is a small riverside settlement occupying the narrow strip of land between the river's southern bank and the extensive surrounding bushland. The township was created in 1884 when the Fagan brothers subdivided their 100ac grant. By the early 20th century the Hawkesbury had become a major destination of holiday-making Sydneysiders. Visitors travelled upriver in fishing boats armed with fishing rods and prawn bait.

2 HAWKESBURY RIVER MARINA

Drive to the end of Brooklyn Rd (about 4km) and turn left into Dangar Rd, which leads you to the Hawkesbury River Marina.

The main places to go in Brooklyn are the marina and McKell Park. Both are located at the north-eastern tip of the settlement, where there are wharves, two slipways, a chandlery, restaurant, water taxi service and ferry service.

3 MCKELL PARK

A driveway leads past the marina to a large car park, beyond which is McKell Park.

McKell Park has two tiers. Walk up the steps to the upper level. On the southern side is a view down to Parsley Bay where there is a good concrete boat ramp and car park, at the end of George Street. Also on the upper level are picnic, barbecue and playground facilities and, at the eastern end, a short walk to a modest lookout over the Hawkesbury and across to Dangar Island. Walk down the steps by the lookout to the bottom tier to more picnic, barbecue and playground facilities.

4 OLD SYDNEY TOWN

Return to the Pacific Hwy and continue north for about 15km to the signposted turn-off on the left which leads directly to the car park for Old Sydney Town.

Old Sydney Town is a carefully researched theme park with street theatre based on colonial history. It is essentially an attempt to re-create Sydney *circa* 1800, including Sydney Cove, the Tank Stream (Sydney's initial freshwater source), soldiers' huts and other rudimentary buildings with thatched or shingled roofs in a bush setting. There are a large number of actors in period costume, re-enacting daily life with all of its chores. There is a courtroom scene, a classroom, a pistol duel, floggings, working bullock drays that will take you to the nearby animal park, soldiers, convicts, tradespeople, old inns serving contemporary recipes, a windmill, church, a gaol and Lieutenant Dawe's Observatory, all carefully re-created just as they stood at Sydney Cove.

5 AUSTRALIAN REPTILE PARK AND WILDLIFE SANCTUARY

Adjacent to Old Sydney Town is the Australian Reptile Park and Wildlife Sanctuary.

Located in a bushland setting, the reptile park has Australia's largest reptile collection of alligators, lizards, crocodiles, giant galapagos turtles, kangaroos, koalas, platypus,

Historic houses at Old Sydney Town.

echidnas, Tasmanian devils, emus, dingoes and snakes. On display are alligator handling, the feeding of enormous Eric the Croc, reptile demonstrations, a platypusary, a noctarium and the milking of snakes—the venom is distributed throughout the world for the creation of antivenenes and for use in research. There are picnic and barbecue areas, a nature walk, playground, swimming pool and kiosk.

6 BULGANDRY ABORIGINAL ENGRAVINGS

Return to the Pacific Hwy and continue north for 500m to the T-intersection. Turn right into Wisemans Ferry Rd and drive to the next T-intersection. Turning left into what is an extension of the Pacific Hwy. Follow the highway for about 1.2km and turn right into Woy Woy Rd. A further 2.7km along is a signposted turn-off to the visitors' car park for the Bulgandry Aboriginal Engravings site.

It is a short walk from the car park to the flat rock surface. A pathway has been constructed around the circumference of the site for optimum viewing and minimal damage to the engravings. There are good information boards nearby which look at what is known of the Guringgai people and the etchings.

The figures are of men, women, marine life, kangaroos and canoes. Although a good surviving example of Aboriginal engravings, erosion has taken its toll and the figures are sometimes indistinct, however, the information boards are helpful in providing clarity. The engravings are clearest at dawn or dusk, or after rain. It is a further 2km drive to Staples Lookout, on the left, which offers a commanding view eastwards over the park to Woy Woy Bay.

7 BLACKWALL MOUNTAIN LOOKOUT

Follow Woy Woy Rd for 7km. At the T-intersection, turn right into Rawson Rd and follow it to its end. Turn right into Edward St and take the immediate left into Allfield Rd, then turn right into Blackwall Rd. After 900m, take the turn-off to the left. The high embankment on your right is the edge of Blackwall Mountain. To access the lookout you must take the first right into Bayview Cres. Near its end is a right turn into another roadway.

The walk from this point to Blackwall Mountain Lookout is steep but relatively short. Just past the water tank the road forks. Take the left track. The lookout provides a good view to the south. The geometric layout of residential East Ettalong is below. The roar of the traffic is at odds with the tranquillity of Brisbane Water which lies beyond the suburb and the densely forested shoreline of Wagstaff on the other side. Close your eyes and imagine how it looked before white settlement.

8 THE MOUNT ETTALONG LOOKOUTS

Head back down Bayview Crescent and turn left into Blackwall Rd, then left into Memorial Ave. The next left is into Maitland Bay Rd. At its end turn right into Picnic Pde and then right into The Esplanade. Follow the shoreline for 1km and turn right into Kourung St. Take the second left down Barrenjoey Rd and turn right at

The wharf at Patonga Beach.

the roundabout into West St. At its end, the road bends to the left as Sydney Ave. Follow Sydney Ave around to the right, where it becomes Hobart Ave, and then take the sharp left into Mount Ettalong Rd. Continue for 3km to the signposted turn-off to the left onto Patonga Drv, which will take you to the Mount Ettalong lookouts.

The Mount Ettalong lookouts are the finest on the entire western shore of Brisbane Water. Probably the best view to be had is by walking immediately east of the road's end, towards the cliff face. Immediately below is Pearl Beach. Beyond that it is easy to see Green Point at its southern end, then a desultory strip of beach. South of that the land ends at the estuary of the Hawkesbury, which lies at the western end of Broken Bay. The views over the bay, usually dotted with white sails, are excellent. Lion Island lies in the middle. The land to the far left with the lighthouse is Barrenjoey Head.

Note the unusual honeycombed weathering of the sandstone at the lookout, created largely by windblown sand particles. The official lookouts lie a short distance to the north of the car park. Just follow the signs. The northernmost lookout faces northwards up Ocean Beach to Ettalong and Wagstaff. From here, the shallowness of Brisbane Water is apparent from waves breaking offshore over the shoals and sandbars. To the east is Brisbane Water National Park. A directional plate indicates various locations in the distance and how far away they are.

9 PATONGA

Return to Patonga Drv and turn left. It is about 5.2km to Patonga.

Patonga is the southernmost beach on the Central Coast. The waters are calm because of its sheltered location within a recessed bay, making it a good beach for family bathing. There is a wharf, a boat ramp and a children's play area. Brisk Bay faces in a south-easterly direction across to West Head, Pittwater and Barrenjoey. Follow Patonga Drive to the roundabout with the war memorial set in the middle of the circle.

Turn left into Bay Road which will take you to the southern tip of the Patonga peninsula where there is a caravan park.

10 PEARL BEACH

Return along Bay Rd and Patonga Drv. After 5km (about 200m before the turn-off to the Mount Ettalong lookouts) turn right into Pearl Beach Rd, which winds its way down the mountainside to the beach. Turn right into Diamond Rd just before the road's end. Any of the next three lefts will take you to Pearl Pde by the waterfront, where there is a reserve, picnic and barbecue area, children's playground and tidal baths.

Pearl Beach is true to its name. Here the residences more effectively blend with the vegetation, which has been left relatively intact and is noticeably greener and lusher than elsewhere on the western shoreline. The houses are less obtrusive and in a finer balance with the environment so that the area appears as bushland with houses rather than houses with a bit of bush. The fishing is said to be good off the rocks for jewfish and tailor.

Head back along Pearl Beach Rd and turn right into Patonga Drv. Return the way you came along Mount Ettalong Rd and Barrenjoey Rd for as far as you can go, then drive through the roundabout and continue north on Memorial Ave. At the T-intersection, turn left into Blackwall Rd. Continue along Blackwell Rd to its end and turn right into Brisbane Water Drv which leads, after 8km, to the Pacific Hwy. Turn left and, after 5km, turn left again, onto the freeway. From here it is 38km to Hornsby.

Pearl Beach in summertime.

36 AROUND BRISBANE WATER

■ DRIVING TOUR ■ 75KM ■ 1 DAY ■ BEACHES AND BEAUTIFUL COASTLINE

Beachside holiday resorts, glorious sandy beaches with excellent surfing and small villages are all a part of the attraction of the state's Central Coast.

*I*n summertime the area around Brisbane Water is pure holiday magic. There are small boats on the water and the shoreline is sprinkled with anglers tossing their lines in, hoping to catch something for lunch or dinner. The beaches are popular haunts for swimmers, sun-lovers, families and holiday-makers, and, for those wanting to get fit, there are some excellent bushwalks in Boudi National Park and around the edges of this glorious stretch of water.

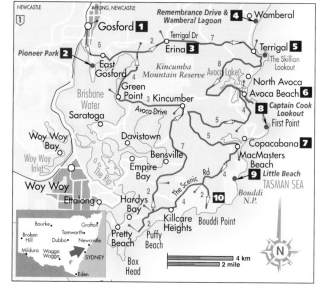

1 GOSFORD

The Gosford Visitors Information Centre is located on the corner of Mann St and Burns Crescent, adjacent to the train station. The centre is clearly signposted and the obvious place to start an investigation of the area.

Located at the northern end of Brisbane Water, Gosford is the region's commercial and administrative centre. The area around Gosford is characterised by steep hills and valleys with extensive state forests to the west and north-west and the Tuggerah Lakes to the north. Tourism, orchards, poultry, prawning, fishing, oysters, plant nurseries and retirees form the basis of the local economy, although many residents commute to Sydney.

The first white settlers to the area were drawn by the local supplies of cedar, forest oak, blue gum and other hardwoods. In the 1880s tourism got under way, particularly with the completion of the Sydney to Newcastle railway in 1889 and a new focus on leisure and health in the national culture. The Central Coast quickly became a primary tourism destination of Sydneysiders with fishing serving as the main attraction, although sightseeing and hunting were also popular. Holiday homes began to appear. With the construction of the freeway in the 1960s and the improvement of the rail service in the 1970s, Gosford has virtually become a part of metropolitan Sydney.

2 PIONEER PARK

Head south from the information centre along Mann St for about 1km, passing, on the left, the old courthouse (1849) and Christ Church (1858). From here Mann St bends to the left. Turn left into York St. The first right is Albany St, which runs south for 1.5km along a narrow promontory. At its end is Point Frederick. The road leads into Pioneer Park.

Pioneer Park is a very pleasant park offering attractive views across Brisbane Water. Set within the park is a number of historic gravestones, showing the age of the area.

3 ERINA

Return along Albany St and turn back into York St, which will take you across the Punt Bridge and onto The Entrance Rd in to Erina.

The first land in what is now called Erina was granted to William Bean in 1824, when the area was full of thick scrub and gigantic trees. Some of the tree stumps were hollowed out and used as temporary homes.

This natural resource meant the area became important as a source of hardwood, especially after the building boom in Sydney in the late 1860s.

4 REMEMBRANCE DRIVE AND WAMBERAL LAGOON

About 3km from Punt Bridge, turn right off The Entrance Rd into Terrigal Drv. Follow the road for 5km and turn left into Ocean View Drv. Continue for 2km along Ocean View Drv and turn right into Remembrance Drv.

As you head along Remembrance Drive, Wamberal Lagoon is to your left. The land on either side of the lagoon is a sanctuary for protected birds and animals. The car park at the end of Remembrance Drive has an information sign about the reserve and is a convenient access point to Wamberal Beach, the surf lifesaving club and a kiosk, all just around the corner. Wamberal is a patrolled family beach with moderate surf and a rockpool area. The northern end is for more experienced surfers. The headland on the northern side and a jutting section of beach to the south give Wamberal a pleasant, secluded feeling.

5 TERRIGAL

Return along Remembrance Drv, Ocean View Drv and then left into Terrigal Drv, which becomes The Esplanade as it reaches the beachfront.

Terrigal has an airy beauty. The pleasant ambience probably has something to do with the stand of Norfolk pines along The Esplanade that lend character and beauty to the beachfront. Terrigal is one of the most popular residential, holiday resort and retirement centres on the Central Coast.

Bateau Bay, Wyrrabalong National Park, near Terrigal.

Visitors flock here for fishing, swimming, surfing, boating, waterskiing and the natural scenery. Anglers will find snapper, flathead and jewfish offshore and bream, flathead and blackfish in the surf.

A pathway beneath the trees and opposite the shops follows The Esplanade alongside the beach and over the hill to Broken Head. The northern side of this headland is relatively wide and flat, constituting an open grassy parkland. What makes it distinctive is The Skillion, the narrow section of the headland that rises dramatically on the southern side. The surface is well-grassed so there is a short walk to the top to the lookout. From here you can see south to First Point beyond Avoca Beach and north to Yumbool Point in Wyrrabalong National Park, just south of The Entrance.

6 AVOCA BEACH

The road continues past The Skillion and becomes the Scenic Hwy, which winds westwards and then south. There is a roundabout after about 5km. Turn left into Avoca Drv. A little over 2km brings you to another roundabout. Turn left into the continuation of Avoca Drv. At the next roundabout turn left and the Avoca Beach car park is to your right.

Avoca Beach is a popular holiday resort and surfing area towards the southern end of a continuous stretch of residential coastline from MacMasters Beach in the south to The Entrance in the north. In recent times the area has become a popular holiday retreat for the wealthy residents of Sydney's North Shore. Its wooded hills and quietness are seen as ideal for family holidays and outings where the emphasis is on beach activities.

Avoca Beach is a long pleasant and popular beach enclosed at either end by rocky headlands. The beach has a surf lifesaving club and is considered a major surfing beach, with the surf at the northern end considered the best. Avoca is ideal for fishing and its length makes it good for beach walking and exercise.

7 COPACABANA BEACH

Turn off Avoca Drv into Cape Three Points Rd and follow it south until it becomes Copacabana Drv. As the road bends to the right turn left into Pampas St and then left into Simone Pl, which runs along the length of Copacabana Beach.

Copacabana is another popular patrolled surfing and holiday beach. Cockrone Lagoon lies just behind the beach. A pleasant family spot for a swim or paddle, the lagoon's eastern neck almost reaches to the beach and then expands westwards, effectively dividing the hinterland in two. So while it is possible to walk all the way along Copacabana Beach to MacMasters Beach, it is a 10km drive by car.

8 CAPTAIN COOK LOOKOUT

Follow Simone Pl north along the beachfront and take the road to the right (Del Monte Pl) which leads to First Point. A signposted side road leads to the car park for the Captain Cook Lookout, which lies at the end of a short path.

At Captain Cook Lookout a cairn bears a plaque which explains that, when sailing offshore in 1770, Cook looked south along the

The Skillion at Terrigal.

coastline and noticed it had three prominent headlands. These he imaginatively named First Point, Second Point (Mourawaring Point at the southern end of MacMasters Beach) and Third Point (Bombi Point south of Little Beach). The three can be seen from this lookout, which is one of the best on the coast. Not only are the views to the south excellent but from here it is possible to look north beyond Avoca Beach to The Skillion at Terrigal.

9 LITTLE BEACH

Return to the top of Copacabana Drv and turn left into Cullens Rd. Follow the road west for over 4km into Kincumber and then turn into The Scenic Rd. Continue heading south-east for about 6km. Turn left into Grahame Drv and follow it to the car park.

An easy walking track leads from the car park down to Little Beach, in the north-eastern section of Bouddi National Park. Little Beach is well-named, being located within a very small and rocky bay. It is a popular yet secluded surfing, picnic and camping spot.

10 BOUDDI NATIONAL PARK

Return along Grahame Drv and turn left into The Scenic Rd. After about 2km turn left into Mount Bouddi Rd.

Mt Bouddi Road leads to a picnic area and a walking track to an excellent lookout at Mount Bouddi. This track also leads down to Maitland Bay and north-east to Little Beach.

In your vehicle, return along Mount Bouddi Road and turn left into The Scenic Road. It is a little over 2km to the park's information centre, on the left-hand side of the road, opposite Maitland Bay Drive. There is a large car park beside the centre and it is from here that the walk to Maitland Bay begins. It is not too long. The bay has a sense of seclusion and privacy because it is deeply recessed behind Bouddi Point and protected by the very steep rockface which adds to the sense of enclosure. The beach is beautiful and so is the forestry around it. Maitland Bay was originally known to Europeans as the Boat Harbour. In 1898 the 880-tonne paddle-steamer *Maitland*, seeking

shelter in Broken Bay from gale-force winds, hit submerged rocks off Bouddi Point. Twenty-seven people died in the attempt to reach the beach with a line to secure the boat's position and facilitate access to the shore. If you walk around the bay and clamber out to the slippery rock ledge off Bouddi Point, you can walk over to the ship's boiler. Other remnants are a short distance away.

Continue south-west along The Scenic Road for about 500m to the Marie Byles Lookout, which has an information board and pointers indicating interesting locations in the distance. The views are spectacular. Barrenjoey Lighthouse at Palm Beach is visible to the south-west.

Follow The Scenic Road for another 2km to its end. Beach Road leads to the surf lifesaving club at Putty Beach. Alternatively, head up the very short and steep Nukara Avenue. At the top it splits three ways. Take the middle path. This dirt road, which heads to the Tallow Beach car park, offers views over Putty and Tallow beaches and south to Barrenjoey Head and its lighthouse.

Return to the four-way intersection and along The Scenic Rd. After about 1km, turn left into Wards Hill Rd. At the T-intersection 2km further along, turn left into Empire Bay Drv. Follow the road to cross Brisbane Water on the The Rip Bridge. At the T-intersection, turn right into Memorial Ave. At the next T-intersection, turn left into Blackwall Rd and follow it to its end. Turn right into Brisbane Water Drv which leads, after 8km, back to the Pacific Hwy at West Gosford.

Low tide at Avoca Beach.

37 AROUND LAKE MACQUARIE

■ DRIVING TOUR ■ 115KM ■ 1 DAY ■ BAYS, INLETS AND PICNICS

Lying south of Newcastle, Lake Macquarie is a vast coastal saltwater lake which attracts many holiday-makers with its excellent fishing, its quiet beaches and its tranquillity.

Lake Macquarie is the largest coastal saltwater lake in the southern hemisphere, measuring 24km in length, 3.2km at its widest point and 9.7m at its deepest. The lake's foreshore consists of 174km of bays, beaches and headlands. The eastern side of the lake is well developed and tourist oriented, while the western side is quieter and more rural, with scrubby woodland fringing the shores and the Watagan Mountains in the background. Lake Macquarie is an ideal place to explore, to have a picnic and to enjoy the still waters of a lake so near to the ocean.

1 CATHERINE HILL BAY

Take the Swansea exit off the Newcastle Fwy and follow the old Pacific Hwy to Doyalson. From Doyalson, continue for another 12km and take the signposted turn-off on the right to Catherine Hill Bay.

Catherine Hill Bay is a quiet, old mining village. The village is named after the schooner *Catherine Hill* was wrecked in the bay in 1867. Coal was discovered and mined by the New Wallsend Company, which bought up the land, built a jetty and opened the mine in 1873. The coastal location was ideal for shipping. The enterprise employed between 70 and 100 men, whose cottages, still lining the roadside, formed the basis of the township. Approximately 1000 tonnes of coal a week was taken by horse-drawn skips from the mine to a loading chute on the jetty. A post office opened in 1874 but closed in 1877, when the township virtually ceased to exist. Then the Wallarah Coal Company re-opened the mines in 1889.

2 UNITING CHURCH AND LOOKOUT

Follow the road in from the highway for a further 2km. Turn left into Clarke St, right into Lindsley St and then left into Flowers Drv, which leads past the bay. Follow Flowers Drv up the hill. To the right is the Uniting Church.

A right turn into the driveway by the church leads to a viewing area that offers an excellent elevated perspective over the beach. At either end are two headlands which mark the bay's boundaries. At the southern end is

the coal-loading wharf with the colliery on the hillside behind it.

3 THE SECOND LOOKOUT AND MIDDLE CAMP

Return to Flowers Drv and continue northwards. Turn right into Northwood Rd, which leads out to a bluff overlooking the beach below. Return to Flowers Drv and continue northwards.

You will soon find yourself in a residential area known as Middle Camp, which is situated in a gully surrounded by high hills. Lining the roadside are rows of 19th-century miners' cottages, some of which are now available as rental accommodation. They are simple, look-alike, box-like rectangles with verandahs and no fences, all situated close to the street.

4 SWANSEA

Another 1.5km will take you back to the Pacific Hwy. Turn right and continue north to Swansea, 5km away.

Swansea is the largest town on Lake Macquarie. There is no appreciable tidal range within the lake, although the tidal race at Swansea channel can be strong. The Swansea channel has six boat ramps and a public wharf by the southern side of the bridge. At one time Lake Macquarie was a bay, but it was almost enclosed by the development of sandbars created by the wind, waves and tides.

5 SWANSEA LOOKOUT

Turn right at the roundabout, opposite McDonald's, into Bowman St. Turn right into Park Ave and follow it south for 1km then turn right into Scenic Drv. Head up the steep hill for 1km and you will see an unsignposted right turn that will take you up to a lookout area.

The lookout offers 360° views of the lake and is a good spot from where to examine the lake's entrance. The headland by the

entrance is known as Reids Mistake after Captain William Reid who, in 1800, became the first European to make his way into the lake. Sent from Sydney to collect coal from the Hunter River, Reid mistook the entrance, ventured inside and met some members of the Awabakal people, who directed him to some coal at the headland. It was only upon

Raffertys Resort at Lake Macquarie.

Pelicans on one of the Lake's many small jetties.

Late afternoon on the edge of the Lake.

his return to Sydney that he realised his error. The lake was known as Reids Mistake until 1826, when it was renamed in honour of Governor Lachlan Macquarie.

6 BLACKSMITHS BEACH

Return to the highway and continue north over the bridge. Turn right into Ungala Rd and drive to the surf lifesaving club at its end.

Blacksmiths Beach is popular with surfers. The surf lifesaving club is a good spot from where to access the beach. There is a break-water nearby and just offshore is Moon Island, a breeding site for birds. To the north the beach is known as Nine Mile Beach, which stretches northwards to Redhead Point. That stretch is unpatrolled and considered dangerous for surfing and swimming.

7 PELICAN FLAT

Return to the highway and continue northwards. Turn left at the first set of traffic lights into Turea St. At the T-intersection turn left into Ninag St, then turn right at the next T-intersection into Lakeview Pde, and proceed to the lake's edge.

By 1860 there were some 30 or 40 Chinese living at Pelican Flat, Swansea's western peninsula. They caught and dried fish and grew vegetables. The first town allotments at Swansea went up for sale in 1863, and were taken up by anglers and sailors. By 1877 there were 120 people at Pelican Flat and a dredge was at work deepening the shallow channel. The name of the settlement was changed from Pelican Flat to Swansea in 1887.

8 BELMONT

Return to the highway and continue north for about 4km to Belmont.

Belmont is a suburban tourist resort on the eastern side of Lake Macquarie. The flotilla of bobbing boats and white, flapping sails that crowd the bay are a symbol of the town's central activity, although fishing and swimming are also popular.

The town's name comes from a weather-board guesthouse named Belmont, which was built in the 1860s. The first town allotments went on sale in 1868, taken up by miners who worked at nearby collieries. The improvement of the roads in 1883 and the arrival of the railway later in the decade prompted more substantial development.

9 TORONTO

Proceed along the highway to the large intersection. Turn left into Macquarie St. At the end of the road, turn right into Brooks Pde and continue past the rock pool and boat ramp. Veer left into Ross St, which becomes Croudace Bay Rd. At Speers Point there is a roundabout. Turn left into Five Islands Rd which continues south as Toronto Rd.

Toronto is set at the western end of a long peninsula that protrudes from the north-western shore of Lake Macquarie. The western side of the settlement is bordered by dry, unattractive scrub while the eastern side of the town and the peninsula are green and leafy with more expensive residences along the lake foreshores. Fishing, sailing and rowing are the mainstays of local recreational activities.

Toronto was established by the Excelsior Land Investment and Building Company which purchased the Ebenezer estate in 1885 with plans to create a tourist resort on the shores of the lake. The town was named in honour of world-champion sculler Edward Hanlan, who hailed from Toronto in Canada. The company built the Toronto Hotel in 1887.

10 TORONTO FORESHORE

As you approach Toronto, Toronto Rd becomes Carey St. Turn left into Victory Pde.

Victory Parade descends past the Toronto Hotel and Toronto foreshore park on the left. There is a rock pool to the east and a boat ramp to the west. From here are views northwards across to Kooroora Bay and

north-east to Bolton Point, both on the next peninsula. Every Sunday afternoon at 1:00pm there is music in the park.

Toronto Railway Station Heritage Centre is located at the western end of the park. It is the old railway station, now restored, which houses the Lake Macquarie Historical Society's collection of historical photographs and other memorabilia. Situated opposite the park and on a hill overlooking the lake, Toronto Hotel (1887) has ornate iron posts and fencing the verandah and balcony with ornate cast-iron lacework.

11 THE PENINSULA

Follow Victory Pde as it becomes Brighton Ave. At the T-intersection turn right into Ambrose St which becomes Excelsior Pde and then Skye Point Rd. Skye Point Rd follows the northern side of the peninsula out to its eastern edge. The road then bends around and heads back westwards along the southern side of the peninsula as Coal Point Rd.

There are three small plots of parkland left at the end of the promontory. Gurranba looks northwards to Green Point and Rocky Point on the north-eastern shore and to Speers Point at the northernmost tip of the lake; Birriban gazes north-east to Belmont jetty, east to Lake Head, Pelican Flat and Swansea and south to the long, narrow Wangi peninsula. Threlkeld looks south directly across to Fishing Point and west to Rathmines, both on the next peninsula to the south.

At the south-western tip of the peninsula is Kilaben Park, where there is a wharf and swimming pool, and views eastwards out to Skye Point and beyond to Swansea.

12 MORISSET

Coal Point Rd becomes Barina Ave and then Jarrott St. At the intersection veer left into Excelsior Pde which becomes Mountwaring Rd and then Wangi Rd. As you approach Morisset the road becomes Wamsley St then, once across Dora Creek, it is known as Macquarie St. Before you reach the shopping strip, turn left into Fishery Point Rd which leads out along the peninsula. It is necessary to take a distinct left turn after about 2km along this road in order to continue out to the peninsular.

Morisset is not a tourist town, but there is a pleasant drive out along Morisset Peninsula. On the north-eastern tip is Shingle Splitters, the name serving as a reminder of the days when the timber industry was important. Some of the casuarinas they didn't cut down remain. The fringes of the promontory are residential but there is much bushland adjacent to the roadway and the large Sunshine Park camping reserve at the eastern tip of the peninsula.

At Casuarina Point Reserve there is a boat ramp, a swimming pool, and views to the Wangi Wangi peninsula and the stacks of Wangi Point Power Station and Vales Point Power Station.

Return from Sunshine Park along Fishery Point Rd and then turn left, back into Macquarie St, which leads through the main part of town. As you pass through the roundabout, Macquarie St becomes Dora St. Before long you will come to the merging lanes which lead back onto the Sydney to Newcastle Expressway.

38 WALKING HISTORIC NEWCASTLE

■ WALKING TOUR ■ 10KM ■ 1 DAY ■ AN ELEGANT AND HISTORIC PROVINCIAL CITY

Newcastle is an elegant and historic city. A pleasant walk around the city offers insights from convict to modern times.

To think of Newcastle as simply a steel city driven by the coal deposits in the hinterland and its huge steel mill is being one-eyed. In reality, Newcastle is an elegant city full of gracious historic buildings located on a series of hills overlooking the Pacific Ocean and the Hunter River. This walk through historic Newcastle begins at the city's visitors centre and takes in Fort Scratchley, the old convict swimming pool, the cathedral and the Botanic Gardens.

1 STATIONMASTER'S RESIDENCE

The visitors centre is located within the old stationmaster's residence (1858) at 92 Scott Street. Beautifully restored, the building has fine iron columns supporting a porch with ornate cast-iron lacework.

2 THE OLD COURTHOUSE COLUMN AND COALMINING MONUMENT

Head east along Scott St. Near its end, Parnell Pl runs off to the left.

This thoroughfare was hit by shells from a Japanese submarine in 1942. To the immediate right is a small park with a large column that belonged to the old 1841 courthouse which was demolished in 1899. At the end of Parnell Place is a complex intersection, to the side of which is a monument to Newcastle's coalmining and shipping industries with a series of informative plaques.

3 FORT SCRATCHLEY

From this intersection a small driveway heads off up the steep hill to Fort Scratchley.

Being an obvious place for a warning beacon, a signal mast was set atop the hill in 1804 and it was named Signal Hill (although known as Fort Fiddlesticks to the convicts). In 1813 the mast was replaced by a coal-fire beacon which burned until Nobbys Lighthouse was established in 1858. When fear of a Russian invasion gripped the colony in

the 1870s, it was decided that Newcastle, as a coal and steel producer, needed to be properly fortified. The fort, designed by Lieutenant-Colonel Peter Scratchley, was built between 1881 and 1886. *The Heritage of Australia* notes that Fort Scratchley 'is one of only two examples of late 19th-century military fortifications in New South Wales'.

The fort's defence purposes were truly put to the test in June 1942, when a Japanese submarine attacked Newcastle. The guns then discharged the only shots ever fired in hostility from the Australian mainland. The military relinquished the site in 1972 and it is now the Newcastle Region Maritime and Military Museum, open weekends and public holidays. In the rock platform below Fort Scratchley are the ocean pools known as the Soldiers Baths, built in 1882.

4 NOBBYS HEAD

Immediately above Fort Scratchley, on a very narrow promontory, is Nobbys Head.

At Nobbys Head a lighthouse stands sentinel over the Hunter estuary. Beyond the headland is the rocky mass of the southern breakwater. Lieutenant Shortland sought shelter at Nobbys while searching for escaped convicts in 1797. There he found coal and this discovery resulted in a visit by Lieutenant James Grant who called it Coal Island. Coal was mined there until 1817.

Using convict labour and rock fill from the Fort Scratchley area, work began on the construction of a pier out to the island in 1818. The pier was not completed until 1846 and it was rebuilt in 1864. In 1855, Nobbys was reduced in size from 61m to 27m, and a lighthouse was erected in 1857 to replace the

coal-fire beacon of Fort Scratchley. It has since been replaced. You can walk along this artificial promontory, with Nobbys Beach to your right, past the lighthouse and along the breakwater to its terminus. Towards the end of the pier are five sculptures reflecting various aspects of Newcastle and its history.

5 NEWCASTLE BEACH

At the roundabout, take the left into Shortland Esplanade.

To the left are a large ocean bath and an old and large children's wading pool at the northern end of Newcastle Beach.

6 THE BOGIE HOLE

From the southern end of the beach, Shortland Esplanade begins to rise up the hill. You will come to a signposted side-track which leads down to the Bogie Hole at the bottom of the cliffs.

This large excavation in the rocks tells us something of the nature of Newcastle in the early 19th century. It is a bathing pool built by convict labour for the personal pleasure of Major James T. Morriset, the military commandant from 1819 and 1822 who did much to improve the breakwater, roads and barracks in the settlement. Known for many

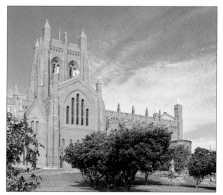

Christ Church Anglican Cathedral, Newcastle.

Customs House, Newcastle.

years as Commandants Bath, the pool was opened to the public in 1863. As one stands and watches the waves washing over the pool the extent of the achievement and the indulgence of the commandant becomes apparent. The convicts must have dug this hole between waves, waist high in water.

7 KING EDWARD PARK

Follow the path up the hill to King Edward Park.

In a gully you will see the lovely octagonal band rotunda (1898) with its fine cast-iron decoration. This natural depression was once the site of a paddock for the Australian Agricultural Company's horses that worked in a nearby pit. It now features a sunken garden.

Notice the army fortification zone on the hilltop. The fortifications were established in 1890 but rebuilt during World War II when it was known as Park Battery. A cement fortress and a series of pillboxes remain. From this point there are excellent views towards the harbour and the Anglican Cathedral on a nearby hill.

8 THE OBELISK

Wander down The Terrace and observe the fine Victorian terrace houses (c.1890) which give the street its name. At the bottom, turn right into Reserve Rd then take the left into Wolfe St. There is a signposted set of steps to your right leading up to The Obelisk.

A windmill built on this site in 1820 became a major navigational aid for shipping. Its demolition in 1847 provoked protests from mariners and, consequently, the obelisk was erected as an alternative marker in 1850. An early water reservoir was situated under this spot in 1885.

9 BARKER STREET

Proceed along Wolfe St and turn right into Ordnance St and left into Baker St.

Near the hilltop is an enormous mansion named Jesmond House. Built in 1870, it was apparently considered Newcastle's most fashionable house at the time. Highlights include the elaborate staircase leading to the second-storey verandah with its beautiful central pillar, ornamental cast-iron fencing and ornate columns. At 11 Barker Street is Bryn-Y-Mor Lodge (c.1880), built as stables for Jesmond House. Note Shalamah at 4 Baker Street and the beautiful houses opposite the bottom of the street. Turn left into Tyrrell Streer. To the left is an attractive series of Victorian terrace houses dating from 1870 to 1890.

10 CHRIST CHURCH

Go back to Ordnance St, turn right into Wolfe St and then right into Church St.

To the left is Christ Church Anglican Cathedral. Like some medieval castle, the cathedral is one of Newcastle's most impressive buildings. Originally designed by the distinguished architect J. Horbury Hunt in 1869, work did not commence until 1883. Even then, Canon Selwyn's determination to wrest control from Hunt slowed construction which ceased again in 1885 and did not recommence until 1891. Selwyn's determination finally led to Hunt's dismissal in 1895. Although the building was dedicated in 1902, the chancel remained incomplete until 1912. The nave was finished in 1928, the tower in 1979 and the central spire still awaits construction. There is a separate timber bellcote on the grounds, 72 stained-glass windows, a wealth of religious adornment within and fine views from the grounds.

11 CHURCH STREET

Continue eastwards along Church St.

At the corner of Bolton and Church streets is Newcastle East Public School, the city's first school, which was established in 1816 with a convict teacher. It is the oldest school still in use in Australia and was moved to this site in the 1830s. The present building dates from 1908. On the other side of Bolton Street is the Grand Hotel (1891) and on the other side of Church Street are the imposing archway and pillars of justice of the courthouse (1890).

12 MILITARY BARRACKS

Continue on Church St and head east, turning right into Watt St.

On the right is the entranceway of the James Fletcher Psychiatric Hospital. Newcastle's first underground coal shaft was sunk 18m inside this driveway in 1814. The hospital was formerly the site of a military barracks. The commandant's house, main barracks building and gatehouse were all built in 1841 and remain standing today.

Head down Watt Street, which was effectively Newcastle's first thoroughfare. It started its life as a track down which convicts pushed barrows of coal from the coal shaft to a wharf near the site of the present Customs House.

13 HUNTER STREET

Turn left into Hunter St.

To the immediate right, on the corner, is the old Public Works Department (PWD) building (now Hunt and Hunt Lawyers), originally a post office (1860) but redesigned by colonial architect James Barnet in 1872 for the PWD. The upper floor was added in 1877.

Next door is the police station, a two-storey sandstone building designed by Mortimer Lewis, built in 1859 and extended by James Barnet in 1890. It now houses the Wilderness Shop, the John Paynter Gallery and the police station museum which features the original padded cell and exercise yard of the old lockup.

Next door, on the corner of Hunter and Bolton streets, is the post office (1903), a fine piece of Edwardian Classical architecture designed by W.L. Vernon. The design was apparently based on Palladio's Basilica at Vicenza.

14 LONGWORTH INSTITUTE

Turn right down Bolton St then left into Scott St.

At 127–131 Scott Street is an excellent two-storey red-brick baroque building with an elaborate facade designed by Frederick Menkens. It was built in 1892 for brewer and alcohol merchant Joseph Wood as offices and auction rooms, which later became the Longworth Institute (a library and art gallery), and is now the Air Force Club.

15 RAILWAY STATION

Head east along Scott St.

The railway station (1878) is considered a major example of Victorian railway architecture with five buildings, symmetrically arranged. The line to Sydney was not completed until 1889.

16 CUSTOMS HOUSE

Opposite the railway station is the former Customs House, a large and graceful building adorned by a prominent clock tower.

One of Newcastle's most impressive architectural monuments, Customs House was designed by James Barnet and built in 1876–1877 with the Watt Street wing added in 1898–1900. This entire block of land was once occupied by a convict stockade, established in 1805 under the supervision of the explorer Dr Charles Throsby.

The position of these civic buildings, standing virtually adjacent to and overlooking the city and harbour, reflects the integration of what is very much a working harbour into the city's public life.

Continue along Scott St, back to the visitors centre.

Ships moored in Newcastle Harbour.

Newcastle's famous tram offers city tours.

CHAPTER 7
THE HUNTER VALLEY

39 HISTORIC HUNTER

■ DRIVING TOUR ■ 154KM ■ 1 DAY ■ A DRIVE THROUGH THE HISTORIC HUNTER VALLEY

The Hunter Valley, famous for its coal and vineyards, is rich in interesting historic buildings. Towns like Morpeth and Dungog have both charm and sophistication.

Most Australians, when they hear the words 'Hunter Valley' mentioned, automatically think of vineyards and fine wines. In fact, the Hunter Valley is a far larger and more complex area than this simple labelling describes. To the north, on the edges of the Great Dividing Range, are a number of particularly attractive and interesting historic townships which, because the traffic in the region tends to be move northwards or head towards the wineries, have remained largely unchanged. Here, in these quiet valleys, is an opportunity to explore rural New South Wales as it was a century ago.

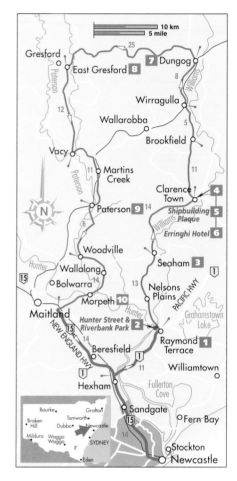

1 RAYMOND TERRACE

If you are approaching Raymond Terrace from the south, turn right at the traffic lights into William St, the main shopping strip and continue down to King St.

Raymond Terrace was gazetted in 1837 and land sales began in 1838. A courthouse, police station, steam-driven flour mill and punt were soon established. The town became an important shipping centre in the 1840s for wool carted by road from New England. Shipping continued into the 1920s. King Street was the business centre of Raymond Terrace from 1840 until a flood in 1955 shifted trade around the corner. The attractive 19th-century timber buildings with post-supported verandahs are well preserved. Some date back to the 1840s. The two large trees halfway along the street, to the left, are called the 'marriage trees', because they were used for wedding ceremoniess before the town's churches were erected.

2 HUNTER STREET AND RIVERBANK PARK

Return to William St and continue down towards the Hunter River.

On the corner of William and Hunter streets is the Junction Inn. The oldest portion dates from 1836 when it served as Kings Hotel, a post office and the business premises of the first European settler, James King. Attractive Riverbank Park, adjacent to the Hunter River, is located on the site formerly occupied by a wharf and a large group of stone buildings that were erected in the 1830s as part of James King's business enterprises.

Morpeth Bridge across the Hunter River.

3 SEAHAM

Return up William St and turn left onto the Pacific Hwy. Take the second left, opposite McDonald's, into William Bailey St and proceed across the bridge. After 2km there is a fork in the road. Take the road on the right to Seaham. After 11km turn right into East Seaham Rd (signposted for Raymond Terrace) and then turn right into Warren St.

To your left is the small but attractive St Andrew's Anglican Church (1860), a quaint little building made of rubble stone. It stands adjacent to Seaham Swamp Nature Reserve. Head back the way you came along East Seaham Road and turn right, continuing north. On your right you will pass Seaham Weir, a large body of water well-stocked with bass and mullet from November to February.

4 CLARENCE TOWN

Continue north for about 12km to the T-intersection and turn right for Clarence Town.

Clarence Town is a small, sprawling and tranquil township situated by the banks of the Williams River. When the river system was the main mode of transport within Australia, Clarence Town was a busy and important river port. Timber was loaded here for export in the 1850s. By the 1880s dairying, grazing and fodder production had become the town's economic mainstays and they remain so to this day.

5 SHIPBUILDING PLAQUE

You will enter Clarence Town along Queen St. A sign on the right-hand side of the road directs you along a gravel driveway down to the boat ramp, which leads to a small park with picnic facilities.

The park is located beside a green, tree-lined and beautiful section of the wide, deep and placid Williams River. A plaque commemorates the 150th anniversary of the launching of the paddlewheel steamer *William IV* from the Deptford Shipyards, Clarence Town, 500m downstream on the west bank of the river on 14 November 1831. *William IV* was the first ocean-going steamer built in Australia. The boat left Clarence Town under sail and its engines were fitted in Sydney.

6 ERRINGHI HOTEL

Return along the gravel drive, turning right into Queen St. Turn right at the next intersection into Grey St.

The Erringhi Hotel (1913) was erected on the site of the George and Dragon Inn, built there in 1842. This two-storey symmetrical building has elaborate cast-iron lacework on the upstairs balcony railing and the eaves of the posts, and carved timber bargeboards around the gables.

7 DUNGOG

Return along Grey St and head towards Dungog, which is 24km away. As you enter Dungog, Clarence Town Rd meets up with Lord St. Turn right into Mary St, then take the first left into Dowling St, which is the main thoroughfare.

Dungog is located in a valley surrounded by rolling hills. It is a moderate-sized Australian country town with a typically wide main street. Dungog serves as a base for an exploration of the fine countryside to the north, where you will find Chichester Dam, state forests and Barrington Tops National Park—all ideal places for bushwalking, scenic drives, swimming, photography,

The former CBC Bank, Dungog.

The Anglican Christ Church in Dungog.

horseriding, cycling, camping, trail-bike riding and canoeing.

The main street of Dungog, named after Chief Justice James D. Dowling, is an urban conservation area. With its old shops and facades, many dating from the late 19th and early 20th centuries, the street has a somewhat antiquated look and feel. One of the oldest surviving buildings in town is the Anglican Christ Church (1858), located at the corner of Dowling and Chapman streets. Next door is the masonic lodge (1894). On the other side of Chapman Street is St Andrew's Presbyterian Church (1901), a substantial and attractive building with arched lancet windows. Further along the block is the School of Arts building, now an historical museum with displays on local industry and history. Almost opposite is the Royal Hotel and next door to that, at 72 Dowling Street, is Kirralee (1910), a gracious and carefully restored Edwardian house with wide verandahs and stained-glass work on the door. At the corner of Dowling and Hooke streets is the former CBC Bank (1874), now the National Bank. Note the iron gate, cedar doors and fittings, arched facade and cast-iron lacework.

8 EAST GRESFORD

Turn left into Hooke Rd from Dowling St. Turn right into Common Rd and take the first left. Less than 2km out of town is another turn-off to the left to East Gresford, 24km away.

Gresford and East Gresford are two small settlements 2km apart. They make an obvious base for an exploration of the area to the north where you will find lovely Allynbrook, Lostock Dam, Mount Allyn and the mountainous terrain of Chichester State Forest and Barrington Tops.

9 PATERSON

Continue south for 21km to Paterson.

Paterson is a tiny but attractive little hamlet settled amid mountains on the Paterson River, which has its source in Barrington Tops to the north. A good way to see Paterson is to obtain a walking tour pamphlet and map from the Paterson Country Cafe in King Street, opposite the Courthouse Hotel. Of particular interest is the Courthouse Hotel, which started as the Cricketers Arms in 1864 on the river ank north of the present village site. A major flood in 1875 made the building uninhabitable. It was demolished and moved to the current site and rebuilt as the Courthouse Hotel. That building was badly damaged by flood and then fire in the 1930s and, in 1960, the manager's wife was tragically burned to death in another fire.

On the other side of the railway crossing is St Ann's Presbyterian Church. Many early settlers in the area were Scots and St Ann's was built in the late 1830s. The building has arched lancet leadlight windows with timber tracery. Over the road is the Paterson Courthouse Museum in King Street. The building was erected in 1857 with additions completed in 1865. Its dominant feature is the arcaded porch with its three monumental arches. Court sessions ceased in 1967.

10 MORPETH

Head south on the main road to Maitland. Morpeth is 20km away. At the T-intersection turn left and cross the Morpeth Bridge. At the next T-intersection turn right into Swan St, which is Morpeth's main thoroughfare.

Morpeth is an historic inland river port on the banks of the Hunter River. With its beautiful riverside setting, the genuinely historic feel that emerges from the mellowed stonework of its many old buildings, the modest and eminently walkable size of Morpeth and the willow trees lining the riverbank, the town is becoming popular with travellers. The main street has a profusion of arts and crafts, antique and curio shops housed in historic buildings and is very much geared towards tourism.

The best way to explore Morpeth is to walk through the town. Start at the corner of Tank and Swan streets. The large symmetrical gabled building on the corner is the old Campbells Store (c.1850), built of locally quarried sandstone and brick with flagged sandstone paving and timber posts supporting an awning. There are large blow-ups of interesting historic photographs with explanatory text adorning the walls. Next door to the store is the Surgeons Cottage, a smaller sandstone building with hipped roof, decorative cast-iron columns and a sandstone verandah built for a Dr Bennett.

Just around the corner, in Green Street, is an old slab cottage dating back to the 1820s which has been restored and relocated to this site. Returning to Swan Street, there is a series of terrace houses on the right (numbers 153–163) built about 1850. Just beyond the terraces is the CBC Bank building (1889). Designed by the Mansfield brothers, the bank has an impressive interior, featuring Italian fireplaces, porcelain servants' bells, red cedar woodwork, a fine staircase, quality panelling and original bank fittings including a huge cedar counter, ledger desk and cupboard.

The CBC Bank initially set up shop in Taylors Bonded Stores (1850). This impressive sandstone building is situated opposite the Classical Revival courthouse which was completed in 1862. The latter features round-headed windows, channelled stone, pilasters, architrave and pediment. It now serves as a local history museum. Further down Swan Street, just past the post office (1861–1866) is the Royal Hotel. The hitching posts out the front, where patrons tethered their horses, serve as a reminder that this is one of the town's earliest inns.

Head out of town along Swan St, which becomes Morpeth Rd. After 5km you will reach East Maitland. Turn left onto the New England Hwy and, after a further kilometre, turn left into High St. When you reach the roundabout, turn right into Lindesay St. Near its end, Raymond Terrace Rd bends off to the left. Follow this road for 14km to the T-intersection. Turn right at the signpost for Raymond Terrace, 2km away.

Palms make the streetscape attractive in Raymond Terrace.

40 HUNTER VALLEY MINING TOWNS

■ DRIVING TOUR ■ 125KM ■ 1 DAY ■ EXPLORING THE HUNTER VALLEY MINING TOWNS

The wealth of the Hunter Valley has been its vast coal deposits. Towns like Cessnock, Kurri Kurri and Maitland are essentially coalmining towns.

The Hunter Valley is a rare combination of attractions. The area contains some of the state's most beautifully preserved historic towns and it is famous, particularly over the past thirty years, as one of the country's premier wine destinations, producing wines of both national and international reputation. Perhaps not so well known, however, is that it is one of the country's most important coal-producing regions. The valley is unusual in that within a single district there is a successful mix of the intensely working-class activity of coalmining with the vigorous activity of winegrowing—but that is part of the attraction of the Hunter Valley.

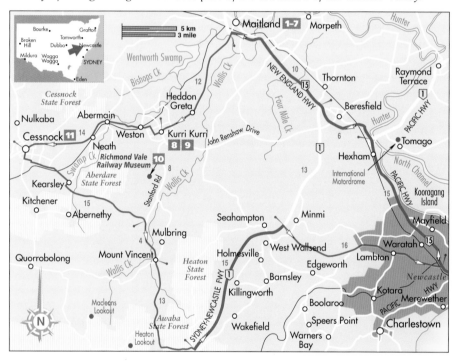

1 MAITLAND
Starting in Newcastle, head out of the city on Hunter St, turning into Industrial Rd which eventually becomes the old Pacific Hwy. In turn, this becomes the New England Hwy. The city of Maitland is 32km north-west of Newcastle.

Maitland Post Office, Maitland.

Maitland is situated on flood plains adjacent to the Hunter River. Consequently, the city has had 15 major floods since 1819. The last flood was in 1955, when 11 people were killed, which prompted the construction of levees, spillways and channels to mitigate the effects of the flood water. Maitland was once the principal town of the Hunter Valley and as such it boasts many historic buildings of considerable quality.

2 REGENT STREET
Continue past Maitland Park (the swimming pool is on your left), through the first roundabout and cross the railway line. At the next roundabout, take the turn that heads back east and continue along Regent St.
Regent Street is a classified urban conservation area full of lovely old houses, the most striking of which are the mansions Benhome, at no. 30 (now the headquarters of the Maitland Benevolent Society) and Cintra, at no. 34, a beautiful and imposing two-storey Classical Revival house set in

spacious grounds with fine gardens. Cintra was designed by William Pender and built during Maitland's boom period (1880) of rendered brick. The house has extensive and intricate cast-iron lacework and Corinthian columns and a tower capped with cast-iron decoration. The tall gates open onto a gravelled carriage loop driveway that leads to the gabled, sandstock-brick stables.

3 MAITLAND COURTHOUSE
Return to the corner of Regent St and turn north across the Long Bridge until you reach the corner of High and Sempill sts.
Here is the town's elegant Victorian courthouse and police station, built of dressed sandstone with a large clock tower topped by a copper-clad dome set around a fine courtyard. It was designed by government architect W.L. Vernon and completed in 1895.

4 WALKA WATERWORKS COMPLEX
Turn right into Sempill St, which heads north as Oakhampton Rd. After about 3km turn left into Scobies Lne, which leads to the Walka Waterworks complex.
Constructed between 1879 and 1885 as part of the first water supply scheme for Newcastle, Walka Waterworks was the first permanent, clean water supply and, at the time, the largest industrial complex in the Hunter Valley. Demand continually outstripped supply, however, and Chichester Dam was constructed in 1913. One of the largest and most intact 19th-century industrial complexes in the Hunter Valley, Walka Waterworks was classified by the National Trust in 1976 and restored and reopened in the 1980s. The complex's distinguishing features are the fine Italianate architecture and ornate brickwork of the pumphouse, the striking chimney, large storage area, the old sandstone wall enclosing the large reservoir full of waterbirds, and the working model of the original pump which is on display inside the main pumphouse.

5 WEST MAITLAND (CENTRAL PRECINCT)
Return to Semphill St via Oakhampton Rd, turn right into High St and left into Ken Tubman Drv. Just beyond the next roundabout is Church St. This is a walk around West Maitland.
Maitland Railway Station is located beyond the roundabout at the southernmost end of Church Street. The current Italianate-style building dates from about 1880. In Church Street the Grand Junction Hotel (1916) and Sherbourne, an excellent 19th-century building of Italianate design, have finely detailed facades. The Grossman House Museum and Brough House (Maitland City Art Gallery)

The magnificent Kurri Kurri Hotel.

are inverted mirror images of one another. These two elegant red-brick Victorian town-houses were built in 1860–1861 by Samuel Owens and Isaac Beckett. Both feature cedar joinery, marble fireplaces, sandstone quoins, two-storey verandahs atop Doric columns and intricate cast-iron lacework, shuttered windows and French doors.

Over the road is St Mary's Rectory (1880–1881), a fine building with elaborate ornamentation. The detailed, decorative Gothic Revival sandstone church next door was designed by Edmund Blacket and its construction (1860–1867) was overseen by the distinguished architect J. Horbury Hunt. The bell is from Sydney's St Andrew's Cathedral. The quite remarkable tower and spire were added in 1885–1886 and dominate the city skyline.

Continue to the northern end of Church Street and turn into High Street. This street, with its civic and commercial buildings, is classified by the National Trust. High Street was originally a bullock track around which the settlement grew in a piecemeal and unplanned fashion. A number of the shop facades are interesting and the original dates and business names are still on some of the upper storeys. At the corner of Church and High streets is a relic from the past, a Black-boy hitching post from the United States, made in the 1880s and initially erected outside the post office in 1886. The hitching post has been on this site since 1892.

The ANZ Bank building (1869) is one of Maitland's architectural highlights. A rare colonial example of a Byzantine design, the building features round-headed windows and a two-storey arcaded verandah which bends around the corner into Elgin Street.

6 EAST MAITLAND

Return to your vehicle and head back towards Newcastle for 2.5km until you cross Wallis Creek and enter East Maitland.

On the far side of the bridge are two buildings built by John Smith. One of the original 11 ex-convict grantees, Smith became a noted local businessman. Probably the original Black Horse Inn, the building at 46 Newcastle Street is thought to date from the 1820s. Englefield is a Georgian structure built in 1837 which became the new Black Horse Inn in the 1840s. Smith's flour mill began operations in 1844 and the building (a timber ground storey topped by a stone second storey) is located at 99 Newcastle Street, by the corner with Mill Street.

Also in Mill Street is Caroline Chisholm Cottage (1840). The cottage became an immigrants' home set up by Caroline Chisholm in 1842. The original shingled roof still lies beneath the iron.

7 GAOL AND COURTHOUSE

Turn right into High St and continue north until you reach the roundabout. Turn left and continue along Lindesay St until you reach the Maitland Gaol. The courthouse is in John St, the next street south.

The gaol was designed by colonial architect Mortimer Lewis and completed in 1848. The structure consists essentially of a pair of two-storey buildings with gatehouse, cells and outer wall and remains in operation today. This was the site of the state's last official flogging, in 1905.

The brick-and-stone Neoclassical court-house opposite was built about 1860. The facade of the central courtroom features a gable with a clock in the pediment. There are two flanking wings, an arcaded porch and terracotta roofing.

8 KURRI KURRI

Head west out of East Maitland towards Maitland and at the first roundabout take the signs to Cessnock and Kurri Kurri, which is 12km south of Maitland.

Kurri Kurri is an old coalmining town. Coal was discovered in the district by William Keene in 1856 but the full potential of the Greta coal seam was not recognised until 1886, when geologist T.W. Edgeworth David did some exploratory work. The first colliery of the South Maitland Coal Field (Richmond Vale) was opened in 1891 and many others soon followed. Kurri Kurri was laid out on crown land in 1902 to serve the growing community of miners and their families. The pits began to close from the late 1950s and wine slowly supplanted coal as the centrepiece of the local economy.

9 KURRI KURRI HOTEL

Continue along Mulbring St (which becomes Victoria St) until you reach the roundabout at Lang St. Turn left and continue until you reach the roundabout at the corner of Lang and Hampden sts.

By far the most impressive pub (it is really the town's only historic building of high quality) is the Kurri Kurri Hotel, opposite Rotary Park. Built in 1904, the hotel is an unusual and relatively ostentatious building that stands out in what is an otherwise undistinguished streetscape. Three storeys high, the building sports ornate cast-iron lacework on the verandahs with extravagant verandah brackets, large decorative brick arches, inset pedimented doors and windows and quality joinery.

10 RICHMOND VALE RAILWAY MUSEUM

Continue south-east on Hampden St until you reach Railway St. Take the bend to the left into Stanford St, which is signposted for Wyong. About 3km south along this road, at Pelaw Main, is Richmond Vale Railway Museum and Richmond Main Heritage Park.

The railway museum is based around the private Richmond Vale Railway which operated from 1856 to 1987, making it

Australia's last operating steam railway. The railway once conveyed miners between the Pelaw Main and Richmond Vale collieries, both owned by industrial magnate John 'Baron' Brown. The track covered 36km. The locomotives are now heritage protected and take visitors for rides along the track on the first three Sundays of each month. The old Richmond Main Colliery is also heritage listed. Buildings include the administrative centre, the powerhouse and workshops, including the blacksmith's.

11 CESSNOCK

Return to Kurri Kurri shopping centre (3km) and continue out of town on Cessnock Rd. Cessnock is 11km away.

The Cessnock area began to be established in 1823 and became a major mining and timber centre at the turn of the century. Settlers harvested cedar and rosewood and convicts were employed to clear the surrounding land to plant maize, wheat, tobacco and potatoes. A man called John Campbell was granted 2560ac in 1826 along Black Creek, where the town is now situated. He named the property after Cessnock castle in Ayrshire, Scotland, which belonged to his baronial grandfather. The Cessnock Inn was established here in 1856 for those travelling between Wollombi and Maitland. By 1858 there were about 11 residents here.

Coal was discovered by William Keene in 1856 but the full potential of the Greta coal seam was not recognised until 1886, when T.W. Edgeworth David did some exploratory work. The first colliery (Richmond Vale) was opened in 1891 and was linked by rail with Maitland. Closed in 1967, it is now a mining museum. The local mining operations were very large, even by world standards.

Leave Cessnock on Aberdare Rd and travel for 31km until you reach the Sydney to Newcastle Expressway. Continue north on the expressway for 15km to the Newcastle Link Rd. The centre of Newcastle is 19km to the east.

Statue of a miner, Kurri Kurri Workers Club.

41 VINEYARDS AND WINERIES OF THE HUNTER VALLEY

■ DRIVING TOUR ■ 40KM ■ 1 DAY ■ EXPLORING HUNTER VALLEY VINEYARDS

The premier wine region in New South Wales is the Hunter Valley where, for over 130 years, fine grapes have produced fine wine. It is a popular weekend and day trip destination.

Grapes were being grown in the Hunter Valley as early as the 1860s but it wasn't until a century later that the region gained a reputation as a fine winegrowing area. The success of the Hunter Valley is symbolic of the way Australian life changed after World War II. The huge immigration from southern Europe—particularly from Italy and Greece—created an environment where the drinking of wine was seen as a socially acceptable and integral part of Australian life. By the 1970s the vineyards had become a popular weekend retreat for Sydney-based wine lovers.

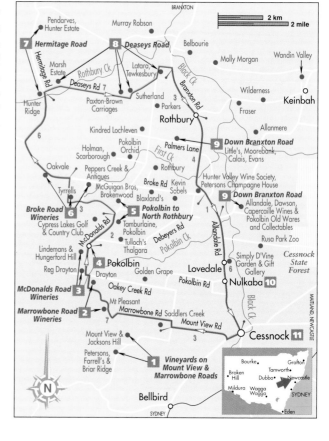

1 VINEYARDS ON MOUNT VIEW AND MARROWBONE ROADS

Start at the centre of Cessnock, where Maitland Rd, Wollombi Rd, Allandale Rd and Vincent St all meet at what is left of Black Creek. Head west on Wollombi Rd and turn west onto Mount View Rd. After about 3km there is a T-intersection. A right turn will take you on to Oakey Creek Rd and a left turn is a continuation of Mount View Rd. Continue on Mount View Rd.

As you drive down Mount View Road, to your right are Mount View Estate, Jackson's Hill Vineyard and Petersons. A little further along, to your left, are Briar Ridge Vineyard and, to your right, Farrell's Limestone Creek Vineyard.

2 MARROWBONE ROAD WINERIES

As you continue, Mount View Rd becomes Marrowbone Rd.

Along Marrowbone Road is McWilliams Mount Pleasant Winery where there is a newly opened wine and food area with picnic and barbecue facilities. The first vineyard was established here in the 1880s, supplying local vignerons with wine grapes, but it was not until the 1920s that winemaking on the property began.

Just before that intersection with Oakey Creek Road is Drayton Family Wines, where there are picnic, barbecue and play facilities. The oldest winery in the Pokolbin area, Drayton was established about 1860.

3 MCDONALDS ROAD WINERIES

Turn into McDonalds Rd and head north.

McDonalds Road is named after one of the first settlers of this beautiful area, John McDonald, who obtained a land grant in the area in 1825. His descendant established a winery in 1870. The roadway runs south–north, connecting Oakey Creek Road with Branxton Road. At the western end of Oakey Creek Road, McDonalds Road heads off to the right. On this corner is Reg Drayton Wines, which is open every day. A short distance along, to the right, are Hungerford Hill and Lindemans.

4 POKOLBIN

After you pass Lindemans vineyard you are at Pokolbin, in the heart of the Hunter Valley.

Pokolbin is not a town and although some refer to it, for historic reasons, as a village this is also stretching things somewhat. There is little centrality about the area, which is essentially a district bisected by a number of roads along which are picturesque vineyards and those businesses that complement the wineries: accommodation, restaurants, galleries, nurseries, gift shops.

Viticulture in the Hunter Valley is often considered to have commenced with James Busby. In the 1820s Busby studied oenology, wrote a treatise and guidance manual on the subject and briefly taught viticulture at a Liverpool farm school. In 1831 he undertook a tour of French and Spanish vineyards which resulted in two published journals of

Peppers Guesthouse in the Hunter Valley.

The Hunter Valley's premier wines start at the grapes.

the trip. He returned with 700 carefully wrapped cuttings of European vines, sending half to the newly established Royal Botanic Gardens in Sydney. The rest he took with him to the family estate of Kirkton, just north of Belford. There he established what was probably the first vineyard in the district.

The Drayton family established a vineyard at Pokolbin in the late 1850s and the Tyrrells Estate was set up in 1859 by a nephew of the first Anglican Bishop of Newcastle who produced his first batch of wine in 1864. Vineyards really sprang up from the late 1870s but the depression of the 1890s dealt the industry a blow which was further crippled by the influx of cheaper wine from South Australia when customs barriers between the states were removed after Federation in 1901.

It was not until the 1960s that the wine industry of the Lower Hunter really began to boom with the closure of local mining operations and the reorientation of Australian tastes with the influx of European immigrants after the World War II. By the 1980s winegrowing had superseded mining as the centrepiece of the local economy.

5 FROM POKOLBIN TO NORTH ROTHBURY

Continue until McDonalds Rd crosses over Debeyers Rd.
To the right is Pokolbin Estate Vineyard and a little further north, Thompsons Road heads off to the left. On the corner is Cypress Lakes Golf and Country Cub. Almost opposite this turn-off is Tamburlaine Wines.
Turn left off McDonalds Rd into Campbells Lne.
Almost opposite the turn-off is Brokenwood. Just beyond it, to the right, is the Small Winemakers Centre. The next intersection is with Pokolbin's other main thoroughfare, Broke Road. On the corner is McGuigan Hunter Village, a large complex containing McGuigan Bros Winery and Cellars, the Hunter Valley Cheese Company, the Cellar Restaurant, the Vineyard Resort and Convention Centre, aqua golf, putt-putt golf, a children's adventure playground, barbecue facilities, a gift shop, eateries and a

miniature steam train that operates on weekends as well as school and public holidays.

6 BROKE ROAD WINERIES

Turn left into Broke Rd and head west.
Broke Road joins the village and district of Broke in the west to Allandale Road in the east. Starting from the intersection of McDonalds and Broke roads and heading west, you will pass Peppers Creek Winery and Antiques at the corner of Broke and Ekerts roads and then, at the end of a little side road on the left, Tyrrells Winery, with picnic and barbecue facilities. The second oldest winery in the Pokolbin area, Tyrrells was established in 1859 by Edward Tyrrell, a nephew of the first Anglican Bishop of Newcastle, who produced his first batch of wine in 1864. An old slab hut built by Edward Tyrrell remains, along with antiquated hand presses and wooden casks. The winery hosts Jazz in the Vines in October. Further along the road are Chateau Francois and Oakvale Winery and Cottage which also contains Bacchus Books (established in 1893) and the Butterflies Gallery and Garden Cafe.

7 HERMITAGE ROAD

Continue on towards Broke and turn north on Hermitage Rd, which runs north to Belford on the New England Hwy.
Hardy's Hunter Ridge Wines is to the left, just south of Deaseys Road. On the other side of Deaseys Road, to the right, are the Hunter Estate Winery and Cellars, the Hunter's largest winery, located at the Hunter Resort.

8 DEASEYS ROAD

Turn right into Deaseys Rd.
Deaseys Road is a gravel road that runs eastwards from Hermitage Road to McDonalds Road. To the left are Marsh Estate (specialising in red and white table wines), Terrace Vale, along a little side road on the left, Paxton–Brown Carriages which offer a leisurely horse-drawn ride about the vineyards and Hunter Valley Hot-Air Ballooning and, just before you reach McDonalds

Road, Sutherland Wines. Past the corner, on opposite side of McDonalds Road, are Latara Wines which specialises in semillon and Tewksbury Estate, which has a good range of red and white table wines.

9 DOWN BRANXTON ROAD

Turn right onto Branxton Rd and head back towards Cessnock. About 4km south of Rothbury you will reach Palmers Lne.
To the left are Moorebank Vineyard a picnic ground; Calais Estates, which has picnic and barbecue facilities; Little's Winery with a gallery and shaded picnic area (open every day 10.00am–4.30pm, and Carindale Wines, which possesses a small art gallery. Further south is Lesnik Family Wines, which offer a wide range of wines from table reds to liqueurs. Between Broke Road and Cessnock, on Lovedale Road (Lovedale Road heads east off the main road, which is now called Allandale Road), are Pokolbin Old Wares and Collectables, Capercaille Wines which has a gallery and picnic facilities, and Allandale Winery with a gallery and fine views.

10 NULKABA

Head south along Allandale Rd, which originally led through the farms that bordered Black Creek and Anvil Creek.
With a view to the future development of a village, land was reserved here for a church and school during the first surveys of the area in 1829. St Luke's Anglican Church was built in 1867, the original slab-construction St Patrick's Catholic Church in 1872 and a school in 1877. Intended as an administrative centre for the district, a village was laid out in 1884–1885 as 'The Village of Pokolbin' but became known as Cessnock later in the decade. That name was transferred to the town now known as Cessnock in 1908 and the local name, Nulkaba, was officially adopted in 1927.

As you drive north you can see, to the left, just past the cemetery, St Patrick's and then, to the right, the interesting sight of some large and unusual-looking pottery kilns (c.1880). They are now located in the grounds of Potters Tavern.

11 CESSNOCK

Cessnock lies 1km further south.
Cessnock became a major mining centre at the turn of the 20th century, so are only a few heritage buildings that exist. However Cessnock and its surroundings have many interesting attractions to see, including the memorials of the Bellbird mining disaster and Rothbury riots depicting the region's strong mining heritage, and the restored historic timber building of Marthaville in Wollombi Road. This is the former house of George Brown, who was a builder, saw miller, prospector, magistrate, coroner, councillor and vigneron in early Cessnock.

In the sandstone country of this area, evidence of Aboriginal settlement is apparent in the many caves and shelters which hold hand stencils, tribal stencils, tribal markings and other art images.

42 UP THE HUNTER VALLEY

■ DRIVING TOUR ■ 124KM ■ 6 HOURS ■ FROM THE HISTORIC HUNTER VALLEY TO HORSE COUNTRY

Moving north-west from the Hunter Valley with its grapes and coal mines the traveller roams through rich farming country which is famous for its outstanding beef cattle and horse studs.

The New England Highway from Maitland to Murrurundi passes through some of the richest grazing country in New South Wales. This is a region famous for its elegant homes (Belltrees, near Scone, is the family home of Patrick White, the Nobel Prize-winning author), its fine horse studs and pleasant undulating countryside.

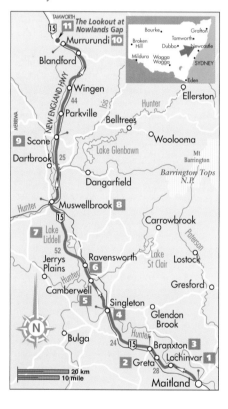

1 LOCHINVAR

Starting in Maitland, follow the New England Hwy west for 14km to Lochinvar.

The land was granted in 1823 to Leslie Duguid, a founding director of the Commercial Bank of Sydney. A village was laid out in 1840 and a bridge built over the Hunter River in 1874. St Helena Close heads off the highway to the left. It leads to St Helena House, which was built in 1869 by French winemaker Philbert Terrier, who was invited to Australia in 1857 to teach viticulture and viniculture. The house is now a restaurant. A roadside stop to the left on the outskirts of Lochinvar offers a fine prospect over the valley. Lovedale Road runs off to the right to the winery area.

2 GRETA

Continue along the New England Hwy for another 8km to Greta.

Greta has several older buildings that reflect the fact they were constructed in the early to mid-19th century. The township was surveyed and named in 1842 but it wasn't until the establishment of the Anvil Creek Coal Mine in 1874 that the first development was prompted. Four hotels, four churches, a school and school of arts soon appeared.

Entering Greta from the east, the town's historic buildings are virtually all situated on the left-hand side of the highway within one block of Wyndham Street. Tattersalls Hotel has been recently renovated. Two doors down is the post office with a modest gallery display, then the old council chambers (1912), which contains local historical records, a 19th-century photographic display, coalmining material and items pertaining to the postwar immigrant staging camp. Next door is the gracious if somewhat dilapidated brick courthouse (*c.*1890) with arched windows and slate gambrel roof. There is an arcaded verandah on three sides with a pediment over the entry.

3 BRANXTON

Branxton is 4km west of Greta, along the New England Hwy.

Branxton is a small settlement with a number of interesting historic buildings. Just beyond the Dalwood Road turn-off is Elderslie Road and just past that is Branxton Inn Licensed Restaurant and Gallery, situated in a building that dates back to 1862. Take the next left into Church Sreet. On the left, as you go up the hill, is St John's Anglican Church (1871–1879), a brick building with a tower designed by the distinguished architect J. Horbury Hunt. Over the road is the courthouse, made of brick with a gabled roof and attractive front verandah. Adjacent is the police station (1880, designed by colonial architect James Barnet), a symmetrical, single-storey brick building with a front verandah topped by a stepped gabled roof and pediment over the doorway.

Take the first right into Drinan Street. At the end of Drinan Street turn right into Clift Street, which will lead back to the highway. On the corner of Drinan and Clift streets is the old Branxton Methodist (now Uniting) Church (1865). On the corner of Clift Street and the highway is the Victoria Building (*c.*1860). Originally a general store, it is now a coffee shop.

4 SINGLETON

Continue north-west along the New England Hwy for 34km to Singleton.

The area around Singleton was officially opened up for settlement in 1823. Benjamin Singleton established a punt service across the river and the ford became a favourite river crossing for people heading north. He opened a flour mill on the riverbank in 1829 to process grain and a post office was established at his inn the same year. Proper roads were in place by 1831. It was Singleton's grant which, when subdivided in 1836, formed the basis of the town.

The Old Court Theatre, Kingdon Street, Scone.

Singleton has some fine heritage buildings. Many of the commercial and administrative buildings date from the boom period, which occurred after the arrival of the railway in 1863. Start on the eastern side of town on pleasant, tree-lined Dangar Road, which contains a number of older buildings of architectural quality including Lonsdale at the corner of Dangar Road and Boundary Street. This impressive late Victorian residence with its decorative verandah and fine landscaping was built in 1890 and extended in 1907.

At the corner of Bishopsgate and Goulburn streets is the Christian Israelite Church. Opposite is a complex of Anglican buildings situated in a beautiful churchyard ringed with jacaranda trees. Facing on to Goulburn Street is the All Saints Sunday School (1864). The two main buildings are the All Saints Anglican Church and the beautiful and rather elaborate Victorian Gothic rectory. The latter was built in 1875 and features steep gables, chimneys, a red slate roof and beautiful, gabled dormer windows.

5 CAMBERWELL

Proceed north-west along the New England Hwy for 13km to Camberwell.

In the tiny village of Camberwell is St Clement's Anglican Church, which was built between 1844 and 1855.

6 RAVENSWORTH

Ravensworth is 6km beyond Camberwell.

At the tiny settlement of Ravensworth is a huge open-cut coalmine (on the roadside to the right) which exclusively supplies coal for domestic power generation. If you take a right turn into Hebden Road, near the school, you will see Ravensworth House to the right 3.5km along the road. The house was built in 1840 and was possibly designed by the prominent architect John Verge.

7 LAKE LIDDELL

Follow the highway for about 17km to the turn-off on the left to Bayswater Power Station where there is a visitors centre.

Bayswater Power Station Visitors Centre is open weekdays with free tours by appointment only on Tuesdays and Fridays 1.00pm–3.00pm. You can walk around the lake and there are displays inside the centre.

8 MUSWELLBROOK

Follow the New England Hwy for another 15km to Muswellbrook.

Muswellbrook was laid out and gazetted in 1833. The first post office was established in 1837 and that year, when Edward Denny Day was made first police magistrate of the district, a mounted police force, police barracks and courthouse were established.

The town's newly opened Tourist Information Centre is located at 87 Hill Street. A heritage walk brochure is available at the centre, along with maps and general information about the area. Inquiries about visits to the many local horse studs should be made here.

The Court House, Scone.

The buildings in town of particular interest include Eatons Hotel, a lovely old two-storey building with roundheaded French windows and an enormous verandah featuring fluted cast-iron columns. A tribute to its age is the opening beside the main entrance which was designed to allow access to the stables at the rear. On Hill Street is St John's Presbyterian Church, designed by W.L. Pender and erected in 1913–1915, with an arched lancet doorway, fine cedar door, impressive spire and beautiful interior, especially the ceiling, organ and pulpit. The headstones of early Presbyterian settlers John and Janet Ferguson, who died in 1843 and 1851 respectively, are built into a nook on the western side of the church.

The next building is an earlier St John's, erected in 1843. The Reverend John Dunmore Lang, a significant figure in colonial church history, preached here in 1850. It is now a Sunday School Hall. On Bridge Street is the post office (1885), which stands in front of the old telegraph office (1861). Next door is the old School of Arts (1871, extended in 1913), which is now the town hall. On the first floor is the Muswellbrook Regional Gallery. Over the road, occupying the first town allotment ever sold (in 1834) is the Royal Hotel (1893). There have been licensed premises on the site since 1835.

9 SCONE

Proceed north out of Muswellbrook along the New England Hwy for 26km to Scone.

Scone, a pleasant rural centre of wide, tree-lined streets, is an important stock-selling centre noted for its horse and cattle studs. The town is known as the Horse Capital of Australia and claims to be the second-largest horse-breeding area in the world, after Kentucky in the United States.

Of interest in the town are the Belmore Hotel (1866), an attractive symmetrical building with side wings, stone quoins and iron columns supporting a timber verandah. At the intersection with St Aubins Street is the Royal Hotel with a fine cast-iron lacework balcony. Guernsey Street was the main street of the town in the 1840s and

it contains a number of interesting old corrugated-iron buildings with some featuring pressed metal bay windows. St Luke's Anglican Church was built in 1883–1884 to replace an older church erected in 1841. It is of an early English Gothic design and is set among well-established trees. The Scone Historical Museum and Records Centre is situated in the old lockup (the town's second) and constable's quarters, both being built in 1870. There are two cells to the rear of the gaol which were intended as holding pens for those awaiting trial or transfer. The main display presents cultural artefacts grouped in periods that relate to different aspects of local history, including pre-colonial settlement and the goldmining days.

10 MURRURUNDI

Head north out of Scone along the New England Hwy for 44km to Murrurundi.

Murrurundi is a small rural town. The main street has been declared an urban conservation area. Buildings of interest in the town include the Haydonton Inn, made of local bricks in the early 1850s. A little further north, almost opposite Brook Street, is a skin and wool store built about 1856 of handmade thumbprint bricks. Over the road is the White Hart Hotel. The original dining room remains from the timber structure erected in 1842. The old Royal Hotel (1863) has a hipped roof, upstairs verandah and quoins. Cobb & Co used it as a changing depot until 1867. To the rear of the building are the old stables (best seen from Murulla Street), built in 1860 of local sandstone.

11 THE LOOKOUT AT NOWLANDS GAP

Proceed north from Murrurundi along the New England Hwy.

Just north of Murrurundi the highway rises up and over the Liverpool Range via the Murrurundi Gap, otherwise known as Nowlands Gap after William Nowland, a farmer from Singleton who discovered this route across the mountains in the late 1820s. Today there are truck stops at Nowlands Gap which provide excellent views south over Murrurundi and the upper Hunter Valley.

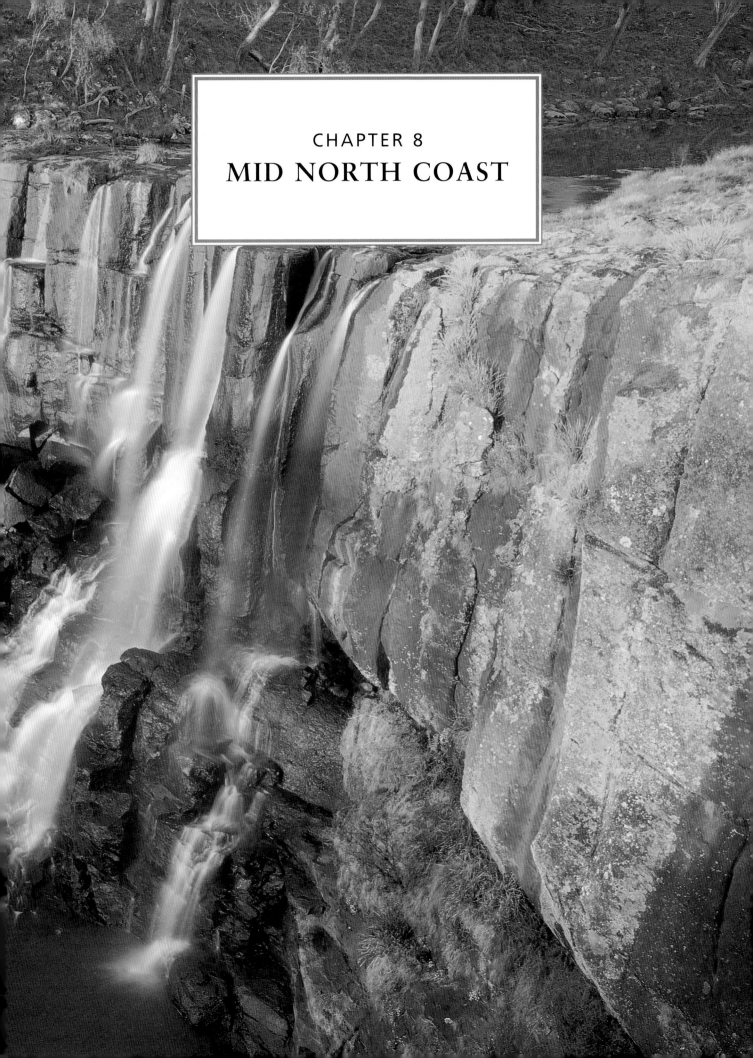

CHAPTER 8
MID NORTH COAST

43 PORT STEPHENS—THE SOUTH SIDE

■ DRIVING TOUR ■ 124KM ■ 1 DAY ■ EXPLORING THE BEACHES AND SOUTHERN COAST OF PORT STEPHENS

One of the hidden treasures of the New South Wales coast is the area around Port Stephens where holiday-makers, anglers, surfers and people seeking quietude in the sun.

Too often Sydneysiders, going for a seaside holiday, get in the car and just drive and drive. They roar past Newcastle and Port Stephens on their way north without realising that this section of the Central Coast is absolutely delightful. Port Stephens is a pretty seaside resort with good accommodation and a marvellous marina. Nearby are virtually pristine beaches where, even in summer, it is easy to find a stretch of beach all to yourself. Port Stephens is a secret well worth sharing; a delightful stretch of coastline with that lazy holiday feeling.

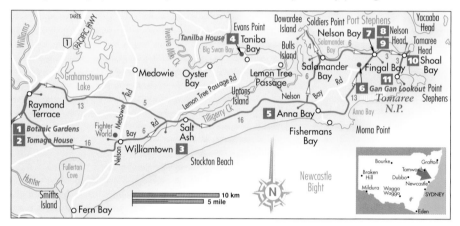

1 BOTANIC GARDENS

Start at the intersection of the Pacific Hwy and William St in Raymond Terrace. Head south along the highway for about 5km until you see, to your left, the signposts indicating the turn-off to the attractive Hunter Region Botanic Gardens.

These beautiful grounds were developed and are maintained on a volunteer basis. Walks have been established through the wildflowers and other native vegetation. The visitors centre has a botanic library. While donations are non-compulsory, they are certainly welcome.

2 TOMAGO HOUSE

Continue south for another 2.5km and take the left turn into Tomago Rd. About 4km along this road you will see a small sandstone chapel in an open field to your right. Just beyond it a signpost indicates the entry to Tomago House.

Tomago House was built for barrister Richard Windeyer, who acquired 30 000ac of land in the Hunter Valley between 1838 and 1842. Planning an elaborate agricultural estate, Windeyer initially purchased 850ac in the area, drained the swamps near Grahamstown and began work on the homestead in 1843.

Tomago House is a gracious and elegant mansion of finely tooled sandstone shipped by barge from the Raymond Terrace quarry. The drawing room and dining room are particularly impressive with large bay windows looking out across pleasant grounds and French doors opening out to a flagged sandstone verandah with delicate cast-iron columns. The modest chapel was designed by Maria Windeyer and her sister, and was built of sandstone rubble left over from the mansion's construction. The chapel was intended for the worship of the family, neighbours and the estate workers. The cedar pews, lectern and joinery are original.

3 WILLIAMTOWN

Continue along Tomago Rd for about 13.5km and then turn left at the T-intersection into Nelson Bay Rd, following the sign for Nelson Bay and Williamtown. After about 1.5km turn left, at the roundabout, into Medowie Rd. Another 500m will bring you to the entrance of Fighter World, located in the grounds of the Williamtown RAAF base.

Fighter World is an RAAF museum. Displays include nine decommissioned fighter aircraft, several cockpits for the young to sit in, a very large collection of handcrafted and entirely accurate wooden aeroplane models, as well as missiles, weapons, other military items, a video, educational displays, games, souvenirs and a refectory. There is also a viewing platform from which to watch the base's Hornets landing.

4 TANILBA HOUSE

Return along Medowie Rd to the roundabout and turn left, back into Nelson Bay Rd. After 6km, turn left at the roundabout into Lemon Tree Passage Rd. Continue for 10.2km and turn left, passing through two sets of gateways, then take the gentle left into Diggers Drv. It reaches Peace Pde which becomes Tanilba Ave. You will see some stone fencing and a temple. Turn left into Admiralty Ave and then follow this loop road around to the entrance of Tanilba House.

The beautiful and elegant Tanilba House is one of Australia's oldest buildings and one of the principal attractions of Port Stephens. The foundations were laid in 1837 by Lieutenant Caswell, brother-in-law of Robert Hoddle who designed the city of Melbourne, and the house was built of quartz porphyry stone from a nearby quarry.

Rocky coastline at Fishermans Bay, Port Stephens.

The mortar came from lime produced by burning oyster shells.

Rather than being a museum piece, Tanilba House has a very comfortable, rustic and lived-in feel. Indeed, it is still inhabited and, for a small entry fee, you will join a brief tour of the house on Wednesdays, weekends, and every day during school and public holidays.

A focal point is the flagged verandah, covered with creepers that gently filter the light, creating an atmosphere of tranquillity. The views over the lawn, the fine gardens and the bay are excellent. The small gaol and exterior kitchen are reminders of the days of convicts and servants. There are interesting historic displays and a remarkable book collection with items dating back to the 17th century.

5 ANNA BAY, BOAT HARBOUR AND ONE MILE BEACH

Return along Lemon Tree Passage Rd and turn left back onto Nelson Bay Rd. After about 17km turn right into Gan Gan Rd. It is a further kilometre to the intersection of Gan Gan Rd and Morna Point Rd at Anna Bay.

Anna Bay is the first of a number of small settlements that lie between Newcastle Bight and Port Stephens. They are all characterised by caravan parks, quiet beaches and pleasant walks.

6 GAN GAN LOOKOUT

Follow Morna Point Rd southwards and turn right to explore Birubi Point or left for Fishermans Bay. Continue eastwards along Gan Gan Rd for the turn-offs to Boat Harbour and One Mile Beach. You will come to a T-intersection 7.7km from Anna Bay. Turn right into Nelson Bay Rd. From here it is about 500m to Lily Hill Rd (on the left), which will take you up to the Gan Gan Lookout car park.

This lookout is one of the highlights of the area. The view is breathtaking, especially at dusk. From here it is possible to look south to the opposite side of the peninsula; south-west down to Newcastle and the cargo vessels in its harbour; west to the mountain boundary; north-west over Soldiers Point; and north-east over Hawks Nest to the two gigantic headlands that loom over the port's entrance, Nelson Head and Nelson Bay. Lily Hill Road is named after the abundance of enormous Gymea lilies to be found at the top the hill. The stalks, which grow to 5m, are edible and were used by the Aborigines for spears.

7 NELSON BAY

Return to Nelson Bay Rd and follow it for another 1.5km to the centre of Nelson Bay.

Nelson Bay is a coastal resort town at the mouth of Port Stephens. A group of Chinese fishermen established a base here early in the 19th century. They cured their catch and sent it back to China and to Chinese merchants in Sydney and Melbourne. The first survey of Nelson Bay was carried out in 1874. A post office and school were established in 1883. By 1886 there were about 30 residents. The villagers led a peaceful life based around fishing until

The marina and shops at Nelson Bay.

developers arrived in the late 1960s. Today, Nelson Bay has everything the visitor could want. Boats are moored in the harbour. It is pleasant to walk west along the harbour-front as far as you can go then follow the walkway which juts out into the waters of Port Stephens. If you look due west you will see the string of lights that indicates Soldiers Point stretching out almost to the northern shore of the port.

Halifax Park is located off Victoria Parade (behind the visitors centre). A bicycle and walking track follows the shoreline west to the next beach at Dutchmans Bay, where the white sand and attractive beach is surrounded by casuarina and eucalypt.

8 NELSON HEAD

From the visitors centre, follow Victoria Pde eastwards along the shoreline. The road bends to the right, at which point it becomes Shoal Bay Rd. Victoria Pde continues on through some lovely parkland to Little Nelson Beach. Drive through this section and you will see a steep narrow road heading up the hill which leads to another car park outside the lighthouse complex.

Nelson Head separates Little Nelson Beach to the west from Shoal Bay to the east. On Nelson Head sits the Inner Lighthouse, dating from 1872 but still operating and classified by the National Trust. Originally lit by three kerosene lamps, electric lights were installed in 1946. The system was recently automated. The cottage was built in 1875. This small cluster of buildings incorporates a modest historical display. There are also films, panoramic views, a tea room and a gift shop.

9 LITTLE NELSON BEACH

Return down the steep hill to Little Nelson Beach.

Little Nelson Beach has a car park, a large boat ramp, a wharf and a children's play area. In the clearing over the road from the picnic and play area are several Aboriginal canoe trees—trees which, in the distant past, had a large chunk of bark carved out and lifted off in the rough shape of a dugout canoe. The cuts are still plainly visible and are surviving remnants of the land's occupation by the Worimi people before

European settlement. The dense bushland area behind this small beach (the area adjacent to the enormous anchor) is a flora reserve.

10 SHOAL BAY AND TOMAREE NATIONAL PARK

Continue up Dixon Drv to the intersection with Shoal Bay Rd and turn left. Keep to the left, following the shoreline past the Shoal Bay shops to the end of the road, where there is a car park and picnic area at the base of Tomaree Head.

Shoal Bay was supposedly named by Governor Lachlan Macquarie because of its sand shoals. There is a holiday park at Shoal Bay and you can hire aquatic equipment on the beach (in season).

At the easternmost edge of Shoal Bay is Tomaree Head (168m high), which marks the north-eastern tip of Tomaree National Park. Its beaches are attractive and ideal for swimming and fishing. The park is full of birdlife and, from July to February, wildflowers.

Adjacent to the car park is the start of a fairly arduous walking track to the summit of Tomaree Head. En route is Fort Tomaree, which was established on the headland during World War II. Two large gun emplacements lie along the main track.

11 FINGAL BAY

From the Tomaree Head car park, return along Shoal Bay Rd, taking the first substantial left into Tomaree Rd. A further 1.5km will bring you to a T-intersection. Turn left into Marine Drv. After 1.1km you will see a park adjacent to the beach at Fingal Bay where there is a playground and a kiosk.

Fingal Bay has a resort, a patrolled beach, boat ramp and fishing from both the beach and from Fingal Head. Whales can sometimes be spotted offshore between September and November or, less frequently, from late May to July. They like to rub their barnacles off on a reef 50m offshore.

Return along Marine Drv and Tomaree Rd and then turn left, back into Shoal Bay Rd. Follow Shoal Bay Rd all the way back to Nelson Bay and then head south-west along Stockton Rd which soon becomes Nelson Bay Rd. Continue westwards for about 28km and then turn right into Richardson Rd which, after another 17km, reaches a T-intersection with the Pacific Hwy.

44 PORT STEPHENS—THE NORTH SIDE

■ DRIVING AND WALKING TOUR ■ 115KM ■ 1 DAY ■ FORGOTTEN COASTLINE

The northern coastline of Port Stephens is peaceful and pleasant. It lies neatly between Myall Lakes and the quiet waters of the port.

*I*n the mid-1990s, after John Howard became Australian Prime Minister, the Australian public were introduced to the tiny seaside resort of Hawks Nest. It was revealed that Mr Howard and his family had been taking their summer holidays at Hawks Nest for decades. What was the appeal? Curious visitors found that Tea Gardens and Hawks Nest and the northern coast of Port Stephens were notable because developers and tourism had bypassed them. They were sleepy seaside resorts on the edge of the Myall Lakes National Park, where families had managed to keep the quiet pleasures to themselves. Today, not much has changed.

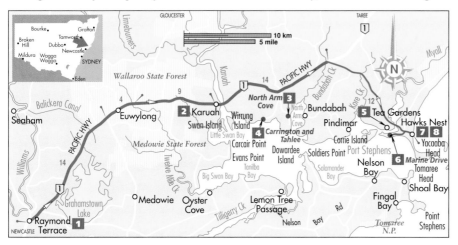

1 RAYMOND TERRACE

Start at the intersection of the Pacific Hwy and William St in Raymond Terrace. Grahamstown Lake is to your right as you head north along the highway.

Raymond Terrace's riverbank location makes it a good spot for waterskiing, boating and riverside picnics. There are two boat ramps in town: one off Riverside Park in Hunter Street and the other on the northern side of the Fitzgerald Bridge, which is a good place to stop to have a look at the river junction.

Grahamstown Lake is adjacent to the Pacific Highway just north-east of Raymond Terrace and is very beautiful. This lake is less developed and populated than Lake Macquarie with quiet, gentle foreshores and lengthy stretches without a sole residence in sight.

2 KARUAH

Continue in a north-easterly direction along the Pacific Hwy. Karuah is 28km from Raymond Terrace.

Karuah is a small town on the banks of the Karuah River. Once occupied by the Worimi people, the area was originally known to Europeans as Sawyers Point. Governor Lachlan Macquarie named the river the Clyde. The indigenous placename, thought to mean 'native plum tree', was later adopted for both the waterway and township.

Today, Karuah is the gateway to the northern arm of Port Stephens. There is a holiday resort in town, and beside the river,

a boat ramp and picnic spot where there are boats for hire: just turn off the highway on the western side of the bridge. Fishing is a popular pastime.

3 NORTH ARM COVE

A further 7.2km beyond the Karuah bridge turn right into Tahlee Rd. After 1km a branch road appears to the left signposted for North Arm Cove.

At the end of World War I proposals were made for the development of this area as a major industrial port city. Walter Burley Griffin, who was responsible for the layout of Canberra, put forward one design. When Griffin's company went into liquidation, wealthy realtor Henry F. Halloran bought up the land and subdivided it in expectation of the sales and the linkage of the 'city' to the main railway line but nothing came of the proposal. Today, North Arm Cove is a very attractive little settlement amid forest on the shore of Port Stephens. The Aboriginal name for the point was Weepi.

4 CARRINGTON AND TAHLEE

Return along North Arm Rd until it rejoins Tahlee Rd and turn left. It is 3km to the tiny settlements of Carrington and Tahlee.

Carrington and Tahlee have strong historical associations with the Australian Agricultural Company (AAC), which was formed in 1824 to take advantage of a report recommending

that wealthy settlers should be given land and convict labour in order to develop the local economy. The company aimed at producing fine wool for English mills and crops for the English market. It was granted half a million acres on the northern side of Port Stephens in 1826 and a base of operations was established at present-day Carrington with 80 settlers, 720 sheep and some horse and cattle.

A remnant from the company's days is the old church (adjacent to Tahlee Road), which was erected in 1846–1847 as the Church of the Holy Trinity. The church was closed in the early 1860s but was restored and reopened in 1888 by R.H.D. White. The building ceased its life as a church in 1949 and is now privately owned and not open to the public. Other reminders include a kiln (1834), used for making the settlement's building bricks, the boat harbour, tarring pits, claypits and the company bell. Garden Island lies just offshore.

Tahlee House is 600m beyond the church, built by convict labour in 1826 for the AAC's first manager, Robert Dawson. A fine example of colonial architecture, the sand-stock brick homestead, impressive reception and ballroom wing and outbuildings are beautifully situated upon extensive grounds that run from the shoreline up the eastern side of the hill on which the house is located. Additions to the original structure were made by subsequent occupants in 1832, the mid-1830s and, most notably, in the 1880s when Robert White rebuilt the verandahs, erected the large timber billiards room and ballroom and did much of the landscaping and the planting of exotic species.

A stone and brick slipway below the house, known as the Boat Harbour, was used to build the steamer Karuah under the direction of AAC superintendent Sir Edward Parry in 1831. There is also a cottage reputedly dating back to 1825. The company sold Tahlee House in 1853. The complex is currently owned by a Bible college that is happy for visitors to look around on weekdays. About halfway between the church and Tahlee House, on elevated ground, is the old AAC cemetery.

5 TEA GARDENS

Return along Tahlee Rd to the Pacific Hwy and turn right. After 7km there is a turn-off on the right, signposted for Tea Gardens and Hawks Nest. Tea Gardens is about 8km from the highway.

The small township of Tea Gardens is separated from the town of Hawks Nest by the mouth of the Myall River, which runs from the Myall Lakes down to Port

Collecting worms for fishing on the beach at Salamander Bay.

Stephens, and joined to it by the Singing Bridge, named for its tendency to act like a wind harp in a strong south-westerly breeze. The local economy has traditionally revolved around seafood and timber. While today there is still a fishing cooperative and woodchip mills still work the forests, BHP's sandmining operations are probably the principal source of local income if not the predominant employer.

The first Europeans to work in the area were timber-getters, who took an interest in the forests (mostly red cedar) along the Myall River early in the 19th century. The timber was hauled by bullock train to mills, then carted by punt downriver. Ships bound for Newcastle and Sydney picked up the timber, unloading the stone they carried for ballast on the banks of the river, much of which was used in the construction of the rock walls which are still in evidence today. The mouth of the Myall River was crossed by punt until a ferry service was established in 1928, to be replaced by the bridge in 1974.

6 MARINE DRIVE

As you enter Tea Gardens, turn left off Myall St into Coupland St. At its end turn right into Marine Drv, which follows the riverbank of the Myall River south to the bridge.

This frontage is Tea Gardens' most impressive feature. The streetscape is pleasant and at the end of the road there is a children's park, swimming pool (open from October to April), a noticeboard with information for anglers plus pedestrian access to the bridge. Dolphins can occasionally be seen in these waters.

At Tea Gardens, visitors can pursue a range of activities, mostly relating to the proximity of water: boating, swimming, surfing, windsurfing, waterskiing, diving, fishing and canoeing.

On the wharf opposite the Tea Gardens Hotel Motel are the departure times for the ferry to Nelson Bay, on the southern peninsula of Port Stephens. There are two caravan parks and three boat ramps along Marine Drive, and it is from this location that you can hire a boat or houseboat and join the various river, lake, fishing, deep-sea fishing and dolphin-watch cruises.

7 HAWKS NEST

Turn off Marine Drv into any side street and then turn left, back into Myall St, to cross the bridge that separates Tea Gardens from Hawks Nest.

The quiet seaside township of Hawks Nest, with both ocean and river frontage, is located at the northern head of Port Stephens. The eastern edge of Hawks Nest faces the ocean, its beaches rim the forests and lagoons of nearby Myall Lakes National Park.

Hawks Nest was named after a large tree that was a favourite nesting place of hawks, situated near the old hotel and used as a navigational marker in the early days. One pioneer was Frank Motum, who arrived from England in 1877. With his family, Motum established a hauling business shipping fish to the Newcastle and Sydney markets.

Aquatic activities are a major attraction at Hawks Nest. The proximity of Myall Lakes National Park also makes bushwalking, birdwatching, camping and the exploration of four-wheel-drive tracks popular.

Once across the bridge, you will find yourself on Kingfisher Avenue. To your left is a reserve noted for its koala colony. There have been further sightings along Mungo Brush Road and in the national park.

8 HAWKS NEST BEACH

At the end of Kingfisher Ave turn right into Tuloa Ave and then left into Booner St. Follow Booner St to its end and turn right into Beach Rd and continue along to the parking area. Walk the short distance across to the beach.

Hawks Nest beach is very long and very beautiful. Cabbage Tree Island (at 26ha) looms just offshore. The island was named after the cabbage tree palms in the two gullies on the its western side, the only known nesting site of Gould's petrel. The one island in southern Australia to include rainforest habitat, Cabbage Tree was also the first gazetted flora and fauna reserve in New South Wales.

It is well worth the 2–3km walk (about two hours) along the spit that separates Hawks Nest from Yacaaba Head, the enormous headland at the north-eastern tip of Port Stephens. When you reach the base of the promontory, a sign stands adjacent to a well-developed path declaring the Yacaaba Head Walk. The path leads around the base of Yacaaba to its pebbly southern side, where you can look out across the mouth of the bay to the southern peninsula of Port Stephens. Just offshore is an area known as Dolphin Hole which dolphins frequent on a daily basis to socialise and rub their bodies on the smooth pebbles.

Millions of years ago this was low-lying and relatively flat country until a massive volcanic disturbance thrust the land upwards. Lava, subsidence and millions of years of erosion produced a dramatically undulating landscape of hills and valleys. The headlands and offshore islands represent some of the ancient volcanic peaks from this topography and the rocky outcrops are the product of lava flow.

Return along Beach Rd, and back across the bridge, then follow Myall St for 8km, back to the Pacific Hwy and turn left. It is 44km back to Raymond Terrace.

View of Yacaaba Head, Hawks Nest, from Tomaree Head.

45 AROUND THE BARRINGTON TOPS NATIONAL PARK

■ DRIVING TOUR ■ 405KM ■ 1 DAY ■ HISTORIC TOWNS AND MOUNTAIN COUNTRY

A favourite retreat from Sydney and ideal for bushwalking and horse riding, the Barrington Tops area is characterised by great natural beauty and extensive wilderness areas.

The coastal towns of Nelson Bay and Forster and the beautiful Myall Lakes lie to the east. Behind the hinterland are the towns of Dungog, Stroud and Gloucester, where time has stood still. And beyond the towns the low coastal hills rise into the beautiful wilderness that is the Barrington Tops National Park. Here, dirt roads wind through cool-climate and dense forests. Although the coast is less than an hour's drive away, you feel you are in a part of New South Wales that has not changed for tens of thousands of years.

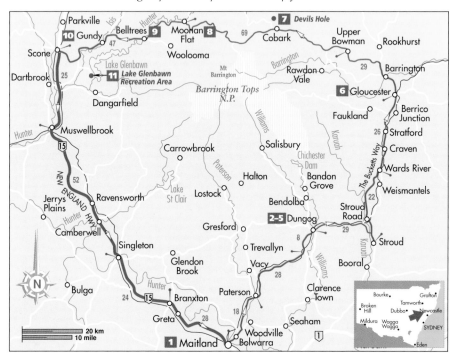

1 MAITLAND

Maitland is situated on the Hunter River flood plains. The city has had 15 major floods during the period of European settlement. The last flood was in 1955 when 11 people were killed, which prompted the construction of levees, spillways and flood channels. So prominent have floods been to Maitland's history that there is a major artistic presentation in the grounds of the visitors centre.

2 DUNGOG

Head north from Maitland via Belmore Rd, which will take you through Bolwarra. This road becomes Maitland Rd. Turn right alomg Paterson Rd. Paterson is 18km north of Maitland. From Paterson continue north for another 5km and turn right onto the Dungog Rd. At the end of this 23km road turn left, heading north to Dungog (another 7km).

Dungog is essentially a cattle-raising, dairying and timber town. The first Europeans in the area are thought to have been stockmen in

search of wayward cattle. The thick stands of cedar in the area soon drew timber-getters. The land for a township to be named Upper Williams was set aside in 1830, but the name the name Dungog was adopted in 1834.

It was at this time that settlers petitioned the authorities for a military post to deal with bushranging in the area. Captain

Thunderbolt and his wife had been involved in plundering homesteads in the Munni, Monkerai, Main Creek and Underbank districts. The hilly terrain made for natural cover. The town courthouse was built between 1835 and 1838 as a barracks and stables for troopers, who successfully drove Thunderbolt north over Gloucester Tops and out of the area.

3 APEX LOOKOUT

Proceed to the northern end of the main street, turn left into Brown St and drive up the hill. Turn left into Hospital Rd at the T-intersection. On the right, 100m along, is the hospital (established in 1892). Opposite is a parking area and the lookout.

The Apex Lookout, at the western edge of town, provides an interesting view over Dungog. From this position it is clear that the town is nestled in a valley surrounded by mountains.

4 HISTORIC BUILDINGS

Return along Hospital Rd, turn back into Brown St and proceed downhill to Lord St.

Near the intersection of Brown and Lord streets are several buildings of historical interest. Behind the police station, on the hillside, is the courthouse. The police residence was originally a lock-up dating from 1884. Over the road is St Joseph's School (1888) and St Mary's Catholic Church. On the north-eastern corner is the Courthouse Hotel (1868) with cast-iron lacework on the balconies and eaves.

5 DOWLING STREET

Continue along Brown St for one block, back to the main street (Dowling St), turn left and proceed north for one block to the Hooke St intersection.

The main street of Dungog, named after Chief Justice James D. Dowling, is an urban conservation area. At the corner of Dowling and Hooke streets is the Bank Hotel, an attractive building with an upstairs balcony, cast-iron fencing and decorative columns.

The Courthouse Hotel in Dungog.

The Bucketts viewed from Gloucester.

Diagonally opposite is the former CBC Bank (1874), now the National Australia Bank. This fine two-storey building has an upstairs balcony with cast-iron lacework on the columns and eaves. At 206 Dowling Street is Coolalie (1895), a beautiful two-storey brick building with cast-iron lacework on the eaves and a lovely garden. Across Mackay Street is the old School of Arts building, now an historical museum with displays on local industry and history. Almost opposite is the Royal Hotel and next door to that, at 72 Dowling Street, is Kirralee (1910), a gracious and carefully restored Edwardian house with wide verandahs and stained-glass work on the door. One of the oldest surviving buildings in town is the Anglican Christ Church, located at the corner of Chapman and Dowling streets. Building of the church commenced in 1849 and was completed in 1858.

Horse sculpture from cedar at Hookes Creek Forest Resort near Gloucester.

6 GLOUCESTER

Return north along Dowling St and head out of town. The road soon will lead you eastwards (signposted for Stroud and Gloucester). After 22km you will reach a T-intersection. Turn left onto the Bucketts Way and head due north for another 49km to Gloucester.

Gloucester, known as the gateway to Barrington Tops, is a charming country town nestled in a valley under a range of impressive monolith hills called the Bucketts. It is the principal town of a cattle-raising, dairying and mixed farming district. Robert Dawson, the first manager of the Australian Agricultural Company (AAC) that was formed in England in 1824 with the object of raising fine wool and agricultural products, established an outstation which he named Gloucester after the English town because the landscape reminded him of the county of Gloucestershire.

The main attractions in the town are The Homestead (c.1830), located opposite the saleyards, on the western side of the Bucketts Way at the southern end of town. It is a single-storey sandstock brick residence built by the ACC on what was then the main north coast road. It is currently a private residence.

Just to the north, at the corner of the Bucketts Way and Oak Street, is St Clement's Historic Park. Gloucester's first church was built here by the Australian Agricultural Company in 1860. Just behind the park is the Upper Bowman School Museum, which is a typical 19th-century, one-teacher rural schoolhouse with original furniture. From here the Bucketts Way is known as Church Street. At 12 Church Street is the Gloucester Folk Museum, located in the former shire chambers (1909). The Wunderlich pressed-metal ceilings are of interest and, to the rear of the building, are the police lockup and an explosives store from the former goldmining town of Copeland, 14km west of Gloucester.

7 DEVILS HOLE

About 60km from Gloucester, via Barrington Tops Forest Rd, is the Devils Hole Lookout Day Use Area.

The Devils Hole Lookout Day Use Area offers fine views over the Barrington wilderness and adjoining farmlands. It is one of several lookouts signposted along the Barrington Tops Forest Road.

8 MOONAN FLAT

About 93km from Gloucester is a signposted turn-off to the right into Moonan Flat.

Moonan Flat is a peaceful little village in a beautiful setting ringed by the Mount Royal Range. The township was founded in the 1870s to serve the goldminers of the Denison diggings, where the bushranger Thunderbolt held up an hotel in 1867. It was initially proclaimed as Macqueen but known locally as Moonan.

The Victoria Hotel dates from about 1890, while the tin building behind the pine tree is an old bunkhouse built in 1860. It was originally associated with a set of stables (now gone) used by the Cobb & Co coach service which travelled this route.

9 BELLTREES

The main road becomes surfaced 2.5km beyond Moonan Flat. The turn-off to the left to Belltrees is 14km from Moonan Flat.

Belltrees is an 18 000ac horse, sheep and cattle property and an excellent example of a colonial country seat. Established in 1831, Belltrees was built on land granted to Hamilton Sempill, who became the manager of the Segenhoe property in 1830. He named the property Belltrees after the English estate of an ancestor.

When Sempill returned to England, Belltrees passed on to explorer W.C. Wentworth who sold the property in 1853 to the sons of James White. By 1912 it covered 160 000ac, was enclosed by 3200km of fencing and incorporated 64 buildings. The property is still owned, run and occupied by the White family, who raise Belltrees Black Angus cattle and polo ponies.

As you enter the estate off Gundy Road a dirt drive leads past a number of outbuildings. To the left, set back from the road, is the gracious, two-storey brick homestead, which was built in 1907 by Henry White. The homestead features a fine cast-iron verandah on the upper floor, projecting gables from the front roof section, elegant columns, and shuttered windows.

10 GUNDY

Continue along Gundy Rd for another 15km to Gundy.

When gold was located nearby at Stewarts Brook and Moonan Brook, Gundy became a small service centre to the miners and their families. An inn and church were built. By 1881, when the population had risen to 60 there was also a school, post office and stores. In recent years Gundy was used as the setting for the films *Smiley* and *The Shiralee*.

As you enter the town, to the left is St Matthew's Anglican Church (1869). Further on is the Linga Longa Inn. The property of Bellevue, which gave its name to the village, lies behind the old Catholic church. The homestead (c.1872) is a couple of hundred metres off the road on private property.

11 LAKE GLENBAWN RECREATION AREA

Continue along the Gundy Rd towards Scone. After about 11km there is a turn-off on the left into Segenhoe Rd (signposted for Lake Glenbawn and Aberdeen). After a further 2km turn left (signposted for Lake Glenbawn) and continue on for 5.3km to the turn-off (left again) that will take you up to Brushy Hill.

Brushy Hill has two separate lookouts with spectacular views across beautiful Lake Glenbawn. To the east are Mount Woolooma, the Mount Royal Ranges and Barrington Tops. To the north is the Liverpool Range and to the south and west the valleys of the Upper Hunter.

The lake is a popular spot for waterskiing, swimming, sailing, canoeing and sailboarding. The foreshores consist of open woodland with an abundance of birdlife (including galahs, eastern rosellas, pelicans and king parrots) and both kangaroos and wallaroos to be seen in the early morning and at dusk.

Return the way you came until you reach Segenhoe Rd. Cross over Segenhoe Rd and continue on for 7km until you reach a T-intersection at the southern end of Scone. Turn left onto the New England Hwy, which will take you back to Maitland (131km).

46 EXPLORING THE MID NORTH COAST LAKES

■ DRIVING TOUR ■ 151KM ■ 1 DAY ■ THE TRANQUIL BEAUTY OF MYALL LAKES

To the north of Newcastle lie the beautiful Myall Lakes and the quiet settlements of Seal Rocks and Mungo Brush. This is a great area for swimming, fishing and bushwalking.

To appreciate the beauty of this area you must experience it. Bulahdelah, a small township on the Pacific Highway, gives little indication of the lakes that lie to the east of the town. Travellers crossing the Myall River, however, will notice the houseboats moored at the river's edge. Hire one of these houseboats and you are in a magic world of silent lakes, a myriad of native birds, and coastal scrublands that reach to untouched beaches. Myall Lakes is in an area where, because it is a national park, the development of the coastline has been successfully halted.

1 SEAL ROCKS

Seal Rocks is a small, sleepy and isolated beach town south of Forster–Tuncurry. The town's fame rests largely on its beautiful lighthouse and the sense of isolation it enjoys. The very ordinary dirt road that separates the town from the main road (Lakes Way) has kept development at bay and the locals are well pleased with this barrier to excessive development.

Despite resistance to the upgrading of the connecting road, change seems inevitable. There are some very real attractions at Seal Rocks: unspoilt surfing beaches; a noted diving spot; idyllic picnic areas; the nearby Myall Lakes National Park; and, most notably, the spectacularly beautiful Seal Rocks lighthouse—officially known as Sugarloaf Point Lighthouse—which overlooks an unspoilt beach and the group of rocky outcrops offshore that give the area its name.

The jagged and dramatic Seal Rocks are reached by driving to the eastern end of the small township. There are a couple of convenient roadside stops along the way,

however, which offer excellent views over the ocean, beach and shoreline. The view from the parking area opposite the general store and post office is particularly impressive.

2 LIGHTHOUSE AND SEAL ROCKS

Follow the main road to its end, park your car and walk through the gate. It is a few hundred metres to the lighthouse and lookout.

Just before you reach the lighthouse, you will pass a spectacular sea cavern where the ocean surges through a tunnel it has carved at the base of an enormous rock wall. The lighthouse was built in 1875. Before its conversion to mains electricity in the 1960s, one of the lighthouse keepers wrote a detailed account that recalls a time when the beacons and their keepers were vital to shipping around the coast: 'There is an old saying amongst sailors to the effect that more wrecks occur near lighthouses than on

unlit parts of the coast. There are several reasons for this. The most important are that lights are placed where shipping hazards are the greatest and where sea traffic is high.'

No doubt he had Seal Rocks in mind when he made this observation because some 20 wrecks have occurred around there since the lighthouse was established. As recently as 1985 the *Catterthun*, bound from Sydney to China, sank with a loss of 55 lives. It is unknown how many were wrecked before the lighthouse went up, however. The anchor of the steamer *Rainbow*, which sank offshore in 1864, is located just outside the general store. Its boiler is still be seen on Boat Beach. A sign within the grounds declares:

The Sugarloaf Point Lighthouse is built on the point of land bearing that name. The 44-foot [14m] tower of brick and cement was erected and apparatus installed at a cost of $19,000. The light, which is 258 feet [79m] above high water, came into use for the first time on 1 December, 1875. The main white flashing light, visible at sea from a distance of 22 miles [35km] was originally of 122,000 candle power, but was increased to 174,000 candle power on 1 April, 1923. The light is produced by a kerosene vapour burner with the optic, from where 16 equidistant powerful rays are slowly revolving ranging far over land and sea. In addition to the main light, a green subsidiary light of 150 candle power is set at a lower altitude. This green light, visible from a distance of only 3 miles [5km] is designed to alert close cruising

A view of Seal Rocks from the lighthouse.

Boats on the Myall Lakes at Bulahdelah.

Quiet cottages on the edge of Myall Lakes.

vessels of imminent dangers. Sugarloaf Point lighthouse is operated by a staff of three trained lightkeepers and is one of 56 manned lights in use on the Australian coast.

It is not possible to enter the building but the access path leads you to a spot within metres of the lighthouse and its out-buildings. Another path leads you around the buildings to the lookout over Seal Rocks, a collection of rocky islets which are home to the northernmost colony of Australian fur seals. During the summer breeding months the seal population on the rocks can be seen from the mainland.

3 BULAHDELAH

Head out of town on Seal Rocks Rd. After 12km you will reach a T-intersection with the Lakes Way at Bungwahl. Turn left and follow the Lakes Way to its end (24km). Turn left onto the Pacific Hwy and you are immediately on the outskirts of Bulahdelah.

In recent times Bulahdelah has become a popular departure point for an exploration of the area's many state forests and Myall Lakes, which lie to the east. The name Bulahdelah comes from the language of the Worimi people and is thought to mean 'meeting place of two rivers'. The explorer John Oxley gave the name to the mountain that looms to the east. Known locally as Alum Mountain, it was once an important source of the mineral alunite used as a fertiliser and in the textile industry. The area around the mountain has been declared a state forest reserve, Bulahdelah Mountain Forest Park.

People wanting to spend time exploring the Bulahdelah area should visit the town park, where there is a placard listing the region's attractions and a good map showing where to find the various places.

4 BULAHDELAH MOUNTAIN FOREST PARK

About 400m short of the bridge over the Myall River turn left into Meade St, which leads past the State Forestry Commission District Office to the entrance of Bulahdelah Mountain Forest Park.

At the entrance to the park there are information boards, as well as picnic, toilet and children's play facilities. The Twin Dams Nature Trail heads off from here on a 650m ramble through swamp forest, moist and dry eucalypt forest and small pockets of rainforest above Twin Dams, which were built for the alunite mining about 1880. The picnic area was once an alunite stockpile site. The ore was transported down the mountain by cable-operated carriers. A tramline then took skip trucks along Church Street to the river, where the ore was loaded onto barges.

A narrow, steep and rocky road (1.5km) leads from the picnic area at the base of the mountain. At the road's end you will notice what appear to be two trails heading off into the bush, a set of concrete steps near the information board and another trail on the other side of the picnic spot. The two trails join up to form one short track that will take you to the old Tunnel Quarry site.

The concrete steps are a good spot to start the Alunite Trail. They lead up to a track that takes you past the Kimberley Quarry and Ladysmith Quarry sites. Follow the path to the Big Quarry site, where there is a lookout that faces west. The view over Bulahdelah is excellent. When you return to Ladysmith Quarry, follow the steps down the hill to the fence. The track heading down the mountain is the old tramway and leads down to the lower picnic area. The track to your left will take you back to the upper picnic site. The whole walk is about 40 minutes return.

5 BULAHDELAH COURTHOUSE

Return along Meade St and turn left, back onto the highway. After 200m turn left into Crawford St. You will soon come to the courthouse on the corner of Crawford and Anne sts.

The courthouse (1886), situated on a hill to the east of town overlooking the Myall River, is the town's one building of historic interest (1886). It has recently been repainted and restored as a museum. Investigate the cells behind the courthouse.

6 MYALL LAKES NATIONAL PARK

From the courthouse proceed out of town along Anne St which soon becomes Lakes Rd, a poor-quality, unsealed track. Bombah Point is 15km from Bulahdelah, on the Broadwater.

There is a ferry across the Broadwater at Bombah Point, located within the beautiful Myall Lakes National Park, which combines long beaches, freshwater and saltwater lakes, swamps and rugged headlands. The lagoons—Myall Lake, Boolambyte Lake, Two Mile Lake and the Broadwater—are linked by narrow straits which form a continuous waterway. To the east, between the lakes and sea, are high sand dunes with varied vegetation cover. There are 40km of almost unbroken beaches within the national park. This natural combination has produced one of the largest lake systems in Australia.

The area was once inhabited by the Worimi and Birpai people and there are numerous middens on the coast and on Broughton Island. There was relatively little economic activity in the area until sand-mining began in the late 1960s, leading to major struggles between conservationists and mining interests.

A variety of ecosystems exist in the park. Myall Lakes National Park is a very popular holiday spot and its extensive waterways are ideal for sailing, surfing, canoeing, power-boating, kayaking, windsurfing, sunbathing, swimming, camping, waterskiing and bush-walking. The park is at its best from August to October.

The ferry operates every half-hour from 8.00am to 6.00pm. From this point, Mungo Brush Road, a sealed road, leads south-east to Hawks Nest. It is 1.6km to a parking area on the left, from where you can begin a series of bushwalks. Another 4.3km will take you past the Mungo Brush campsite, where you can enjoy the Mungo Brush Rainforest Walk, or embark on the 21km Mungo Track.

A further 6.1km will bring you to the start of the Dark Point walk to the left and the Wallflower Walk to the right. The former leads over a series of vast, denuded and impressive sand dunes, created when the sea level was higher, past an ancient Aboriginal midden to an absolutely beautiful and unspoiled part of coastline looking out over Broughton Island.

It is 7.3km to the other end of the Mungo Brush Walk (signposted on the right-hand side of the road) and 12.3km to the intersection of Mungo Brush Rd and Kingfisher Ave. Turn right into Kingfisher Ave, which leads across the bridge into Tea Gardens. Follow this road for 10km to the T-intersection and turn right onto the Pacific Hwy. From here it is 30km to Bulahdelah and a further 3km to the turn-off, on the right, back into the Lakes Way. Follow the Lakes Way for 24km to the turn-off, on the right, into Seal Rocks Rd. It is a 12km drive back to your starting point.

The Sunken Cavern near Seal Rocks lighthouse.

47 THE HEART OF THE MID NORTH COAST

■ DRIVING TOUR ■ 120KM ■ 1 DAY ■ FISHING, SURFING AND BUSHWALKING

An area of holiday resorts which range from beautiful, chic destinations like Blueys Beach to popular camping and caravan stays like Forster and Tuncurry.

The New South Wales Central Coast is an area of lakes, unspoilt forests and sleepy townships. In summertime the area is a popular family holiday destination, where towns such as Forster and Tuncurry offer the usual array of fish and chip and fast-food shops and dolphin-watching cruises. There remains an 'away from it all' feeling about this area, however. Blueys Beach and Pacific Palms are holiday resorts for people who don't want the hurly-burly of a tourist resort. Their peaceful beauty is characterised by pristine beaches and surfers on the eternal search for the perfect wave.

1 FORSTER

Forster and Tuncurry sit on opposite sides of the entrance to Wallis Lake. The two towns are fronted by the ocean to the east and the lake to the west and represent the typical holiday resort with all the strengths (plenty of accommodation, places to eat takeaway food and the local seafood, good fishing, surfing and swimming areas, a casual atmosphere) and weaknesses that such destinations have.

The first European settlers on the townsite were the Godwin family, who set off from Gosford in 1856. The townsite, then known as Minimbah, was first surveyed in 1869 and renamed in 1870 after the Secretary of Lands, William Forster. Timber-getting, milling, shipbuilding and fishing were the principal industries in the early days with sailing ships and then steamships carrying fortnightly cargoes to Sydney. The first oyster lease at Forster was granted in 1884. Today, fishing, oyster leases and tourism are the mainstays of the local economy. The area has a number of good surfing beaches and rock pools, as well as lookouts and pleasant coastal walks.

Of interest in the area are Tobwabba Art, an award-winning Aboriginal Art Centre located at 10 Breckenridge Street—featuring works (paintings, artefacts and decorative works) by artists descended from the area's original inhabitants—and the Curtis Collection of vintage cars (including the first Australian car), motor-cycles, horse-drawn vehicles (an original Cobb & Co stagecoach is on display), telephones, cameras, toys, police displays, bottles and musical instruments.

2 CAPE HAWKE

Head south out of Forster along the Lakes Way. On the outskirts of town is a roundabout. Turn left into Cape Hawke Drv. It is 3.5km out to Cape Hawke, one of the most northerly points of Booti Booti National Park.

There is a very steep 440m path that winds its way to the summit of the hill. As you climb the headland, the views are increasingly spectacular. At the top (233m above sea level) is a cairn recording that Captain Cook sighted and named Cape Hawke on 12 May 1770. Below the lookout is McBrides Beach, a lovely and secluded spot.

3 BOOTI BOOTI NATIONAL PARK

Return to the Lakes Way and proceed south for 6.2km. To your left is The Ruins camping ground, which contains the information centre for Booti Booti National Park.

The stretch of coast from Forster to Pacific Palms is a spit that separates Wallis Lake from the ocean. This spit is part of Booti Booti National Park. The 26km long lake is noted for its sailing and saltwater fishing. There are several picnic spots along the Lakes Way that face out onto the lake; the northernmost is at Booti Point.

The information centre, situated within the camping ground, has a leaflet outlining the Booti Hill Walk (3.2km) which heads south from the camping ground past Booti Hill (169m) and around the headlands above Lindemans Cove to Elizabeth Beach. The ocean views are impressive. Adjacent to Booti Hill and Lindemans Cove is a rainforest. If you wish to return, there is an easy-going path back to the campground that runs beside Wallis Lake and the Lakes Way.

Surfers checking out the waves at Blueys Beach near Forster.

4 PACIFIC PALMS

Drive south along the Lakes Way for 3.5km and turn left into Lakeside Cres which passes Charlotte Head and then veers south as Boomerang Drv, adjacent to Boomerang Beach.

Pacific Palms is the name given to a strip of the mid north coast from Tiona Park, just north of The Ruins camping ground, to Tarbuck Bay in the south. This is a holiday area of small settlements. Not surprisingly there is a feeling of relaxation and serenity. Fishing is a popular pastime and beach anglers will usually be rewarded with tailor, bream, whiting and mulloway. The headlands and rocks are good for drummer, blackfish, bream and tailor; the lakes for bream, whiting and flathead; and Charlotte Head is generally considered the best spot for land-based game anglers after tuna and kingfish.

5 BOOMERANG BEACH AND BLUEYS BEACH

Continue south past Boomerang Beach and turn left into Headland Drv, where you can park your car at its end.

From the car park a path leads to the northern side of Boomerang Point over-looking Boomerang Beach. Blueys Beach is on the southern side of this headland. These two beaches and their hinterland make up the core of Pacific Palms. They are both noted surfing beaches. Blueys Beach is named after a cow called Bluey that fell from the southern headland into the sea. In recent times the houses above the beach, which enjoy an uninterrupted view over the Pacific Ocean, have greatly increased in value and the area has become fashionable.

6 SMITHS LAKE AND SANDBAR

Return along Headland Drv and turn left into Boomerang Drv. If you follow Boomerang Drv around the corner you will soon pass the Pacific Palms Visitors Centre on the right-hand side of the road. A further 3.6km west you will reach a T-intersection. Turn left onto the Lakes Way. After 5km turn left into MacWood Rd and follow the signs to Smiths Lake.

At the southern end of the district, occupying a peninsula that juts out into Smiths Lake, is a pretty village of the same name situated within beautiful bush surroundings. Opposite the boatshed is John DeBert Reserve, a beautiful lakeside spot where there is a boat ramp and picnic, barbecue and toilet facilities. Birdlife is abundant here.

Smiths Lake township is on the western rim of Symes Bay. From the verandah of the boatshed it is possible to look east across

The Amish Country Barn, Nabiac.

to Sandbar, which is literally a sandbar separating Smiths Lake from the ocean.

7 THE GRANDIS

Return to the Lakes Way and continue west along the Lakes Way for 24km to a signpost inviting you to turn right into Stoney Creek Rd. Drive the 5km to the formidable Grandis.

The Grandis is a huge, 400-year-old flooded gum (*Eucalyptus grandis*) which, at a height of 76m, is said to be the second tallest tree in New South Wales.

8 WANG WAUK FOREST WAY

Continue along Stoney Creek Rd for another 6km until you reach the T-intersection. Turn right onto the Pacific Hwy. After 1km turn left into Wang Wauk Forest Way.

Wang Wauk Forest Way will take you into the Bulahdelah and Wang Wauk State forests. The signs along Forest Drive will direct you to Shortys Camp (5km) and the old trestle bridge, where there are picnic, barbecue and toilet facilities.

Just beyond the Wang Wauk Forest Way turn-off is a short side-road to the left (sign-posted on the right-hand side of the road) which will lead you into the O'Sullivans Gap Flora Reserve rest area. An information board describes a 1.25km walking trail through some beautiful, untouched rainforest.

9 NABIAC

Proceed north along the Pacific Hwy for 36km to Nabiac.

Nabiac has missed the developments of the north coast. Consequently, it stands as a memento of what towns on the mid-north coast were once like. The charming old St Paul's Church of England, the public school (1884), the old timber shops and the wealth of timber houses make this small and quaint village a worthwhile stopover and a sharp contrast to the modern development within the other seaside towns. Walk across the pedestrian bridge from the western part of town and you will see an old-style buggy out the front of the Nabiac Amish Country Barn, a modest but interesting craft shop-cum-eatery owned by Australia's only Amish Mennonite family. There are some lovely handmade wooden toys and pieces of furniture on the premises.

10 TUNCURRY

From Nabiac proceed north along the Pacific Hwy for 5km and then turn right on the road signposted for Forster–Tuncurry. After another 6km, turn right again onto the Lakes Way. It is 11km to Tuncurry.

Bluey's Beach near Forster.

The bridge which joins Forster and Tuncurry.

Tuncurry was known as North Forster until 1875 when John Wright, his foreman, a sawyer and a builder set up camp there in 1875. They established cordial relations with the local Aborigines and adopted their placename of Tuncurry, which is thought to mean 'good fishing place'. By 1878, Wright had established a sawmill, store, shipbuilding yard and houses for his employees. He built a school in what is now Peel Street, which was replaced by a government school in 1881, and the settlement's first church (the Latter Day Saints) opened in the old school-room. The settlement was proclaimed a village in 1893. The first hotel and hall were built there the following year, an iceworks in 1895 and a butter factory in 1917. Two enterprising Italian migrants transformed the fishing industry of Tuncurry in the 1890s.

With the building of the bridge from Tuncurry over to Forster in 1959, the two towns blurred, with traffic passing easily from one centre to the other. Prior to the opening of the bridge, a ferry service joined the two towns. One of the town's few claims to fame is a remarkably elaborate and original toilet near the caravan park. The structure resembles a church or a public hall.

The Bar is located at the southern end of Nine Mile Beach, which extends northwards from Tuncurry to Hallidays Point. To get there, cross the bridge, take the first right into Wharf Street, turn right again at the first main cross street (Beach Street) and take the first right into Rockpool Road. The Bar is a good surfing area with a rock pool, grassed areas, kiosk, showers, toilets, children's play-ground, and a pleasant bathing and picnic area with barbecue facilities. You can walk out to the end of the breakwater where dolphins can sometimes be seen at play.

The Tuncurry Bicentennial Flora Park is located off Myers Drive in west Tuncurry. There is a walking trail in the park, plus seating, a range of local flora and about 60 bird and animal species.

Tuncurry's main road leads across the bridge over the Wallis Lake inlet, back to Forster.

48 PORT MACQUARIE AND THE HINTERLAND

■ DRIVING TOUR ■ 90KM ■ 6 HOURS ■ HISTORIC PORTS AND TIMBER TOWNS

Port Macquarie is one of the most popular family holiday destinations on the entire New South Wales north coast. It is surrounded by a wide range of family attractions.

*I*n a very real sense the area around Port Macquarie has become a forgotten part of the coastline and hinterland of New South Wales. While some holiday-makers make Port Macquarie their destination, most people heading north from Sydney drive quickly through this section of coastline on their way to the warmer waters of Coffs Harbour through to Queensland. This is a pity. The district is full of historic interest—Port Macquarie was an infamous penal colony—and the hinterland is characterised by rolling green hills and areas of dense forest which sustain the local timber industry.

1 PORT MACQUARIE

Port Macquarie boasts a history dating back to convict times, superb nature reserves, interesting historical buildings, lovely beaches with good surfing and excellent fishing opportunities, a fine museum, beautiful walking tracks around the head-lands and beaches, numerous amusements for children, and a koala hospital. It is the largest town on the New South Wales coast between Newcastle and Tweed Heads. Captain Cook sailed past this section of the coast in 1770, as did Matthew Flinders in 1802. However, the first European to investigate the Hastings River Valley was the exporer John Oxley, in 1818. He named the river after the Governor-General of India and, when he arrived at its estuary, named the town site after Governor Lachlan Macquarie. Port Macquarie was seen as a suitable site for a penal colony and so, in 1821, three ships set sail with 44 military personnel aboard and 60 convicts chosen for their skills and good behaviour. St Thomas'

Anglican Church was built between 1824–1828 and a Female Factory, where women made nails and other items, was erected in 1825.

In recent times, Port Macquarie has changed from a fishing town to a prosperous holiday and retirement destination. The population more than doubled between 1966 and 1981. The beaches in the area are excellent. To the north of town and across the Hastings River is the 16km long North Beach. Off Stewarts Street is Town Beach, situated at the mouth of the Hastings River. Seven other beaches extend southwards from Town Beach.

Attractions in the town include Tacking Point Lighthouse, the third oldest lighthouse in the country. Lighthouse Road heads off to the left, running parallel with the coast and out to the lighthouse. There are also walking trails from Lighthouse Road to Miners Beach.

Just off Stewart Street (near the Lord Street corner) is Gaol Point Lookout, from where there are pleasant views over the river mouth, the harbour and Town Beach. The Lions Club has created a very interesting historic map for the site, which conveys what the settlement looked like in the early 19th century.

Between Murray Street and Hay Street is the Port Macquarie Museum, housed in a convict-built store erected about 1836. The museum contains numerous historical docu-ments and artefacts. In the courtyard are re-creations of 19th-century shopfronts. Other features include a charming Victorian parlour, colonial farm equipment and sugar mill crushing machinery dated from the mid-19th century.

Roto House, located in Roto Place off Lord Street just south of the Hill Street intersection, is an historic (1890) 10-room country house built of red mahogany. Restored and furnished with period furnish-ings, the building is open for inspection. Roto House is surrounded by Port Mac-quarie Nature Reserve, a 12ha section of forest that is essentially a treatment and

Tacking Point Lighthouse, Port Macquarie.

relocation centre for injured koalas. The reserve is open daily.

2 THE BIG BULL

Return to the centre of Port Macquarie and head out of town along the Oxley Hwy towards Wauchope. About 9km from the Pacific Hwy turn right into Redbank Rd and follow it for 3km.

The Big Bull is a working dairy farm with an educational display, animal nursery, restaurant, hay rides, hands-on milking displays and a 14m bull offering panoramic views from the bull's eye lookout over the Hastings River, green pastures and the Broken Bago escarpment.

3 WAUCHOPE

Return to the Oxley Hwy. Wauchope is 2km away.

Wauchope is a thriving service centre affectionately referred to as 'the heart of the Hastings'. Within the town are the solid old courthouse, located in Hastings Street, and the old bank building (1888), now a solicitor's office, which stands in Cameron Street just off the High Street.

4 TIMBERTOWN PIONEER VILLAGE

Head west out of town along the Oxley Hwy for 2km.

The major attraction in the Wauchope area is the Timbertown Pioneer Village, which has literally dozens of houses re-creating an old timber town of the 1880s. There is a blacksmith, a leatherworker and other craftspeople, a railway station, steam train, steam sawmill, shops, bakery, pub and barbecue facilities. This is a very good pioneer town set on 87ac. At the edge of the Timber-town car park is the Wauchope Historical Society, located in a small timber church which has been reconstructed on the present site. Inside the church is an interesting display of photographs, memorabilia and equipment associated with the local timber industry. The museum is a perfect complement to the Timbertown Pioneer Village.

5 TAREE

Head south from Wauchope along the Bago Rd for 14km to rejoin the Pacific Hwy at a point 8km north of Kew. Continue heading south along the highway for 62km to Taree.

Taree is situated 16km inland from the mouth of the Manning River and consequently has developed more as a service centre and stopover point than as a tourist destination.

One of the town's delights is Fotheringham Park, which lies between the Pacific Highway and the Manning River just north of the bridge. In the Bicentennial year a community project established a very unusual Herb and Sculpture Garden with tiles, two sculptured and tiled posts and a range of interesting herbs which can be picked by locals wishing to add a little flavour to the evening meal.

The town's historic buildings are worth exploring. The Taree Heritage Walk is a pleasant walk along the riverbank and around the main streets (Albert Street, Victoria Street, Macquarie Street and Pulteney Street) in the city centre. A brochure of the walk is available from the Manning Valley Information Centre on the Pacific Highway in Taree (north of the town). One of the buildings of interest in the town is the Taree Public School, a grandiose building dating from 1902. The oldest building in town is St Paul's Presbyterian Church (1869), which is a typical Victorian Gothic Revival building. The church is located in Albert Street, one street west of the Pacific Highway.

Over the road from St Paul's is the magnificent courthouse (1897), which has a two-storey courtroom with single storey offices on either side. There is a small police station out the back. The courthouse is particularly attractive because of the trees and shrubs planted around it. Nearby is the huge St Mary's Catholic Church, which was built in the 1930s to replace the original 1870s church. The presbytery was built in 1890.

Located 5km south of Taree and clearly signposted from the Pacific Highway is the Kiwarrak State Forest. Within the forest is a 16km signposted drive that passes Breakneck Lookout and the delightful picnic area known as The Pines.

There is no better way to experience the Manning River and the area around Taree than to take a Manning River Cruise, which leaves from the wharves near Fotherington Park.

6 OLD BAR

Head south along the Pacific Hwy for 4km and turn left onto the signposted road that leads straight out to Old Bar. This road passes the turn-offs to Manning Point (8km along on the left) and Saltwater (9km along on the right).

Located 15km south-east of Taree, Old Bar is the southern entrance to the Manning River. It was first discovered by Europeans when John Oxley passed through the area in 1818. Old Bar boasts an excellent surfing beach, good fishing in the estuary and on the beach, and attractive picnic locations near the beach.

7 SALTWATER

About 2km west of Old Bar a side road heads south for 5km through Wallabi Point to Saltwater.

Saltwater is a tiny holiday village notable for the beautiful beach that stretches northwards for 6km to Old Bar. The beach is known as the best and most popular surfing destination near Taree and it also boasts a safe lagoon for toddlers. There are excellent views up and down the coast from Wallabi Point.

8 MANNING POINT

The turn-off to Manning Point is located about 3km west of Old Bar. Follow this side road north for about 4km and then take the signposted turn-off on the right for the final 12km to Manning Point.

Manning Point is a delightful seaside resort town situated on the principal estuary of the Manning River. This is a great place for surfing and swimming, as well as a popular haunt for anglers. Manning Point is also known for its excellent oysters.

9 LAURIETON

From Taree, head north along the Pacific Hwy for 54km to Kew and then turn right and follow Ocean Drv for 8km to Laurieton.

Laurieton is located at the base of North Brother Mountain at the mouth of the Camden Haven River. The result is a setting that combines lagoons and waterways with bushland and views of the mid-north coast. The main attraction in the area is North Brother Lookout. Don't miss it. A signposted winding road (to the north-west of the town) reaches the summit of North Brother Mountain (490m high) and offers a superb view over the coastline, the lakes and the mouth of the Camden Haven River. This is one of Australia's most impressive coastal views.

At the northern end of Laurieton turn right into Bonny Hills Coast Rd. Follow Bonny Hills Coast Rd for 16km to Lake Cathie. Continue north along the coastal road for another 12km to Tacking Point at the southern outskirts of Port Macquarie.

An old steam engine outside Timbertown.

The Camden Haven River at Laurieton.

49 SMOKY CAPE AND SOUTH WEST ROCKS

■ DRIVING TOUR ■ 148KM ■ 1 DAY ■ SPECTACULAR OCEAN VIEWS AND RUGGED COASTLINE

There are still areas of the coast of New South Wales which have escaped excessive development. The area between Crescent Head and Smoky Cape is one such area.

*A*t Kempsey, the Pacific Highway is a long way from the coastline. Here the highway passes through drab stands of gum trees and it requires a special commitment to take the roads to the coast. It is a 19km drive to Crescent Head, 22km to Hat Head and 15km to South West Rocks from the highway. Each village is worth the effort, however. The scenery is spectacular. The surfing is outstanding. The rugged coastline and the quiet beaches are a hidden treasure. This area is pure escape, which is the motivation for people who choose this area as their holiday destination.

1 KEMPSEY

Kempsey is the second-largest town on the mid-north coast after Port Macquarie.The town was named after Kempsey in the Severn Valley, in Worcestershire, England, and was first settled by Europeans when cedar-cutters moved into the area in the late 1820s. At one point there were 200 cutters in the valley. Once this industry was exhausted (by about 1842), the land returned to the pastoralists. At various times beef, sugar cane, maize and dairy cattle have formed the basis of the valley's rural economy. Today, the town has a population of about 10 000 people.

2 HISTORIC KEMPSEY

When crossing the bridge across the Macleay from the south, keep going straight ahead into Belgrave St rather than turning right along the Pacific Hwy.
Kempsey is a service town and consequently the important buildings in the town are public utilities, such as the National Australia Bank building (now a liquor barn) and the post office. The most interesting historical buildings in the town are located near the railway line in West Kempsey. They include the town's elegant courthouse, with rendered pilasters and parapets and distinctive gables, the Royal Hotel and All Saints Parish Church. Nearby is the post office (in Belgrave Street), which is a fine example of High Victorian architecture. It was built in 1879–1880.

3 CRESCENT HEAD

Return south through the town and continue through South Kempsey for 3km until you see the sign-posted left turn to Crescent Head, which is 19km from Kempsey.
Crescent Head is one of the best-kept secrets on the northern New South Wales coast. A delightful sleepy little coastal village, Crescent Head is characterised by beautiful beaches and a headland featuring one of the most spectacular cliffs on the eastern coast of Australia. It is also a well-respected surfing destination which offers good fishing both from the beach and the rocks. The tiny township is well protected environmentally, with the Goolawah Reserve and Limeburners Creek Nature Reserve edging it to the north and the south.

Although the district around Crescent Head had been thoroughly explored by the 1830s, no settlement was established in the immediate vicinity. It is only in recent times that this quiet stretch of coastline has been recognised as an ideal holiday destination. A town eventually emerged and it is presently characterised by 1950s-style accommodation with many fibro holiday homes.

The peacefulness of the town is largely a result of its unusual location. Travellers have to make a deliberate decision at Kempsey to depart from the Pacific Highway and head in a southerly direction. Since most travellers are heading north, they are unwilling to backtrack down the coast. This circumstance seems certain to ensure that Crescent Head will never be inundated by large numbers of tourists.
To reach Crescent Head turn at Baranghi St (beside the service station) into Korogora St and then into Skyline Cres.

Crescent Head is a wonderfully deceptive craggy outcrop. That fine Australian tradition of despoiling the landscape has reached some kind of metaphorical highpoint with a huge, ugly concrete water tower sullying the promontory.

Look south and far below is a beach with the headland tumbling through thick tufts of banksia to a long, pale arc of sand. And

The view from South West Rocks across to the Trial Bay Gaol.

below, on a lower headland, is the solitary grave of Herbert Arnold O'Dell, who died on 1 September 1917 while he was fishing off the rocks at Crescent Head.

The views from Crescent Head are spectacular. It is a sheer fall of nearly 100m into the Pacific Ocean. You can see south to Point Plomer and north to Hat Head. The wind from the south buffets the banksias that seem to cringe against its force.

4 GLADSTONE

There is a less than perfect road from Crescent Head to Gladstone—a mixture of sealed road and dirt. Head back towards Kempsey for 1km and then turn north and continue for 26km to Gladstone.

The tiny settlement of Gladstone has a street appropriately named Memorial Avenue where there are markers beside the trees recording the names of the men from the village who were killed in World War II. Gladstone is recognised as an historic village and its attractions include the Old Lodge Pottery, Darkwater House (which sells handicrafts and morning and afternoon teas) and the Gladstone Hotel (which claims to have the best beer on the Macleay River). The Gladstone Courthouse (1885) and police station (1898) are heritage listed.

5 HAT HEAD NATIONAL PARK

Continue north from Gladstone on the South West Rocks Rd for 8km until you reach Kinchela. Turn east to Hat Head and continue on Hat Head Rd for 12km.

Hat Head village is located in the heart of Hat Head National Park. The area is characterised by excellent surfing beaches and good fishing. It is also noted for the whales and dolphins off the coast and the many coastal birds that live in the heathland flora which characterises much of the area. Hat Head National Park covers 6445ha and offers camping facilities.

6 JERSEYVILLE

Return to Kinchela on Hat Head Rd (12km) and turn north on South West Rocks Rd for Jerseyville (11km).

Jerseyville was named after Governor Villiers of New South Wales who also happened to be the Earl of Jersey. Today it is nothing more than a few houses, including a particularly beautiful old house on the far side of the river.

7 SMOKY CAPE LIGHTHOUSE

A further 4km along Arkaroon Rd is the turn-off to Smoky Cape. Turn off to the east on Lighthouse Rd and continue for 4km until you reach the parking lot at Smoky Cape.

Smoky Cape Lighthouse is on the edge of the Hat Head National Park. Perched atop a cliff, the lighthouse offers wonderful views to the north and south and heart-stopping views to the waves and rocks far below. The first European to sight the headland was Captain Cook who, in 1770, named it Smoky Cape Range. The lighthouse, coach house, stables and the lighthouse keeper's cottage were designed by colonial architect James Barnet and completed in 1891. The lighthouse is built in a distinctive octagonal shape and the cottage has been located in a shelf cut into the rocks on the headland.

8 ARAKOON STATE RECREATION AREA

Return along Lighthouse Rd for 4km and turn north on Arakoon Rd for Arakoon (another 3km). Follow the signs to Trial Bay Gaol (1km).

This recreation area, which includes Trial Bay Gaol, was established in 1965. There is a good camping area located below the gaol and a number of excellent walks ranging from the short (Little Bay to Gap Beach takes about 45 minutes) to a long and relatively difficult walk along the coast from Trial Bay to the Smoky Cape Lighthouse. The most important historical site in the area is the Trial Bay Gaol (located to the east of the small settlement of Arakoon), which has a museum as well as the beautifully preserved ruins. The area is under the control of the National Parks and Wildlife Service. There is a self-guiding brochure available that directs the visitor through the points of interest.

The gaol was built between 1877 and 1886 to house prisoners of good conduct. Built of grey granite quarried on the site, the gaol is characterised by its hexagonal structure with three cell blocks radiating from the main entrance. The gaol's purpose at the

The lighthouse at South West Rocks.

time was to house cheap labour to help with the construction of a 1.6km long breakwater around the bay. The project was not completed and the gaol closed in 1903, to be reopened in 1915 to intern Germans during World War 1. The anti-German feeling at the time had led to the interning of German people. Although life was hardly pleasant, the internees established their own band, turned part of the gaol into a tennis court and one visitor described the evenings as being more like a pleasant beer hall than a gaol.

On the cliffs to the east of the prison is a monument to the Germans who died while interned at Trial Bay. The gaol was closed permanently in 1917 and the moveable parts of the building were auctioned off in 1922.

9 SOUTH WEST ROCKS

Return to Arakoon (1km) and then drive 3km along Phillip Drv until you reach South West Rocks.

South West Rocks is one of those coastal towns often bypassed by holiday-makers. It is one of the quietest and most attractive towns on the mid-north coast. The township was established in 1896 and grew as a result of the opening of a new mouth to the Macleay River. A pilot's station was constructed in 1902 and the town slowly grew up around this activity. The name of the town is a result of the pilot officer instructing vessels to anchor in Trial Bay so the rocks would be south-west of their anchorage. The locals decided upon the name for the town in the 1910s.

Today, the township of South West Rocks is strictly a tourist destination. There is lots of accommodation, good foreshores, pleasant beaches and good fishing. The town also has some particularly beautiful stands of Norfolk pines. Located in Ocean Drive is the old Boatman's Cottage, which operates as the local tourist information centre. The cottage is also a museum with an interesting display of the maritime history of the local region. In the grounds is the small *Macleay*, the Macleay River's first powered pilot boat.
Return to Kempsey, which is 31km to the south.

The Kempsey Post Office.

Trial Bay Gaol near South West Rocks.

50 THE PUB WITH NO BEER

■ DRIVING TOUR ■ 171KM ■ 6 HOURS ■ AUSSIE MYTHS AND TIMBER COUNTRY

Australia's most famous contemporary folk song is 'The Pub With No Beer'. Its setting in the hinterland behind Macksville has attracted tourists to this timber and cattle area.

One of Australia's most potent contemporary myths is the story of the pub with no beer, a symbol of the type of tragedy that could overwhelm a decent Aussie male. The song, which became a huge hit in Australia, tells the story of a pub that runs out of beer and how these difficult circumstances lead to changes in the lives of its regular patrons. The original Pub With No Beer is at Taylors Arm, a delightful village some 30km from Macksville. The town is typical of the area, which is characterised by charming small villages and sleepy towns that provide sustenance and services for the surrounding dairy and timber districts.

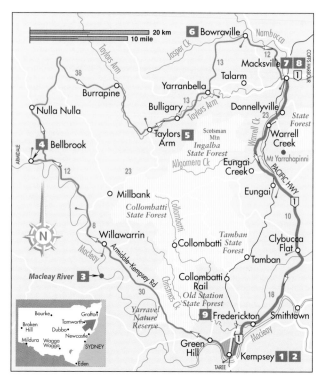

1 KEMPSEY

Kempsey is a large and important rural centre popular as a stopping point for people making the journey north along the Pacific Highway. Its location on the Macleay River—approximately halfway between Sydney and the Queensland border—ensures that weary travellers use it for a necessary break. At various times, beef, sugar cane, maize and dairy cattle have formed the basis of the valley's economy.

2 HISTORIC KEMPSEY

When crossing the bridge across the Macleay from the south, keep going straight ahead into Belgrave St rather than turning right along the Pacific Hwy.

Kempsey is a service town and consequently the important buildings in the town are public utilities such as the National Australia Bank building (now a liquor barn) and the post office. The most interesting historical buildings in the town are located near the railway line in West Kempsey, and they include the elegant courthouse built in the Classical style with rendered pilasters and parapets and distinctive gables. Nearby is the post office (in Belgrave Street), which is a fine example of High Victorian architecture. It was built in 1879–1880.

3 MACLEAY RIVER

The journey from Kempsey to Bellbrook is 39km.

The drive from Kempsey to Bellbrook is a particularly pretty one. The road follows the Macleay River and there are a number of spots offering spectacular views of the river making its way through the valley.

4 BELLBROOK

Bellbrook is classified by the National Trust as a heritage village but most travellers will be surprised by the listing because the only building of real historic importance seems to be the pub. The area was settled by timber-cutters and graziers in the 1830s. For most of the century there was active antagonism between the local Aborigines and the settlers and so the settlement was slow to develop and of small scale. It wasn't until 1882 that a post office was built and it was duly named Bellbrook. Although rather unassuming from the outside, the Bellbrook Hotel is fascinating inside with many of the original features and much of the historic charm carefully retained.

5 TAYLORS ARM

Continue for 38km from Bellbrook on the unsealed mountain road, which passes through the locality of Nulla Nulla and the tiny village of Burrapine until it reaches Taylors Arm.

The former Cosmopolitan Hotel (1903) is your reason for stopping in this small and isolated settlement for it was the subject of the famous song 'The Pub with No Beer'. It is claimed that the song's origins lie with a verse written by Dan Sheahan of Ingham, in Queensland. The song is usually credited to bush worker Gordon Parsons, however, who may well have transformed Sheahan's verse. At any rate, it became a national folk song in

All Saints Anglican Parish Church, Kempsey.

the hands of country and western singer Slim Dusty. The Cosmopolitan is now officially called The Pub with No Beer.

6 BOWRAVILLE

Take the road from Taylors Arm towards Macksville for 14km and turn north on an unsealed road which, after a further 12km, reaches the timber town of Bowraville.

Bowraville is situated in the heart of the Nambucca Valley. The town promotes itself as 'the verandah-post heritage town' because most of the older buildings are characterised by old-style verandahs which provide shade for the footpaths. The township, originally named Bowra, grew up in the 1850s and 1860s. It was renamed Bowraville in the 1870s to avoid confusion with the Southern Highlands township of Bowral. No-one knows with any certainty what the word *Bowra* means. Various sources claim it to be a local Aboriginal word meaning either 'cabbage palm', 'bullrout fish', 'scrub turkey' or 'bald head'. There is also a suggestion that the name comes from a European, Captain Bowra, who was sent up the Macleay River to search for cedar.

Bowraville was primarily a timber town that grew to meet the needs of the local timber-cutters.By the 1870s it boasted two hotels, a number of general stores, a black-smith's shop, tailor, local post office, a school and several churches. A decade later, while timber was still the dominant industry, the district became an important dairy and pig-raising area. People who are interested need only to take a short walk down the hill from the Bowra Hotel to see the size and scale of the local timber mills.

The town has remained relatively static throughout the 20th century but by the 1960s this part of the New South Wales coast was attracting people interested in alternative lifestyles. The area has seen the development of such varied activities as macadamia farms, avocado growing and even deer and ostrich farming. The town's main street has been carefully re-created so that it maintains a certain old-world charm.

There is no substitute for simply getting out of your vehicle and walking up and down the main street of Bowraville. There are a number of attractive buildings, including the Bowra Hotel with its wide verandah, the Bowraville Folk Museum and particularly the wooden churches at the northern end of town. The Old Bank Gallery

The Pub With No Beer at Taylors Arm.

in the main street is also worth visiting because it has fine displays of paintings and craft made within the local area.

7 MACKSVILLE

Take the road from Bowraville to Macksville, which is only 11km away.

Macksville is a pleasant town of 2900 people located on the banks of the Nambucca River. It is a fishing and oyster-farming centre that services a productive area noted for its bananas and other tropical fruits, along with vegetables, grazing, dairying and timber. A small settlement known as Nambucca, or Central Nambucca, emerged in the 1870s at the same time as Bowraville and Nambucca Heads. All three were centres for the settlers, timber-getters, anglers and miners living in the district.

The town's present name derives from two Scotsmen, known as Angus Mackay and Hugh McNally, who subdivided their selections for a township that became known as 'Mack's Village'. A park in town is named after Frank Partridge, a local man who won the Victoria Cross in 1945 for leading a successful attack against Japanese bunkers in the Bougainville campaign. He was also famous as a competitor on the television game show *Pick-a-Box* against Barry Jones.

The delightful old Star Hotel (1885), located in River Street (turn right just before the Macksville Bridge), doesn't seem to have changed in the last half century. It still has the old Tooths advertisements on the walls depicting 1950s sports heroes. Local red cedar was used for the bar and the staircase.

8 MARY BOULTON'S COTTAGE

Continue 2km east of the Star Hotel along River St.

Mary Boulton's Cottage is a charming replica of a rough-sawn timber house considered typical of those used by the early European settlers, although the timber rather than earthen floor and internal fireplace would

then have been considered luxuries. The cottage is set in a pleasant garden on the riverbank. The display includes an array of antiquated utensils, furniture, costumes, horse-drawn vehicles, tools and other memorabilia from the past. Mary Boulton is a descendant of some of the valley's earliest European settlers.

9 FREDERICKTON

Return 2km to the corner of River St and the Pacific Hwy, and turn left to continue southwards through Macksville. After 46km you will reach the small town-ship of Frederickton.

Frederickton is one of those places where it would be so easy to pass through the town and barely notice the attractive and historic hotel and miss the opportunity to walk down to the banks of the Macleay River.

The area around Frederickton was first settled by Europeans in the 1820s. Until the early 1840s, the primary European interest was in cedar and once this was exhausted (about 1842) the land returned to the pastoralists. At various times beef, sugar cane, maize and dairy cattle have formed the basis of the district's economy.

Turn right at the first road at the northern end of the town and continue along the road until you reach the public school and headmaster's residence. Designed by the distinguished architect J. Horbury Hunt, these simple Gothic-style buildings were constructed in 1880. They are notable for the belltower, the stained glass windows depicting wildflowers and birds, and the windvane (in the shape of a quill) as well as the excellent location of the complex on a hill surrounded by mature trees. The build-ings represent an excellent example of a Victorian school complex and were built of sandstock bricks which unfortunately have been cement rendered.

Continue on the Pacific Hwy for another 7km and you will reach Kempsey.

Mary Boulton's Cottage, Macksville.

51 THE BELLINGER VALLEY

■ DRIVING TOUR ■ 284 KM ■ 1 DAY ■ WATERFALLS AND IDYLLIC RURAL BEAUTY

Nestled behind the Pacific Ocean and edged by the Great Dividing Range, the Bellinger River Valley is a verdant escape from the city rat-race.

There are places along the northern coast of New South Wales where tourism and development have been avoided. The Bellinger Valley, an area of extraordinary beauty characterised by rich fields of fodder for the local dairy and cattle herds and a peaceful meandering river, is one such gem. Even Urunga, at the mouth of the Bellinger River, has avoided over-development and the valley, from the Dorrigo plateau to the coast, is a peaceful destination full of charm. Here is an opportunity to explore one of the most attractive hinterlands on the New South Wales coast.

1 URUNGA

Urunga is one of those secret places where people come to retire and where, because it is bypassed by the Pacific Highway there is a charming old-world, untouched feeling. The town is far removed from the commercialism that characterises so much of the New South Wales north coast. Urunga is a pleasant, sleepy little place located between the Bellinger and Kalang rivers with some beautiful walks around the foreshores, plenty of fishing and sporting activities such as golf and bowls, and lots of sun and salt air. It is easy to spend a couple of hours gazing out over the river from the lounge of the Golf and Sports Club, and there is no sense of urgency or an overwhelming feeling of tourism. As one retiree said, 'It's a secret. Don't tell too many people about it.'

By 1868 a pilot station had been built at Urunga (then known as Bellinger Heads) to help the sailing ships across the bar and up the river. The mouth to the river was always dangerous and inevitably it saw a number of dramatic shipwrecks, including that of the *Violet Doepel*. By 1892 a breakwater had been constructed to help shipping but the effort was in vain because the improvement in rail and road meant that by 1933 the pilot station had been closed down.

On the river to the east of town and opposite the caravan park in Morgo Street is the Bellinger Valley Historical Museum, which is open from 2.00pm–4.00pm on Wednesday. The town's Bicentennial exhibition, tracing the local history from the time of Aboriginal settlement some thousands of years ago is in the Urunga Library in Bonville Street, and is open for inspection during library hours. The museum is worth visiting on any weekday because outside is the headstone of James Thrower (it is a rare thing to see a headstone without a grave) and the museum itself is located in the old Literary Institute, a charming old wooden building constructed in 1896. The inscription on Thrower's gravestone reads: 'Sacred to the memory of Mr James Thrower late master of the cutter Comet of Sydney who suddenly departed this life in a boat while engaged in sounding the bar of the Bellinger River. His vessel laying at anchor June 4th 1846.'

On the hill above the boardwalk, at 4 Morgo Street, and looking out to the heads at Urunga is the old Pilot's Cottage (which is not open for inspection). The cottage boasts one of the most pleasant views available and some unusual statues of pelicans above the front gate. The front view can be accessed by a narrow lane further up Morgo Street. The lane leads out to a small park that offers fine views over Urunga Heads.

2 BELLINGEN

Proceed north along the Pacific Hwy for 4km and then turn left onto the Waterfall Way. It is 12km to Bellingen.

Bellingen is an attractive township in the heart of the Bellinger Valley. It is a town in transition. Traditionally a rather substantial town on the Bellinger River servicing the surrounding dairy farmers and timber-cutters, in recent times it has seen an influx of people fleeing from the city including, most famously, television reporter George Negus and pianist David Helfgott.

The valley was progressively settled throughout the 1850s. By 1857 the North Coast Steam Navigation Company had been established and by 1865 there was a pilot station to guide ships through the Bellinger Heads. In 1869 both the police station and

Bellingen and the Bellinger Valley from the Rotary Lookout.

the courthouse were built in Bellingen and this largely determined the town's pre-eminence over the rival claims of smaller settlements at Fernleigh and Raleigh. By the late 1880s Bellingen had reached a point where the local School of Arts was built (1887) and by the 1890s, the first Church of England (1896) had been completed. In 1900, the town's most admired commercial building, the Hammond and Wheatley Emporium, was established.

There is a brochure available around the town (published by the Rotary Club and Heritage Council) that suggests walks around the town. The first walk takes half an hour and basically goes from Church Street down the main street to Prince Street and back up again. It includes the courthouse and police station, Shire of Bellingen Administration Centre, Bellinger Valley Historical Museum and the Yellow Shed, an interesting craftworks and garden centre located in an old Workers Recreation Hall. The second walk includes the delightful Hammond and Wheatley Emporium, Federation Hotel and the Old Butter Factory.

3 GRIFFITHS LOOKOUT

Leave Bellingen and continue towards Dorrigo. At the top of the steep escarpment (24km from Bellingen), turn left into Maynard Plains Rd off the main Dorrigo–Bellingen Rd near the Lookout Motor Inn. Continue for 1km and then turn south. The lookout is a further 5km away.

Located on the edge of the escarpment and offering outstanding views of the Bellinger Valley, Griffiths Lookout is one of the highlights of any trip to this area. On a clear day it is possible to see from this vantage point to the Pacific Ocean. Griffiths is one of the most impressive lookouts on the eastern coast of Australia. The view across rolling cattle country dissolves into timber country before tumbling down into the Bellinger Valley.

4 DORRIGO NATIONAL PARK

Drive 6km back to the main Bellingen–Dorrigo road and turn left towards Dorrigo. You will see signs to the Dorrigo Rainforest Centre 3km further along the road .

The obvious starting point for any exploration of the Dorrigo National Park is the Dorrigo Rainforest Centre, which is situated 2km east of Dorrigo near the top of the escarpment. The centre has experienced staff who will not only explain the flora and fauna of the rainforest but also provide detailed information on the walks available.

View across the estuary to the ocean at Urunga.

The park is approximately 8000ha of rainforest and incorporates subtropical rainforest, warm and cool temperate rainforests and dry rainforest. In the national park are impressive stands of sassafras, red cedar, coachwood and yellow carabeen. There are over 60 species of bird, including the satin bowerbird, the rufus scrub bird, the brush turkey and the lyrebird.

5 DORRIGO

Continue north-west along Waterfall Way for another 3km to Dorrigo.

Dorrigo sits near the edge of the New England escarpment and is only a few kilometres from the steep mountain road that rises into the Bellinger Valley. This country town is pleasant and unassuming, and services the rich agricultural lands surrounding it. The first European into the Dorrigo was an escaped convict named Richard Craig. Craig lived with the local Aborigines and, pursuing their hunter-gatherer lifestyle, wandered between the coast and the Dorrigo plateau throughout the year.

The first official European in the district was Land Commissioner Oakes, who sighted the mouth of the Bellinger River on 3 August 1840. By 1841, timber-cutters had entered the Bellinger River searching for red cedar. They set up camps and moved from one stand of trees to the next.

By 1865 a track had been constructed from Dorrigo down the mountain to the Bellinger Valley, which ensured access to the coast. Before the track was opened, it had taken Dorrigo settlers up to six months to make the return trip to the coast.

6 DORRIGO STEAM RAILWAY AND MUSEUM

As you arrive in Dorrigo, the main road from Bellingen becomes Karabin St and then Myrtle St. Turn left from Myrtle St into Cudgery St, cross the river, turn right into Rosewood St and then, on the far side of the railway line, turn right into Tallowood St.

The Dorrigo Steam Railway and Museum boasts the largest collection of railway rolling stock in the southern hemisphere. It has 55 locomotives, 280 carriages and wagons, 13 railmotors and a Silver City Comet set. The museum is yet to be opened to the general public but if you drive down Tallowood Street you will get a good idea of the vast amount of equipment that has been accumulated by this unusual museum. There is a plan to reopen 70km of branch line so that some of the rolling stock can be

James Thrower's headstone, Urunga.

The Pilot's Cottage, Urunga.

Hammond and Wheatley in Bellingen.

used to provide round trips and day trips for visitors.

7 DANGAR FALLS

Return to the town centre, turn left into Hickory St and then into Vine St. Continue for another 2km and you will see Dangar Falls clearly signposted.

These small and pretty falls are well worth a visit. There is an attractive picnic spot that offers excellent vantage points. From here it is possible to get down to the banks and walk along the river below the falls.

8 OTHER WATERFALLS IN THE AREA

There are a number of other impressive waterfalls in the area that are well worth visiting. The Ebor Falls, located 48km from Dorrigo on the Armidale Rd are some of the best to see.

At Ebor Falls, the Guy Fawkes River drops 115m over columned basalt rock. There are barbecues, tables, running water and toilets plus three viewing platforms with sweeping views of the falls and the Macleay Valley.

9 WOLLOMOMBI FALLS

Proceed west for another 38km along the Waterfall Way. A signposted side road to the left leads to Wollomombi Falls.

The sensational Wollomombi Falls are Australia's longest single-drop falls, where after local rain the Wollomombi River plummets 220m over the cliff to the gorge below. Situated at 1160m above sea level, there are gorge rim walks (including a wheelchair track) that take you to two outstanding lookouts, and a track for the fit that takes you down the gorge to the Chandler River where you can swim if the weather is suitable. The track is hard going and takes five hours' return.

Return to Urunga via Ebor, Dorrigo and Bellingen. The total distance is 131km.

CHAPTER 9
NORTH COAST

52 AROUND COFFS HARBOUR

■ DRIVING TOUR ■ 63KM ■ 5 HOURS ■ BANANAS, FISH AND AVOCADOS

Over the past decade, the area around Coffs Harbour has developed rapidly so that now it challenges Queensland's Gold Coast as a popular holiday destination.

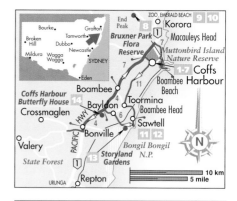

The countryside around Coffs Harbour is characterised by a richness created by heavy rainfall and long summers which produce rainforests and paddocks of high grasses. This is Banana Country. Here, the hills are covered with banana plantations which, in season, are notable for the blue plastic sheets used to cover the bunches of bananas. As a symbol of the area, the Big Banana, one of the first 'Bigs' in Australia, stands on a hill to the north of Coffs Harbour at the gateway to a theme park, where travellers can gorge themselves on every possible banana concoction.

1 COFFS HARBOUR

Coffs Harbour is a major coastal resort town noted for its banana plantations, its fishing, its appeal to retirees seeking the warm north of the state and its family-orientated holiday-makers. The area was opened up for selection from 1863, although there was little settlement until 1880. Because of the fertility of the land along the river flats, higher prices were asked for blocks near the river, which initially slowed development.

The first school opened in 1885 and a town was proclaimed and laid out in 1886. Early settlers experimented with fruit crops, dairying, goldmining and sugar cane. Improved access by road, rail and air in subsequent years saw the expansion of the tourism industry. Today, Coffs Harbour is one of the major tourist destinations in the state. Consequently, the population rises dramatically in summer.

The harbour became the base of a large and active fishing fleet in the 1970s. Tourism, bananas, fishing, timber and engineering now constitute the mainstays of the local economy. In recent years, seaside estates have been developed along 30km of local coastline.

The town beaches, south to north, are Boambee Beach (which extends south to Sawtell), Jetty Beach and Park Beach. Further north are Diggers Beach, Campbells Beach, Mid Sapphire Beach, Moonee Beach, Shelly Beach, Emerald Beach, Fiddamans Beach and Sandys Beach.

2 COFFS HARBOUR HISTORICAL MUSEUM

Turn right off the Pacific Hwy at Park Ave. Continue east until you reach Earl St and then turn left until you reach High St.

The Coffs Harbour Historical Museum at 191 High Street, near the Earl Street corner (east of the Mall). It has Aboriginal artefacts (mostly large and carefully crafted pebble tools), 'cedar-getters' implements, mining and farming relics, and the lantern from the South Solitary Island Lighthouse, made of brass and hand-cut prism glass, which was in use between 1880 and 1975.

The view south from the point at Sawtell.

3 THE NORTH COAST REGIONAL BOTANIC GARDEN

Continue east (towards the harbour) down High St until you reach Hardacre St. Turn left and continue along until you reach the Botanic Garden.

The North Coast Regional Botanic Garden covers 20ha and displays both native and exotic flora, rainforest areas and prolific birdlife. The park is surrounded on three sides by Coffs Creek and offers various self-guided walks. This is a pleasant retreat and is ideal for quiet picnics away from the hustle and bustle of the town centre.

4 BEACON HILL LOOKOUT

Return down Hardacre St until you reach High St. To access Beacon Hill Lookout, turn right off High St into Edinburgh St as you head towards the harbour.

Beacon Hill Lookout offers excellent views over Coffs Harbour, Jetty Beach and Muttonbird Island. The lookout is ideal for getting an orientation on the harbourside area of the city.

5 THE OLD JETTY AREA AND MUTTONBIRD ISLAND

Return to High St and continue east until you reach Camperdown Street. Continue and turn right at the next turn which takes you across the railway lines to the Esplanade, Jetty Beach and the Boat Harbour.

The old jetty dates from 1892 when it gave a boost to the local timber industry and provided a crucial outlet for other regional produce. This is a very pleasant area for a

The famous Big Banana, Coffs Harbour.

A fruit sculpture at the Big Banana complex.

stroll—along the jetty, Jetty Beach, the Foreshore Park and out to Muttonbird Island (measuring 600m by 200m) which is joined to the mainland by a breakwater that constitutes the northern arm of the harbour. Surrounded by rugged rocks, the island is home to what is thought to be the largest colony of wedge-tailed shearwaters in New South Wales, which breed on the island in the summer, along with the mutton-birds. From this vantage point humpback whales can also be seen from May to September during their annual migration.

6 PET PORPOISE POOL

Not far from the jetty, in Orlando Street, is the Pet Porpoise Pool, situated near the entrance to Coffs Harbour Creek. The pool has performing porpoises, sea lions, sharks, penguins and other marine animals, a reef tank and a native fauna sanctuary, as well as a cafe and souvenirs.

7 THE BIG BANANA

Continue heading north on Orlando St for 2km until you reach the Pacific Hwy. Turn right and drive north for 1.5km. On your left you will see the huge parking area for the Big Banana.
The Big Banana is located 3km north of Coffs Harbour on the western side of the Pacific Highway. Within the complex is a monorail tour which incorporates the Aboriginal Dreamtime Cave, featuring the Dreamtime story of the Gumbaingerri tribe, a skywalk to the lookout, toboggan rides, an icerink, a bill-abong complete with bunyip, an audio-visual theatrette, historical exhibits, hydroponic glasshouses containing an array of unusual exotic species, a tissue culture laboratory, gift shop, produce centre, packing shed and hilltop restaurant with excellent views.

8 BRUXNER PARK FLORA RESERVE

Leave the Big Banana and head north for 2km until you reach Bruxner Park Rd, which heads north-west off the highway into Orara State Forest. Continue for another 2km until you reach Bruxner Park Flora Reserve.
Bruxner Park Flora Reserve (407ha) was named after Lieutenant-Colonel Bruxner, a committed conservationist and advocate of creating nature reserves. The reserve's dense rainforest growth of vines, orchids and ferns is bisected by a walking track that takes in a picnic area at Park Creek. A scenic road leads to Sealy Lookout, from where there are excellent views of Coffs Harbour, the coastline and surrounding hills.

9 NORTHERN BEACHES

Continue north on the Pacific Hwy. There are a number of attractive beaches along the coastline that offer the visitor good swimming away from the crowds.
Moonee Beach, 10km north of the Big Banana, is a large beach with a small settlement and a foreshore lined with pine trees. It has good facilities. Emerald Beach (17km north of the Big Banana) is also attractive, though Sandy Beach (a further 2km north, on the other side of Bare Bluff) is quieter and more secluded.

10 COFFS HARBOUR ZOO

Return to the Pacific Hwy from Bruxner Park Flora Reserve. Coffs Harbour Zoo is located 14km north of Coffs Harbour.
The award-winning Coffs Harbour Zoo has nearly 400 different animals, continual animal presentations, an animal nursery and a rainforest aviary, all set in landscaped gardens. Children can hand-feed kangaroos, waterbirds and wallabies.

11 SAWTELL

Return 14km to Coffs Harbour. Turn left at Park Ave, right at the roundabout into Gordon St, left into Albany St and continue until you reach the major roundabout at Hogbin Drv. Head south for 7km and you will reach another roundabout. Turn left into Sawtell Rd and it is a further 3km to the centre of Sawtell .
Sawtell is a peaceful and typical coastal retirement and family holiday destination. The *raison d'être* of this tourist town is the pretty beach that lies between Boambee Head and Bonville Head. These two rocky promontories sit adjacent to the estuaries of Boambee Creek and Bonville Creek.
Sawtell has a small shopping centre (with a very distinctive and quite luxuriant median strip), lookouts from the two headlands, some good walking areas near the river and the beach, a fine picnic area and play-ground near the mouth of Boambee Creek, good fishing (particularly for blackfish) in the creeks and the ocean, a saltwater tidal swimming pool at Bonville Head and safe swimming at Boambee Bay.

12 SAWTELL BEACH

Continue through town and follow the signs to Sawtell Beach.
This attractive beach lies between two rocky headlands—Boambee Head to the north and Bonville Head to the south. Sawtell Beach has a surf lifesaving club and a grassy fore-shore reserve runs along its length. There is a children's playground and picnic and barbecue area at Boambee Head (off Sawtell Road), a fine ocean pool at Bonville Head (via Boronia Street) and lookouts at both heads.

13 STORYLAND GARDENS

When Sawtell Rd crosses Middle Creek it becomes Lyons Rd, which veers westwards back out to the Pacific Hwy. Along this road is Storyland Gardens.
Storyland Gardens is for the entertainment of children. It features sculptures of famous characters from fairytales—Snow White, the Three Little Pigs and Red Riding Hood among them—all within their own story-land settings. The whole is contained within a forested area. The owners actually live in a large shoe (as in the Old Woman Who Lived In A Shoe), which has a kiosk in the toe. There are landscaped gardens, a large fish pond full of koi, a playground, a bird aviary, small animals and barbecue facilities.

14 THE COFFS HARBOUR BUTTERFLY HOUSE

Follow Lyons Rd to the highway and turn left. Proceed south for 300m to the Strouds Rd intersection, where you will see the Coffs Harbour Butterfly House.
Within the Coffs Harbour Butterfly House you will find an array of native butterflies in a subtropical rainforest setting with attractive gardens and tea rooms.
Return north along the Pacific Hwy for 11km to Coffs Harbour.

The fishing fleet at Coffs Harbour.

53 GRAFTON TO GLEN INNES

■ DRIVING TOUR ■ 182KM ■ 6 HOURS ■ ACROSS THE GREAT DIVIDING RANGE

The drive from the coast through the New England Ranges passes through large areas of untouched forest and environmentally important national parks.

Grafton is famous for its jacaranda trees. In season, the streets of this elegant town turn a glorious purple as the trees bloom. Beyond the city lie some of the most attractive national parks in New South Wales. The traveller winds up the Clarence Valley and into the Great Dividing Range arriving in the sharp and crisp world of Glen Innes. In summer it is a delightful relief to pass from the heat and humidity of the coast to the cool area of the New England Ranges. In wintertime the traveller can move from the balmy coast to snow-covered mountains in the space of less than two hours.

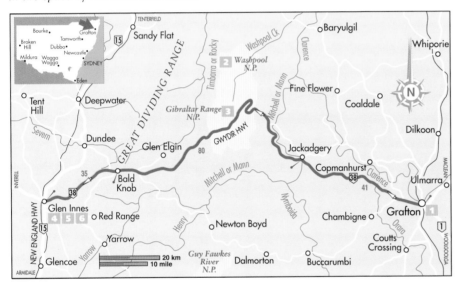

1 GRAFTON

Grafton is a very beautiful and gracious city centre characterised by its wide streets, elegant Victorian buildings and a superb location on the banks of the Clarence River. The city is famous for its trees, particularly the jacaranda stands which were planted in 1907–1908. A sensible place to start an exploration of Grafton is the Clarence River Tourist Centre, at the corner of Spring Street and the Pacific Highway in South Grafton. The centre has a theatrette and Aboriginal art on display, as well as all the information you need about the area, including a brochure on Grafton's beautiful collection of trees, the Heritage Trail and a self-drive tour of the area.

Within the city centre are a number of impressive buildings. Most of the city's civic architecture is on Victoria, Fitzroy and Prince streets, while Oliver, Mary and Alice streets have a number of fine residences. Of interest are the post office (1874), with its weighty sandstone colonnades, and the Classical Revival courthouse (1877–1880) in Victoria Street, with its colonnaded and stone-flagged verandah. Adjacent is the former police station (1881), which was conceived as an harmonious complement to

the courthouse. All three buildings were designed by colonial architect James Barnet.

Across the road are three historic buildings. At 58 Victoria Street is the Post Office Hotel (1860). Next door is Foott Law & Co Solicitors (c.1880) and, at no. 54, is Fitzgeralds Chambers (1908)—a two-storey Classical Revival building.

Christ Church Cathedral is located on the corner of Victoria Street and Duke Street. The foundation stone was laid in 1874. Designed by the architect J. Horbury Hunt, the principal construction work was carried out between 1880 and 1884. The salmon-coloured bricks were locally manufactured from over 100 different design moulds. The roof trusses in the sanctuary and nave are of particular distinction.

Also in Victoria Street at no. 85, is Roches Family Hotel (c.1870). At no. 95 is 'Istria' (1899), an early Edwardian residence. The cottage at no. 140 Victoria Street remains virtually unchanged since it was built in the 1860s and at no. 150 is 'Arcola' (1907), arguably the town's best example of Edwardian architecture.

South Grafton is a real surprise. For those who think all the old buildings are concentrated in Grafton, this 19th-century river

town is worth a visit. It has a number of impressive buildings, including St Matthew's Anglican Church (1886), at the corner of Through Street and Summerland Way (the road that leads across the bridge). St Matthew's contains stained-glass windows from the English chapel of the Duke of Grafton, after whom the town is named.

2 WASHPOOL NATIONAL PARK

Head north-west out of Grafton along the Gwydir Hwy (Ryan St). After 88km turn right into Coombadjha Rd and Washpool National Park.

The World Heritage-listed Washpool National Park contains the largest undisturbed rainforest in NSW and the world's largest remaining undisturbed stand of coachwood forest. The plateau upon which the park stands rises to 1200m above sea level and the Washpool and Coombadjha Creeks have carved gorges through the plateau.

Less than a kilometre along Coombadjha Road a side road to the left heads off to The Granite where there is a picnic area and a 700m walking track to a lookout that takes in the south-eastern section of the park. Coombadjha Road continues past three clearings—the Bellbird Rest Area, the Coachwood Picnic Area, and the Coombadjha Creek Rest Area, from where there are two walks, the 1.1km Coombadjha Nature Stroll and the Washpool Walk (10km return).

3 GIBRALTAR RANGE NATIONAL PARK

Return to the Gwydir Hwy and continue west for 3km. Turn left into Mulligans Rd and Gibraltar Range National Park.

Gibraltar Range National Park is located in high granite country, dominated by eucalypt forest. The park is an ideal place for bushwalking. The large numbers of wildflowers bloom in the warmer months and there is a great diversity of wildlife within the park.

Several roads lead to particular attractions in the national park. Mulligans Road is the main access road, leading, after 10km, to the Mulligans Hut Rest Area on the western bank of Little Dandahra Creek. There are campsites, showers, toilets, fireplaces and tables and various swimming holes along the creek.

Five walking trails depart from Mulligans Hut Rest Area, leading to the beautiful Dandahra Falls, the Barra Nula Cascades, the Atrichornis/Murrumbooee Cascades, Tree Fern Forest and The Needles. The Needles are six separate granite outcrops which, according to Aboriginal lore, are six sisters turned to stone by the curse of their pursuer.

There is also a picnic area just off the highway in Mulligans Road and two walking tracks depart from a point about 3km along the road. One heads south to Anvil Rock (4km return). The other heads south-west to the spectacular Dandahra Crags (5km return).

Further along the Gwydir Highway, Boundary Falls Road heads off to the left and will take you to the falls of the same name. From there you can walk 1km downstream to the beautiful Lyrebird Falls.

4 CENTENNIAL PARKLANDS AND THE AUSTRALIAN STANDING STONES

Return to the highway and continue westwards for 63km to Glen Innes. As you arrive on the outskirts of Glen Innes take Watsons Drv on your left, which leads to Martins Lookout and the new Centennial Parklands.
Centennial Parklands and the Australian Standing Stones is clearly signposted. This is where 1000 trees were planted in the late 1970s. There are panoramic views of the town from Martins Lookout, picnic, barbecue and toilet facilities, a replica crofter's cottage which supplies refreshments, souvenirs and information, and the Australian Standing Stones. The standing stones are intended as a tribute to the Celtic peoples who contributed to the development of Australia and who were predominant in the early European history of the district. It is based on the Ring of Brodgar, a megalithic stone circle in the Orkneys, although it is given a distinctively Australian flavour by the superimposition of the Southern Cross on the design. Like those earlier stone arrangements, the stones function as a seasonal clock delineating the summer and winter solstices. Further information can be obtained from the visitors centre.

5 GLEN INNES

Return along Watsons Drv to the Gwydir Hwy. Turn left and continue on until you reach Meade St. Turn left and just over the road is the tourist information office.
Glen Innes is a town known for its fine parks which are especially attractive in autumn. The first European in the area was the

An old water cart outside the Land of the Beardies History House and Research Centre.

explorer John Oxley, en route to Port Macquarie in 1818. By 1835, two bearded convict stockmen, Chandler and Duval, assigned to Captain Dumaresq, were the first Europeans working in the area north of Armidale. They did much to open up the area to settlement by advising and guiding prospective settlers to new lands where they selected stations in the late 1830s. For this reason the district was initially known as 'Beardy Plains' or 'Land of the Beardies'.

The present town site was laid out in 1851 and was named after the station's former owner, Major Archibald Clunes Innes, former commandant of the Port Macquarie penal settlement. Glen Innes was gazetted in 1852 and the first land sales took place in 1854, the year the first post office opened. The area became a noted sheep-raising and wheat-growing area and the first flour mill opened in the 1850s.

The town's information centre is located at 152 Church Street (the New England Highway), between Bourke and Meade streets. A few doors south of the visitors' centre, the museum houses the 1922 power generators that supplied Glen Innes with electricity before the introduction of the grid system in 1956.

The information centre's heritage walk brochure begins at the corner of Grey Street and Ferguson Street (the Gwydir Highway), where you will find the town's oldest inn, the Royal Hotel, built around 1860, although it is much altered. Heading south on Grey Street there is the courthouse, designed by James Barnet and built in 1873–74 of basalt with grey granite quoins. The bushranger Thunderbolt (Fred Ward) was apparently tried in the first courthouse (built in 1858). Aboriginal outlaw Black Tommy was also tried here, in 1876. He was acquitted but, accused of murder and horse-stealing, was shot to death by local constables 18 months later.

At the north-eastern corner of Meade and Grey streets is the two-storey masonry post office and over the road is the two-storey rendered masonry of the Great Central Hotel, a typical 19th-century country hotel situated on the first town allotment to be sold, in 1854. Diagonally opposite is the rendered brick Imperial Hotel (1901). On the south-western corner is the ANZ Bank, built of rendered masonry in 1884 as the Bank of New South Wales.

6 LAND OF THE BEARDIES HISTORY HOUSE AND RESEARCH CENTRE

Head north on Grey St until you reach Ferguson St. Turn left and continue west until you reach West Ave. Set slightly above the road is the history house.
The Land of the Beardies History House and Research Centre is a quality folk museum located in the town's first hospital (1875). One of the largest in New South Wales, the building is set in extensive grounds that include a reconstructed slab hut. The museum has a fine collection of 19th-century relics and is set out to demonstrate the material culture of the colonial era.

The South Grafton Post Office.

54 ALONG THE CLARENCE RIVER—GRAFTON TO YAMBA

■ DRIVING TOUR ■ 60KM ■ 5 HOURS ■ COASTAL RIVERLANDS

From Grafton to Yamba, the northern rivers, fed by the area's heavy rainfall, have provided rich river flats which are ideal for cattle grazing and cropping.

As the traveller continues north the temperature gets warmer, the annual rainfall increases and the rivers form broad floodplains as they make their short journeys from the escarpment to the sea. This is an area of great richness where dairy and beef cattle graze on green pastures, where sugar cane is grown and mixed farming is practised on some of the country's most fertile land. The drive from Grafton to Yamba is an opportunity to experience subtropical farming at its most successful while exploring the charming river ports of Ulmarra and Maclean before arriving at the peaceful holiday town of Yamba at the mouth of the Clarence River.

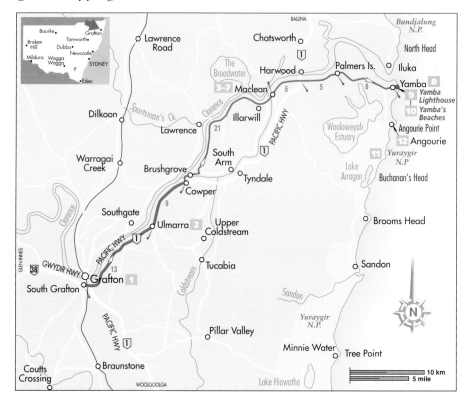

1 GRAFTON

Grafton is a very beautiful and gracious city centre characterised by its wide streets, elegant Victorian buildings and a superb location on the banks of the Clarence River. The city is famous for its trees, particularly the jacaranda stands which were planted in 1907–1908. A sensible place to start any exploration of Grafton is the Clarence River Tourist Centre, at the corner of Spring Street and the Pacific Highway in South Grafton. The centre has a theatrette and Aboriginal art on disply, as well as all the information you need about the area, including a brochure on Grafton's beautiful collection of trees, the Heritage Trail and a self-drive tour of the area.

2 ULMARRA

From South Grafton, follow the Pacific Hwy north-east towards Maclean. It is 12km to Ulmarra. Turn left at the newsagents into River St, or take the next left at the service station into Coldstream St.

The Police Station, Ulmarra.

Ulmarra is one of those towns you could pass through and think you had missed nothing. The Pacific Highway manages to miss the best part of the town by a block and it leaves the hasty traveller with the impression of a tiny, uninteresting settlement. In fact, if the traveller turns into River Street or Coldstream Street, the buildings and setting create a fine impression redolent of the town's past as a 19th-century river port.

Ulmarra was established when Thomas Small bought the land in 1857. By 1871 the township boasted a population of nearly 1000 people. Sugar cane failed as a crop and eventually dairy farming started to dominate. It was as a result of this that the town developed as an important river port.

Along River Street are some older buildings of interest. There is a fine example of a Federation-era single-storey timber court-house, an interesting timber police station with a wide country verandah around it, a charming timber post office and a particularly grand masonic hall with elaborate doors.

So convincing is the authenticity of the buildings that the Commercial Hotel (built in 1929 and characterised by fine iron-work and a large verandah) was used in the television series *Fields of Fire* as a Queensland pub. The hotel is located in Coldstream Street, which runs parallel to River Street. Other structures of interest are the wharf, the council chambers, the old church and a number of other buildings that have remained largely untouched since they were built. Bailey Park, which runs down to the river, is particularly attractive.

3 MACLEAN

Return to the Pacific Hwy and continue in a north-easterly direction to Ferry Park on the Pacific Hwy, at the southern turn-off to Maclean (22km).

Maclean is situated on the Clarence River, which is a major source of the nation's seafood. This town is also at the southern limit of the Australian sugar crop, which extends north from here to Cairns. Timber,

The main street of Maclean.

maize, mixed crops and tourism help to buttress the local economy.

The Lower Clarence Information Centre at Maclean can furnish information regarding deep-sea fishing charters, a self-drive tour of significant Aboriginal sites in the area and whale-watching cruises, as well as boat hire, river cruises and horseriding. The Centre also has tide charts, fishing guides, and a brochure on historical walks around Yamba.

4 TWO CHURCHES

Follow Cameron St into Maclean. As you approach the river, turn right into River St which follows the coastline north.

At the southern end of River Street, near the Church Street intersection, is the former Methodist (now Uniting) Church (1890). Continue along River Street. As it bends to the left, turn right into Wharf Street. To the immediate right is the Free Presbyterian Church, which has been in continuous use since its construction in 1867 by the early Scottish settlers.

5 BICENTENNIAL MUSEUM

Continue along Wharf St for 500m. At the intersection of Wharf St and Grafton St is the Bicentennial Museum.

The cottage was built in 1879 from local sandstone and has been set up as a Maclean house of the 1880s with contemporary artefacts. Adjacent to the museum the large folk museum display includes a number of particularly fine examples of sulkies and carriages.

6 THE LOOKOUT AND THE PINNACLE

Continue up Wharf St for another 1.5km to the lookout.

The lookout offers fine views over the town and the district's cane fields, east along the Clarence River to Yamba and Iluka at the river's mouth, and along the coast. The Pinnacle, a balancing rock formation and cave network, is 200m from the lookout.

7 MACLEAN'S HERITAGE BUILDINGS

Head west along Taloumbi St for two blocks, then turn right into Woodford St and proceed north for two blocks. Turn left into Stanley St.

To the right is the former brewery (1870), which has been converted into two houses but still retains the archway into the courtyard and the charm of the original building. Return along Stanley Street and turn left, back into Woodford Street. To the right, on elevated land, is St Mary's Catholic Church (1894), a beautiful stone Gothic building with a tower capped by battlements. The grounds offer attractive views over the valley.

8 YAMBA

Head north out of town along River St and follow the road as it veers eastwards. After 6km the road crosses the Pacific Hwy. Cross the highway and continue east for another 10km to Yamba.

Yamba is a quiet seaside town on the southern side of the Clarence River estuary. The town's economy is based on its substantial fishing fleet and its appeal as a quiet holiday destination beside the sea.

Pelicans at the moorings at Yamba.

The Yamba breakwater was built in 1893 and the population swelled to 350, dropping to 250 when that work ended in 1903. The population reached 689 in 1919 and its reputation as a holiday destination was assisted by the arrival of the Sydney railway at South Grafton in 1923. Further harbour works were carried out from 1952 to 1971 and improvements at this time saw a steady growth from about 1000 people in the late 1960s to the present 4572, although that number swells dramatically, if temporarily, in holiday periods.

Yamba's reputation for recreational fishing was greatly encouraged by the inauguration of an annual fishing contest in 1958, initially hosted by famous radio personality Jack Davey, who retreated to Yamba to relax and fish. The Yamba Family Fishing Festival is now held in September or October.

The first shipment of fish to Sydney occurred in 1884. Prawn trawling commenced in 1946 and has steadily expanded to the point where over 600t of prawns are trawled annually, together with 1300t of fish. Clarence oysters have also supplied the nation since the 1880s.

9 YAMBA LIGHTHOUSE

Follow the main road (which becomes Wooli St) into Yamba. Near its end turn right into Yamba St and then take the first left into High St. At its end turn right into Clarence St and take the first left into Pilot St.

Yamba Lighthouse stands 41m above the sea and offers fine views of the coastline (it is a popular whale-watching site in the winter months). The lighthouse's beams can be seen 17km out to sea. Nearby is a replica of the original 1879 lighthouse, erected by volunteers for use as a community radio station.

10 YAMBA'S BEACHES

Yamba has a number of beaches that are ideal for swimming and surfing. Yamba Beach (patrolled in summer) is the main beach in town. It has a rock pool for safe swimming and is located on the southern side of the lighthouse, below Flinders Park. On the other side of the lighthouse is Turners Beach, which is also patrolled in summer. Whiting Beach is a stillwater beach suitable for young children. It extends from the western side of the breakwall out along the sand spit known as Hickey Island. Convent Beach extends eastwards from the rock pool at the eastern edge of Yamba Beach to Yamba Point. On the other side of Yamba Point is Pippi Beach (also patrolled in summer), which extends south to Angourie.

11 YURAYGIR NATIONAL PARK

Head back out of town along Wooli St and turn right into Angourie Rd. Just before you reach Angourie, turn right onto Lakes Boulevarde. After about 500m a sign directs you into the park. About 1.5km further on there is a turn-off on the right to Mara Creek, from where a pedestrian suspension bridge leads to picnic facilities.

The 10km Angourie Walking Track starts at Mara Creek Picnic Area. Considered one of the finest coastal walks in the country, it is at its best in spring and early summer when the wildflowers are in bloom and drawing the maximum amount of birdlife.

12 ANGOURIE

Return from the national park the way you came in, until you reach the intersection of Lakes Boulevarde and Angourie Rd. Turn right into Angourie Rd.

Angourie has become a popular haunt for surfers. The town is tiny but boasts its own surfboard manufacturer, which demonstrates where the town's priorities lie. At the beginning of the town there are signs to the lookout, which overlooks the beach and headland where most of the surfing is done, and the Blue Pools, an interesting and large rock pool set in bushland just behind the beach. The pool was created when a rock quarry filled with freshwater from a subterranean spring. The quarry supplied the material for Yamba's breakwater. In fact the Angourie Road was established in the 1890s as a tramline for the transportation of the stone. Angourie Road leads to Angourie Bay Picnic Area. Some of the coast's best surfing is to be had at Angourie Point, adjacent to the picnic area.

55 AROUND BYRON BAY

■ DRIVING TOUR ■ 157KM ■ 1 DAY ■ IN THE LAND OF CITY ESCAPEES

The hills roll down to the sea. The valleys are green and peaceful. The surfing is some of the best on the coast. No wonder Byron Bay is one of the state's most popular holiday destinations.

*I*n the mid-1960s many city dwellers began to question their lifestyle. The urgency of daily life and the pressures of living in a large city led many to choose a slower, more relaxed alternative. The hinterland around Byron Bay became a retreat for hippies and surfers. Slowly, as the beauty of the region was more widely appreciated, the area became a chic option and movie stars, television producers and advertising executives bought up land. Today, the coastline around Byron Bay is charming, sophisticated and not overdeveloped.

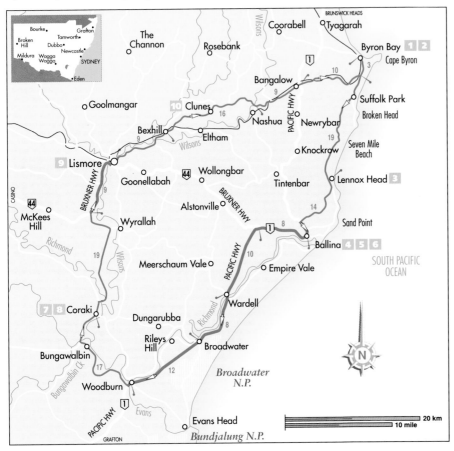

1 BYRON BAY

There can be few towns in Australia with a more complex identity than Byron Bay. On the one hand the town has, historically, been associated with the alternative lifestyle movement of the 1970s and therefore seen as a kind of interesting hippie retreat in northern New South Wales. On the other hand, Byron Bay has been seen as an up-market retreat for wealthy southerners. And over the past 20 years the town has acquired a reputation as the residence of the rich and famous, with Paul Hogan and Linda Kozlowski moving into a mansion in the hinterland (which they have subsequently sold), John Cornell and Delvene Delaney doing the same and owning a local hotel,

and Olivia Newton-John finding the place an ideal retreat from Los Angeles. Olivia, too, has since moved on.

2 CAPE BYRON LIGHTHOUSE

Two main roads from the Pacific Hwy lead into Byron Bay from the west and the south, and meet at a roundabout in town. From this roundabout head east along Lawson St with the ocean to your left. At the end of the street turn left into Lighthouse Rd. Take the first right into the one-way road, which is signposted for the lighthouse.

Byron's greatest attraction is its outstanding lighthouse. Located only 300m south of Australia's easternmost point, Cape Byron, the lighthouse was completed in 1901 and stands 22m high (113m above sea level).

This is an ideal starting point for the delightful Cape Byron Headland Reserve and Walking Track that heads both north and south from the lighthouse. The northerly track winds around the cliffs before dropping down to Little Wategos and Wategos Beach, and the southerly track heads down the ridge towards Captain Cook's Lookout. Both walks offer exceptional views of the Pacific Ocean and the hinterland and are true highlights of any visit to Byron Bay.

3 LENNOX HEAD

Return to the roundabout and turn left, heading south along Jonson St. When you come to the next roundabout turn right, continuing south along Bangalow Rd. Make sure you follow this road to the left. Bangalow Rd continues south as Broken Head Rd through Suffolk Park. About 20km from the main intersection at Byron is a signposted turn-off on the left to Lennox Head.

Lennox Head is one of those small townships that is characterised by a large and beautiful headland (hence the name) to the south and a long, 'seven mile' beach which, in the words of the surfing community, is a place where 'the magical right-hand break' occurs. To some people Lennox Head is the surf capital of the far north coast.

In the 1860s James Ainsworth took up land behind Seven Mile Beach and in 1922 Lennox Head was created as a private subdivision. The idea was to sell the blocks of land for weekender and holiday accommodation with Lake Ainsworth being the main attraction of the area.

The Pat Morton Lookout offers excellent views north from Lennox Head across Seven Mile Beach and south to Rocky Point and Skenners Head. It is an easy distance to walk from town, along the oceanfront reserve and climb the headland to enjoy this view. Below it is The Point, where surfers come from all over the world to enjoy the near-perfect waves. Dolphins and sometimes whales are commonly seen from the headland.

4 BALLINA

Return to the highway and continue south. After about 6km there is a fork in the road. Keep to the left, following the Coast Road into East Ballina. When you pass the Gunundi Conference Centre (to your left), turn left into Shelly Beach Rd. After 1km turn right into Beach Rd, then right into Harbourview St, and then right again to the lighthouse.

Ballina is a service centre for traffic moving through to Queensland but it is also a holiday destination. As early as 1842 a boat named *Sally* had brought cedar-cutters to the area and a settlement had developed at East Ballina. There was a natural sequence with the timber being cut, the land being planted with corn and then with sugar cane. Quickly sugar cane came to dominate and by 1875 there were 75 sugar mills operating along the length of the Richmond River.

The Ballina lighthouse must be one of the smallest lighthouses on the Australian coast. First established in 1866 it turned automatic in 1926 and is now located incongruously in a park near the water. The lighthouse was built to a design by colonial architect James Barnet.

5 MUSEUM GROUP

Return along Harbourview St and Beach Rd and turn right at the T-intersection, back into Shelly Beach Rd. Turn right at the helipad into Compton Drv. At the T-intersection turn left, back onto the main road. Cross over Missingham Bridge and turn left into Kingsford Smith Drv which soon bends to the right as River St. Take the first left into La Balsas Plaza.

By the corner of River Street and La Balsas Plaza is the tourist information centre which is combined with two museums. There is the FNC Family History Group and the Naval Museum, as well as a maritime museum. On the waterfront is the MV *Florrie*, which was built at Brisbane Water in 1880 and traded on the Richmond River as a passenger vessel and tug. In front of this collection of museums and information centres is MV *Richmond*, which operated on the Richmond River for nearly 50 years. Perhaps the most famous exhibit at the Ballina Maritime Museum is the 12m long and 6m wide *Las Balsas*, which landed at

The Big Prawn in Ballina.

Cape Byron Lighthouse.

The courthouse in Lismore.

Ballina on 21 November 1973. The balsa-wood raft floated across the Pacific from Ecuador, a journey of 3760 nautical miles, which it achieved in 178 days.

6 THE BIG PRAWN

Head west along River St (the Pacific Hwy). A little over 3km from the courthouse, to your right (opposite Quays Drv) is the Big Prawn.

This manifestation of the Australian fascination with Big things (along with the Big Pineapple, the Big Banana and the Big Cheese) has the usual collection of gift shops.

7 CORAKI

Continue west along the Pacific Hwy which eventually veers south to Woodburn, about 17km from the centre of Ballina. Cross the river and take the immediate right onto Casino Rd. Coraki is 17km away.

Coraki is an interesting and historic river port located at the junction of the Richmond and Wilson rivers. Throughout the 19th century the town was the most important river port in the district largely because of the entrepreneurial efforts of William Yabsley, who built a shipyard, opened a general store and conducted a school for both his family and the apprentices who worked in his shipyard.

By the 1890s, Coraki was the most prosperous town in the district. As the 20th century evolved, however, and as both Lismore and Casino grew in importance, Coraki became a smaller and quieter community.

8 HISTORIC CORAKI

As you enter Coraki follow Richmond Pde with the river to your right.

Richmond Parade has the Richmond River on one side. On the other side are the police station, located in the former courthouse (1888); the ANZ Bank, in the former ES&A Bank building (1911); and further along are the historic Club Hotel and the Coraki Hotel.

9 LISMORE

From the northern end of Queen Elizabeth St in Coraki turn right, heading across the river. Follow this road north for 12km and then, instead of veering left to the Bruxner Hwy, turn right. After 2km you will come to a T-intersection at Whyrallah. Turn left here and it is 12km to the T-intersection with Ballina St at Lismore. Turn left at Ballina St and proceed to the second round-about, where you will find the information centre.

Lismore has become a major base for those wishing to pursue creative endeavours and alternative lifestyles. Thus the city has a high

The view from Cape Byron Lighthouse.

concentration of painters, woodworkers, ceramists, filmmakers, musicians, poets, designers and dancers, and there are many galleries, studios and theatres in the area. The Lismore Visitor and Heritage Centre is located at the corner of the Bruxner Highway and Molesworth Street. The centre features the 'Rainforest Experience', a section on the history of the area and a large gallery of local arts and crafts for which the area is noted. Nearby, Heritage Park has barbecue facilities, a playground and miniature-train rides.

Proceed up Molesworth Street. To the left are the old council chambers. Upstairs is the Richmond River Historical Society Museum, which features colonial furniture made of local cedar and other pioneering relics, geological specimens, Aboriginal artefacts and a photographic collection. Opposite the museum is the Art Nouveau post office (1897) with its fine brickwork, sandstone masonry and massive tower.

Proceed north along Molesworth Street for one block. The T&G Building, at the Woodlark Street corner, was built in 1891 to an Italian villa style. Continue along Molesworth Street for another block and turn right into Zadoc Street. The imposing Classical Revival courthouse (1883) with its grand stairway is opposite St Andrew's Anglican Church which overlooks the river. Turn right into Keen Street then, at its end, turn right into Orion Street. At the Leycester Street corner is St Carthage's Roman Catholic Cathedral (1892–1907), which has a rich interior, fine woodwork and stained-glass work.

10 CLUNES

At the end of Rotary Drv turn left into Uralba St. At the second roundabout, turn right into Dawson St. When you reach the T-intersection, turn right into Brunswick St (the Bangalow Rd) and it is 18km to Clunes.

In 1892, Clunes was the meeting place for a group of dairy farmers who went on to establish the North Coast Dairying Cooper-ative, or Norco, as it is more familiarly known. The road leads past St John's Presbyterian Church (1910) and St Peter's Anglican Church (1906). After St Peter's, take the next sharp left to see the Methodist (now Uniting) Church and manse. Opposite is Coronation Hall (1910).

Return to the Bangalow Rd once again and continue on for 15km to the Pacific Hwy. Cross the highway and proceed along the Bangalow Rd for a further 11km, entering Byron Bay from the south.

56 BYRON BAY, MURWILLUMBAH AND NIMBIN

■ DRIVING TOUR ■ 195KM ■ 1 DAY ■ SEEKING AN ALTERNATIVE LIFESTYLE

The hinterland behind Byron Bay has become a popular retreat for people seeking an alternative lifestyle. The small towns and the hidden valleys are peaceful and beautiful.

If the area around Byron Bay is characterised by an elegant alternative lifestyle, the area to the north of Byron Bay is the true, 'get back to nature' area. Here, the hills are alive with the sound of hippies who, since the 1960s, have managed to carve out comfortable and interesting life-styles by either engaging in farming or craftwork and living a subsistence lifestyle in which they grow most of their own produce. And the towns reflect this lifestyle. Nimbin is the most famous town in Australia for people living an alternative lifestyle, and it is closely followed by Mullumbimby. The larger centres of Lismore and Murwillumbah also have a certain laid-back ambience.

1 BYRON BAY

Byron Bay continues to try to maintain the delicate balance between popular tourist destination (the development of the area, while contained, has been considerable over the past decade) and away-from-it-all retreat. To visit Byron Bay is to enjoy the surfing, embrace the relaxing lifestyle, visit the lighthouse, and go for walks around the coastline and the township.

2 MULLUMBIMBY

Head out of Byron Bay on Jonson St and proceed to its northern end. Turn left at the roundabout, cross the railway line and take the first right into Shirley St. Follow this road for 6km and then turn right onto the Pacific Hwy. After 8km take the signposted turn-off on the left for Mullumbimby, which is 4km away.

Mullumbimby is situated on the Brunswick River. Tourism is important to the local economy in a region noted for its bananas, avocados, pineapples and other tropical fruit, dairy products, macadamia nuts,

The weekly markets at Mullumbimby.

cattle, pigs and timber. The town's name is thought to derive from the language of the Bundjalung people, with *muli* said to mean 'hill'. The full name has been interpreted as meaning 'small round hill'—a reference to Mount Chincogan (309m), beneath which the town is situated.

The townsite was surveyed in 1887 and the village was proclaimed the following year. When the railway arrived in 1894, dairying and agriculture took off and the town prospered, acquiring its own municipal government in 1908. The fertile river flats and subtropical climate also proved ideal for the cultivation of bananas and other tropical fruits.

3 MULLUMBIMBY'S HISTORIC BUILDINGS

From Byron Bay you will enter town along Argyle St. At the T-intersection turn left into Station St, take the first right into Burringbar St and the first left into Stuart St. On the south-western corner of the third intersection (with Myocum St) is the museum.

Brunswick Valley Historical Society Museum is located in the former post office (1907), adjacent to Saltwater Creek. The museum is

open on Wednesday and Friday afternoons and at other times by arrangement.

Return along Stuart Street and turn left, back into Burringbar Street. The next major intersection is with Dalley Street. On either side of the intersection are the police station and courthouse (1908), both designed by government architect W.L. Vernon.

4 BRUNSWICK VALLEY HERITAGE PARK

Turn left into Mill St which bends to the right as Brunswick Tce.

To the right, adjacent to the river, is Heritage Park, a reserve with a walking track and over 200 rainforest plants which are all labelled. The species include red cedars, coolamons, grevilleas, black apple, giant water gum, rosewood, flooded gum, swamp mahogany and hoop pines.

5 BRUNSWICK HEADS

Proceed south along Brunswick Tce, which finishes at a left turn into Burringbar St. At its end turn left and then take the first right, back into Argyle St. Continue to the Pacific Hwy (4km) and turn left. Brunswick Heads is 5km away.

The Freemason Hotel, Nimbin.

Brunswick Heads is a charming mixture of quiet holiday retreat and large commercial fishing fleet. The town is simple and unassuming. Access to the town's main beach is relatively complicated, involving crossing Simpsons Creek via two bridges. There is an ambience of peacefulness and an easy sense of holiday-making pervading this quiet town.

By the 1870s there were nearly 100 cedar-cutters working in the hinterland. The town's importance diminished dramatically with the arrival of the Sydney to Brisbane railway line in the late 1880s. The residents had hoped the railway line would pass through Brunswick Heads. Instead, the line was routed through Mullumbimby.

Brunswick Heads is a popular fishing, surfing and swimming holiday destination. There is an interesting quasi-pirate ship located in the river near the main beach. Canoes and paddleboats can be hired near the pirate ship booth

6 MURWILLUMBAH

Return to the Pacific Hwy and continue north for 32km. You will reach a roundabout on the eastern riverbank at the outskirts of town. In the park opposite is the information centre.

Murwillumbah spreads along the banks of the Tweed River by the foothills of the McPherson Ranges. The town is surrounded by sugar cane, which is the major industry of the Tweed Valley. Dairying and bananas also contribute to the local economy.

The townsite was surveyed in 1872. Settlement remained limited until the railway arrived in 1894 from Lismore, however. A lift-span bridge was built over the river in 1901 and the settlement was declared a municipality in 1902. A hospital was built in 1904 and the Murwillumbah branch of the Norco butter factory opened in 1906, signalling the emergence of dairying in the area. Banana plantations also began to appear in the early 20th century.

Tourist information can be obtained at the World Heritage Rainforest Centre, which is located in Budd Park, on the eastern bank of the Tweed River, at the corner of the Pacific Highway and Alma Street.

7 MURWILLUMBAH'S HISTORIC BUILDINGS

Turn left at the roundabout and proceed across the bridge. Take the first right, then the first left, and keep to the left as Wharf St leads into Main St.

To the right are W.L. Vernon's Federation-style courthouse (1909), the police station (c.1905) and their outbuildings. Further along, on the other side of the Queensland Road intersection, are the Catholic Church, the associated school and the timber presbytery.

Turn into Queensland Road. Bent Street heads off immediately to the right. At this corner is the local history museum, located in the former council chambers (1910).

8 MOUNT WARNING NATIONAL PARK

Proceed to the western end of Main St and turn left, just before the roundabout, into Nullum St. Take the first right into Wollumbin St and then the first left into Riverview St (the Kyogle Rd). After 10km take the signposted right turn onto the Mount Warning Rd and travel 6km to the Breakfast Creek Picnic Area at the park entrance by the base of the mountain.

Mount Warning (1157m high) receives the first rays of sunlight on the Australian mainland each day. It is located in a 2210ha rainforest park which was given a World Heritage listing in 1986. The mountain, with its Dreamtime connections, is significant to the indigenous people who know it as 'Wollumbin'. The European name was bestowed by Captain Cook to warn mariners of offshore reefs which he encountered in May 1770.

The Mount Warning Summit Track is strenuous, steep and rocky in parts. It is an 8.8km hike (including the return trip) through subtropical and temperate rainforest, wet sclerophyll forest and heath shrubland which takes about four hours to complete.

9 UKI

Return along the Mount Warning Rd and turn right, back into the Kyogle Rd. You will soon come to Uki.

Uki is an attractive village which began as a service centre to a cedar-getting area. The village prospered with the emergence of dairying in the 1890s. The school (1895) and Holy Trinity Anglican Church (1921) remain in the main street. The village shrank when dairying declined after World War II.

10 NIMBIN

Follow the Kyogle Rd south-west for another 29km and then take the signposted left for Nimbin, which is 14km away.

There was a time when Nimbin was a sleepy little dairy village hidden in the hills behind Lismore and Murwillumbah. Situated on the edge of the Nightcap National Park, Nimbin was an isolated settlement in which things had barely changed since the arrival of Europeans in the 1840s. Then, in 1973, the Australian Union of Students chose the Nimbin Valley as the venue for an experimental Aquarius Festival. The festival was to be 'a total, cultural experience through the lifestyle of participation' and attracted students, alternative lifestylers and hippies from all over Australia.

The 'alternative society' has been able to prosper in this is impossibly rich land with a rainfall that averages 1500–2000mm per year. The climate is ideal, particularly in the pockets of rich rainforest, for the growing of bananas, pawpaws, mangoes and kiwifruit.

For most visitors Nimbin is a different world. To wander along the main street of Nimbin is to experience this world-the cafes are full of wholesome food and the shops are full of crafts. This is the heart of the Nimbin experience. The Rainbow Cafe is probably the most famous of all the venues on the main street. The Nimbin Museum records the town's hippie history.

11 NIMBIN ROCKS

Follow the Lismore Rd south out of town for about 3km. To the right are the remains of an ancient, eroded volcanic dyke known as the Nimbin Rocks. The rocks have been estimated as 20 million years old. The rocks have special significance to the local Aborigines, who regard them as a sacred burial site.

Continue south for another 26km to Lismore. As you come in on the Nimbin Rd, veer left into Terania St. At its end turn right into Bridge St. Turn left at the roundabout, follow Woodlark St and at the third roundabout turn left into Dawson St. When you reach the T-intersection turn right into Brunswick St (the Bangalow Rd) and follow it for 44km to Byron Bay.

The timber-cutter memorial in Knox Park, Murwillumbah.

57 MURWILLUMBAH, THE GOLD COAST AND THE HINTERLAND

■ DRIVING TOUR ■ 205KM ■ 1 DAY ■ RIVERS, RAINFOREST AND HOLIDAY BEACHES

The border between New South Wales and Queensland is well-known for its high rise development surrounded by subtropical rainforest, rich riverflats and undulating, fertile valleys.

State borders are artificial dividing lines. The line between New South Wales and Queensland blurs on the coast where, as you drive from Murwillumbah, you enter the southern edge of the huge Gold Coast development between Tweed Heads and Coolangatta. You then wind into the hills behind the coast only to gaze out from Queensland back onto the coastal plains of New South Wales. This journey mixes great and peaceful rural beauty with the full-on development of one of Australia's most popular holiday destinations.

1 MURWILLUMBAH

Murwillumbah is a pleasant town on the Tweed River. The town is located 31km from the river mouth at Tweed Heads, the border between New South Wales and Queensland. In recent times the Pacific Highway which joins Sydney and Brisbane has bypassed the township and so it has become a quieter and more sedate service centre. Murwillumbah is surrounded by fields of sugar cane, which is the major industry of the Tweed Valley. There is also some dairying and banana growing.

The Aborigines who lived in the area before European settlement probably used the word Murwillumbah to describe either a good place for camping beside the river, or a good place to catch possums. There is no accurate record available. The first European into the area was the explorer John Oxley, who named the Tweed River in 1823. Five years later Captain Henry Rous, after whom the smaller river is named, surveyed the area, and by the late 1830s, timber-cutters were already at work on the rich forests of the hinterland.

As early as the 1860s, sugar cane was being grown along the valley. There was no real need for an organised settlement at the time and it wasn't until 1872 that a site for a town was finally surveyed.

If you want to explore the area further a visit to the visitor centre is advised. Known as the World Heritage Rainforest Centre, it is located in Budd Park, on the eastern bank of the Tweed River, at the corner of the Pacific Highway and Alma Street (the main road through Murwillumbah).

2 CONDONG SUGAR MILL

Head north-east along the Pacific Hwy towards Condong, which is 4km away.
The Condong Sugar Mill (established in 1880) is located on the left-hand side of the Pacific Highway. From July to November visitors can view the sugar cane being processed.

3 TWEED HEADS

The road follows the river and each side is given over to sugar cane. Pass through the tiny township of Tumbulgum. There is a turn off to the coast north of Tumbulgum, towards the Avocadoland Plantation Restaurant. The highway then swings north and crosses the Tweed River before reaching Tweed Heads.
Tweed Heads is the beginning of the Gold Coast proper. Although it is in New South Wales, Tweed Heads is a twin town with Coolangatta which is just across the border. Both towns developed independently but by the 1960s, as the Gold Coast began to expand, the line between the two centres began to blur. Today, Tweed Heads is a true centre for retirement. The town must have one of the largest bowling clubs in Australia (on the right-hand side of the road as you enter the town). Equally, the Twin Towns Service Club is a monument to the people who have retired to the area. The club attracts entertainment for senior citizens.

4 NERANG

Leave Tweed Heads via Griffith St to reach Coolangatta. Head north along Marine Pde, turn right into Musgrave St and continue north for about 1km to rejoin the Gold Coast Hwy. At Tugun, the Pacific Hwy and the Gold Coast Hwy diverge. Take the Pacific Hwy fork to the left. Continue through West Burleigh, Mudgeeraba and north to Nerang.
The town of Nerang is a perfect example of what has happened on the Gold Coast from the overspill of population from both Brisbane and the Gold Coast. Once a quiet little town, Nerang now looks like a large slab of suburbia with wide roads, recent project home developments,

Next door to Coolangatta is popular Kirra Beach.

modern shopping complexes and the usual features of a large centre of population and commerce.

Looking at Nerang today it is hard to imagine that back in 1842, after the land around Moreton Bay had been opened up for settlement, the river was first surveyed. Settlement occurred quickly and for a short time, in 1862–1864, cotton was grown. The crop was replaced in 1865 by sugar cane. In 1865 the town was surveyed and the following year residential land was sold. .

The town grew rapidly in the 1870s. A hotel was built (1872), a post office (1874) and a school (1876). In 1889 the railway arrived, thus ensuring the town's continuing survival.

5 HISTORIC RIVERMILL

Head south out of Nerang along Price St as it becomes the Beaudesert–Nerang Rd (Highway 90). About 4km out of town, branch to the right, following the Canungra–Beaudesert–Warwick signpost. This is still the Beaudesert–Nerang Rd. About 7km further along this road, by the Coomera River is an historic mill.

To the west of Nerang, on the Nerang River, is an historic mill which has been turned into a popular tourist attraction. The mill was built in 1910 and at the time was Australia's first arrowroot mill. Today it has a good-quality restaurant, a museum and a number of interesting displays to engage the tourist. The mill is open between 9.00am–5.00pm.

6 BINNA BURRA LODGE

Two roads can be taken at this point. The road to Advancetown leads to Natural Bridge and into New South Wales. If you feel you have time, or if you would like a quiet day walking in the bush, turn right onto the road signposted for Beechmont and the Binna Burra Lodge. Beechmont is 21km south. When you get there, pass the roundabout next to the Beechmont School and turn left. Follow this road, which winds up the Beechmont Range, for 10km to reach the lodge. There are a number of lookouts on the way which provide dramatic views back across the Gold Coast hinterland.

Another popular attraction in the area is Binna Burra Lodge, which is located on the eastern side of Lamington National Park.

The lodge is ideally located. The views across the valleys are dramatic. The lodge provides a range of activities to tempt the visitor to stay for a few days. There are bushwalking tracks to the falls and the nearby caves, plus guided bushwalks and organised horseriding through the rainforest. The Lamington National Park is said to have over 500 waterfalls and, typical of the area, the vegetation moves from eucalypt forests to tropical rainforest. The park covers 20 200ha of subtropical rainforest with waterfalls, superb views and excellent bushwalking tracks.

7 NATURAL BRIDGE

Return the way you came, through Beechmont, back to the turn-off for Advancetown. Turn right and drive south through the Numinbah Valley to Natural Bridge. Once again, you will rise up the mountain range. At times the journey seems effortless but then a steep incline will lift you to new vantage points where you can see both the Gold Coast and the hinterland. About 1km north of the border is a side road signposted for the Natural Bridge.

Located in Springbrook National Park, the 'bridge' consists essentially of a creek that disappears into a huge hole in the roof of a cave to emerge below in a water pool. The access road leads to a car park in a delightful shady grove with birds wandering through the rainforest and the sound of the stream as it passes through the valley below. A clearly signposted track leads down through the rainforest—notice the vines in the trees and staghorns as well as the huge trees rotting on the forest floor—to the creek below. The most distinctive trees in the area are the hoop pines, which abound here in the national park. The track crosses the creek and moves upstream, firstly offering a view of the falls and then the opportunity for the walker to clamber down to creek level to inspect the Natural Bridge falls or to enter a cave where there is a particularly good vantage point. The falls are small but impressive. The water has cut a cave in the rock and the forest light shafts down through the opening. The path moves beyond the falls, crosses the creek again, and climbs back up to the parking lot. Glow worms can be seen in the cave at night.

8 CHILLINGHAM

Head south across the border into New South Wales. From here there is a wonderful view of northern New South Wales across the undulating hills and the road making its way down into the valley. The road slowly heads east across the fertile valley of the Rous River and passes through a series of attractive and peaceful villages. It is about 13km from the Natural Bridge turn-off to Chillingham.

Although little more than a general store and a couple of houses, Chillingham is the first stopping point on the New South Wales side of the border. The general store offers a range of specialist products from the local area and serves an excellent cup of tea.

From Chillingham continue down the valley towards Murwillumbah. The upper reaches of the Rous River valley are planted with sugar cane and, if the visitor travels through the region at the right time of year, there are walls of sugar cane on either side of the road. At one point, close to Murwillumbah, the road crosses the river and takes a sharp turn to the right. If you decide not to take this turn, you will follow the Tweed River on the inland side before being able to cross some kilometres beyond Murwillumbah at Tumbulgum.

The lighthouse at sunset, Tweed Heads.

CHAPTER 10
NORTHERN
NEW SOUTH WALES

58 AROUND TENTERFIELD

■ DRIVING AND WALKING TOUR ■ 182KM ■ 1 DAY ■ FEDERATION, SADDLERY AND SACRED SITES

The New England Ranges are spectacular and full of pleasures for those eager to bushwalk and explore their rugged, unspoilt beauty.

O*ne of the very best Aboriginal cultural tours available in New South Wales is the Woollool Woollool Aboriginal Cultural Tour, which leaves Tenterfield and heads north to Bald Rock, the largest granite monolith in Australia. The tour is the very essence of Australia. Run jointly by Aboriginal and European guides, the tour combines the ancient history of the district with the more modern history to reveal that this area of the New England Tablelands was vital to the federation of Australia's states and was made internationally famous by Peter Allen's song 'Tenterfield Saddler'.*

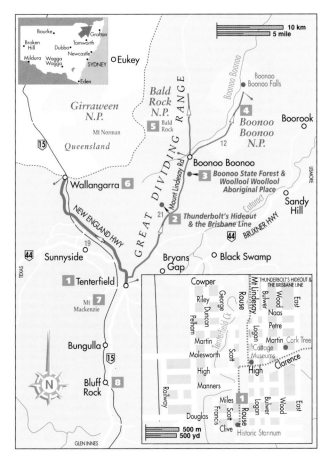

1 TENTERFIELD

Tenterfield is situated in a valley at the northern end of the New England Tablelands in an area of rugged mountains and rural vistas. The town claims to be the Birthplace of the Nation as it was here, in 1889, that Henry Parkes made his famous Federation speech, which led the establishment of Australia.

The Tenterfield area is devoted to sheep and cattle, although orchards, farm crops, a silica mine and a growing tourism sector all contribute to the local economy. The first white settlers arrived in the late 1830s. From 1847 until the late 1860s, most of the wool of New England district passed through Tenterfield en route to the coast. Court hearings were established at Tenterfield in 1847. In 1849 a post office was set up and the first publican's licence was issued for the Georges Inn, on the site now occupied by the Royal Hotel. A townsite was surveyed on the Tenterfield station that same year and was

gazetted as Tenterfield in 1851, by which time police buildings and huts had been established.

Tenterfield was declared a municipality in 1871. The most memorable single event in the town's history occurred at the Tenterfield School of Arts in 1889 when five times the Premier of New South Wales, Henry Parkes, delivered his famous speech calling for the federation of the Australian colonies. His speech is credited with setting off the chain of events that culminated in the declaration of the Australian Commonwealth in 1901.

J.F. Thomas, the man who defended 'Breaker' Morant, was a native of Tenterfield and, for 16 years, was the owner of the local newspaper, the *Tenterfield Star*, which pressed for Federation and was the first country paper to advocate the formation of the Country Party. Noted Australian entertainer Peter Allen was also born here in 1944, as Peter Woolnough, the grandson of George Woolnough, celebrated in Allen's song 'Tenterfield Saddler'.

The information centre is located at 157 Rouse Street (the New England Highway), on the corner with Miles Street. Here you can obtain a pamphlet on the self-guided heritage walk. Inquiries can be made at the centre for the guided tours to sites of Aboriginal significance within the Bald Rock and Boonoo Boonoo national parks.

On the corner of Manners and Rouse streets is the Sir Henry Parkes Memorial School of Arts. The building began its life as a working man's institute in 1876. It was here that Henry Parkes delivered his famous speech. The museum houses a collection of Parkes memorabilia. Over the road is the

two-storey, rendered brick post office (1881), a Victorian Classical building with a metal mansard roof, arched colonnades and clock tower. Also at this corner is the Exchange Hotel (1890).

Head north along Scott Street and turn right into Molesworth Street where you will find the masonry courthouse (1882), designed by colonial architect James Barnet, with an outstanding glass skylight. The trees were planted in the 1880s. To the rear of the courthouse, facing Martin Street, are the gaol with its unusual masonry dormer, the police station and the brick police and warden's residences (1874). The whole complex is integrated by fencing and landscaping.

At the end of the block turn left into Rouse Street. To the left is the Criterion Hotel (1872). On the other side of the road is the masonic lodge (1877). Cross back over Molesworth Street. In the next block, to the left, is the State Bank building (1891). Turn left into High Street, once the town's main thoroughfare. To the right, at 123 High Street, is The Saddler's Shop, which achieved widespread fame through Peter Allen's song, written as a tribute to

Woollool Woollool guides on Bald Rock.

his grandfather, George Woolnough, who worked here from 1908 until his retirement in 1960. Made of locally quarried, hand-cut blue granite with 50cm thick walls, the building was erected in the 1860s and initially served as a residence before becoming the premises of the Australian Joint Stock Bank in 1874. In original condition, the doors and joinery are of red cedar. It is still a saddlery specialising in quality handmade saddles and Australian clothing.

2 THUNDERBOLT'S HIDEOUT AND THE BRISBANE LINE

Return along High St and turn left, back into Rouse St. At the fourth intersection turn right into Naas St and then take the first left into Logan St which heads north-east as the Mount Lindesay Rd. About 12km from town is a sign on the left-hand side of the road indicating the whereabouts of Thunderbolt's Hideout.

Leave the car and follow the directions for 300m to some large granite boulders that form two caves, believed to have been used by the bushranger Thunderbolt (Fred Ward). In Ward's day the summit of the boulders was a natural vantage point over the road, then the main route to the north. An information sheet at the visitors centre outlines the exploits and local sites associated with the outlaw.

A further kilometre up the road, to the left of the cement wall, are some upright posts. Designed as tank traps, they are remnants of the Brisbane Line fortifications from World War II. This was the second line of defence in case of an invasion from the north. In the course of the war, there were up to 10 000 troops stationed in the Tenterfield area.

3 BOONOO STATE FOREST AND WOOLLOOL WOOLLOOL ABORIGINAL PLACE

Proceed north on the Mount Lindesay Rd. About 18km from Tenterfield, you will come to Linbrook Rd, clearly signposted to the right, which leads through the Boonoo State Forest.

Within the Boonoo State Forest is a rest area known as the Basket Swamp and the Bark Hut Picnic and Camping Area. Also within the 370ha reserve is Woollool Woollool, an impressive stone outcrop with one mushroom-shaped rock protruding above the other boulders (1040m above sea level at its peak). A spot of great natural beauty, it is a designated sacred site of the Bundjalung people. Woollool Woollool was a *wayangali*, a clever man with special rights to this centre of spiritual power. His spirit is reputed to have returned to the site upon his death, rendering it approachable for others. A dry weather road comes to within 3km of the site, with a four-wheel-drive track leading the remainder of the way.

4 BOONOO BOONOO NATIONAL PARK

Return along the park road and then turn right, back into Mount Lindesay Rd. About 22km from Tenterfield the Mount Lindesay Rd brings you to the locality of Boonoo Boonoo. Here a clearly signposted road on the right heads north-east to Boonoo Boonoo Falls.

At Boonoo Boonoo Falls, the Boonoo Boonoo River gathers in beautiful pools before plummeting 210m into the gorge below. There is a picnic area, and a graded walking track descends from the main parking area to a viewing platform with excellent views of the gorge and the falls. There are remnants of sluicing operations in the Morgans Gully area near the park entrance, a reminder of the days when there was goldmining in the area.

5 BALD ROCK NATIONAL PARK

Return again to the Mount Lindesay Rd. A further 5km north, Bald Rock Rd heads off to the left, leading to the Bald Rock picnicking and camping area.

From the picnic area the Bungoona Walk is an easy 2.5km trek past some interesting granite boulders to the summit of the aptly named Bald Rock. Signs and white markings lead to a more direct route marked up the north-east face.

Bald Rock is the largest exposed granite monolith in Australia, being 750m long, 500m wide and 200m high (1341m above sea level at the highest point of its featureless pate). South Bald Rock, a smaller granite dome, is a mere 5km away and can be reached via a marked trail from the rest area. It is actually west over the state border, in Girraween National Park.

6 WALLANGARRA

Return along Bald Rock Rd and turn right, back into Mount Lindesay Rd and follow it south, back to Tenterfield. At the end of Logan St turn right into Naas St and then take the first right into Rouse St. At the end of the block turn left into Cowper St and follow it as it curves to the right becoming Wallangarra Rd (the New England Hwy). It is 19km to Wallangarra.

Wallangarra was established in 1888 when the railway line was extended to the state border. Customs excise officers were immediately relocated from Tenterfield and Stanthorpe to a purpose-built customs house where duties were imposed upon those crossing the border. Resentment of these duties helped to fuel the push towards Federation. It is now possible to go on a 30-minute guided walk through Customs House Corner precinct and other historic attractions.

7 MOUNT MACKENZIE GRANITE DRIVE

Return to Tenterfield, entering the town along Cowper St. Turn right into Rouse St and hen right into Molesworth St. At its end turn left into Neagles Lne and when you come to the T-intersection turn right onto Mount McKenzie Rd.

Mount Mackenzie Granite Drive provides a fine overview of the town and district from several vantage points to the west of town. It also takes in some of the district's striking granite outcrops. The 38km (one-hour) circular route to the west of town is detailed in a leaflet available from the visitors centre which also draws attention to various sites, including Ghost Gully, a dry creek bed featuring interesting erosion formations, and Mount Mackenzie Lookout (1298m above sea level). There is a parking area with picnic and barbecue facilities at the summit.

8 BLUFF ROCK

Return to Rouse St (the New England Hwy) and turn right, heading south out of town. About 10km from Tenterfield is Bluff Rock.

Bluff Rock is an unusual granite outcrop rising steeply from the highway. Although the rock is on private property, it is clearly visible from the roadside. There is a rest area on the northern side of the road. The rock's speckled appearance is caused by large crystals of pink feldspar.

It is said that in 1844 a shepherd named Robinson was murdered by Aborigines who ultimately fled to the rock, pursued by a posse of whites who then decimated the tribe by throwing them off the top of the rock. *Return 10km back to Tenterfield on the New England Hwy.*

Dense undergrowth and huge granite boulders characterise the whole district.

59 HISTORIC ARMIDALE

■ WALKING TOUR ■ 4KM ■ 2 HOURS ■ HISTORIC ARMIDALE

Now a thriving service centre and home to the University of New England, Armidale is a rural city of great charm and elegance.

*A*rmidale is one of the most gracious inland towns in Australia. The wealth generated by the large properties surrounding Armidale has ensured a streetscape characterised by elegant historic buildings—both public and private—and a remarkable 10 per cent of the town's central area given over to parks and gardens. Beyond Armidale, the high country, where it snows every winter, is sheep country. The area is notable for its impressive granite outcrops and its dramatic and beautiful national parks.

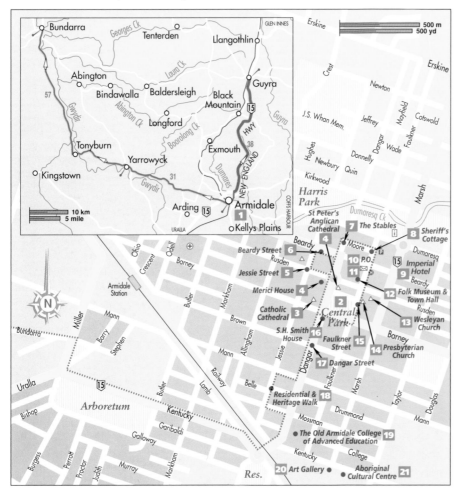

1 ARMIDALE

Armidale is an attractive and graceful city with tree-lined streets and a large number of historic buildings. Grazing and the production of high-grade fine wool are the major sources of local income. There are many well-established and wealthy grazing families in the area. The affluence of the district is apparent in some of the city's fine heritage buildings.

There is plenty of impressive scenery around Armidale, including forests, mountain gorges, waterfalls and four national parks. Armidale itself has plenty of parkland and a reputation as a major educational and ecclesiastical centre. The University of New England was the first to be established outside of the capital cities. The town boasts two major cathedrals facing Armidale Central Park, and St Nicholas's, which is registered on the National Estate. The collection at the New England Regional Art Gallery is considered the best of any country gallery in Australia.

Armidale's Tourist Information and Coach Centre is located in Curtis Park, on the corner of Dumaresq and Marsh streets. There is information on self-drive scenic and heritage tours of the district, heritage walks of Armidale and Hillgrove, horseriding in the area, fishing in a district noted for its trout, guided trout fishing tours, gem fossicking, farm holidays, sightseeing, abseiling, rafting, swimming and picnic spots.

2 CENTRAL PARK

A logical place to start a walking tour of Armidale is in Central Park, which is the centre of the city. Bounded by Faulkner, Barney and Dangar streets and Tingcombe Lane, the park is an attractive, dignified reserve which was dedicated in 1874 as a recreational area. The band rotunda was built as a 1902 Boer War memorial. The well-established trees are beautiful, particularly in autumn.

3 TWO CATHEDRALS

The two most obvious landmarks on the edge of Central Park are the two cathedrals. The Anglican Cathedral of St Peter, built in 1875, stands on the northern side of the park while St Mary's and St Joseph's Catholic Cathedral, on the other side of Dangar St, is the city's most dominant building. A Gothic Revival structure it was built in 1911–1912.

4 ST PETER'S AND MERICI HOUSE

Nearby, on the corner of Dangar and Rusden streets, is the splendid High Victorian Gothic design of St Peter's Anglican Cathedral. Considered one of Australia's most interesting and innovative ecclesiastical designs, the cathedral was primarily built between 1871 and 1878. The brickwork is outstanding and the detailing is exceptional, within and without the building. There is a museum in the belltower with items relating to parish and diocesan history.

Also on Dangar Street is Merici House, which was built as St Mary's School in 1862. Angela Merici was the founder of the Ursuline Order of nuns, who began teaching at the school in 1883.

5 JESSIE STREET

Head west along Rusden Street to the corner of Jessie Street. On the north-eastern corner is Minto, built in 1894 as the Central Hotel. On the north-western corner is the town's second Baptist Church, built in 1918 to a Gothic Revival design. Duck down Jessie Street. On the left is the Ursuline Convent, built in the 1860s.

6 BEARDY STREET

Return along Jessie Street and turn right into Beardy Street. On the right, at no. 208, is the State Bank building (1887–1889), which has

University of New England in Armidale.

The Armidale Post Office.

a decorative facade and elegant interior. Outside Woolworths is Armidale's only remaining hitching post. Nearby is the charming and elegant New England Hotel (1897).

7 THE STABLES
Slightly north, along Dangar Street, at the corner of Moore Street, is an 1872 cottage known as The Stables, situated behind the National Bank building. There is a hoist over the main door to service the loft. The building is currently a gift shop.

8 SHERIFF'S COTTAGE AND COURTHOUSE
Walk down Moore Street to Faulkner Street. On that corner is the Sheriff's Cottage, a simple, single-storey brick magistrate's residence with timber verandah. Built in 1870 it was originally the town lock-up. The cottage lies behind the simple brick courthouse (1859–1860) on the north-western corner of Beardy and Faulkner streets. Note the grand portico and squat clock tower.

9 IMPERIAL HOTEL
On the south-eastern corner of Beardy and Faulkner streets is the two-storey brick and stucco Imperial Hotel (1889). Armidale's oldest surviving hotel, this highly ornamented building features extensive cast-iron frieze work on the verandahs and extravagant parapets. The interior retains an air of Victorian opulence.

10 POST OFFICE AND LANDS BOARD OFFICE
On the south-western corner is the two-storey Classical brick and stucco post office (1880). Next door, at 164–66 Beardy Street, in the mall, is the Lands Board Office (*c.*1882), now a series of shops.

11 LANDS DEPARTMENT OFFICE
Return to Faulkner Street. Next door to the post office, at no. 108, is the Lands Department Office (1886), a two-storey High Victorian public building with an elegant and elaborate verandah and balcony.

12 FOLK MUSEUM AND TOWN HALL
Further south on Faulkner Street, on the corner with Rusden Street is the old School of Arts and Mechanics/Literary Institute. The original corner section was built in 1863. The building is now a folk museum with local artefacts. Next door (along Rusden Street) is the two-storey High Victorian town hall (1882–1883) with its decorative stuccoed brick facade.

13 WESLEYAN CHURCH
East along Rusden Street is the Wesley Uniting Church (1893). The hall was the town's first Wesleyan Church (1864). The pipe organ was made in 1879.

14 ST PAUL'S PRESBYTERIAN CHURCH
Further south on Faulkner Street, to the right, opposite Tingcombe Lane, is St Paul's Presbyterian Church (1881–1882), a Gothic Revival design with a tall steeple, wrought-iron ornamentation, arched lancet windows and rose window.

15 FAULKNER STREET
Adjacent to the church, at 139 Faulkner Street, is Solomons Cottage, built of English bonded brick in 1872 to a Georgian design. Next door, at the Barney Street corner, is New South Wales' first masonic temple, which has a fine leadlight gallery. Diagonally opposite, at 128 Faulkner Street, is Lindsay House (1880s).

16 S.H. SMITH HOUSE
West along Barney Street, at the corner with Dangar Street, is S.H. Smith House, built in 1889 of Flemish brickwork. The building originally served as the New England Ladies' College, which closed in 1904. In 1960 it was joined with Southhall, a two-storey building dating from 1886.

17 DANGAR STREET
Turn left into Dangar Street. To the left, at no. 133, is Arran Cottage, built in 1863 for one of Armidale's first doctors. The house behind it, at 133 Dangar Street, was built in 1862.

18 RESIDENTIAL AND HERITAGE WALK
The following walk can be considered either as a separate tour or an extension of the preceding one. It starts precisely where the last walk concluded.
Head south along Dangar Street, across Brown Street and, to the left, is Armidale City Public School which opened in 1861. The school shifted to its present site in 1865. Before then, this was the town's first cemetery and police barracks. Opposite the school, at 160 Dangar Street, is the former Hilton School (*circa* late 1880s). The house at 176 Dangar Street was built about 1900.
Turn right into Mann Street. At no. 146 is Linden Hall, built about 1880. Turn left into Jessie Street and then left again into Mossman Street. At no. 145 is The Turrets, built in the 1860s. The house's name derives from the turreted bay windows. There is an interesting old buggy shed on the grounds.

19 THE OLD ARMIDALE COLLEGE OF ADVANCED EDUCATION
Turn right into Dangar Street and then left at Kentucky Street. To the left is the Armidale College of Advanced Education, now part of the University of New England. From 1863 to 1920, this was the site of the town gaol, where six hangings took place. The building also doubled as an insane asylum. The college purchased the site in 1927 and the current building opened in 1930, the first regional teacher's college in New South Wales. Situated atop a hill amid formal gardens, it is a Classical design building featuring an impressive art collection within.

The college's Educational Museum is situated opposite, to the right of Kentucky Street. It consists of three 19th-century school buildings.

20 NEW ENGLAND REGIONAL ART GALLERY
A little further along Kentucky Street, at the corner with Marsh Street, is the New England Regional Art Gallery. Its collection is considered by many as the best of any country gallery in Australia, with a particularly impressive collection of Australian paintings from the late 19th and early 20th centuries, including Tom Roberts, Norman Lindsay and Arthur Streeton. There are also pieces by Kandinsky and Rodin.

21 ABORIGINAL CULTURAL CENTRE AND KEEPING PLACE
Adjacent to the gallery is the Aboriginal Cultural Centre and Keeping Place with visual and performing arts programs designed to preserve and inform about Aboriginal and Torres Strait Island art and culture.

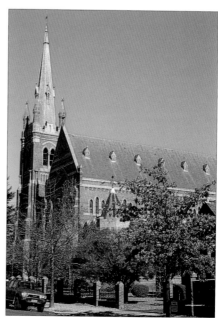

St Mary's and St Joseph's Catholic Cathedral.

60 TAMWORTH TO MOREE

■ DRIVING TOUR ■ 378KM ■ 1 DAY ■ INTO THE NORTHERN SLOPES

The road from Tamworth to Moree is famous for its bushrangers and the fertile northern slopes which have proved ideal sheep country for over a century.

*I*n the past twenty years, Tamworth has established itself as Australia's Country Music Capital. Beyond Tamworth lie the New England Ranges and the northern slopes with their deep valleys and rugged granite outcrops. Further west is Moree, where people travel for thousands of kilometres to bathe and relax in the hot, curative mineral springs.

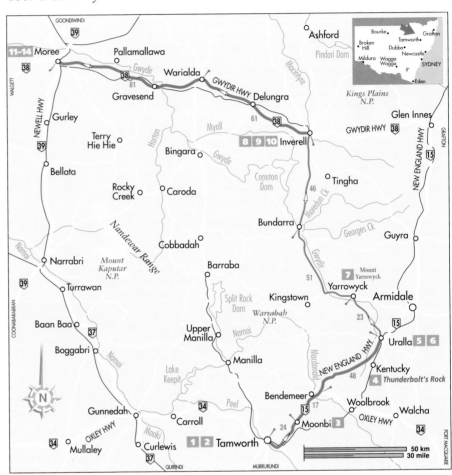

1 TAMWORTH

Known as the Country Music Capital, Tamworth is thought of as a sort of Australian equivalent to Nashville in the United States. The focus of this promotion is the Australasian Country Music Festival, held every January. The association of the city with country music started in the late 1960s, when local radio station 2TM discovered the scale of the potential country music audience when it began broadcasting its program 'Hoedown'. Tamworth capitalised on the success by establishing the Country Music Awards in 1973.

2 COUNTRY MUSIC CAPITAL

A good starting place for exploring the city's country music connections is the Tamworth Information Centre at the corner of Peel and Murray streets. Just behind the centre is the Tamworth Songwriters' Association Songwriter Tribute, a memorial to Australian country music songwriters such as Tex Morton, Slim Dusty, Stan Coster, Joy McKean and Gordon Parsons.

Head west along Peel Street for five blocks and turn right into Brisbane Street. In the first block, to your right, is the Australian Country Music Foundation Museum, which includes a collection of Slim Dusty memorabilia. Nearby is The Winners Walkway, a landscaped memorial in Treloars Arcade dedicated to those who win the Golden Guitar Award.

3 MOONBI

Leave Tamworth on the Armidale Rd (the New England Hwy). Moonbi is 20km away.
Moonbi, at the foot of the Moonbi Ranges, is the largest poultry-producing area in the state outside Sydney, hence the Big Chook in the park on the left-hand side of the highway.

A few kilometres further north along the highway is Moonbi Lookout at the top of the first Moonbi Range, where a huge granite boulder offers a view over the agricultural valley below.

4 THUNDERBOLT'S ROCK

Continue along the New England Hwy. Thunderbolt's Rock is 61km from Moonbi.
To the right of the highway is the large granite outcrop known as Thunderbolt's Rock. The rock has, unfortunately, been attacked by graffitists. The notorious bushranger Thunderbolt (Fred Ward) used the outcrop as a vantage point and hide-out. Blanchs Inn, where Thunderbolt's final ride started, was located about 300m further south of the rock, on the opposite side of the road. A few old bricks remain and a depression in the ground indicates where the cellars were located.

5 URALLA

Continue along the highway for 8km, which crosses East St, becoming Bridge St. At the corner of Bridge and Salisbury sts is the information centre.
Uralla calls itself Thunderbolt Country and the town's chief claim to fame is the grave of the bushranger. Uralla emerged in the 1840s around a shepherd's out-station on the banks of Rocky Creek. The town really began with the discovery of gold at Rocky River in 1851, which started a gold rush when the find was publicly announced the following year. The village was gazetted in 1855.

Although the mines continued to prove highly profitable in the 1860s, the area also prospered from pastoral and agricultural pursuits. Wheat was a major focus and Samuel McCrossin established a large mill at Uralla in 1870. Still standing today, the mill now houses a museum.

6 URALLA VISITORS CENTRE AND THUNDERBOLT

Uralla's visitors centre in Bridge Street has pamphlets outlining a self-guided heritage walk. At this same corner is a lifesize statue of Thunderbolt on a horse. Nearby, just along Salisbury Street is a plaque dedicated to Constable Walker, who killed the bushranger to the south of Uralla in 1870. Also at the corner is a stand which plays pre-recorded information relating to Thunderbolt's life and death.

If you start at the visitors centre and head south-east along Salisbury Street you will reach McCrossin's Mill Museum, located in the three-storey flour mill built of brick and granite in 1870. Adjacent to the museum are old stables built in the 1860s in association with McCrossin's post office and store, which was located where McRaes Store stands today.

The museum's many displays include a Thunderbolt exhibition which features an effigy of his body on the table the corpse was originally laid out on, and original paintings relating to the bushranger's demise.

7 MOUNT YARROWYCK ABORIGINAL ART SITE

Return along Salisbury St and turn right into Bridge St. Take the first left into Hill St, the second right into Uralla St and then the first left into the Bundarra Rd. About 23km from Uralla you will pass the Armidale turn-off on your right. Continue along the Bundarra Rd for about 1km to a small signpost directing you to turn right onto a gravel road.

This gravel road leads to a car park and picnic area where there are plaques pointing out the highlights of the 3km loop walk. The walk includes seeing Aboriginal rock art within a small shelter, on the south-western slopes of Mount Yarrowyck. There on a 2.7m rock surface, are red ochre paintings dominated by bird-track motifs.

8 INVERELL PIONEER VILLAGE

Return along the gravel road and turn right, back into the Bundarra Rd. After about 1km, turn left and follow the signs for Torryburn and Kingstown. Ignore the Kingstown turn-off (after 17km) and veer right, heading due north to Bundarra, which is 80km from Uralla. At Bundarra, branch right and follow the signs for Inverell rather than for Bingara. It is 43km to Inverell. As you enter the town, the pioneer village is to your right.

Inverell Pioneer Village is a collection of 19th-century homes and buildings, relocated in landscaped environs to give the impression of a colonial village. Included in the village is

Statue of Thunderbolt in Uralla.

a printing office, Paddys Pub (1874), a miner's hut, the Nullamanna Church, a hall, Goonoowigall school, a blacksmith's hut, telephone exchange, farrier's shop, shearing shed, a cottage that houses a collection of gems and minerals, and an 1841 homestead with a stringybark roof from the Tingha area which serves as a museum housing artefacts of the period 1840–1925. There are also old steam and traction engines.

9 INVERELL

Inverell is a service centre to a mixed farming district. Mining has been a staple of the area since the 1870s with tin, sapphires, zircons and diamonds all being commercially exploited.

Colin and Rosana Ross established a store near a popular crossing on the Macintyre River in 1853 to cater to early settlers and teamsters headed north to the Darling Downs. The residents petitioned for a townsite to be laid out in 1855. By 1859 there was a Presbyterian Church (most of the early settlers were Scottish), two stores, two inns and a collection of bark huts and tents. Merino sheep were fundamental to the district in the early days. From 1866, small selectors moved into the area and began farming wheat.

10 INVERELL'S HERITAGE

From the pioneer village, continue north along the main road. When you come to the T-intersection turn left onto Glen Innes Rd. At the roundabout, turn left into Campbell St.

About 700m along Campbell Street, to the left, is the tourist information centre, located in the Water Towers Complex which was once Inverell's water source. Within the centre is a mining museum with a gem and mineral display and a working sapphire model.

Walk along Evans Street and turn right into Otho Street. To the right are the post office (1904) and the Classical courthouse. The town's fourth, the courthouse was built in 1886–1889 and has a splendid clock tower.

Opposite is the CBC Bank building (1890), a two-storey Italianate building with the old stables still to the rear. Turn left into Rivers Street and, after two blocks, right into Lawrence Street. To the left is the Church of England, designed by distinguished architect J. Horbury Hunt. Continue along Lawrence Street and turn right into Granville Street. To the right is the Presbyterian Church, the town's second, built to a Gothic design in 1878. Cross over Vivian Street to Sinclair Park, home of the Bicentennial Memorial which features a series of panels depicting the history of the Inverell area.

11 MOREE

Head back along Otho St to the T-intersection. Turn left, cross over the river and then, at the fork, take the left turn into the Gwydir Hwy. It is about 137km to Moree.

Moree promotes itself as the Artesian Spa Capital. The town's hot artesian spa bath complex has evolved from the Moree bore, which was originally sunk to a depth of

The golden guitar on the outskirts of Tamworth.

Thunderbolt's Rock near Uralla.

850m in 1895 to obtain irrigation water. The complex is located at the corner of Anne and Gosport streets. The mineral-rich water emerges at 41°C and is pumped into the pool complex via underwater spa jets and, for therapeutic and pleasurable effect, by above-pool spouts. The pools are emptied and cleaned each night.

12 MOREE'S HERITAGE BUILDINGS

There are a few buildings of note in Frome Street. The Edwardian-style Moree Club was originally the residence and private practice of Dr McGill, who, in 1900, allegedly became the first Australian motor car owner when he bought his jalopy in Sydney and drove it to Moree. It is said that he soon returned to horse power. The brick and stone courthouse with gambrel roofs, built in 1903, has venerable old jacaranda trees for shade.

At Frome and Heber streets is the Federation-style Lands Office building (1894) with gambrel roofs and enormous verandahs added in 1910.

13 MOREE PLAINS GALLERY

The Moree Plains Gallery, at the corner of Heber and Frome streets, has an ever-changing display of art works, though the collection of Contemporary Aboriginal Art and Artefacts from the Kamilaroi region is on permanent display.

14 MARY BRAND PARK

Mary Brand Park, at the corner of Gwydir and Frome streets, is named after the woman who, along with her husband, opened a store in 1852. The store proved to be the beginning of the town. In 1861 Mary established the town's first inn on this corner. The park contains a replica slab hut and Meei Cottage, which is typical of an 1890s residence.

61 GOONDIWINDI TO COONABARABRAN

■ DRIVING TOUR ■ 519KM ■ 1 DAY ■ UP THE NEWELL HIGHWAY

Vast plains stretch endlessly to the west and low-lying hills indicate the edge of the Great Dividing Range. These are the state's Western Plains.

This is cotton country. Years ago the rich soils on the slopes from Coonabarabran to Goondiwindi were used for sheep and cattle grazing but in more recent times such towns as Wee Waa, Narrabri and Goondiwindi have become centres for the lucrative cotton-growing industry. In season it is common to find the edges of the local roads littered with cotton balls. These towns are typical country service centres surrounded by beautiful countryside, particularly the Warrumbungle Ranges near Coonabarabran.

1 GOONDIWINDI

Goondiwindi is a rambling Queensland settlement on the banks of the Macintyre River. Pronounced 'gun' rather than 'goon', Goondiwindi is a typical Darling Downs town which has become important because of its unique position at the junction of the Cunningham, Newell, Bruxner, Barwon and Leichhardt highways on the border between New South Wales and Queensland. This fame, which is based largely on location, has been compounded by a racehorse named Gunsynd that became known as the Goondiwindi Grey and was the subject of a Tex Morton hit that reached no. 5 in 1973, titled 'The Goondiwindi Grey'. The town has made much of this famous horse and beside the river in Apex Park is a plaque commemorating its racing glories.

Goondiwindi grew up in the 1840s as a riverside camp for the teamsters bringing supplies from northern New South Wales to the outlying properties in western Queensland. This importance was greatly increased when Queensland became a separate colony in 1859 and the Macintyre River became the border. The establishment of a customs house ensured the settlement's continuing importance. The Customs House

was probably first built in 1859 but over the years it has gone through a number of alterations. Between 1872 and 1894 the building operated as a centre for staff policing and controlling illegal trading between Queensland and New South Wales.

Located on the town side of the main bridge across the Macintyre, the old Customs House has been converted into the Goondiwindi Museum and is now a typical rural folk museum containing many interesting local artefacts.

Apart from the Customs House (and the charming old cottage beside it) the other superb building in town is the Victoria Hotel, at 81 Marshall Street. The Victoria Hotel (1898) is a beautifully preserved and highly original Queensland country pub with wide verandahs and an unusual tower which makes it look more like a wedding cake than a pub. The pub sees itself as a monument to Gunsynd with a good collection of equine memorabilia.

2 MACINTYRE GINNERY

Follow Marshall St east for a couple of kilometres to the Macintyre Cotton Gin where the local cotton is processed.

In the picking season the streets of the town are filled with the roar of huge trucks as they make their way from the cotton fields to the ginnery. The gin is open between 8.00am–5.00pm daily between April and September. The processes inside the gin are both simple and fascinating. Following yellow lines, the visitor can watch the raw cotton balls being fed into the machine and can follow the series of processes that clean and prepare the cotton so that by the end it is ready to be semi-automatically baled and shipped away for carding, drawing and roving.

3 MOREE

Return along Marshall St and turn left into McLean St (the Newell Hwy) and it is 127km to Moree.

Moree promotes itself as the Artesian Spa Capital. The town's hot artesian spa bath complex has evolved from the Moree bore,

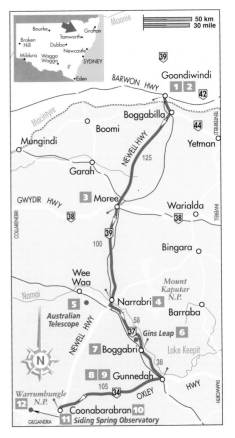

which was originally sunk to a depth of 850m in 1895 to obtain irrigation water. The complex is located at the corner of Anne and Gosport streets. The mineral-rich water emerges at 41°C and is pumped into the pool complex via underwater spa jets and, for therapeutic and pleasurable effect, by above-pool spouts. The pools are emptied and cleaned each night.

4 NARRABRI

Follow the Newell Hwy through Moree (there are no complicated turn-offs). It is another 97km to Narrabri.

Narrabri is located in the Namoi River Valley and is well known as a producer of wheat, fat lambs, beef and, especially,

The Old Gaol Heritage Centre, Narrabri.

The Dorothea Mackellar statue in Gunnedah.

Siding Spring Observatory at Coonabarabran.

cotton. The first squatting run was the Nurrabry, taken up in 1834. A hotel was licensed in 1858 and the town was proclaimed in 1860. A post office and police station were established but a catastrophic flood devastated the township in 1864.

Bridges over Narrabri Creek were built in 1877 and the Namoi in 1879. The railway arrived at Narrabri West in 1882 and a settlement began to develop around it. Cotton was introduced in 1962. Intensive research and improved irrigation have created the largest cotton yields in Australia, bringing renewed prosperity to the town.

Narrabri Shire Visitors Centre is located at the corner of Tibbereena and Lloyd streets. There is a pleasant and easy walk around the town. From the visitors centre, follow the bank of the creek through the parkland to the Tibbereena and Denison Street intersection. Walk along Denison Street and take the first left into Maitland Street. To the right are the brick police residence (1878–1879), the second court-house (1886–1888) and, at Maitland and Bowen, the original brick courthouse (1864–1865)—all designed by colonial architect James Barnet.

Turn right into Bowen Street. To the left is Gallipoli House, originally the Narrabri Steam Flour Mill (1881). Opposite is the Heritage Centre, located in the old lock-up which was built in 1882 and functioned as such for a century. Another Barnet design, the centre houses a large collection relating to local and family history. At the eastern end of Bowen Street is the Keys Flour Mill (1911). Over Logan Street is the railway station (1897). Return along Bowen Street and turn right into Nandewar Street. At the corner of Dewhurst and Nandewar streets is St Cyprian's Anglican Church (1895), a fine building designed by the distinguished architect J. Horbury Hunt.

5 AUSTRALIA TELESCOPE
Head out from the centre of town towards Coona-barabran, along Dangar St (the Newell Hwy) and take the very clearly signposted right turn into Ugoa St. Keep watching for the directional signs to the Australia Telescope, 24km away.

A radio helioscope was first established at this location by the CSIRO in 1967. In the 1980s the helioscope was replaced by the most powerful telescope in the southern hemisphere, capable of receiving radio waves from deep space by means of six gigantic dishes. There is a visitors centre at the complex with push-button displays and videos.

6 GINS LEAP
Return to Narrabri town the way you came. At the end of Ugoa St turn right into Cooma Rd (the Newell Hwy). At the second roundabout turn left onto the Boggabri/Gunnedah Rd. About 49km from the turn-off, on the right-hand side of the road, is a rock formation known as Gins Leap.

The naming of Gins Leap is said to derive from the death of an Aboriginal woman who leapt from here while fleeing a tribal elder or suitor. There is a picnic area and an interpretive sign at the site where the Rock Inn once stood. Used as a coaching stopover, the inn was built about 1850, before Boggabri existed.

7 BOGGABRI
Continue south along the main road for 4km into the town of Boggabri.

Boggabri is a small country town by the Namoi River. Boggabri is basically a town servicing the surrounding area which is given over to wheat, wool and cotton. There are large grain-holding facilities and huge, but as yet unexploited, coal reserves under nearby Leards Forest. The Boggabri Museum is located in Brent Street, two blocks west of the Royal Hotel.

8 GUNNEDAH
Head south on the main road to Gunnedah, which is 37km away.

Gunnedah is an important country service centre sustained by wool, beef cattle, pigs, poultry, sheep, lucerne, barley, cotton, oilseeds and sorghum and three coalmines. The town's information centre is situated in Anzac Park, at the eastern end of South Street.

9 DOROTHEA MACKELLAR MEMORIAL
Gunnedah calls itself Town of My Country, a reference to the poet Dorothea Mackellar (1885–1968), who is memorialised in a life-size bronze statue located in Anzac Park. Dorothea spent a great deal of time on a local property from 1905 (the year she wrote her best-known work, 'My Country', which is thought to have been inspired, in part, by the local terrain) until the late 1930s. Also in Anzac Park is the Water Tower Museum, which houses a collection of local memorabilia and photographs. A spiral staircase leads from the third floor to an observation deck from where there are fine views of the town.

10 COONABARABRAN
Head west along South St. Drive through the roundabout (the road veers slightly to the left) and continue out of town along the Oxley Hwy. It is 100km to Coonabarabran.

Coonabarabran is known as the Gateway to the Warrumbungles. Wool and wheat are the economic mainstays of the town, although it has capitalised on tourism. The visitors centre is located in John Street (the Newell Highway), adjacent to the swimming pool and War Memorial Park. The centre features a display on ancient Australian megafauna. The display includes the most complete skeleton in Australia of a diprotodon, the largest known marsupial. Something like a buffalo-sized wombat, the diprotodon roamed the area 34 000 years ago.

11 SIDING SPRING OBSERVATORY
If you are coming through town from the south, turn left at the clock tower, which is located at the corner of John St (the main road) and Dalgarno St. Take the second right into Namoi St and the third left into Eden St, which heads west out of town as the National Park Rd. Continue west along the National Park Rd. In the Warrumbungle Range, 24km from the town centre, is the turn-off to Siding Spring Observatory.

Siding Spring Observatory is a complex of international importance with the largest optical research telescope in Australia (3.9m). Visiting the complex is a hands-on experience with an interactive exhibition, a theatrette, a science gift shop and cafeteria.

12 WARRUMBUNGLE NATIONAL PARK
Continue along the National Park Rd, beyond the observatory turn-off, for another 3km.

Warrumbungle National Park is one of the state's most popular parks. Easily accessible, the park has good facilities and provides excellent opportunities for family recreation. Splendid wildflowers bloom in spring and early summer. There are 180 species of birds and plenty of other fauna within the park, including koalas and kangaroos.

Close to the park's entrance is a signposted parking area to the left, at the start of the short walking track to the outstanding Whitegum Lookout (1.1km return). In all there are 30km of walking tracks of varying lengths, qualities and grades of difficulty. They are outlined in material available from the visitors centre in the park or at Coonabarabran.

Return along National Park Rd to Coonabarabran.

The park beside the Castlereagh River, Coonabarabran.

CHAPTER 11
CENTRAL
TO FAR WEST

62 SHEEP COUNTRY

■ DRIVING TOUR ■ 150KM ■ 6 HOURS ■ EXPLORING PASTURE LAND

The slopes and plains beyond the Great Dividing Range are famous for their herds of fine wool sheep. This is the area which rode to prosperity on the sheep's back.

This is the state's sheep country. The towns here pride themselves in the rich grassy pastures which turn brown in summer and then green with the winter rains. Grazing on these pastures are some of the best merinos in the country. The towns are service centres—sometimes small like Boorowa, or main highway stopover places like Yass (now bypassed), or railway towns like Cootamundra which rejoices in the fact that it was where the young Don Bradman grew up.

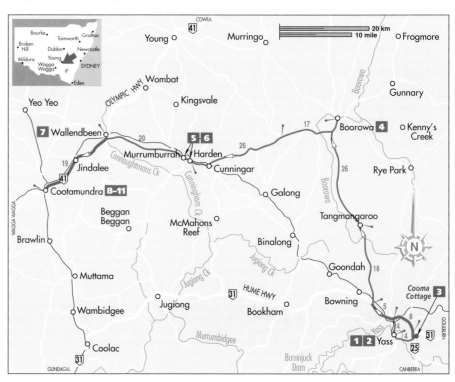

1 YASS

Yass is a rural town located on the Yass River, a tributary of the Murrumbidgee River. Although traditionally centred on wool, merino studs and agriculture, a number of wineries and vineyards have sprung up to the south of town. The plains of Goulburn and Yass were joined by a bush track as early as 1825. A village began to develop about 1830 when settlement began on the south bank of the Yass River. The first survey was conducted in 1834, a local storekeeper became the first unofficial postmaster in 1835 and the township was gazetted in 1837. In 1839, the explorer Hamilton Hume returned to Yass and purchased Cooma Cottage, where he lived with his wife until his death in 1873. Hume made a substantial contribution to the development of the wool industry in the area.

2 HISTORIC YASS

Today the visitor should begin an exploration of the district by first visiting the Yass Visitors Centre in Coronation Park in the main street. Nearby in Comur Street is the Hamilton Hume Museum, where the displays relate to the history of Yass from the pre-colonial period, including a photographic collection and a display on the wool industry. The Parallels exhibition looks at the correspondences between the Yass of the 1890s and that of the 1990s.

From the museum, walk along Comur Street to the Lead Street intersection and turn left. To the right is the Yass Railway Museum at the old railway station which was built when a tramway was opened in 1892. The tramway became a railway line in 1917 and closed in 1988. The station has the shortest platform in Australia.

Since the town was bypassed in 1994 by the highway, the main street has had a major

facelift with an emphasis on heritage. Old buildings have been repainted, wrought-iron verandahs restored and heritage lights installed. Between Lead and Meehan streets, to the left, are the old Mechanics' Institute (1869), now the F.L. Kelly building, the former Bank of New South Wales (1886), now the Sheep's Back Gallery; the old AJS Bank building (1885), now the Westpac Bank; and the Royal Hotel (1849), the town's oldest continually licensed premises. Bushranger Frank Gardiner was arrested at the Royal in 1854 when it was known as Harts Hotel. The National Bank building over the road dates from 1872. The Classical Revival post office (c.1880–84) is an imposing edifice by James Barnet with a three-storey clock tower and cast-iron hitching posts.

3 COOMA COTTAGE

Head south along the main street and follow the road as it veers to the left. Cooma Cottage is 4km from the town centre, near the Barton Highway connector.

Cooma Cottage is a single-storey colonial house with gabled coach-house. The original section is an intact weatherboard bungalow with verandah, dating from 1835, when it was erected for pastoralist Cornelius O'Brien. From 1839 until his death in 1873, Cooma was the home of explorer Hamilton Hume who added numerous brick and stuccoed sections, a pavilioned wing and Classical Revival portico.

The cottage is now a museum with a display relating to the life of Hume and an educational program for schoolchildren that teaches history through role-play.

4 BOOROWA

Continue on from Cooma Cottage to the bypass and turn left. After 4km turn left again onto the Hume Hwy and follow it for about 14km, then take the signposted right to Boorowa. It is 44km north to Boorowa.

Boorowa is surrounded by rich pasture land and has been a centre for wool and wheat production since it was first settled by Europeans in the 1840s. The town came into existence in 1850. No-one knows exactly where the name comes from, but it is thought to be a Wiradjuri word for turkey.

In the 1860s Boorowa became infamous as part of the area where the bushranger Ben

Harden–Murrumburrah Historical Museum.

Hall and his gang went on a robbing spree. At the time, the town was known as Burrowa. Today, the town is a quiet rural community which, because it is not on a main road, has a special kind of untouched old-world charm. Of particular interest is the court house on the corner of Marsden and Queen streets. This symmetrical building was designed by the colonial architect and completed in 1884. It has a distinctive double-height courtroom and Roman arches. Equally interesting is St Patrick's Catholic Church (completed in 1875), the first Roman Catholic church to be built west of the Great Dividing Range.

5 HARDEN–MURRUMBURRAH

Head back towards the Hume Hwy for 4km then take the signposted turnoff on the right to Harden. After 34km you will reach a T-intersection. Turn right and it is 5km to Harden.

Harden–Murrumburrah is located on Murrimboola Creek. The separate names are misleading as they form, in reality, one town. The town came into existence when the superintendent of the Murrumburra run, James Kennedy, opened an inn in the late 1840s which was the first authorised business to be conducted on the townsite. Gold was discovered a few kilometres to the north-west of the present townsite in 1854 but serious prospecting didn't begin until 1856. The first school was established in 1862–1863 and St Mary's Roman Catholic Church was built in 1868. Until 1880 Harden was known as Murrumburrah North. The town had become an important rail centre when the railway station was built there in 1877.

6 HISTORIC HARDEN–MURRUMBURRAH

A suitable place to start exploring the town is the Harden–Murrumburrah Historical Museum, located in the old School of Arts building in Albury Street. Displays include a blacksmith's and wheelwright's premises (1874–c.1940), historic garments from 1880, the impressive Harden railway

The Globe Bed and Breakfast, Yass.

refreshment room bar of oak and brass, railway memorabilia and artefacts, a chemist's shop exhibition with items dating back to 1890, a music room, an early Australian kitchen, a vintage bathroom and thunderbox, a child's bedroom and a photographic collection.

The town's interesting historic buildings include the distinctive CBC Bank (now the National Australia Bank) in Neill Street—a beautiful, single-storey Federation building erected *circa* 1905 of brown brick with an unusual slate-clad hipped and gabled roof featuring terracotta ridge-capping—and the Methodist Church in Albury Street (between Lucan and Stair streets) which was erected in 1890 with additions in 1900 and 1933 (now the local scout hall).

Murrumburrah was declared an historic village in 1990 and it certainly has an old-world feel as though time has stood still since the 1950s. The Murrumburrah courthouse (1880), at the corner of Albury and Vernon streets, is a two-storey brick building with single-storey wings.

The foundation stone of St Mary's Catholic Church was laid in 1868. It was extended in 1895–1896 with granite for the tower quarried 3km north-west of Murrumburrah and carted to the site by bullock and horse teams.

7 WALLENDBEEN

Head west out of town along the main road for 17km to Wallendbeen.

Wallendbeen station, taken up by Alexander Mackay, had several brushes with Ben Hall's gang. A Mr Barnes was shot to death near the Mackay home while fleeing John O'Meally and John Vane in 1863 and, six weeks before Hall was killed in 1865, the gang held the cook and a visiting piano-tuner in the dining room of the homestead while they stole three horses.

The village of Wallendbeen was laid out after the railway arrived in 1877. Today wheat, triticale, canola and mustard seed are grown locally, along with large numbers of sheep and cattle. There is also a deer farm.

8 COOTAMUNDRA

From Wallendbeen, follow the signs to Cootamundra (rather than Young or Stockingbingal) 20km south-west along the Olympic Way.

Cootamundra is a prosperous rural service centre whose fortunes depend on its location as a major junction on the Sydney to Melbourne railway line. Goldmining started in the area in 1862 and, while it was never discovered in the town, gold attracted large numbers of miners to the region. The first church—Roman Catholic—was built in 1870 and the first school was completed in 1875. The year 1877 was a watershed one for the town. In that year the town got its first newspaper, the *Cootamundra Herald*, and the paper was able to record the rail connection between Cootamundra and Sydney. Today, Cootamundra is a prosperous and well-known country town. The name Cootamundra Wattle evokes images of the

The National Trust CBC Building, Harden.

Australian bush at its most beautiful (when it flowers in July and August) and the connection with Donald Bradman gives the town a potent link with one of Australia's greatest citizens.

9 SIR DONALD BRADMAN'S BIRTHPLACE

Located at 89 Adams Street, this cottage is an ultimate shrine for cricket lovers. Sir Donald Bradman is regarded by many as Australia's greatest sporting hero. He was born in Cootamundra on 27 August 1908 and his parents moved to Bowral three years later. The birthplace now houses Bradman memorabilia and interesting material on the history of Cootamundra. Located next door to Bradman Cottage, Memorabilia Cottage has a display of old-style memorabilia—everything from convict-made bricks to tobacco tins and a Trafalgar drip safe.

10 JUBILEE PARK

Jubilee Park, located in Wallendoon Street, is now part of a major project which will see bronze busts of all the Australian cricket captains featured on a Captains Walk. Stage One, completed in 1998 and unveiled as part of Sir Donald Bradman's 90th birthday celebrations, featured busts of Arthur Morris, William Murdock, Unaarrimim (the Aboriginal captain of the team that played England in 1868), Richie Benaud, Allan Border, Mark Taylor, David Gregory, William Lawry, Robert Simpson, Ian Chappell and Greg Chappell. When the project is completed, it will be topped off by a full-size statue of The Don in cover-drive stance.

11 POST OFFICE

On Wallendoon Street, an extraordinary four-storey tower stands above the post office making it one of the town's most prominent landmarks. Built in 1881 and classified by the National Trust, the post office was designed by the Office of the Colonial Architect and is characterised by four-panelled windows and doors, a timber verandah and the clock tower with its ornamental fleche and weathervane.

Outside the post office is the Tree of Knowledge, a peppercorn tree which is thought to have been planted around 1891.
Head out of Cootamundra on Gundagai Rd. The Hume Hwy is 38km away at Coolac. Head north on the Hume Hwy. Yass is 85km away.

63 BATHURST TO COWRA

■ DRIVING TOUR ■ 136KM ■ 1 DAY ■ HISTORIC TOWNS AND FIELDS OF PLENTY

A necklace of charming towns greets the traveller who wanders from Bathurst, through Millthorpe and Carcoar, to Cowra with its fascinating Japanese Gardens.

The fertile plains and slopes between Bathurst and Cowra are characterised by herds of sheep, hillsides covered with the bright yellow flowers of the canola plant, and undulating countryside which is home to delightful historic townships such as Millthorpe, Blayney and Carcoar. The driving is easy, and the buildings and streetscapes (Millthorpe's main street belongs to another era) are delightful. This is the New South Wales countryside at its very best.

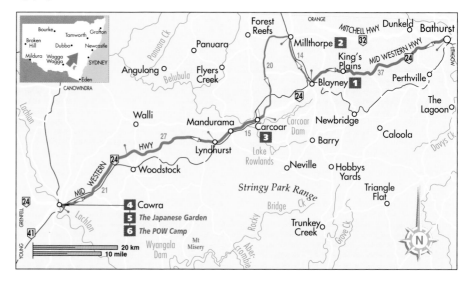

1 BLAYNEY

From Bathurst, continue on the Great Western Hwy for 37km until you reach Blayney.

Blayney is a farming town with avenues of deciduous trees that are especially attractive in autumn. Before European settlement, the area is thought to have been occupied by the Wiradjuri or Gundungura people. The first European to travel through what is now Blayney Shire was surveyor George Evans, in 1815. Unofficial occupation of the district began in 1821. The first land grant was issued to Thomas Icely in 1829. A mill was operating on the future town site of Blayney by 1837, along with an inn and several houses.

Blayney has a few historic buildings of interest in Adelaide Street, between Martin and Burns streets. They include the post office

Millthorpe's Golden Memories Museum.

(c.1880) and courthouse (1880), both Victorian Classical designs. The Presbyterian Church (1885) is situated between Burns and Church streets. The church hall is the original church (1861). The Anglican Church (pre-1890) is located at the corner of Adelaide and Church streets. Heritage Park in Adelaide Street and Carrington Park in Church Street are both pleasant recreation reserves.

2 MILLTHORPE

Head north from Blayney for 14km until you reach the small historic township of Millthorpe.

Millthorpe is a picturesque, compact and historic village set amid gently rolling hills. Classified by the National Trust, the village has a number of fine historic buildings, as well as cobbled, bluestone-bordered streets, an art gallery, gift shops, a museum and two hotels.

Millthorpe's commercial area was extended after the depression of the 1890s and many of its largely brick buildings date from that period. The town's decline after World War I means that it was spared redevelopment and so many of its buildings have survived with very little alteration.

Tourist information can be obtained at the Old Mill Cafe, located in one of the town's original bakeries at 12 Pym Street. Opposite the cafe are Denise's and Nice 'n' Natural, located in the town's old general store. Further south along Pym Street is Bulletproof Furniture and Gallery, located in the old produce shed. The gallery sells bush furniture, woodcrafts, gifts and collectables. Beyond that are the Railway Hotel (established 1884) and the railway station (1870s), which occupies the highest point on the railway line between the Blue Mountains and the Indian Ocean.

Return to the Old Mill Cafe and continue on to the intersection with Victoria Street where you will see the former Grand Western Lodge Hotel (1901), an imposing two-storey brick-faced structure with a two-storey verandah, cast-iron balustrades, an enormous stuccoed central parapet, pictorial leadlight glazing and keyhole windows.

At the corner of Victoria and Park streets is one of the town's finest buildings, the former Bank of New South Wales and manager's residence with original bank vault and banking counter. It was built about 1895 of stuccoed brick in a Late Victorian Free Classical style and is now Rosebank Guesthouse. Opposite is the Commercial Hotel (1877) and nearby is Ada's Place, a studio and gallery housed in a fine old bluestone stable.

Turn into Park Street. On the right is Millthorpe Public School. The school residence adjacent dates from 1876. On the other side of the road is the Golden Memories Museum, which has 10 000 items dating back to 1880, including a colonial kitchen, pioneers' gallery, rural technology display and antiquated rural farm equipment. There is also a craft cottage on the site.

3 CARCOAR

Follow the signs to Carcoar. It is 19km back to the Great Western Hwy. Carcoar is located off the main road, a further 3km along.

Carcoar is a lovely little historic town with an English-village feel located just off the Mid Western Highway. The town is nestled between steep hills in a small green valley around the oak-lined banks of the Belubula River. Carcoar has been classified by the National Trust because of the number of intact 19th-century buildings it possesses.

The Post Office (c.1880) in Blayney.

Icely Street is the main access road into Carcoar from the highway. Just before the Coombing Street intersection, to the left, is the public school. The date on the belltower (1884) indicates the year in which the Board of Education purchased the Carcoar Hotel (built in 1860) and used that building as the basis for the present structure. On the other side of the road is the old Presbyterian manse (1862). Cross Coombing Street. On the left is the former saddlery, established in 1844 (the second storey was added in 1860). Opposite is the town's second police station (1884) built as a sergeant's residence. The police were first stationed at Carcoar in 1836.

Continue along Icely Street. To the left is the former Courthouse Hotel (1870) with its neat picket fence and attic windows. It is now a private residence. Next door is the School of Arts building (1901).

Opposite, at the Belubula Street intersection, is the former courthouse, a Victorian Classical building erected in 1882 to replace the original 1841 structure. Considered one of colonial architect's James Barnet's 'best small country courthouses', the building is made of brick with stuccoed pilasters and consists of a two-storey central section with single-storey wings. There is a fine timber colonnade to the facade and an Italianate clock tower. The verandah ironwork is hand-forged. The interior sports an elaborate painted frieze, fine cedar joinery and original fittings. Next door to the courthouse, in Belubula Street, is the post office, a two-storey brick building dating from 1879 with unusual ironwork to the upper floor (the single-storey structure at the front is a later addition).

4 COWRA

Return to the Great Western Hwy and continue heading south west for another 59km until you reach Cowra.

Cowra is noted for its historical and natural attractions, the magnificent Japanese Garden and Cultural Centre, quality restaurants, wineries, galleries, craft shops and horse-riding. The public identity of the town has become bound up with the Cowra breakout of 1944 (in which Japanese prisoners of war attempted to escape from a local camp during World War II) and the subsequent association with Japan. These events have prompted the town to pursue an internationalist and pacific agenda which is celebrated by the annual Festival of Understanding.

Cowra Visitor Information Centre is located on the western side of the bridge, in Olympic Park, on the Mid Western Highway. The centre screens a very good nine-minute film about the Cowra breakout and Cowra's subsequent role in the world peace movement.

5 THE JAPANESE GARDEN AND CULTURAL CENTRE

From the Visitor Information Centre, head back across the bridge. When you enter the main shopping centre, on Kendal St, turn left on Brisbane St which becomes Scenic Drv and takes you to the Japanese Gardens.

The magnificent Japanese Garden and Cultural Centre was erected on a 5ha site as a symbol of the historical ties between Cowra and Japan. The development was funded by the Australian and Japanese governments and by private donations but is maintained on a non-profit basis by tourism.

The garden was designed by Ken Nakajima, a world-renowned figure in traditional Japanese landscape gardening, in liaison with the School of Environmental Design from Canberra College of Advanced Education.

The garden was designed to reflect the total Japanese landscape. The mountain represents all Japanese mountains. A stream flows down the mountain through a waterfall to a lagoon (representing the mountain ponds) and on to a larger koi-filled lake which equates with the ocean. Japan's cities are represented by the buildings, the trimmed hedges suggest rolling hills and each gravel path offers new perspectives to convey the variety of views when meandering through the Japanese landscape. The garden was also designed to blend in with the indigenous environs. Consequently, gum trees surround the garden.

A traditional tea house sits on an island. There are wooden footbridges, a wisteria pergola, bonsho (calling bell), temple lantern, a lookout over Cowra and the valley, manicured shrubs and lawns, and a delicate and symbolic arrangement of rocks. The 113 species of flora includes water lilies,

cherry trees, wisteria, chrysanthemums, magnolia and Australian natives and there are over 120 bird species in the garden. The overall effect is one of serenity and harmony.

Traditional Japanese design has been employed in the construction of the Cultural Centre, which houses a display of Japanese art including the Somenishiki Ornamental Vase, 500 hand-carved Japanese dolls, Nanga paintings and a fossilised chrysanthemum estimated to be over 70 million years old.

Within the complex is the Bonsai House (with Bonsai display), a pottery house, gift shop, nursery and the Chabana Restaurant, which fuses Japanese and Australian elements and provides views over the garden. In the car park is a Japanese rock sculpture which symbolises peace.

In early October, when the cherry blossoms bloom, the centre becomes the focus of Sakura Matsuri, the Cherry Blossom Festival, during which there are demonstrations of Japanese arts and crafts, recitals on the shakuhachi flute, tea ceremonies, martial arts demonstrations, kite flying and Japanese food.

6 THE POW CAMP

To the north of the Cultural Centre, Sakura Ave leads by the remnants associated with the POW camp.

At the corner of Sakura Avenue and Farm Road (Evans Street) is a memorial cairn and a monument to the many Italian POWs in the camp who took no part in the breakout. A walking track begins from the memorial cairn that takes in the remains of the campsite. A lage concrete slab on the land on the western side of Sakura Avenue marks the site of the camp gaol. To the south-west of the slab is the site of four water storage tanks and due south of that is the original entry road. The Australian Military Forces quarters were located on the other side of Sakura Avenue, most of which is now private property.

A guide map and pamphlet available from the Cowra Visitor Information Centre contains excellent material relating to the camp and the general context of its existence.

The Japanese Gardens and Cultural Centre in Cowra.

64 BATHURST AND THE HISTORIC WEST

■ DRIVING TOUR ■ 204KM ■ 1 DAY ■ CAVES AND TOWNS WHERE TIME HAS STOOD STILL

There is a charm to all these tiny towns—Rockley, Tuena, Trunkey Creek, Blayney—which are now remnants of their former glory.

To the south of Bathurst lie some of the most attractive and untouched historic locations in New South Wales. The charming and sleepy township of Rockley, the attractiveness of Trunkey Creek, the tranquil bush peacefulness of the Abercrombie Caves—easily accessible from a good sealed road—are all attractions that combine to make this pleasant trip a journey through the past.

Bathurst Courthouse.

1 BATHURST

Bathurst is situated in central western New South Wales. Its history is evident through its various historic buildings, such as the courthouse and restored workmen's cottages. An array of arts, crafts and antiques attract visitors to the area, and the many shops, galleries and theatre shows entertain the locals and tourists alike. Bathurst comes alive every year with the AMP Bathurst 1000 and FAI 1000 Classic motor races.

2 BEN CHIFLEY'S HOUSE

The visitors centre is located at 28 William St, on the Durham St corner. Head back towards Sydney on Durham St until you reach the road which, instead of curving left, goes straight ahead between two parks. Drive to Havannah St, turn right and continue until you reach the roundabout at Rocket St. Continue one block further to Brilliant St and turn left. Chifley's house is at 10 Busby St.

Ben Chifley, the son of a blacksmith and Prime Minister of Australia between 1945 and 1949, was born at Bathurst in 1885 and maintained his connections with the city until the end of his life. He joined the New South Wales Railways at the age of 17 and, at 26, became the youngest locomotive driver in the state. Chifley became a union representative in 1913 but was demoted to cleaner because of his involvement in the Great Strike of 1917. He entered parliament as the member for Macquarie (the local seat) in 1928 and became the treasurer and minister for postwar reconstruction in John Curtin's government. When Curtin died in the last month of World War II, Chifley became prime minister. From 1949 until his death in 1951, Chifley was leader of the opposition. He was interred at Bathurst.

The modest house that Ben Chifley shared with his wife between 1945 and 1949 is open to the public between 2.00pm and 4.00pm every day except Sunday, when the open hours are 10.00am–12.00pm.

3 ROCKLEY

Return to the roundabout and head south on Rocket St. Rockley is 31km further south.

Rockley is one of those remarkable villages where, because it is away from the main road, time has stood still. There can be few

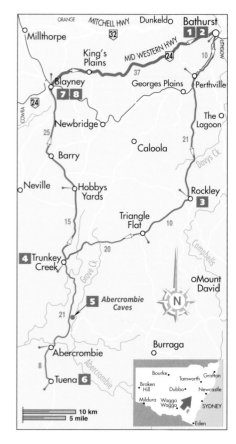

towns in New South Wales which so simply, and with so few alterations, capture rural life around the turn of the century. It is hardly surprising that Rockley has been listed by the National Trust as an Historic Village.

The first European into the Rockley district was Surveyor Evans, who arrived in 1813. By 1818 land in the area had been granted to William Lawson. The actual townsite was not granted. It was held as a stock reserve until 21 February 1829, when Governor Darling granted it, as part of a parcel of 1920ac, to Captain Steel, who named his property Rockley after his birthplace in Wiltshire, in England.

The discovery of gold in the Campbell and Isabella rivers and around Abercrombie Caves in the late 1840s drew settlers to the area. At its peak, the town was home to some 3000 people. The town's prosperity is reflected in the solidity of its churches and public buildings.

Time passed Rockley by. Around the turn of the century, the copper mine closed and slowly people drifted away. As a result, the village remains largely untouched. It is this near-perfect preservation that has resulted in the entire village being listed by the National Trust.

The former Abercrombie Shire Chambers (1912), Rockley.

The Trunkey General Store, Trunkey Creek.

Of particular interest are the Rockley Mill Museum, a handsome red-brick building over the road from Peppers Creek. The mill was built in 1864. It is a typical small town museum with displays of historic mill machinery, historic clothing, old police records for the district and old newspapers. St Patrick's Roman Catholic Church (1870) and St Peter's Anglican Church (1867) were both designed by M.E. (Edward) Gell, a prominent local architect who designed a number of important buildings in Bathurst.

There is the post office was built in 1879, although it did not open for six months after its completion because the furniture and fittings were not transported from Bathurst where they had sat on the railway station. Other buildings of interest include the Club House Hotel (1872), the former Butcher's, Baker's and Saddlery (1871) which is now used as a tea room, the former Bank of New South Wales (1878) which was once held up by the bushranger Ben Hall, the Methodist Church (1859), the School of Arts (1890) and the police station.

Of particular interest is the former Abercrombie Shire Chambers (1912), now a private home. Ben Chifley was president of the Abercrombie Shire Council from 1937 to 1940 and regularly travelled from his home in Bathurst to attend the council's fortnightly meetings.

4 TRUNKEY CREEK

Continue on to Trunkey Creek, which is 30km further south.

Trunkey Creek is a quiet, attractive and tiny old goldmining village. All that remains from the gold days are some mud huts, brick chimneys and abandoned mine shafts and mullock heaps in the hills. The village is little more than a wooden church, a few houses, a hotel-general store and a cafe.

5 ABERCROMBIE CAVES

Continue south for another 21km until you reach the signposts to Abercrombie Caves, which are only 2km from the main road.

Abercrombie Caves is the most accessible cave system in New South Wales. This particularly attractive collection of limestone caves offers the usual array of stalagmites and stalactites. There is a river with a couple of particularly beautiful pools and the caves themselves contain an array of columns and shawls with such names as Hall of Terpischore, Angel's Harp, Plum Pudding and Diamond Cascade.

The caves are run by the New South Wales state government's Caves Reserve Trust which offers a number of attractive walks in the area, a series of guided caves inspections, and, for those not wanting to join an organised cave inspection, there is the Arch Cave, a self-conducted walk over a small hill and beside Grove Creek.

6 TUENA

Return to the main road and continue on for 10km (on mostly unsealed road) to the tiny village of Tuena.

Tuena (the name is said to derive from a local Aboriginal word translated as 'string of waterholes') is one of those old goldmining towns that experienced rapid growth and then equally rapid decline. Gold was discovered at Tuena in 1851. It is claimed that a certain Reverend Douglas, travelling to Tuena for a christening, stopped to boil his billy at Limestone Creek, turned over a stone and found a nugget of gold. Miners poured into the area. At its peak, Tuena had a population of more than 10 000 people but by 1869 the gold was gone and the population had dropped to below a hundred. Today, the town is no more than a few historic buildings on the less-than-perfect dirt road about halfway between Bathurst and Goulburn.

A walking tour of the town's historic buildings is available from Parsons General Store (1860), which features old cedar counters and a museum display. The wlk takes in the Bookkeepers Cottage (1861), a wattle-and-daub building that was used for tallying gold; the Goldfields Inn (1866), which is the oldest licensed wattle-and-daub hotel in Australia; St Mark's Anglican Church (1886); the Tuena Public School (1889); St Margaret's Presbyterian Church (1890), built of local stone; a suspension footbridge; the police station (1900); and a number of other less important buildings.

7 BLAYNEY

From Tuena, turn back north and continue past Abercrombie Caves and through Trunkey Creek for 64km until you reach Blayney.

Governor Gipps proposed the creation of a village named Blayney in 1842, to be located 9km north-east of the present site at Kings Plains which had been surveyed in 1828. That spot proved unsuitable, however, and the village was established on its present site in 1843.

The district was given over to farming, although it received a push along when gold was found at Carcoar, Browns Creek and Kings Plains. Goldmines were established, and copper and iron were also extracted. Samuel Marsden's copper mine operated until 1900.

The arrival of the railway in 1874 spurred on development and Blayney replaced Carcoar as the major service centre to local farmlands. It became a municipality in 1882. By the turn of the century a butter factory and freezing works were the major employers in the town. Blayney's agricultural show is held in March.

8 BLAYNEY'S HISTORIC BUILDINGS

Blayney has a few historic buildings of interest in Adelaide Street, between Martin and Burns streets. These include the post office (c.1880) and courthouse (1880), both Victorian Classical designs. The Presbyterian Church (1885) is situated between Burns and Church streets. The church hall is the original church (1861). The Anglican Church (pre-1890) is located at the corner of Adelaide and Church streets. Heritage Park in Adelaide Street and Carrington Park in Church Street are both pleasant recreation reserves.

Head east out of Blayney on the Great Western Hwy. Bathurst is 38km away.

The Archway entrance, Abercrombie Caves.

65 OBERON AND THE BLUE MOUNTAINS

■ DRIVING TOUR ■ 242KM ■ 1 DAY ■ BEYOND THE BLUE MOUNTAINS

Beyond Sydney lie the Blue Mountains which, in many ways, are more interesting on their western edge than they are on their more popular and accessible eastern edge.

*I*t is one of the best-kept secrets of the Blue Mountains that the best views, and the most spectacular scenery, is not around Katoomba and Leura but some hundred kilometres further west, at Kanangra Walls. The road is difficult but with added bonuses of the excellent Jenolan Caves and the gracious ghost town of Hartley the journey is a marvellous mixture of history, exploration and dramatic views.

1 OBERON

Head out of Bathurst on the Great Western Hwy towards Sydney until, 3km from town, you turn right towards Oberon on the Oberon Rd. Continue on this road for 39km to Oberon.

Oberon is a chilly highland town. Prime lamb and beef cattle are the main rural industries, although vegetable production, tree nurseries, nut tree plantations and bulb farms all play their role. Timber processing by CSR Limited and Boral Timber is a significant secondary industry with wood taken from New South Wales state forests, radiata pine plantations and private forest growers.

Gold was discovered on the Fish River in 1823 and settlement along the river, and of the area between Oberon and Taralga to the south, began that same decade. Oberon was proclaimed a village in 1863 on the site known as Bullock Flats. Tourist information is available from Cobweb Visitor Information Centre and Craft Shop in Oberon Street. The centre has eight tapestries, hand-stitched by 70 local needle-workers, which reflect Oberon's landscape, historic buildings and primary industry.

There are only a small number of historically significant buildings in the town. St Barnabas' Anglican Church (1869) in Queen Street is of some interest. There are two buildings of note in the main street. Ramsgate (1906) is a two-storey Victorian residence, built by storekeeper Albert Fox of Ramsgate in Kent. The house features verandahs on both floors, a rubble-stone and cast-iron fence and decorative effects in wood and cast iron. The Art Deco Malachi Gilmore Hall (1937) is named after the Irish immigrant who was the original European owner and donator of the land upon which the hall stands.

2 KANANGRA BOYD NATIONAL PARK

Continue out of Oberon towards Jenolan Caves. Travel 25km (the road varies from good to ordinary) before turning off to Kanangra Boyd National Park. Continue on this dirt road for 26km until you reach the parking lot at Kanangra Walls.

Kanangra Walls offers the most spectacular views in the entire Blue Mountains. There are two excellent lookouts: the first looks over the Kanangra Creek Gorge with Mount Cloud-maker to the north-east and the main ridge of the Blue Mountains beyond; the second takes in Kanangra Falls and the rugged ravines at the head of the gorge. From this second lookout the Waterfall Walk takes you down into a gully to Kalang Falls. The longest trail is the Plateau Walk, which branches off the Lookout Walk before you reach the first lookout. The Plateau Walk takes in the heath-covered plateau of Kanangra Tops, from where there are excellent views of Kanangra Walls, Mount Colong to the south and Pindari Tops to the west.

3 JENOLAN CAVES

Return 26km to the turn-off on the Oberon to Jenolan Caves Rd and turn towards Jenolan Caves, which are only 5km away. The road is steep and difficult, although it is sealed all the way.

Jenolan Caves are deep in a valley on the far side of the Great Dividing Range. After winding downhill the road reaches the

The pond on the Town Common, Oberon.

The Shamrock Inn, Hartley.

Grand Arch, which is the largest open cave in Australia. The arch is 24m high, 55m wide and 127m long.

The first European to discover the caves was the bushranger and escaped convict James McKeown. There is some confusion over when this occurred. Some time between 1838 and 1841 is the best guess. Certainly McKeown's captors, James and Charles Whalan, returned to the caves many times and in 1846 the Arch Cave was discovered. The Elder Cave was discovered in 1848 and the Lucas Cave in 1860. The government declared the whole area a reserve in 1866 and appointed Jeremiah Wilson the first keeper the following year.

There are 22 major caves in the Jenolan system. Of these, nine—the Imperial, Chifley, Jubilee, Lucas, Skeleton, River, Orient, Temple of Baal and Ribbon—are 'dark caves' opened for guided inspection. The caves feature the usual range of formations with such quaint names as Gem of the West, Gabriel's Wing, Lot's Wife and the Bishop and Three Sisters. Beyond the caves (and everyone who visits the site should inspect at least one cave) are excellent bushwalks.

4 HARTLEY

Continue on from Jenolan Caves for another 44km until you reach the charming village of Hartley.

Hartley, at the base of the hill, was a town designated by early settlers and the government as a future regional centre. Unfortunately, particularly for the residents of Hartley, it was bypassed by the railway and, over a period, fell into disuse. Today we are left with a remarkable remnant of a town largely unchanged since the mid-19th century. Hartley is no more than a couple of dozen buildings but all have been beautifully preserved.

The town was established in 1815 as an important stopping point for travellers who had crossed Victoria Pass. Governor Lachlan Macquarie, who visited the valley in 1815, named it the Vale of Clwyd because it reminded him of a vale in North Wales. By the 1830s there was a need for a police station and courthouse between Penrith and Bathurst, and Hartley was chosen. By 1837 both the courthouse and the police barracks had been built. By 1840 a town, with 16 streets laid out in a grid system, had been surveyed. Most of this town was never completed.

There were 62 residents and 12 houses in 1846. By 1856, as a result of the gold rushes, the town had doubled in size. It was one of the major stopping points on the route from Sydney to the Turon goldfields and, accordingly, there were butchers, blacksmiths, and hotels to serve the weary diggers and bullock drivers.

The future of the town came to an abrupt end in 1869 when the railway line across the mountains was routed through Lithgow. The town's importance declined and by 1887 the functions of the courthouse had been transferred to Lithgow.

Today, Hartley is a remnant of past times. It is controlled by the New South Wales National Parks and Wildlife Service which provide a range of informative books and brochures on the town. The centrepiece is the Hartley Courthouse, which was designed by colonial architect Mortimer Lewis and completed in 1837 for £1476. The building contains a well-preserved courtroom and a couple of fascinating lock-ups, where early convicts scratched their names, their sentences and their crimes into the timber-lined walls.

Over the road is St Bernard's Presbytery, built in the late 1850s, which has been well preserved. Once a home for the priests who held mass at St Bernard's Church (1848), the presbytery is now a private residence. St Bernard's was built from stone quarried at South Bowenfels and timber handsawn in nearby pits. The church has a distinctive French influence which, it is believed, was the result of an enthusiasm for French religious architecture by one of the early priests. If you look carefully you can see that the stone bricks have been cut by different stonemasons (they have distinctive styles) and it is possible to see pit-saw marks on the roof timbers. The sandstone altar was hand-tooled to look like marble.

Next to St Bernard's is the Farmers Inn, which dates from the mid-1840s. Originally built as a house by the Finn family, it became an inn to take advantage of the accommodation requirements of miners heading for the Turon goldfields. The building has changed a number of times but at core it was built of sandstock bricks and shingles, both of which can still be seen.

Beyond the Farmers Inn is Ivy Cottage, built in the 1850s by the Finn family and soon became the police magistrate's house. It is claimed that the magistrate, whose major job seemed to be dealing with drunks, hated the location between the Farmers Inn and the Shamrock Inn.

The Shamrock Inn, the last building in the main street, was built in 1856 and enjoyed enthusiastic patronage from the miners who passed through Hartley on their way to the goldfields. The building is notable for its large number of chimneys and the conspicuous sagging of the roof.

Return along the main street to the courthouse and head towards the Great Western Highway. Next to the presbytery is the post office, parts of which date from the mid-1840s. Around the corner, on the way up the hill to St John's Church, are Old Trahlee (two semi-detached cottages dating from the 1840s); Bungarribee, which was the private residence of Thomas Finn; and the Church of St John the Evangelist, completed in 1859 at a cost of £1356 and believed to be designed by Edmund Blacket, the architect who designed the central quadrangle at Sydney University.

Over the road (and now a private residence) is another inn, The Royal, which was opened in 1849 and soon became the local booking office for Cobb & Co. One source around the turn of the century described The Royal as 'one of the twelve hotels which formerly existed in Hartley ... [it] continued in business for a great number of years, and, though not possessed of a license at the present day, is catering successfully for the increasing motor traffic to and from the Jenolan Caves. Few who seek refreshment within its hospitable walls are aware of the important place it formerly occupied in the coaching days, nor of its present day significance as the remaining relic of Hartley's former greatness.'

Return to Bathurst via the Great Western Hwy. The journey from Hartley via Lithgow is 73km.

Lucas Cave at Jenolan Caves.

66 BATHURST AND THE GOLD TOWNS

■ DRIVING TOUR ■ 179KM ■ 1 DAY ■ HISTORIC GOLDMINING TOWNS

Bathurst is a prosperous and thriving country service centre which was once surrounded by goldmining towns. Today it is surrounded by ghost towns.

Gold was first discovered in the area around Bathurst and it was to the hills and valleys to the north of Bathurst that the first gold prospectors rushed, hoping to find their fortunes. Many did indeed find fortunes. But equally, many went away with nothing to show for their backbreaking labours. Today, the historic goldmining towns of Sofala and Hill End are little more than ghostly reminders of a time when every prospector thought his next heave of the pick would make him a rich man.

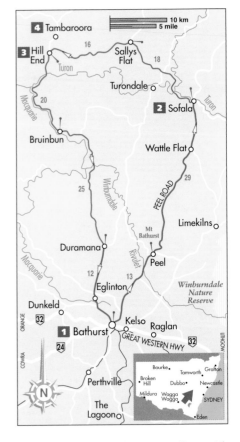

1 BATHURST

Bathurst is Australia's oldest inland city and is characterised by a number of handsome historic buildings. The raising of sheep, cattle and horses, which began with the earliest European occupation of the land, is still practised on large landholdings near the city. Today, however, education is now the largest single industry.

Gregory Blaxland, William Wentworth and William Lawson became the first Europeans to find a way across the Blue Mountains in May 1813, and surveyor George Evans crossed the main range later that year. During the trek Evans camped on the future townsite of Bathurst and made a favourable report of the country he saw. By January 1815, William Cox had completed the considerable feat of building a road over the mountains and in April, Governor Lachlan Macquarie traversed this new route. When he reached the road-building party's depot on the west bank of the Macquarie River, Macquarie proclaimed it 'a site for the erection of a town at some future period' which was to be named Bathurst. Later that year, on this same spot, a government domain, consisting solely of troopers,

government personnel and convict labourers, was established. Private settlement was forbidden on the west bank but Governor Macquarie decided to issue ten 50acre allotments on the east bank to small land-holders in the hope that they would be able to supplement the colony's food supplies.

The depression of the 1840s forestalled expansion but, in 1851, the first payable gold in the country was found at Ophir. This find sparked a remarkable gold rush which fundamentally transformed the entire colony. Bathurst was greatly affected, and became a commercial centre for those en route to the diggings. The town's population doubled in the course of the 1850s to over 4000 inhabitants. There were some 50 grog shops in operation by 1860. The Bathurst Visitors Centre is located at 28 William Street, on the Durham Street corner

2 SOFALA

Head out of Bathurst on the Great Western Hwy towards Sydney. About 2km from the town turn left into Gilmour St and, after another 2km, deviate right into Peel Rd. Sofala is 38km away.

Of all the old goldmining towns in New South Wales, Sofala is one of the most interesting and unusual. It is a village with an authentic old-world charm. In essence, Sofala is nothing more than two streets that have no formal construction and no curbing and guttering and yet it can legitimately claim to be Australia's oldest surviving gold town.

Sofala came into existence as a direct result of the gold rush that was precipitated when Edward Hargraves discovered gold at Summerhill Creek on 12 February 1851. By June that year, a tent city spread across the valley and both the Royal Hotel and a general store were built. By 25 June, more than 200oz of gold taken from the Turon Valley had been sold in Bathurst.

The goldfield was short-lived—the population peaked at 10 000 in September and dropped to 5000 by Christmas. Sofala was a ramshackle temporary town with dozens of pubs and, at its height, an estimated 500 illegal sly grog shops. The fortune of the town was all too brief. By May 1854 there were less than 500 diggers on the field and by 1855, with new gold discoveries occurring at Wattle Flat, Sofala was in decline.

There is a single sheet guide to the village which is available from the Sofala Souvenir Shop in the main street and includes the Old General Store which, with its lacework and

Bathurst Gaol.

The General Store in Sofala.

Re-created goldmine at History Hill at Hill End.

its weatherboard construction is one of the town's most notable buildings. The store was built in the 1860s to meet the needs of the local miners. Over the road from the General Store is the Royal Hotel, which was established in 1862. (The first Royal Hotel in Sofala opened on 7 October 1851.) Now a private residence, the post office was built in 1879 and continued operating until 1989. The gracious two-storey building has been turned into an interesting home. The Gas Hotel dates from late 1851 and, because the timber stump foundations have sunk over time, the building looks as though it was knocked together by a very drunk carpenter. The courthouse (1874) has changed function three times. By 1934 it had become the local hospital and in the early 1960s it became the Community Health Centre. The Hylands Hotel is built on the site of the Globe Hotel (one of the town's original pubs) and still has the original shingles and cellar. It too is now a private residence.

3 HILL END

Head out of Sofala on the Hill End road. This road is unsealed for most of the way and requires additional caution, particularly when rounding curves and bends. Hill End is 35km away.

Hill End is a well-preserved goldmining ghost town. Surrounded by rugged mountain and gorge country, the town is now an important historic site. The roads were carved out in the 19th century and are still largely unsealed.

Alluvial gold was discovered at Hill End (then known as Bald Hill) in 1851 and there were 150 miners on the site within a month. The first stamper battery in Australia was set up about 1856 by the Old Company, which employed Cornish equipment and miners, although initial returns were unremarkable. The stamper battery was located near the township of Tambaroora (5km to the north of present-day Hill End), reinforcing Tambaroora's position as the major settlement. By the early 1860s, Tambaroora had a population of some 2000 people.

By comparison, Bald Hill had only a few hundred residents, a hotel and two stores when it was surveyed and gazetted, mistakenly, as 'Forbes' in 1860. It was renamed Hillend in 1862.

At the time, the Old Company had rights to all reef gold in the area but when it departed in the early 1860s, opportunities were opened up. Steady work began on sites such as Hawkins Hill, and in 1870 worthy returns began to occur. In 1871, as word spread of the escalating profits, speculators moved in *en masse*. They turned syndicates of self-employed reef miners into floated companies with the miners reduced to employee status. They also bought up barren land around town and sold worthless shares to unknowing Sydneysiders.

In October 1872 the Star of Hope Gold Mining Company uncovered what was, at the time, the world's largest specimen of reef gold. Holtermann's Nugget, as it was known, weighed 286kg and measured 150cm by 66cm, with an average thickness of 10cm. That week alone, over 700km of gold were carted away from Hill End by the gold escort. In all, the amount of gold extracted at Hill End was greater than any goldfield in New South Wales other than Canbelego.

By the end of 1872, Hill End had over 8000 people, making it one of the state's largest inland towns with more than a kilometre of shops, five banks, two newspapers, a brewery, 27 pubs, over 200 companies in the field, and stamper batteries pounding ore 24 hours a day. New businesses proliferated while land prices and rents ballooned.

By March 1873 there were four churches, a hospital, improved roads, decent business premises, a public school, three banks and two newspapers. Substantial brick, weatherboard and corrugated-iron buildings replaced the makeshift wattle-and-daub huts. For all that, Hill End proved to be truly a boom (and bust) town. By 1874, cash was scarce on the fields. Miners received a share in prospective profits rather than wages. Hence businesses suffered. Stores closed and the population went into decline-from 8000 in 1872 to 1200 by 1882, and then down to 500 at the turn of the century.

Hill End was proclaimed an historic site in 1967 and placed under the care of the National Parks and Wildlife Service, which began preserving and restoring the buildings on the site. Today, about 100 people manage to make a living from what is now essentially a tourist attraction.

The National Parks and Wildlife Service has an information centre that doubles as a museum and souvenir shop. The centre is located in the Old Hospital Building on the Bathurst Road. It contains material relating to the mining era and a 15-minute audio-visual display. One room has been set up as a hospital ward circa 1870 with the medical equipment of the day. Some of the many photographs taken of Hill End in 1872 by Beaufoy Merlin are also on display. They were commissioned by Bernard Holtermann, who made his fortune at Hill End. A number of photographs have been set up around the town streets to provide insight into how the town looked in its heyday.

Many of Hill End's buildings have been demolished over the years and the on-site photographs indicate what stood on the empty lots. On the other hand, almost all the remaining buildings date from the early 1870s and many have been carefully restored. They include the cottage that belonged to Louis Beyers (late 1860s); the Great Western Store (*c.*1872), which now sells second-hand arts, crafts and collectables; the hospital (1872); Hosies Store (1872); Northeys Store (1873); the school (1872); the Methodist (now Anglican) church (1870); the rough-dressed sandstone of St Paul's Uniting Church (1872); Craigmoor (1875); and the Royal Hotel (1872), which retains original fittings and furniture. The police station and post office date from the turn of the century.

Beyers Avenue forms a corridor leading into town. The various European trees were planted by one of the town's most successful mining figures, Louis Beyers, in 1877 and the mid-1880s.

4 TAMBAROORA

Drive 3km north of Hill End.

Tambaroora is a ghost town that was once a busy gold town rivalling Hill End. Today there is little more than a few decrepit shacks, the foundations of the first stamper battery in the country, imported from Cornwall by the Old Company in 1856, along with the roasting pits used to break the gold-bearing quartz up into manageable pieces for the battery.

Return to Hill End and continue on the dirt road to Duramana and then back to Bathurst. The distance is 60km.

Malcolm Drinkwater at his museum, Hill End.

67 AROUND ORANGE

■ WALKING AND DRIVING TOUR ■ 4KM WALKING AND 82KM DRIVING ■ 1 DAY ■ HISTORIC ORANGE

A substantial and sophisticated rural service centre, Orange combines elegant public buildings, attractive local parks and interesting historic gold villages and vineyards.

Orange is one of the most gracious inland towns in Australia. The wealth generated by the large properties which surround the city has combined, in recent times, with a number of interesting and successful vineyards, to allow the city to develop into something much more than a rural service centre. The restaurants in town are classy, the vineyards attract city clientele, and the historic goldmining town of Ophir offers exceptional scenic beauty.

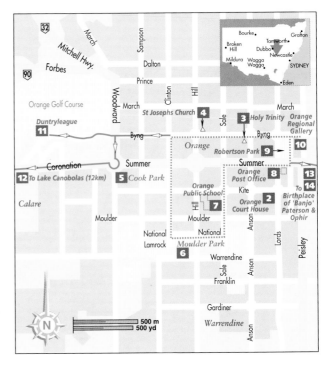

1 ORANGE

Orange is located 261km west of Sydney and 863m above sea level. It lies at the heart of some of New South Wales' most rich and beautiful agricultural land. The area was occupied by Wiradjuri Aborigines prior to European settlement. The first Europeans arrived on 23 June 1813 when G. W. Evans, heading south-west from Bathurst, saw the mountain range (of which Mount Canobolas is the most prominent) to the northwest. The first European to ride through the present town site was Lieutenant Percy Simpson who was heading towards the town of Wellington in 1823. He was accompanied by Chief Constable John Blackman, who gave his name to Blackmans Swamp which was what the settlement was called until the name 'Orange' began to appear on official documents in the late 1820s. The name change was a result of Major Mitchell, who decided the town should be named after the Prince of Orange—Mitchell had fought with the Prince in the Peninsular War in Spain.

A man named John Peisley obtained a license for the Coach and Horses Inn in 1838. A blacksmith and a wheelwright set themselves up near the inn and by 1845 there were more shops including a store, a tannery and a shoemaker.

The discovery of payable gold at Ophir in April 1851 changed the district dramatically. Thousands of people flocked to the Ophir diggings and then gold was discovered nearby at Lucknow. Between 1851 and 1871 the population of Orange grew from 28 to 1456

and businesses sprang up to meet the needs of the many miners who passed through the area on their way to the goldfields.

By the 1870s, the area was known for its high-quality wheat and was gaining a reputation as the finest wheat producing area in New South Wales. Today the city prides itself on being one of the country's food baskets. Produce such as olives, grapes, apples, berries, fine lamb and beef are all grown in the local area and it is of the highest quality.

2 HISTORIC ORANGE

Start a walk around town at the Tourist Information Centre in Byng St. Walk up the street to the corner of Byng St and Lords Pl.

The Orange Court House reputedly stands on a site which was originally used for corroborees by the local Aborigines. Between 1849 and 1851 a simple slab and bark hut was constructed on the site and used both as a watch-house and a courtroom. A sandstone building was completed on the site in 1860–62 and it was in this building that the bushranger Ben Hall was first tried for his alleged involvement in an armed robbery near Forbes on 14 April, 1862. After spending six weeks in custody, Hall was tried and acquitted by a jury. He subsequently went on the infamous rampage, which made him

one of Australia's most famous bushrangers. That building was pulled down in 1882 when the present Neo-Classical building, designed by Colonial Architect James Barnet, was built. It was completed in 1883.

3 HOLY TRINITY

Continue up Byng St until you reach the corner of Anson St.

This beautiful Anglican Church, located on the corner of Anson and Byng streets, dominates the town's architecture. It is a fine example of High Victorian Gothic Revival and was designed by Thomas Rowe in 1879, with the steeple being completed in 1924.

4 ST JOSEPH'S CHURCH

Continue for two more blocks up Byng St until you reach St Joseph's Church.

St Joseph's Church was designed by the prominent Sydney architect, Edward Gell. The nave was completed in 1870 and the transepts were added in 1897. The roof was built of slate and there are unusual gabled ventilators on the ridge of the nave.

5 COOK PARK

Continue one block further on Byng St and then turn left into Clinton St and continue until you reach Summer St (the main street). Cook Park is on the opposite corner.

Cook Park has fountains, a band rotunda, an aviary, a begonia house, a small pond, a sunken rose garden, splendid trees and

Duntryleague—at Orange Golf Course.

Lake Canobalos just outside Orange.

numerous walkways. It is obviously best in spring and autumn but it offers an ideal location for a picnic at any time of the year. The park is famed for its hundred-year-old trees (the first trees were planted in 1880), the interesting John Gale Memorial Fountain (remodelled in the 1920s) and the octagonal Bandstand which was completed in 1908 which still has the original gas fittings and music stands. The City of Orange has produced an excellent Cook Park Heritage Walk brochure which describes all the main features in the park.

6 MOULDER PARK

Continue down Clinton St for two blocks and you will reach Moulder Park which has a pleasant walking path beside the creek.

Located just south of Cook Park, this pleasant location (truly spectacular in autumn) winds along a small creek and is characterised by ducks, reeds and some truly beautiful stands of poplar trees. It is a series of connecting parks which are separated by the streets it crosses.

7 ORANGE PUBLIC SCHOOL

At Sale St turn back towards the town's main street. Continue up Sale St until you reach the Kite St roundabout.

Be amazed at a public school which looks more like a church than a school with its high pointed large-paned sash windows, steeply pitched roof and spire. Orange Public School was designed by G.A. Mansfield and opened in 1880 with the foundation stone being laid by Sir Henry Parkes, a New South Wales' Premier and Founder of Australian Federation.

8 ORANGE POST OFFICE

Complete the walk by returning to Summer St, turning right and heading down to the Post Office.

Designed by J. Barnet and completed in 1879, Orange Post Office is a typical two-storey Classical design with an arcaded facade which has been filled in over the years. It has an interesting balustraded parapet.

Gunnadoo Goldmine, Ophir.

The dirt road between Orange and Ophir.

9 ROBERTSON PARK

Cross over the road and head back to the Tourist Information Centre through Robertson Park.

There are extensive plantings of exotic and native trees and the park, which is located in the centre of the city area, is a pleasant place for a picnic. The park came into existence in 1882 and is located on the original site of Blackmans Swamp. The Whitney Fountain was placed in the park in 1895 and the bandstand was completed in 1915.

10 ORANGE REGIONAL GALLERY

Return to the Tourist Information Centre. Before you return to your car go to local Art Gallery.

Located on the corner of Byng and Peisley streets the Orange Regional Gallery is recognised as one of the best rural art galleries in Australia. It regularly hosts touring art exhibitions and has a fine collection of works by Ian Fairweather, Sidney Nolan, Justin O'Brien, Brett Whiteley and John Olsen.

11 DUNTRYLEAGUE

Return to your car and drive along Byng St until you reach the T-intersection at Woodward St. Across the road you will notice the Orange Golf Club. Cross the road with caution and drive into the Golf Club along the driveway.

Standing like a glorious folly over the western end of town (and towering over the Orange Golf Club) in Duntryleague. It was built in 1876 for local businessman, James Dalton, who was the father of 12 children. Today it is a combination of a guest house and Club House for the Golf Club.

12 LAKE CANOBOLAS

Drive out of the Orange Golf Club and, with care, turn right. When you reach the next roundabout at Summer St head right out of the city towards Lake Canobolas. Continue on the road from 12km west of the city centre.

Lake Canobolas is a pleasant artificial lake which is now so well established that willows and poplars grow on its foreshores and there are excellent picnic and barbecue facilities available. It is said that the name 'canobolas' comes from 'coonoo baloo', a local Aboriginal word meaning 'twin shoulders' or 'twin heads'.

13 BIRTHPLACE OF 'BANJO' PATERSON

Return to Orange. The drive is 12km back to town from the top of Mount Canobolas. Continue through town and head back towards Sydney.

Two-and-a-half kilometres from the Orange Post Office, on the Bathurst Road, you will see Lone Pine Avenue which, when followed north, becomes Ophir Road.

On the way out to Ophir, some 5km from the centre of town, is a simple white monument which declares that this was the location where Australia's most famous, and most loved, bush poet, Andrew 'Banjo' Paterson, was born.

The original house no longer stands but there is a pleasant park area where enthusiasts can enjoy a picnic and appreciate the rolling countryside.

Orange has a reputation for producing famous poets. The great 20th-century poet, Kenneth Slessor, was also born in the town.

14 OPHIR

Continue for another 22km until you reach Ophir. The best road to Ophir is the road to the left—do not take the road to the right unless you are happy doing an extended section of rather ordinary dirt road.

Ophir (it rhymes with 'loafer') is an uninhabited recreation reserve with picnic and camping facilities at the confluence of Summer Hill Creek and Lewis Ponds Creek. It is located in a gorge 29km north-east of Orange. It is here that Australia's first payable gold was located in April 1851. Of interest in the area are the numerous old mines, some of which are still operational and can be inspected. The most interesting is Gunnadoo Goldmine, off the Millers Crossing Road, where visitors are taken about 100m into the mine.

Turn around after you have crossed the creek at Ophir. Return to Orange on the road you came on. It is the best road. It is 29km back to the centre of town.

68 BUSHRANGERS AND OUTER SPACE

■ DRIVING TOUR ■ 138KM ■ 5 HOURS ■ THE ADVENTURES OF BEN HALL AND THE SPACE OBSERVATORY

There is nothing quite so strange as seeing a huge radio telescope surrounded by green paddocks of well-fed sheep. This is one of the attractions on the road from Forbes to Narromine.

Forbes is so famous in the history of Australian bushranging that the song 'The Streets of Forbes' is part of the repertoire of folk singers all over the world. It was here that Ben Hall and his gang held up coaches and robbed local residents. Today, the journey from Forbes to Narromine is a mixture of the old and the new. Near to where Ben Hall carried out his most daring raids a huge radio telescope (64m in diameter) searches the southern skies looking for quasars and pulsars outside the Milky Way.

1 FORBES

Forbes is a substantial country town on the Lachlan River. It has a number of fine parks and gardens associated with the large lagoon known as Lake Forbes. The rural economy is based around the major saleyards complex, abattoir, feedlots, beef and hay exports, wool, wheat, grain seed crops, oil seed crops, fruit and vegetables.

The town did not emerge until gold was discovered by Harry Stephens in June 1861 at what is now King George V Park. The lure of gold initially drew about 30 000 people to the Lachlan goldfields. This tent city was later renamed Forbes. It has been claimed that during the first two years, 8100kg of gold were mined here. Several bushrangers, including Frank Gardiner, Ben Hall and John Gilbert, worked together as a gang, harrying the area between 1862 and 1865.

In 1862, Ben Hall's gang pulled off the largest Australian gold robbery, near

The grave of Ben Hall in the Forbes cemetery.

Eugowra. Hall was arrested but released when gang member Dan Charters refused to implicate his best friend. Hall, however, was shot dead in a hail of gunfire about 20km to the north-west of town on 5 May 1865 and is buried in the Forbes cemetery. John Gilbert was killed shortly after and Frank Gardiner was released from gaol in 1874 on the understanding that he leave the country.

Forbes was declared a municipality in 1870. The railway arrived in 1893 and the local economy expanded to include orchards and dairying. Forbes Railway Arts and Tourist Centre is situated in the old railway station in Union Street.

2 TOWN WALK

A good spot to start your walk is in the scenic parkland adjacent to Lake Forbes, off Gordon Duff Drive. The Vampire Jet on top of the pole was introduced into the RAAF in 1949. The lake has excellent picnic spots around its shores. Follow the lake around to Camp Street and walk along the street, past the all-timber Federation-style Lands Office (1890s). Cross the highway and enter Victoria Lane. To the left is the Classical Revival courthouse (1880). At the end of Victoria Lane, turn right into Harold Street. St Andrew's Presbyterian Church was built of rough stone in 1877. The church has an impressive octagonal belltower and spire, a steeply sloping slate roof and some fine stained-glass windows. Court Street has a number of impressive historic features. At the Harold Street corner is the two-storey stuccoed town hall, capped by a dome on a three-storey octagonal tower.

Almost opposite is the Vandenberg Hotel, with its large timber verandah, cast-iron columns and iron lacework. Originally the Courthouse Hotel, this stuccoed brick building was erected in 1863. Over the road are the formal gardens of Victoria Park. The Grecian design fountain, donated by Mayor Thomas in 1891, and band rotunda are the focal points. St John's Anglican Church is a Gothic Revival edifice with graceful gables, built in 1874–1877. At Court and Lachlan streets is a major element of the local streetscape—the stuccoed brick post office (1879–1881). The ground-floor colonnade and arched first-floor windows are capped by an unusual three-storey clock tower.

3 FORBES CEMETERY

Continue along Johnson St as it doglegs and becomes Bogan Gate Rd. The cemetery is 1km after the dogleg, to the left.

Forbes cemetery contains the grave of bushranger Ben Hall, who was shot to death by a hail of gunfire to the north-west

of town in May 1865. The site of the shooting is indicated with a marker. Fellow gang-members John O'Meally and Warrigal Walsh were buried in unmarked graves (as was Hall initially). Nearby is the grave of Ned Kelly's sister Kate, who married here in 1888 and drowned in the Lachlan River in 1898.

4 PARKES

Return along Bogan Gate Rd and Johnson St to the T-intersection and turn left into Dowling St. Parkes is 33km away.

Parkes is a rural service centre with an expanding economy and population, thanks in part to a wool-combing plant and the

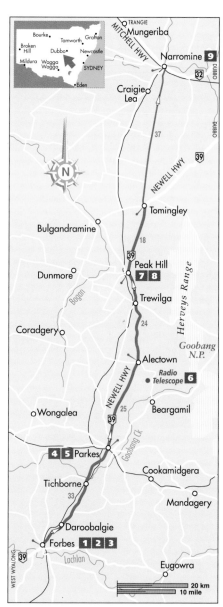

Old mining equipment at Peak Hill.

Elegant buildings grace the centre of Forbes.

North Parkes copper and goldmine, the largest metal mine in New South Wales, which opened in 1994. The town is a major wheat-storage centre in a rural district that also produces other crops, plus wool and livestock.

Reef gold was located a little to the north of the present townsite in 1862. A tent city of 10 000 people emerged almost overnight. It was known as Currajong after the large number of currajong trees in the vicinity. That field was worked for about five years and then rapidly declined. Other major finds were made in the area in 1871, however, and a second rush was soon under way. Between 1871 and 1873 about 1400kg of gold was mined. A hotel was quickly established (on the site now occupied by the Cambridge Hotel), followed by a court of petty sessions, another hotel, the first bank, a Methodist Church and public school.

The tourist information centre is located in Kelly Reserve on the northern outskirts of town, on the western side of the Newell Highway. Kelly Reserve contains an old steam locomotive, barbecues and play facilities and Bushmans Dam, which was originally created to supply water to the miners of Bushmans Hill.

5 PARKES HISTORIC BUILDINGS

At the corner of Currajong and Court streets is an historic precinct featuring the courthouse, post office and police station. The courthouse was built in 1895–1898 to a design of government architect W.L. Vernon. The post office dates from 1880 and the Royal Hotel, at 217 Clarinda Street, was built in 1881. The Henry Parkes Historical Museum, at 316 Clarinda Street, is located in the former masonic temple. The museum has a good display of artefacts from the goldmining and pioneering days, including many items bequeathed to the town by Sir

Henry Parkes, such as his letters and personal library.

One of the earliest surviving buildings is Balmoral Mansion. Built by William Hazelhurst, who owned the Phoenix Mine, the house features some fine cast-iron lacework, Italian marble, a quality wooden staircase and stained-glass windows. Balmoral is located on the eastern side of Hill Street, opposite the school, near the Church Street intersection.

6 RADIO TELESCOPE

Head north out of Parkes along the Newell Hwy (Clarinda St) for 20km and then turn right and follow Telescope Rd for 6km.

In 1959–1961 the CSIRO built the first big-dish antenna radio telescope (64m in diameter) in the southern hemisphere to the north of Parkes. One of the world's most powerful, the telescope has played a vital role in the detection of quasars and of the first pulsars outside the Milky Way galaxy. In 1988 the telescope was joined with the Coonabarabran and Narrabri dishes to form the Australia Telescope.

There is an audio-visual display at the complex and staff are available to answer questions. The visitors centre has interactive displays, computer tours, a working model of the telescope, a hologram, a live connection with the control room computers, project material, souvenirs and posters.

7 PEAK HILL

Return along Telescope Rd and turn left into the Newell Hwy. It is 29km to Peak Hill.

Peak Hill is the second largest town in the shire of Parkes. The town developed in 1889 when gold was discovered in the area and two open-cut goldmines were established. Peak Hill was incorporated as a municipality in 1894 and the railway arrived in 1914, although mining operations ceased in 1917.

As was often the case in goldmining towns, miners and other people, drawn by the economic activity, had taken up land as free selectors and established agricultural enterprises. It was a sign of the town's survival and future that, in 1918, Peak Hill

became the site of the first public wheat silo constructed in New South Wales.

8 GOLDMINE

Head east off the highway for about 300m along Mingelo St to the car park, where a track leads to a viewing platform over the open-cut goldmine.

The goldmine has been established on the site of the two original shafts that were hand-excavated in the late 19th and early 20th centuries—one to a depth of 100m and a length of 200m. There are a number of artefacts—among them old boilers and the remnants of houses—on the walk up to the mine. The artefacts are clearly signposted with extensive information boards detailing their history and origins.

9 NARROMINE

Return along Mingelo St and turn left into the highway. Narromine is 55km away.

Narromine is located near the Macquarie River at the junction of the Mitchell and Newell highways. Although a government reserve had been made in 1849, there was little in the way of a settlement until the railway arrived in 1882. At that time, William O'Neil was the owner of the property 'Narramine', and he had established a hotel at the junction of the road to Trangie (now the Mitchell Highway) and the road to Warren.

The township developed around the railway on land resumed from O'Neil. It was laid out and gazetted in 1883. The first school opened in the same year. The streets were named after early pastoral holdings in the area. A pump station and pump attendant's house were built near the hotel to supply water to the trains at what was the last natural watering place before Bourke.

Narramine was declared a village in 1885. In 1890 a police station was built and O'Neil established a store near the railway. Narromine Visitors Centre is located in Burraway Street. The old courthouse, next to the visitors centre and the police station, has become the town's museum.

Return to Forbes. Travel south 56km to Tomingey. Join the Newell Hwy. Forbes is 100km south.

Parkes radio telescope seen from a sheep paddock.

69 DUBBO TO DUNEDOO

■ DRIVING TOUR ■ 261KM ■ 1 DAY ■ CAVES, GOLDMINES AND PASTURE LAND

An area of undulating slopes and quiet towns and villages greets the visitor who marvels at the perfectly preserved goldmining town of Gulgong and historic Wellington.

The central western slopes of New South Wales are hugely attractive in spring when the paddocks turn green and the fields of canola burst into dazzling displays of yellow. The area is an agriculturally rich one with a number of attractive and interesting towns that are well worth exploring. The town of Wellington is noted for its pleasant public gardens, its interesting historic buildings and the excellent Wellington Caves. Similarly, Gulgong is an almost perfect example of a town that has not changed much from the days when it was a thriving mining centre. By comparison, Dunedoo is a quiet country town and Dubbo is the major rural centre in the district.

Wellington Courthouse.

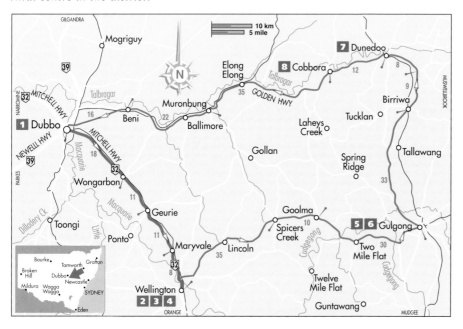

1 DUBBO

Dubbo is a typical, larger Australian country town. Located on the Macquarie River, the town is noted for its excellent historic buildings (including the famous Dubbo Gaol) and the outstanding Dubbo Zoo.

2 WELLINGTON

Head east out of Dubbo along Cobra St (the Mitchell Hwy). It is 50km to Wellington.

Wellington is the second oldest town west of the Blue Mountains and a typical country town. The main street is wide and the park is a delight, with luxurious stands of cool trees and quiet gardens for the visitor.

The first European visitor was the explorer John Oxley. In 1823, inspired by Oxley's glowing report on the area's agricultural potential, Governor Brisbane sent Lieutenant Percy Simpson to establish a camp with convicts and soldiers. The camp was situated about 3km south of the present townsite on the high ground above the Bell River and was, for a short time, the only settlement beyond Bathurst. Wellington was

gazetted in 1846. Cobb & Co established a service through the town in 1865. It became a municipality in 1879 and the railway arrived the following year.

3 HISTORIC WELLINGTON

The visitors centre is located in Cameron Park, which is regarded as one of the best public gardens in New South Wales. Lining one side of Nanima Crescent, the park boasts a sunken garden and superb rose beds. The lily pond was once a children's swimming pool. Cameron Park is linked to Pioneer Park via a suspension bridge over the Bell River.

Start at Cameron Park and head north along the crescent to Warne Street and turn left. At the Raymond Street corner is the former Commercial Hotel (1865), now converted to flats. Head east, back along Warne Street to the Percy Street corner where, to the left, you will see St Patrick's Catholic Church (1914). Adjacent to the church is the Convent of Mercy (1896). Over the road is the Oxley Historical

Museum, situated in an elegant two-storey brick building erected in 1883 as the Bank of New South Wales. It became the Catholic presbytery in 1922. Windora School and Stinson Cottage (an 1851 slab dwelling) have also been rebuilt on the current grounds. Opposite is St John the Baptist's Anglican Church, the town's oldest surviving church, built in 1867 with the transept, chancel and belltower added over the next 25 years. Continue east along Warne Street to the Arthur Street corner. The bell in the fire station tower was used in Lieutenant Simpson's original convict settlement in the area (1823–1831). It was then retained by the Aboriginal mission set up on the same site.

Turn right into Arthur Street. At the Swift Street corner is the Hotel Wellington with a fine belltower and turret. Turn westwards along Swift Street to the Percy Street corner, opposite Cameron Park, where you will find the National Australia Bank (1881), designed by G.A. Mansfield and built of stuccoed brick. Turn left back into Nanima Crescent and then left into Maughan Street. To the right is the Edwardian post office (1904), which has an enormous brick-and-stone arcade that contrasts strongly with the wooden verandah above. At Maughan and Arthur streets is the Late Victorian courthouse (c.1890s), made of brick with stone dressings, a terracotta tiled roof and an unusual entrance arch. Opposite is the Federal Hotel (1894). Turn right into Arthur Street. To the right is the Wellington Public School (1885), retaining the original schoolroom. In the school yard is Oxley's Anchor, one of several anchors donated by the British Admiralty to mark the significant site on the explorer's route. There is also an elm tree under which, in October 1910, the first meeting of the famous Gould League of Birdlovers was held. At one time, the Gould League was an organisation joined by just about every Australian school child.

4 WELLINGTON CAVES

Head south out of town along Arthur St (the Mitchell Hwy) for 8km. There is a signposted right turn which leads to the area's major attraction, Wellington Caves.

The first European to see the caves was probably someone associated with Lieutenant Simpson's settlement (1823–1831), but the first written account was provided by the explorer Hamilton Hume in 1828. He wrote: 'The inside of the cave is beautifully formed, some parts of it are supported by pillars 50 feet high and beautifully carved by nature'.

Two years later George Rankin, a local magistrate, found fossil bones of both a diprotodon and a giant kangaroo in the caves. Rankin returned later with Sir Thomas Mitchell and collected a huge variety of bones from the caves which appear to have acted as a natural trap for fauna. Since that time, the cave has been a steady source of information about ancient geology and fauna.

The caves were vandalised during the 19th century and it wasn't until 1884 that they became a reserve. Two of the caves are open for inspection (by guided tour only)—the Cathedral Cave and the Gaden Cave. The Cathedral Cave is famous for its huge stalagmite known as Altar Rock, which is 32m in circumference at its base and stands over 15m high. It was once thought to be the largest stalagmite in the world. A visit to Cathedral Cave lasts about 45 minutes and a tour of Gaden Cave takes about 40 minutes. Gaden Cave is noted for its unusual and beautiful cave formations.

5 GULGONG

Return along the Mitchell Hwy to Wellington. Proceed along Arthur St, turn left into Maughan St and take the first right into Nanima Crescent. Continue through the roundabout along Lee St and then turn right into Mudgee Rd. It is 72km to Gulgong.

If you wish to gain some insight into how a 19th-century Australian goldmining town looked, then Gulgong—a highly picturesque and well-preserved settlement of single-storey weatherboard, iron, stone and brick buildings with old-fashioned iron-lace verandahs, tiny wooden cottages, horse troughs and hitching rails—is an almost perfect example. The generally antiquated and intimate air also rises from the narrow winding streets, which developed as bullock tracks connecting the major mining claims.

The discovery of gold saw the gazetting of the Gulgong goldfield in 1866 but initial finds were negligible. Tom Saunders discovered a lode on 14 April 1870, however, and sparked a major gold rush. There were 500 people on the site within six weeks and when the town was gazetted in 1872 there were reputedly 20 000 people in the area.

Gulgong became a municipality in 1876 although the gold had already began to dwindle by then. In all, it is estimated that 15 000kg of the precious metal were removed from the Gulgong fields between 1870 and 1880. By 1881, the population was down to 1212 and the boom years were over, although gold was found in small quantities until the end of the century. From that point, wheat and wool production, boosted by the arrival of the railway in 1909, sustained the town.

The Gulgong Visitors Centre is located at 109 Herbert Street. The Gulgong Pioneers Museum, at 73 Herbert Street (at the corner of Bayley Street) is located in the Old Times Bakery (1872–1873). It is a popular and well-awarded country museum. Covering an acre, the museum has a Cobb & Co display, mining equipment, the Gudgeon Cottage, horsedrawn vehicles, a blacksmith's shop, bakehouse, colonial kitchen and an old schoolhouse, as well as Aboriginal and geological artefacts and displays. The Museum of Sight and Sound is devoted to the history of Australian cinematography and sound recording.

The town was particularly well-documented photographically, because of the Holtermann Collection, some of which is on display at the museum. After making a fortune goldmining at Hill End, Bernard Holtermann hired Charles Bayliss and Beaufoy Merlin to photograph the major goldmining towns and areas of New South Wales in order to exhibit them abroad and attract migrants to the country where he made his own fortune. What turned out to be one of the largest wet-plate collections ever made was displayed at international exhibitions in Philadelphia (1876) and Paris (1878). Some of Merlin's photographs provided the basis of the images on the old $10 banknote.

6 GULGONG'S HERITAGE BUILDINGS

Many of the town's buildings date back to the 1870s. In Bayly Street there are the Roman Catholic Church, the convent school and the presbytery, as well as St Luke's Anglican Church (1874–1876). Herbert Street has the courthouse, the post office, Ulan County Council, the library (formerly the Wylandra Shire Hall) and the former Australian Joint Stock Bank. The police station and residence (1878–1879) are in Medley Street.

Mayne Street has the American Tobacco Warehouse, the Greatest Wonders of the World, the Fancy Goods Emporium, the Ten Dollar Town Motel (originally the Royal Hotel) and the Prince of Wales Opera House which appeared on the old Australian $10 banknote. The opera house was originally a bark hut theatre erected for the amusement of the original goldrush inhabitants in 1871. Renowned boxer Les Darcy once fought an exhibition bout there and it was not unknown for female performers to have gold nuggets thrown in their laps.

7 DUNEDOO

At the western end of Mayne St turn right into Crown St which veers to the left as Tallawang Rd. Follow this road to Dunedoo (32km).

Dunedoo is a small town set amid gentle rolling hills and wide valleys adjacent to the Talbragar River. The district was surveyed in 1832 and squatters soon followed, in search of fresh pasturage. The townsite itself was not surveyed until 1868. The name Dunedoo is said to derive from an Aboriginal word for 'swans', which frequented the nearby lagoons.

The railway did not arrive until 1910. Before then, travellers on their way to Sydney had to journey by a horse-drawn vehicle to Mudgee, by Cobb & Co coach to Penrith and then by rail to the city.

8 COBBORA

Head west out of town on the Dubbo Rd. It is 12km to the village of Cobbora.

Cobbora began its life in the 1860s as a postal stop on the run between Mudgee and Mendooran. Two hotels were established and it was declared a town in 1885 when a police station was built. Still standing, the police station is now a private residence and can be seen from the road. It was used in the movie *The Chant of Jimmy Blacksmith*. Cobbora also has an historic cemetery with headstones dating back to 1868.

Dubbo is 76km further on, on the Dubbo Rd (Route 84).

Wellington Museum.

70 EXPLORING AROUND DUBBO

■ WALKING AND DRIVING TOUR ■ 16KM ■ 1 DAY ■ GAOLS AND ZOOS

A thriving commercial service centre, Dubbo draws visitors from all over Australia to its famous and excellent Western Plain Zoo.

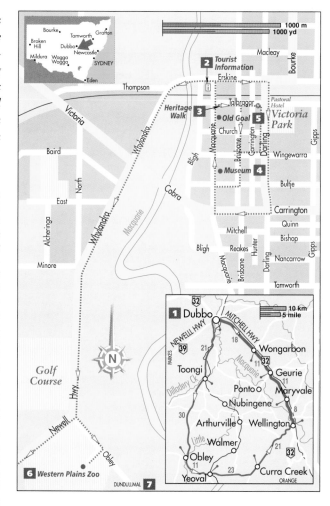

Dubbo is a typical larger Australian country town. Serving as the commercial, industrial and administrative hub of the Central West, Dubbo is also one of Australia's fastest-growing inland cities. It is characterised by a substantial shopping area and a number of historic buildings, including the historic Dubbo Gaol. The area around Dubbo is noted for its wheat and wool production but the major attraction is the excellent Western Plains Zoo, a model zoo where animals roam freely in large open areas mostly protected from the public by deep moats.

1 DUBBO

Dubbo is located on the Macquarie River and noted for its excellent historic buildings (including the famous Dubbo Gaol) and the outstanding Dubbo Zoo. The first Europeans in the area were the explorer John Oxley and his party, who passed the future site of Dubbo in 1818. Oxley noted the quality of the soil, the water supply and the abundance of wildlife, including howling dingoes that kept him awake at night.

In the 1850s, the buoyant markets of Melbourne began to attract stockmen from the north who overlanded their cattle and sheep from New South Wales and Queensland. Dubbo was located just off the Great North Road, which crossed the Macquarie River at Butlers Falls. Consequently, a crude, makeshift bridge was built over the river in the late 1850s and Dubbo became a major trading post on the Great North Road. As late as 1864 there were only two stores and two hotels in town. Rapid change was afoot, however. When the first proper bridge over the Macquarie River was built at Dubbo in 1866, a journalist reported that the village had 'magnificent and commodious' stores, five hotels with a sixth nearing completion, a mill under construction, and a 'well designed court house and lock-up'. The most notable inmate of the lock-up was bushranger Johnny Dunn, who escaped in 1865. He was later recaptured and hanged in Sydney.

Twenty years later, in 1885, a visitor described Dubbo as a 'pretty little town, built on an extensive plateau of squatting land'. He also noted three banks, streets 'mostly lined with neat red brick cottages' and 'a number of substantial shops'. By this time there were also several churches and schools, a library and the town's third and present courthouse was under construction.

Dubbo has grown considerably since World War II, almost doubling its population between 1947 and 1971, and doubling it again since 1971. Dubbo was declared a city in 1966.

2 TOURIST INFORMATION

The obvious starting point for any walking tour of Dubbo is the information centre, which is located by the railway line at the corner of the Newell Highway (Erskine Street) and Macquarie Street.

3 HERITAGE WALK

Walk eastwards along Talbragar Street. Just past Carrington Avenue is the Pastoral Hotel (1890). Return along Talbragar Street, turning left into Brisbane Street. To the left is one of the city's most attractive buildings-the Lands Office building (1897), a two-storey iron and timber structure in the Queen Anne style. Notice the quality of the verandah posts and fencing. A plaque near the door records the height of Dubbo's worst flood (1955). The wooden flaps at the base of the building help it to dry out after flood.

Macquarie Street in Dubbo.

Over the road is the town's most imposing building—the Classical Revival courthouse (1885–1890) with its Corinthian columns and pleasant gardens. It was designed by colonial architect James Barnet and retains the original posts of the first Dubbo courthouse (1852–1859).

Continue along Brisbane Street. To the left is the Holy Trinity Anglican Church (1875–1876), a cruciform stone structure designed by the architect Edmund Blacket, in an Early English rural style. The carved Normandy stone font, tie-beam roof and the timber Gothic pulpit and reading desk were also designed by Blacket. The 18m bellcote was added in the 1920s. On the other side of the road is the Commercial Hotel (1859), the oldest surviving building in the town centre.

Continue along Brisbane Street and turn left into Wingewarra Street. Just beyond Carrington Avenue is St Andrew's Uniting (formerly Presbyterian) Church, built with sandstone from the original 1876 church. It has a fine interior and a fish-scale pattern to the slate roof.

Turn left into Darling Street. To the left is the primary school, which dates from 1873. Opposite the school is Victoria Park. This land was set aside in the original town plan (1849) but didn't become a park until the 1890s.

Return to Brisbane Street. To the left is the Gothic Revival design of St Brigid's Catholic Church, built in 1874 with the sanctuary added in 1881 and the transepts in 1909. Note the pyramid-shaped steeple. Adjacent is the presbytery (1902) and over the road are a pair of late 19th-century cottages.

Walk back along Brisbane Street and turn left into Bultje Street. Just past Macquarie Street, to the left, is the Kemwah building, built in 1881 as the Imperial Hotel. On the other side of the road, at 193 Macquarie Street, is a structure built of local sandstone in 1865 as the Commercial Bank. The original servants' quarters survive in the basement. The building served as the local shire offices from 1909 to 1980 and it is now the Old Shire Gallery, selling antiques, jewellery and fine arts.

4 DUBBO MUSEUM
Turn left into Macquarie St. To the right is the gracious Dubbo Museum.

The Dubbo Museum is located in the former Bank of New South Wales building (1873). This gracious two-storey sandstone building with its cedar staircase, marble fireplaces and decorative ceilings, now contains colonial farm, domestic, Aboriginal and commercial artefacts. To its rear is a collection of 19th-century buildings which have been positioned to form a village square.

Walk north from the museum along Macquarie Street. Just past Wingewarra Street, to the left, is the Commercial Union building, which opened in 1893 as the Bank of Australasia. At the north-eastern corner of Macquarie Street and Church Street is the Colonial Mutual building, an Italianate-style building erected in 1884 for the Australian Joint Stock Bank.

A little further north along Macquarie Street, to the right, is the two-storey Italianate business office of Telstra, built in 1887 as a post office after a design by James Barnet. The clock tower was originally part of the second courthouse.

5 OLD DUBBO GAOL
A further 30m north along Macquarie St is the entrance to the Old Dubbo Gaol.

Dubbo Gaol is a well-preserved prison built about 1871 (the gates and wall were added in 1887) which closed in 1966. Now a museum, it offers an opportunity to see the way the gaol and the judicial system once operated. Features include a sizeable collection of animatronic models that tell the life stories of inmates and staff, a gallows pole with hangman's equipment (eight men were hanged at the gaol), the condemned man's cell (where Thomas Moore relates his story), solitary confinement cells, a graffiti cell, a padded cell, the watchtower, the exercise yard, a display room, bathroom, hospital, kitchen, sanitary disposal block and wood-cutting area.

Jacky Underwood, an accomplice of Jimmy and Joe Governor during their murderous rampage in which ten people were killed was hanged at Dubbo Gaol in January 1901.

6 WESTERN PLAINS ZOO
Head north from the old gaol until you reach the T-intersection with Erskine St. Turn left and continue on Whylandra Rd which becomes the Newell Hwy. Follow the Newell Hwy south out of town for a little over 2km and turn left into Obley Rd. The zoo entrance is 600m along here to the right.

This open-range zoo specialises in large animals (kangaroos would be about the smallest of the mammals and the birds just roam free) and places them in areas that are enclosed by moats, thus giving a feeling of naturalness. The zoo is a *tour de force*.

A koala at the Western Plains Zoo.

There are a number of ways visitors can see the 800 native and exotic species dispersed over 300ha of landscaped parklands. Perhaps the ideal way (although not in the heat of summer) is to hire a bicycle at the gate and slowly cycle around the 6km circular track. It is also possible to drive, and the park provides minimokes for people who want to leave their own vehicle in the car park. There is a guided walk in the morning with zoo volunteers, and people can stay over-night at the Zoofari Lodge.

The park is divided into Africa, Asia, North America, Europe and Australia. Africa comes first, for the obvious reason that it contains many of the most crowd-pleasing species—Cape hunting dogs, zebras, giraffes, hippos, elephants, camels, Barbary sheep, lions, cheetahs, eland, sitatunga and so on—although the Bengal tiger is a highlight. Rare and endangered species, such as the southern white rhinoceros, Galapagos tortoise, the bison and the Przewalski horse are bred at the zoo.

The experience of eating at the park is something of an exotic obstacle race with bees buzzing around your sweet drink and a variety of unusual waterbirds pecking at your shoes in an attempt to persuade you to part with some of your sandwich.

7 DUNDULLIMAL
Continue 2km beyond the zoo, in Obley Rd, to the Dundullimal historic homestead.

The historic timber-slab homestead known as Dundullimal was built about 1840 by wealthy early settler John Maughan as the head station of his 26 000ac sheep station. At that time it housed 20 people, including six convicts. Dundullimal is one of the oldest homesteads left standing in western New South Wales and is located in a pleasant setting on the banks of the Macquarie River.

Information boards, which include old photographs of the house, allow visitors to appreciate the changes that have occurred to the building. There are sandstone stables, working saddlery, blacksmith, woodshop kitchen, gift shop, animal farm, tractor hayride, animal show and the Woolshed Cafe.
Return 4km to the centre of Dubbo.

Old Dubbo Gaol.

Dundullimal historic homestead.

71 THE GREAT GREY PLAIN

■ DRIVING TOUR ■ 208KM ■ 1 DAY ■ IN THE OUTBACK

Beyond the slopes, stretching all the way across the continent, are the great grey plains of Australia—dry, flat sheep country and desert watered by the occasional river.

The flat outback of New South Wales with its tiny isolated towns is full of history and relics. The road from Nyngan to Bourke is a long straight track with never a bend or a turn. On either side of the road, the great grey plains of western New South Wales stretch to the horizon. This is simple country and yet it has its stories to tell and fascinating aspects of outback life to reveal.

1 NYNGAN

Nyngan is located on the Bogan River on the eastern edge of the Great Outback. The town is 583km north-west of Sydney in a region noted for its wool, wheat and cattle. Thomas Mitchell explored the Bogan River in 1835 and recorded the local Aboriginal word *nyingan*, which is said to mean 'long pond of water'. Nyngan was gazetted as a reserve for water in 1865 but a townsite was not reserved until 1880. The townsite was surveyed in 1882 when the Dubbo to Bourke railway was under construction. The track arrived in Nyngan the following year.

Nyngan achieved dubious fame in 1990 when it was deluged with the worst floods of the century. The townspeople laid 260 000 sandbags on top of the established levee but the waters inundated the entire town, causing $50 million worth of damage. Nearly the entire population had to be airlifted out by helicopter. A national relief fund was established to help the town recover.

Most of the town's heritage buildings are located in Cobar and Bogan streets. The town hall (1897), courthouse and post office are in Cobar Street, between Terangion Street and Tabratong Street. On opposite corners of the Bogan and Terangion streets intersection are the Anglican and Catholic churches. Bogan Street also has a number of private homes from the 1890s.

The old railway station in Pangee Street, near the Dandaloo Street intersection, has been restored and converted into an historical museum. The museum houses a display on the 1990 flood and the old telephone exchange, among other items relating to local history.

Adjacent to the railway station in Pangee Strete is a helicopter, a gift from the Australian government to the people of Nyngan to commemorate the occasion in April 1990 when 2000 inhabitants were evacuated, largely by helicopter, because of the breaching of the levee by record floodwaters. The Pioneer Memorial sculpture of a drover, his dog and a mob of sheep, is located at the corner of Pangee and Moonagee streets.

2 GIRILAMBONE

Head north-west out of Nyngan on the Mitchell Hwy. After 43km you will reach the tiny township of Girilambone, which is little more than a petrol station and a long-disused railway station.
Girilambone is said to be a local Aboriginal word meaning 'place of falling stars'. The town began its life around 1880 with the discovery of copper. Mining was carried out into the early 20th century and then ceased.

3 HELENA KERZ'S GRAVE

Turn east at the general store and follow the road marked for Brewarrina for about 1km to a sign to a cemetery. You have to pass through two gates to reach a tiny, lonely graveyard clearly divided by denomination.
In the Roman Catholic section is a headstone that reads: 'In loving remembrance of our dear daughter Helena Kerz. Born 2 December 1878. Died 20 July 1900'. This tribute gives little indication of the events behind Helena Kerz's death at the hands of Jimmy Governor.

Jimmy was a part-Aborigine who had worked as a police tracker before marrying a 16-year-old white woman and obtaining a contract to erect fencing for John and Sarah Mawbey, the licensees of the Breelong Inn, near Gilgandra. A dedicated employee who

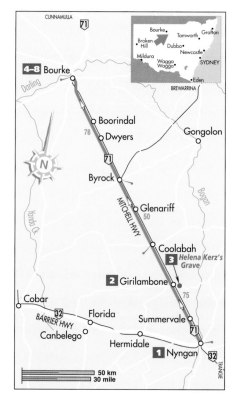

wished to prove himself to white society, Jimmy was initially on good terms with his employers and their family. It seems that Governor's wife, however, who worked in the Mawbey house, was belittled for marrying an Aborigine by Mrs Mawbey and Helena Kerz, the local schoolteacher.

Whatever the contributing factors, Jimmy and Jacky Underwood confronted the women. Jimmy claimed that Mrs Mawbey called him 'black rubbish' and stated that he should be shot for marrying a white woman. Whatever transpired, the two men went into a rage and brutally murdered Sarah Mawbey, three of her daughters and Helena Kerz with clubs and a tomahawk.

Jimmy, his brother Joe, and Jacky then went on a three-month, 3200km rampage, inflicting revenge for past grievances. They murdered five more people, wounded another five, committed seven armed hold-ups and robbed 33 homes. A massive manhunt involving hundreds of policemen and trackers and 2000 volunteers failed to capture the men, who ridiculed their pursuers by advertising their whereabouts and sending satiric letters to the police.

In October 1900, a £1000 reward was offered for their capture and later in the month they were outlawed, which meant they could be shot on sight. By the end of the month Jacky was captured, Joe was shot and

The bridge across the Bogan River at Nyngan.

The main street of Nyngan.

killed near Singleton and Jimmy was captured by a group of farmers near Wingham two weeks after being shot in the mouth. Jimmy and Jacky were hanged in January 1901. In his last days, Jimmy Governor sang native songs, read the Bible and blamed his wife.

4 BOURKE

From Girilambone, follow the Mitchell Hwy north-west for 81km and pass through the tiny township of Byrock. Continue for another 78km to Bourke.

Bourke is located on the Darling River, 110m above sea level. When the explorer Charles Sturt passed through the district in 1828, he thought the whole area was 'unlikely to become the haunt of civilised man'. It wasn't until 1835 that Sir Thomas Mitchell returned to the area and built a fort about 13km south of the town site. Mitchell had bad relations with the local Aborigines and he felt a fort was suitable protection against their attacks. It was named Fort Bourke after the Governor of New South Wales, Sir Richard Bourke (1777–1855). Eventually the district and later the town came to be known by this name.

The area around Fort Bourke was marginal land. The history of the district changed dramatically when in 1859, however, when Captain W.R. Randall sailed the Gemini up the Darling from South Australia. Suddenly, Bourke and Brewarrina and other centres along the river became vital transport nodes. For decades Bourke was the transport centre for the whole of south-west Queensland and western New South Wales. Its port was the only efficient way to transport wool to the coastal markets and at its height in the late 19th century over 40 000 bales of wool were being shipped down the Darling annually. The river transport continued until the last commercial riverboat in 1931.

There is much to see of historical interest in Bourke. The first stop should be at the tourist information centre in Oxley Street, which has

The West Bourke Bridge across the Darling.

an excellent brochure, complete with a detailed map, that highlights the town's most interesting and important buildings.

5 BOURKE'S HISTORIC BUILDINGS

Turn off the Mitchell Hwy into Richard St. After four blocks turn left into Mitchell St at the Anglican church. On the right-hand side, between the fire station and the ambulance station, is the Lands Building.

The Lands Building, now government offices, was built between 1863 and 1865 as the town's first courthouse. It served the town for only a decade before the second courthouse was built in 1875. Today, the first courthouse has been beautifully restored and is one of the most attractive buildings in Bourke.

One of the town's most impressive buildings, and certainly one of the most photographed, is the present courthouse at 51 Oxley Street, which was built in 1899– a true Federation building. The courtroom itself, which is open for inspection, is beautifully preserved and has an appropriate air of solemnity. This courthouse must be one of the first 'project' courthouses in the country, as it is almost identical to the Wagga Wagga courthouse that government architect W.L. Vernon designed at the same time.

A little further down Oxley Street is the post office, which was built in 1880 with the upper floor being added some years later. The post office survived the 1890 flood (the town's

The recreated Fort Bourke Stockade.

worst flood when the river broke its banks and levees) by building its own levee bank.

Much is made of the Carriers Arms Hotel (on the Mitchell Highway, two blocks from Richard Street) in which Henry Lawson reputedly wrote a number of stories and which was a popular Cobb & Co stop-off point. Today the building is singularly unimpressive. When compared to the large number of old and interesting buildings in town, the hotel is a great disappointment.

6 BOURKE WEIR

Drive west along Anson St. About 6km from the centre of town turn right at the fork in the road and you will reach the edge of the river.

The Bourke Weir was opened in 1897 and was designed to maintain a reasonable level of water in the river near the town. Originally a lock, it was nearly 60m long and 11m wide and was the only one built on the Darling River. The lock was concreted and converted into a weir in 1941.

7 BOURKE CEMETERY

Return to the corner of Richard and Anson sts and turn right, heading south along Richard St. Cross the railway line and after 800m you will reach the town cemetery.

There are a number of graves of Afghan camel drivers in the cemetery. They are easy to identify because, unlike the Christian graves, they are all pointing towards Mecca. About 50m further across the cemetery is the grave of John McCabe, a local policeman who was shot by the bushranger Captain Midnight.

8 FORT BOURKE STOCKADE

Head south until you reach Louth Rd. Follow it to the Stockade sign, which is about 11km from the courthouse. Turn right and after another 4km, go left at the double gate. Then, before you reach the fuel tank, turn right along the bush track. The stockade is about 1km further along.

The trip out to Fort Bourke Stockade is actually more interesting than the reconstructed stockade. About 15km out of town the road passes around an extraordinarily beautiful wildlife refuge. The fort itself is nothing more than a few logs in the middle of nowhere. There is no accurate information about what Thomas Mitchell's stockade looked like but it is reasonable to assume that it looked nothing like this re-creation, which would barely hold a single man for half an hour and certainly wouldn't have deterred the 'hostile natives' that Mitchell was so afraid of.

Return to Bourke. The distance is 16km.

Marshy lands beside the mighty Darling River at Bourke.

INDEX